THE OSCAR® STARS
From A-Z

THE OSCAR® STARS

STARS

From A-Z

Roy Pickard

HEADLINE

Copyright © 1996 Roy Pickard

The right of Roy Pickard to be identified as the Author of
the Work has been asserted by him in accordance with the
Copyright, Designs and Patents Act 1988.

First published in 1996
by HEADLINE BOOK PUBLISHING

10 9 8 7 6 5 4 3 2 1

British Library Cataloguing in Publication Data

Pickard, Roy, 1937-
  The Oscar® stars from A-Z
  1.Motion picture actors and actresses
  2.Academy Awards (Motion pictures)
  I.Title
  791.4'3'028'0922

  ISBN 0 7472 1638 X

Typeset by
Letterpart Limited, Reigate, Surrey

Printed and bound in Great Britain by
Mackays of Chatham PLC, Chatham, Kent

HEADLINE BOOK PUBLISHING
A division of Hodder Headline PLC
338 Euston Road
London NW1 3BH

Contents

Acknowledgements

The pictures in this book were originally issued to publicise or promote films made or distributed by the following companies to whom I gratefully offer acknowledgement: Amblin', Close Call Films, Columbia, Enigma, Gladden Films, Samuel Goldwyn, Gramercy, GW Films, Hemdale, London Films, Lumiere Pictures, MGM, Miramax, Orion, Paramount, Polygram, Reversal Films, RKO, Touchstone, 20th Century-Fox, United Artists, Universal, Warner Bros.

Preface

'In the mythology of the cinema the Oscar is the supreme prize,' said no less a director than Federico Fellini when receiving his fourth little gold-plated man. Few in the movie business would disagree, especially the actors, who certainly value the award more highly than any other. An Oscar win can add a million or two to one's asking price, or revive a career that has been flagging for years. Or it can be of no financial significance whatsoever and be treasured simply for its prestige alone.

And the losers and nominees? What of them? Some bask in unexpected glory in front of the TV cameras on Oscar night and make the transition from character actor to star; others fade away in a long, slow dissolve, some to return, many never to be heard of again.

Whatever, they're all here within the pages of this book, all 717 of them, every star, every character actor, every winner, every nominee, discussed in detail and gathered together for the first time in a single volume.

It's an easy book to use, set out in alphabetical order with each entry providing the date and place of the star's birth, his or her Oscar nominations and wins, the names of the characters played and any information that is relevant or amusing. All the A–Z entries are for performers only. When an actor or actress has won in an additional category (for direction, for example) that win is mentioned in the text; so too are honorary and special awards and unusual achievements.

A chronological index provides, for quick reference, every nominee in the six main Academy categories – best film, director, actor, actress, supporting actor and actress – from 1929, the year the awards were first presented at a banquet at Hollywood's Roosevelt Hotel, to 1996. A second index allows you to find, at a glance, just where and how often your favourite films are mentioned in the text.

What I hope you will find within these pages is not only a unique source of reference, but also a flavour of seventy years of mainstream cinema. A kind of history, if you like. A bizarre history, certainly – glitzy, colourful, emotional – but a history nonetheless, one filled with great lines of movie dialogue and amusing comment and rueful reflection from many of the lucky and not so lucky nominees. In short, a bright and breezy 'read and dip'!

My thanks go primarily to the late Margaret Herrick, the first librarian of the Academy of Motion Picture Arts and Sciences (the organisation that first founded the awards back in the late twenties) who – long ago now – suggested the book as a companion to my earlier *The Oscar Movies*. Always unfailingly courteous, always cheerful in her letters, her enthusiasm was infectious, and although we met only in an *84 Charing Cross Rd* way, by letter, the book would not have seen the light of day without her support.

The three volumes I consulted most frequently during the preparation of *The Oscar Stars* were Robert Osborne's official Academy history *60 Years of Oscar*, a fine work that continues to impress; Mason Wiley and Damien Bona's *Inside Oscar*, easily the chattiest and most gossipy of Oscar books; and the splendid *International Film Encyclopedia* by Ephraim Katz. I have drawn also from every kind of obituary I could lay my hands on, and from the 150 or so interviews I have conducted over the years as a radio and magazine journalist. Bette Davis, Henry Fonda, James Stewart, Ingrid Bergman, Gregory Peck, James Mason, Shirley MacLaine, Robert Mitchum . . . memories of them all and many others came flooding back during the compilation of this book.

As for Oscar himself? Well, he's 13½ inches tall, made of britannium, is gold-plated and weighs 8½lb, although he feels heavier when you pick him up. A bald, gleaming little figure standing with a sword on a reel of film, he was designed by MGM art director Cedric Gibbons. When you come right down to it he's not much to look at, but in Hollywood and across the world he's worth his weight in gold.

He still has his detractors among the arty folk of the film world – too crude, too commercial, they scoff, looking down their haughty noses with not a little disdain. Too vulgar as well, much too vulgar. That is, until they win him – and then it's a very different story!

Roy Pickard
September 1996

A

F. Murray Abraham

Born Pittsburgh, USA, 24 October 1939

Oscars (1): Best Actor for Antonio Salieri in *Amadeus* (Orion, 1984)

Madness, envy, treachery, deceit . . . F. Murray Abraham embraced them all as the court composer Salieri in *Amadeus*, beating his nominated co-star Tom Hulce to the winning post by a whisker and then finding that the Oscar hadn't done that much for him after all. Just a few mediocre roles – a gangster in *Mobsters*, a heavy in the comic strip *The Last Action Hero*, a judge in the ill-fated *Bonfire of the Vanities* – have been among his most recent accomplishments. His Inquisitor involved with Sean Connery in the medieval murder mystery *The Name of the Rose* offered him more rewarding opportunities.

Nick Adams

Born Nanticoke, Pennsylvania, USA, 10 July 1931; died 1968

Oscar Nominations (1): Best Supporting Actor for Ben Brown in *Twilight of Honor* (MGM, 1963)

A list of the ten most surprising Oscar nominees would almost certainly include Nick Adams, a young actor who mixed with the fast crowd in the fifties (Dean, Presley and co.) and found himself up for a supporting nod for his accused murderer in *Twilight of Honor*. Perhaps realising he'd been lucky and that this might be his only chance (it was), he lashed out $8000 to help promote his chances. The result of his advertisements didn't exactly have the desired effect, one critic remarking that his photograph in the ads 'ranged in every expression from Upset Stomach to Godzilla to Stopped Up Sinuses to Attila The Hun to Ex-Lax'. The veteran Melvyn Douglas, the year's supporting winner for *Hud*, suffered from none of these things.

Isabelle Adjani

Born Paris, France, 27 June 1955

Oscar Nominations (2): Best Actress for Adèle Hugo in *The Story of Adèle H* (New World Pictures, France, 1975) and the title role in *Camille Claudel* (Orion Classics, France, 1989)

She's tangled with Dracula in *Nosferatu*, played Emily Brontë and Queen Margot, earned awards at Cannes and become the only French actress to be nominated twice for an Oscar – first for her tortured daughter of Victor Hugo in Truffaut's *The Story of Adèle H* and then for her muse and mistress of Rodin, *Camille Claudel*. And she's still only in her early forties. Her chance may still come, although the portents aren't good. Simone Signoret remains the only French performer to win a Best Actress Oscar (for her portrayal in the British film, *Room at the Top*) in the sixty-eight-year history of the awards.

Brian Aherne

Born King's Norton, England, 2 May 1902; died 1986

Oscar Nominations (1): Best Supporting Actor for Maximilian von Hapsburg in *Juarez* (Warner Bros, 1939)

Not quite in the top bracket of Hollywood's 'typical Englishman' so beloved in the movie capital in the thirties, Brian Aherne nonetheless knew how to make the most of his urbane charm and even caused a surprise in 1939 by earning a nomination for his Emperor Maximilian in *Juarez*, which is rather more than can be said for many of the other members of the British colony of the time – Karloff, Alan Mowbray, Nigel Bruce, C. Aubrey Smith, et al. More at home flying his open-cockpit, two-seater biplane than he was in front of the cameras, he lost in 1939 to Thomas Mitchell's Doc Boone in *Stagecoach*. He later said of his *Juarez* co-star Bette Davis: 'Surely no one but a mother could have loved Bette at the height of her career!'

☆

Danny Aiello

Born New York City, USA, 20 June 1933

Oscar Nominations (1): Best Supporting Actor for Sal in *Do the Right Thing* (Forty Acres and a Mule Filmworks/Universal, 1989)

A late starter, whose tough, burly, lived-in features weren't glimpsed on screen until he was forty, Danny Aiello has been enhancing films by Woody Allen (*The Purple Rose of Cairo*, *Radio Days*), Norman Jewison and others for more than twenty years now. New York is his habitat, either as gangster, brutal husband or sympathetic family man. His Oscar nomination was for his role in Spike Lee's *Do the Right Thing* as the owner of the Brooklyn Pizza Parlour, the focal point of the violence that erupts when racial tensions emerge in the sweltering heat of the city. A fine role; an uncomfortable film. Denzel Washington took the year's supporting honours for *Glory*.

Anouk Aimee

Born Paris, France, 27 April 1932

Oscar Nominations (1): Best Actress for Anne Gauthier in *A Man and a Woman* (Les Films 13, France, 1966)

Tall, striking and with an enigmatic beauty that caused one critic to describe her as 'an elusive screen presence', Anouk Aimee has earned just a single nomination in her career, which doesn't sound much until it is put into context, i.e., most French actresses don't win any! Nominated for her glamorous French mother who each weekend visits her child's school in Deauville and who takes time out to fall in love with another visiting parent, she was, unfortunately, little more than an outsider in 1966, when Liz Taylor's blowsy, alcoholic Martha (*Who's Afraid of Virginia Woolf?*) carried all before her and sank all opposition!

Eddie Albert

Born Rock Island, Illinois, USA, 22 April 1908

Oscar Nominations (2): Best Supporting Actor for Irving Radovich in *Roman Holiday* (Paramount, 1953) and Mr Corcoran in *The Heartbreak Kid* (20th Century-Fox, 1972)

They didn't come any brighter or breezier than Eddie Albert – everyone's favourite salesman, piano accompanist and best pal of someone on the skids. *Roman Holiday* wouldn't have been the same without his cigarette lighter-photographer who accompanies Greg Peck and Audrey Hepburn around the eternal city, and *The Heartbreak Kid* would have been a lesser film without his subtle essaying of Cybill Shepherd's wealthy businessman father. Still, two nominations for a career that has spanned more than fifty years and even included a few heavies from time to time somehow seems a less than adequate reward.

Jack Albertson

Born Malden, Massachusetts, USA, 16 June 1907; died 1981

Oscars (1): Best Supporting Actor for John Cleary in *The Subject Was Roses* (MGM, 1968)

To win a Tony is, for many stage actors, the peak of achievement; to earn an Oscar for the same role is a rarity. Jack Albertson managed both for his hostile Bronx salesman bitterly at odds with his wife and never really on terms with his army veteran son in the Pulitzer Prize-winning *The Subject Was Roses*. Not that MGM wanted him for the part. They would have much preferred a box-office name. It was only when the play's author Frank Gilroy stated that he would only sell them the film rights if Albertson repeated his Broadway role on screen that they backtracked. A former vaudevillian and burlesque performer, Albertson was best known in his post-Oscar days for his bedridden grandfather of the young Charlie Bucket in *Willy Wonka and the Chocolate Factory*, and for being among the heroic survivors in *The Poseidon Adventure*.

Norma Aleandro

Born Buenos Aires, Argentina, 6 December 1936

Oscar Nominations (1): Best Supporting Actress for Florencia in *Gaby – A True Story* (Brimmer/TriStar, 1987)

A long way from being the best-known actress in these pages, Norma Aleandro is nonetheless one of the most versatile, earning plaudits the world over for her work as an actress and political activist and as a writer of poems and short stories. Her single Oscar nomination was for her devoted nurse who cares for a cerebral palsy child in pre-war Mexico; her finest role was that of a complacent middle-class woman who is sheltered from the political turmoil around her in Argentina but then discovers that her five-year-old adopted daughter is the offspring of political prisoners. No nomination unfortunately, although she shared the best actress award at Cannes, and the picture, *The Official Story*, was voted best foreign-language film of 1985 by the Academy.

Jane Alexander

Born Boston, USA, 28 October 1939

Oscar Nominations (4): Best Actress for Eleanor Bachman in *The Great White Hope* (20th Century-Fox, 1970); Best Supporting Actress for Book-keeper in *All the President's Men* (Warner Bros, 1976) and Margaret Phelps in *Kramer vs. Kramer* (Columbia, 1979); Best Actress for Carol Wetherby in *Testament* (Paramount, 1983)

She almost made it in 1970, when she gave what for many was the year's finest female performance as the white woman who marries black boxing champion Jack Johnson and suffers shame and humiliation as a result. Glenda Jackson, though, was making a charge for *Women in Love*, and ever since, Jane Alexander has only been there or thereabouts at Oscar time. A pity, for she's one of America's finest. Her subsequent nominations have been for her informer in *All the President's Men*, her abandoned wife and neighbour of Dustin Hoffman in *Kramer*, and her heroic mother trying to hold her family together after a nuclear catastrophe in *Testament*. Her role in *The Great White Hope* was a repeat of her Broadway performance which won her a Tony award in 1961.

Joan Allen

Born Rochelle, Illinois, USA, 20 August 1956

Oscar Nominations (1): Best Supporting Actress for Pat Nixon in *Nixon* (Buena Vista/Hollywood Pictures, 1995)

There were many among the 1995 voters who felt that the talented Joan Allen should have been up for the best actress (she was second in the cast list) and not best support for her Pat Nixon. They had a point. At times her touching, beautifully controlled playing of a First Lady who understood her husband in all his moods, accused him when he was wrong and stood by him when she felt he was right put Anthony Hopkins' title portrayal in the shade. But support it was, and with Mira Sorvino in irresistible form as the good-hearted hooker in *Mighty Aphrodite*, that, to all intents and purposes, was that. The supporting awards of the Los Angeles Critics and New York's National Society of Film Critics offered deserved crumbs of comfort.

Woody Allen

Born Brooklyn, New York, USA, 1 December 1935

Oscar Nominations (1): Best Actor for Alvy Singer in *Annie Hall* (United Artists, 1977)

'Most of the time I don't have much fun. The rest of the time I don't have any fun at all,' said Woody Allen, who was joking at the time, although one only had to glance at his glum, bespectacled countenance to know that he wasn't really joking at all. The star, director and writer of some thirty movies, he has been nominated just the once as an actor, for his little stand-up comic who has a nervous romance with Diane Keaton's Annie Hall. Considering that he looks and sounds exactly the same in every movie, that's probably a fair reward. Where he has really triumphed is as a writer, having earned a total of twelve screenplay nominations from *Annie Hall* to *Mighty Aphrodite*. The surprise is that they failed to nominate him for any of his earlier work, such as *Bananas*, which included exchanges that went along these lines: 'I love you, I love you' – 'Oh say it in French. Oh, please say it in French' – 'I don't know French' – 'Oh, please . . . please!' – 'How about Hebrew?'

Note: Allen has won Oscars for his screenplay and direction of *Annie Hall* and for his screenplay of *Hannah and Her Sisters* (1986). As well as his writing nominations he has earned five mentions as best director – for *Interiors* (1978), *Broadway Danny Rose* (1984), *Hannah and Her Sisters*, *Crimes and Misdemeanors* (1989) and *Bullets Over Broadway* (1994).

Sara Allgood

Born Dublin, Ireland, 31 October 1883; died 1950

Oscar Nominations (1): Best Supporting Actress for Mrs Morgan in *How Green Was My Valley* (20th Century-Fox, 1941)

It didn't seem quite fair that Donald Crisp should win and Sara Allgood should earn just a nomination for *How Green Was My Valley*. They were a pair on screen – as the parents of a Welsh mining family struggling to keep life and soul together at the turn of the century – and they should have been a pair on Oscar night. Mary Astor claimed the supporting award, however, and Sara Allgood went back to doing what she did best, playing amiable mothers, waitresses and landladies, and even, in a moment of weakness, giving shelter to Jack the Ripper in *The Lodger*.

Don Ameche

Born Kenosha, Wisconsin, USA, 31 May 1908; died 1993

Oscars (1): Best Supporting Actor for Art Selwyn in *Cocoon* (20th Century-Fox, 1985)

Rejuvenation was the name of the game in *Cocoon*. Three of them were at it – Hume Cronyn, Wilford Brimley and Don Ameche, all of them given the elixir of youth by some floating friendly aliens. It was Ameche who made it to the podium, pulling off the surprise of the year and earning a just reward for all the singing and smiling and 'You have the girl, you're more worthy of her than me'-type roles he played at Fox in the forties. A national favourite in many popular radio shows, his voice was once described as 'butterscotch baritone'. His trademark was his pencil-thin moustache that always enhanced his ready smile.

Judith Anderson

Born Adelaide, Australia, 10 February 1898; died 1992

Oscar Nominations (1): Best Supporting Actress for Mrs Danvers in *Rebecca* (Selznick/United Artists, 1940)

They didn't come much nastier or more sinister than Mrs Danvers in *Rebecca*, and Judith Anderson gave it all she'd got in Hitchcock's 1940 version, whispering malevolently into Joan Fontaine's ear that it would be so easy to end it all, to lean over and gently jump into the mists far below . . . Somehow, poor Joan resisted, and it was Judith Anderson who met her doom, going up in flames, as mad as a hatter, as Manderley burned to the ground. Marvellous at playing ogres, Judith Anderson was nominated just the once. Her penchant for cruelty included clubbing a cat to death in *The Strange Love of Martha Ivers*. She also sympathised with the Nazis in *All Through the Night*.

Julie Andrews

Born Walton-on-Thames, England, 1 October 1935

Oscars (1): Best Actress for the title role in *Mary Poppins* (Disney, 1964)

Oscar Nominations (2): Best Actress for Maria in *The Sound of Music* (20th Century-Fox, 1965) and the title role in *Victor/Victoria* (MGM, 1982)

'Practically perfect' is how Julie Andrews described herself as *Mary Poppins*. Hollywood agreed, awarding her the best actress prize first time out for her magical nanny, and even nominated her again the following year for a second goody two-shoes, the novice Maria in *The Sound of Music*. Another Julie – Julie Christie, who in *Darling* had a taste for the saltier things in life – put an end to the double; the film *Easy Rider* put an end to Andrews' box-office clout (although not her popularity), as Dennis Hopper and Peter Fonda went for a motorbike ride across America and proved that movies could, unfortunately, be made without decent scripts! Julie Andrews was nominated for a third time, for arguably her best performance, as the drag-artist cabaret star in *Victor/Victoria*.

Ann-Margret

Born Valsjobyn, Sweden, 28 April 1941

Oscar Nominations (2): Best Supporting Actress for Bobbie in *Carnal Knowledge* (Avco Embassy, 1971); Best Actress for Nora Walker Hobbs in *Tommy* (Columbia, 1975)

One of the sixties' most alluring song-and-dance sex kittens, Ann-Margret eyed the Oscars twice in the seventies, dipped her delectable toes in the Academy water and pulled them out again with two nominations – one for her model past her prime and finding sexual satisfaction with Jack Nicholson in *Carnal Knowledge*, the other for her mother of Tommy in Ken Russell's typically exuberant version of the Who's celebrated rock opera. Even bathing in baked beans for dear old Ken didn't do the trick, and Oscars and Ann-Margret were destined never to meet. She's done better on television, essaying a moving Blanche DuBois in a 1984 adaptation of *A Streetcar Named Desire*.

Anne Archer

Born Los Angeles, USA, 25 August 1947

Oscar Nominations (1): Best Supporting Actress for Beth Gallagher in *Fatal Attraction* (Paramount, 1987)

If suffering on screen has anything to do with winning Oscars, Anne Archer should have won hands down for *Fatal Attraction*. As well as having to cope with hubby Michael Douglas' whirlwind affair with a psychotic Glenn Close, she had to remain sane after being hospitalised in a car crash, witnessing the death of a pet rabbit through boiling and an attempted murder in her bathroom. She did retain her sanity but it still wasn't enough. Olympia Dukakis' somewhat less frenetic mom in *Moonstruck* eased in, cool as you like, to take the year's supporting nod without a psychotic or a dead rabbit in sight. It didn't seem fair somehow!

Eve Arden

Born Mill Valley, California, USA, 20 April 1912; died 1990

Oscar Nominations (1): Best Supporting Actress for Ida in *Mildred Pierce* (Warner Bros, 1945)

A sardonic and stylish comedienne who was invariably cast as a wife's best friend or all-knowing sister, Eve Arden had the enviable task of delivering (usually with a mocking glance at her victim) some of the most acid one-liners written for American movies of the thirties and forties. As the friend of the long-suffering Joan Crawford in *Mildred Pierce* (her only Oscar nomination) she says of Crawford's spoiled daughter: 'Veda's convinced me that alligators have the right idea. They eat their young.' In the same film, and in a slightly different mood, she grumbled: 'I'm awfully tired of men talking to me man to man!' Only Groucho Marx, it seemed, got the better of her. In *At the Circus* she says to him: 'I've waited so long for someone like you', to which he replies: 'Someone *like* me. So I'm not good enough for you.' An Emmy award-winner in the fifties for her sharp-tongued but warm-hearted schoolteacher in the TV series *Our Miss Brooks*, she was born Eunice Quedens but changed her name while looking over some cosmetics and spotting the names 'Evening in Paris' and 'Elizabeth Arden'.

Alan Arkin

Born New York City, USA, 26 March 1934

Oscar Nominations (2): Best Actor for Rozanov in *The Russians Are Coming, The Russians Are Coming* (United Artists, 1966) and Singer in *The Heart Is a Lonely Hunter* (Warner Bros, 1968)

The most trivial aspect of Alan Arkin's movie career is that he is the only actor other than Peter Sellers to have played the accident-prone Inspector

Clouseau on film; the most disappointing is that he didn't progress from the promise of the sixties when for a year or two he looked as though he would develop into one of the major performers of the American screen. Instead, he has become one of its most talented and versatile character actors. His Oscar nominations were for his timorous Russian lieutenant who helps run his submarine aground on a sandbar off Cape Cod, and for his heart-rending performance as the deaf mute in *The Heart Is a Lonely Hunter*. He received nothing for his troubled flier Yossarian in the satirical *Catch-22*.

George Arliss

Born London, England, 10 April 1868; died 1946

Oscars (1): Best Actor for the title role in *Disraeli* (Warner Bros, 1929/30)

Oscar Nominations (1): Best Actor for the Rajah of Rukh in *The Green Goddess* (Warner Bros, 1929/30)

A kind of slimline, rather more subtle Charlton Heston of the thirties, in that he essayed a long line of historical roles – Voltaire, Richelieu, the Iron Duke – George Arliss earned his Oscar for his portrayal of the wily British prime minister Benjamin Disraeli, whom he had first portrayed in a 1921 silent. Sensitive, thin-faced and as often as not with a monocle, he was nominated the same year for his Eastern villain in *The Green Goddess*, but alas was not the stuff of matinée idols. He later wrote somewhat ruefully in his memoirs: 'Harry Warner told me that when he decided to do *Disraeli* he did not expect it to pay but he was using me as an expensive bait to hook people into the cinema who had never gone before!'

Note: Although George Arliss was nominated for both *Disraeli* and *The Green Goddess* in 1929/30 he was named only for his performance in the former film on Oscar night. No official reason was given by the Academy. After this third year of the awards performers were nominated for roles in one film only.

Jean Arthur

Born New York City, USA, 17 October 1905; died 1991

Oscar Nominations (1): Best Actress for Connie Milligan in *The More the Merrier* (Columbia, 1943)

Was there really just the one Oscar nomination? The answer for Jean Arthur admirers must be a reluctant yes – for her government girl who allows two men to share her overcrowded apartment in wartime Washington in *The More the Merrier*. Quite how she missed (Jennifer Jones won for *The Song of Bernadette*) is one of the Oscar imponderables; so too is the fact that she was overlooked for a whole gallery of stylish career girls who knew how to put men in their place and keep them there. Frank Capra, Howard Hawks and Billy Wilder were among the directors who made use of her unique talents and husky, squeaky tones. George Stevens was the man who called her 'one of the best comediennes the screen has ever seen'.

Peggy Ashcroft

Born Croydon, England, 22 December 1907; died 1991

Oscars (1): Best Supporting Actress for Mrs Moore in *A Passage to India* (GW Films/Home Box Office, 1984)

The theatre saw the best of Peggy Ashcroft but luckily there was an Indian summer when millions were able to appreciate what the theatre-going few had been witnessing for years. Superb on television as the white-haired Anglo-Indian spinster Barbie Batchelor in *The Jewel in the Crown*, she won her Oscar for another visit to the Indian subcontinent as Judy Davis' chaperone Mrs Moore in David Lean's *A Passage to India*. There should have been more; 16 films in 50 years was not enough, even though it did include some minor gems, such as the kindly crofter's wife in Hitchcock's *The 39 Steps* and a sympathetic Mother Superior in Fred Zinnemann's *The Nun's Story*.

☆

Fred Astaire

Born Omaha, Nebraska, USA, 10 May 1899; died 1987

Oscar Nominations (1): Best Supporting Actor for Harlee Clairborne in *The Towering Inferno* (Warner Bros/20th Century-Fox, 1974)

One of eleven top stars brought together for the disaster movie *The Towering Inferno*, Fred Astaire was also one of the few who managed to get out alive and the only cast member to figure among the year's Oscar nominees. As it turned out, it was a bad year to be nominated, three of the heavies from *The Godfather Part II* – Robert De Niro, Michael V. Gazzo and Lee Strasberg – also receiving mentions. Astaire (for his debonair con man) eventually finished up an also-ran to De Niro and had to be content with the special award he had received 25 years earlier for his 'unique artistry and his contribution to the technique of musical pictures'. He performed two Academy Award-winning numbers at RKO in the thirties – 'The Continental' from *The Gay Divorcee* (1934) and 'The Way You Look Tonight' from *Swing Time* (1936).

Mary Astor

Born Quincy, Illinois, USA, 3 May 1906; died 1987

Oscars (1): Best Supporting Actress for Sandra Kovak in *The Great Lie* (Warner Bros, 1941)

'The chances are you'll get off with life,' said Bogie to Mary Astor at the climax of *The Maltese Falcon*. 'That means that if you're a good girl you'll be out in twenty years. I'll be waiting for you. If they hang you, I'll always remember you.' The lift door clangs like a prison and descends from view. Mary Astor's Oscar role? Surprisingly, no, but for many it should have been, for *femmes fatales* don't come much more *fatale* than her Brigid O'Shaughnessy! Instead, the Academy opted for another of her 1941 offerings, *The Great Lie*, in which she played a selfish, career-minded concert pianist and co-starred with Bette Davis. It was her only award, although if she had starred in a film of her own life, a roller-coaster ride which included teenage romance with John Barrymore, numerous other affairs, bouts of alcoholism, a suicide attempt and a career as a novelist, she might have earned another!

☆

Mischa Auer

Born St Petersburg, Russia, 17 November 1905; died 1967

Oscar Nominations (1): Best Supporting Actor for Carlo in *My Man Godfrey* (Universal, 1936)

A comedian by accident (he began in films playing mainly villains and old men), the Russian-born Mischa Auer made his comedy breakthrough in style as a piano-tinkling gigolo forever hankering after something to eat, in the William Powell–Carole Lombard comedy *My Man Godfrey*. The role brought him an Oscar nomination and a Hollywood career that embraced impoverished princes, distraught waiters, excitable playwrights and even, in Capra's *You Can't Take It With You*, a Russian ballet master who regards a ballerina with awe and then says: 'Confidentially . . . she steenks!' The cause of the famous catfight between Marlene Dietrich and Una Merkel in *Destry Rides Again*, he was an Oscar nominee just the once. After World War II he took his bulging eyes and doleful countenance to Europe, where he helped enliven films starring Martine Carol and Brigitte Bardot. In 1954 he played the proprietor of a flea circus for Orson Welles in *Mr Arkadin*.

☆

Margaret Avery

Oscar Nominations (1): Best Supporting Actress for Shug Avery in *The Color Purple* (Warner Bros, 1985)

Lucky breaks come the way of most movie performers; Margaret Avery's occurred when Tina Turner turned down the role of Whoopi Goldberg's long-time friend in *The Color Purple* and because Steven Spielberg remembered her from a commercial he had once directed. An Oscar nomination was the result, but not the award itself. Three women in *The Color Purple* (Avery, Goldberg and Oprah Winfrey) were nominated for their roles but none came out a winner. Neither did anyone else connected with the film, even though it amassed eleven nominations.

Dan Aykroyd

Born Ottawa, Canada, 1 July 1952

Oscar Nominations (1): Best Supporting Actor for Boolie Werthan in *Driving Miss Daisy* (Warner Bros, 1989)

Even if he never makes another film, Dan Aykroyd's place in cult movie history is assured as one of the destructive Blues Brothers and as one of the zany Ghostbusters! Less bawdy and noisy in recent years, he has developed into something of a versatile character actor, earning his Oscar nomination for his caring and frequently worried son of the aged Jessica Tandy in *Driving Miss Daisy*. An electronic gadget freak working with Robert Redford's shady gang in *Sneakers*, and the silent movie mogul Mack Sennett in *Chaplin* have been among his recent roles.

☆

Lew Ayres

Born Minneapolis, USA, 28 December 1908

Oscar Nominations (1): Best Actor for Dr Robert Richardson in *Johnny Belinda* (Warner Bros, 1948)

Described by one critic as a man 'who chose the wrong vocation', Lew Ayres was best known for his series of roles as the popular Dr Kildare, and for his young German soldier disillusioned by war in Lewis Milestone's *All Quiet on the Western Front*. Unlucky to miss out on a nomination for the latter role, he was subsequently rewarded for his post-war performance as the kindly New England doctor in *Johnny Belinda*. His career was damaged by his stand as a conscientious objector during World War II, when he refused to join the armed services for religious reasons but served with bravery and distinction as an orderly in the Army Medical Corps at three Pacific beachhead invasions. Although he continued to act after the war, he was more at ease studying philosophy and comparative religions than he was before the cameras.

B

Hermione Baddeley

Born Broseley, Shropshire, England, 13 November 1906; died 1986

Oscar Nominations (1): Best Supporting Actress for Elspeth in *Room at the Top* (Romulus, 1959)

Just a couple of scenes were enough to earn Hermione Baddeley her nomination for her music-teacher friend of Simone Signoret in *Room at the Top*; the first as she discreetly interrupts Signoret's lovemaking with Laurence Harvey, the second when she is in full cry after Signoret's hideous death in a car crash and tongue-lashes Harvey with 'You bastard . . . you dirty rotten *bastard* . . . you killed her!' Dramatic stuff for 1959, not enough to win her the award, which went to Shelley Winters (*The Diary of Anne Frank*), but enough to get her to Hollywood, where she exchanged the blowsy, sometimes humorous, sometimes shrewish characters she had been playing on British screens for more squeaky-clean ones at Disney, in *Mary Poppins* and *The Happiest Millionaire*. Her elder sister Angela became famous on the small screen as Mrs Bridges in the TV series *Upstairs, Downstairs*.

Mary Badham

Born 1952

Oscar Nominations (1): Best Supporting Actress for Scout Finch in *To Kill a Mockingbird* (Universal-International, 1962)

She was a joy, was the young Mary Badham, as Greg Peck's little tomboy daughter in *To Kill a Mockingbird*, and easily nabbed one of 1962's supporting nods, even though it was a little hard on the other kids in the picture – Phillip Alford as brother Jem and John Megna as Dill – both of whom were equally deserving. Nineteen sixty-two, however, was not her year, the sixteen-year-old Patty Duke for *The Miracle Worker* beating off her nine-year-old challenger, a situation that was reversed eleven years later when the younger Tatum O'Neal (*Paper Moon*) got the better of Linda Blair in *The Exorcist*. The sister of director John Badham and the daughter of a retired army general, Mary had no previous acting experience before being selected for her role.

Fay Bainter

Born Los Angeles, USA, 7 December 1892; died 1968

Oscars (1): Best Supporting Actress for Aunt Belle Massey in *Jezebel* (Warner Bros, 1938)

Oscar Nominations (2): Best Actress for Hannah Parmalee in *White Banners* (Warner Bros, 1938); Best Supporting Actress for Mrs Amelia Tilford in *The Children's Hour* (United Artists, 1961)

The understanding, warm-hearted mom, aunt and best friend; that was Fay Bainter's lot on screen and it paid dividends at least as far as the Oscars were concerned, allowing her to become the first actress to achieve the Oscar double – nominations for best actress (for her gentle, spiritual housekeeper of Claude Rains in *White Banners*) and best supporting actress (as Bette Davis' Aunt Belle in *Jezebel*) in the same year. A subsequent nominee for her grandmother deceived by a child's lies in Wyler's *The Children's Hour*, she was only occasionally allowed to go off the rails, as she did in *The Shining Hour* when, as a domineering spinster who loathes her sister-in-law, nightclub dancer Joan Crawford, she has a fit of frustrated rage and sets fire to the family home. Such opportunities came her way only rarely.

Carroll Baker

Born Johnstown, Pennsylvania, USA, 28 May 1931

Oscar Nominations (1): Best Actress for Baby Doll Meighan in *Baby Doll* (Warner Bros, 1956)

A thumb stuck provocatively in her mouth, her girlish figure revealed through her skimpy nightie and her bare legs stretched to the tip of her cot-like bed! Few actresses of the fifties made quite such an impact as the twenty-four-year-old Carroll Baker in Kazan's *Baby Doll*, but although she was Oscar-nominated for her retarded child bride the quality follow-up roles didn't materialise and she was reduced to cultivating a vulgar, trashy image – one that served her well in the sixties and seventies, often in sexploitation films made in Italy and Spain. Her best American roles were in *The Carpetbaggers*, in which she enjoyed herself swinging half-naked from a chandelier, and best of all as the legendary MGM star in *Harlow*. In 1983 she appeared as the mother of the murdered *Playboy* centrefold Dorothy Stratten in Bob Fosse's *Star 80*.

Martin Balsam

Born New York City, USA, 4 November 1919; died 1996

Oscars (1): Best Supporting Actor for Arnold Burns in *A Thousand Clowns* (United Artists, 1965)

He began by handing a subpoena to Marlon Brando (it took two of them, Leif Ericson was also in on the act) in *On the Waterfront*, and developed into one of America's most dependable and versatile character actors, as adept at ordinary middle-class husbands as he was with crazed army officers, hijackers and Mafia men. Just one Oscar win in his forty years in the movies – for his agent brother of hack TV writer Jason Robards in *A Thousand Clowns* – was a poor reward, and quite where the voters were when he was playing the sweating jury foreman in *12 Angry Men* is anybody's guess. His biggest disappointment? Not getting the role of HAL in *2001*. He had recorded the dialogue but Kubrick had second thoughts and opted for someone with a slightly more sinister voice. His biggest mistake? Climbing those stairs in *Psycho*!

Anne Bancroft

Born the Bronx, New York, USA, 17 September 1931

Oscars (1): Best Actress for Annie Sullivan in *The Miracle Worker* (United Artists, 1962)

Oscar Nominations (4): Best Actress for Jo Armitage in *The Pumpkin Eater* (Columbia, 1964), Mrs Robinson in *The Graduate* (Avco-Embassy, 1967), Emma Jacklin in *The Turning Point* (20th Century-Fox, 1977) and Mother Miriam Ruth in *Agnes of God* (Columbia, 1985)

Older filmgoers remember Anne Bancroft best as the predatory Mrs Robinson who seduces graduate Dustin Hoffman; younger movie fans recall her singing 'Sweet Georgia Brown' in Polish with hubby Mel Brooks in *To Be or Not To Be*. Somewhere in between lies a body of work that earned her a best actress Oscar – as the teacher of Helen Keller (a repeat of her Broadway role) and nominations for her neurotic mother of eight in *The Pumpkin Eater*, Mrs Robinson in *The Graduate*, an ageing ballet dancer, and a mother superior. No one deserved her Oscar success more. Anyone who could survive a five-year apprenticeship (at Fox in the fifties) that included roles in *Gorilla at Large* and *The Girl in Black Stockings* was due the highest reward possible.

George Bancroft

Born Philadelphia, USA, 30 September 1882; died 1956

Oscar Nominations (1): Best Actor for Thunderbolt Jim Lang in *Thunderbolt* (Paramount, 1928/29)

The trouble with George Bancroft is that no one remembers the roles that made him famous (many of them for Von Sternberg at Paramount in the late twenties) whilst just about everyone recalls his stagecoach driver Curly from the reruns of Ford's *Stagecoach* on the telly. By 1939 he had left most of his villainy behind him but in the final days of the silent cinema and the early years of sound he was as tough and vicious as they came, earning his Oscar nomination for his death-row convict awaiting execution in Sing Sing. He gave it all up in 1942 when he put his hoods, underworld kings and character roles into cold storage and retired to become a rancher.

Ian Bannen

Born Airdrie, Scotland, 29 June 1928

Oscar Nominations (1): Best Supporting Actor for Crow in *The Flight of the Phoenix* (20th Century-Fox, 1965)

A long-serving, reliable Scottish actor who began in romantic leads in lightweight British comedies of the fifties, Ian Bannen has in more recent times found a niche for himself playing devious politicians, seedy criminals and disillusioned spies. The only cast member of Robert Aldrich's *The Flight of the Phoenix* to earn an Oscar nomination, he excelled as Crow, who with his unfailing patter keeps up the spirits of his fellow passengers when James Stewart's rickety old cargo plane crash-lands in the desert. Defeated on Oscar night by Martin Balsam in *A Thousand Clowns*, he was perhaps unlucky to miss out for his alleged child molester in Sidney Lumet's *The Offence* and, in 1987, for his cricket-loving and lady-loving Grandfather George in John Boorman's *Hope and Glory*.

Marie-Christine Barrault

Born Paris, France, 21 March 1944

Oscar Nominations (1): Best Actress for Marthe in *Cousin, Cousine* (Northal Films, France, 1976)

A real enchantress, Marie-Christine Barrault brought a light gaiety and charm to a year when Faye Dunaway was carving up just about everyone who got in her way in *Network*. The charm brought a nomination but nothing more, other than the pleasure of watching her embarking on an illicit affair with her cousin by marriage and discovering that things become rather more passionate than she had imagined. A big success in the States (it was subsequently remade as *Cousins* with Isabella Rossellini and Ted Danson), the film was also nominated as one of the year's best foreign-language productions. Barrault made her screen début in Rohmer's *My Night at Maud's* and is the niece of Jean Louis Barrault.

Barbara Barrie

Born Chicago, USA, 23 May 1931

Oscar Nominations (1): Best Supporting Actress for Mrs Stohler in *Breaking Away* (20th Century-Fox, 1979)

Meryl Streep's domination of every pre-Oscar award in the supporting category for *Kramer vs. Kramer* made her such an odds-on certainty for the Academy Award that the interest rested more on who would make the remaining four places. Barbara Barrie was a welcome surprise, earning her nod for her working-class mom of a teenage racing cyclist in *Breaking Away*. 'I'm not quite right for it,' she had told director Peter Yates just prior to shooting. 'Nonsense,' he replied, 'you're perfect.' The Academy agreed. So too, subsequently, did the TV producers who cast her in the same role in the spin-off television series.

Ethel Barrymore

Born Philadelphia, USA, 15 August 1879; died 1959

Oscars (1): Best Supporting Actress for Ma Mott in *None But the Lonely Heart* (RKO, 1944)

Oscar Nominations (3): Best Supporting Actress for Mrs Warren in *The Spiral Staircase* (RKO, 1946), Lady Sophie Horfield in *The Paradine Case* (Selznick, United Artists, 1947) and Miss Em in *Pinky* (20th Century-Fox, 1949)

One of the grand old ladies of the screen, Ethel Barrymore won her Oscar for playing Cary Grant's Cockney mum in *None But the Lonely Heart*, which is probably as good a way as any of winning a top prize. It didn't stop her trying for more, though – first as a widowed invalid trapped in a spooky old house, then as the wife of lecherous trial judge Charles Laughton, and finally as the kindly head of a decaying Southern family who bequeathes her property to Jeanne Crain. Four nominations in just six years wasn't bad for someone approaching her seventies, although many felt that her all-knowing art dealer who befriends the haunted Joseph Cotten in *Portrait of Jennie* should have made it five in six. In real life, a woman of sparkling wit and humour, she boasted a huge book collection and was an avid baseball fan. She appeared on screen with her two brothers, Lionel and John, just the once, when she played the Czarina in *Rasputin and the Empress*. She said: 'I thought I was pretty good but what those two boys were up to I'll never know.'

Lionel Barrymore

Born Philadelphia, USA, 28 April 1878; died 1954

Oscars (1): Best Actor for Stephen Ashe in *A Free Soul* (MGM, 1930/31)

'I've got a lot of ham in me,' admitted Lionel Barrymore, whose portraits of doctors, patriarchs, attorneys and plain crotchety old men (many of them with a soft centre) emerged with regularity from the MGM sound stages for more than a quarter of a century. An Oscar-winner for his drunken lawyer defending his daughter on a murder charge in *A Free Soul*, he was nominated two years earlier for his direction of *Madame X* and remained the only actor/director to have been nominated for both crafts until Orson Welles entered the lists with *Citizen Kane* in 1941. Confined to a wheelchair in his later years because of a leg injury and arthritis, he began in the business at the Biograph studio, working for D. W. Griffith as a $10-a-day extra. On a good day he wrote two-reelers at $25 a piece!

Richard Barthelmess

Born New York City, USA, 9 May 1895; died 1963

Oscar Nominations (2): Best Actor for the title role in *The Patent Leather Kid* and Nickie Elkins in *The Noose* (both First National, 1927/28)

'When I saw my friends were earning just seven or eight dollars a week in banks I thought I'd better try acting,' said Richard Barthelmess when recalling his start in movies. It was a wise decision. Boyish in looks and all-American in personality, he became a favourite with silent audiences, especially in *Tol'able David*, in which he played a Virginia mountain boy who sees the US mail gets through. Nominated for two roles in the first year of the Awards – for his prizefighter *The Patent Leather Kid* and an alleged murderer in *The Noose* – he retired from films in 1941 because 'the fun had gone out of picture making'. His last major film role was as the failed, supposedly cowardly husband of Rita Hayworth in Hawks' *Only Angels Have Wings*. He enjoyed his retirement as a New York socialite, spending his winters in luxury on Park Avenue and his summers on the shores of Long Island. He left a million dollars.

Note: In the first three years of the awards performers were sometimes nominated for roles in more than one film. When this occurred – as in the case of Richard Barthelmess – the performances have been listed as separate nominations. See also Maurice Chevalier, Ronald Colman and Greta Garbo.

Mikhail Baryshnikov

Born Riga, Latvia, 27 January 1948

Oscar Nominations (1): Best Supporting Actor for Yuri in *The Turning Point* (20th Century-Fox, 1977)

Attempts to turn ballet dancers into movie stars have never really succeeded – Ken Russell's disastrous try with Nureyev in *Valentino* remains forever etched in the memory – but at least Baryshnikov managed an Oscar nomination for his début role as the Russian stud touring the States with a dance company in *The Turning Point*. The acting was so-so, the dancing brilliant, the award nowhere in sight. That went to the somewhat more grizzled Jason Robards who danced not a step but did wonders with his portrait of novelist Dashiell Hammett in *Julia*.

Albert Basserman

Born Mannheim, Germany, 7 September 1867; died 1952

Oscar Nominations (1): Best Supporting Actor for Van Meer in *Foreign Correspondent* (United Artists, 1940)

A close-up, a smile, a gun shot . . . the face covered in blood! Albert Basserman's place in movie history was assured as he featured in one of

Hitchcock's most celebrated murder sequences amid the rain and the umbrellas in *Foreign Correspondent*. A nomination was duly his, but like the equally unlucky Judith Anderson (nominated for Mrs Danvers in *Rebecca* in the same year), the Oscar was not. Nothing more for Hitch, but plenty of cultured old European gentlemen to keep him occupied on screen until his death in a plane crash over the Atlantic in 1952.

Angela Bassett

Born New York City, USA, 16 August 1958

Oscar Nominations (1): Best Actress for Tina Turner in *What's Love Got to Do With It?* (Touchstone, 1993)

Any actress worth her salt should make the most of a life such as Tina Turner's, and Angela Bassett didn't disappoint, either in the knockout production numbers that permeated the film or in the dramatic scenes of her home life with husband Ike Turner. It was all there in a full-blooded, noisy and powerful performance; unfortunately for Miss Bassett (whose voice was dubbed with Turner's original recordings) 1993 was a year of peace and calm in the best actress category, Holly Hunter winning for uttering not a word in *The Piano*. Bassett's earlier role as the Muslim nurse who marries Malcolm X in Spike Lee's biopic failed to make the nomination lists.

Alan Bates

Born Allestree, Derbyshire, England, 17 February 1934

Oscar Nominations (1): Best Actor for Yakov Bok in *The Fixer* (MGM, 1968)

Not really an angry young man of the sixties, Alan Bates was more of an amiable one who was out to have a good time with Charlotte Rampling in *Georgy Girl*, make it to the top in *Nothing But the Best* and discover the pleasures of sex in *A Kind of Loving*. All a bit dated now; not so the performance that won Bates his Oscar nomination as the Jewish peasant wrongly accused of a ritual child murder in Tsarist Russia in *The Fixer*. A neglected film (based on the novel by Bernard Malamud) but a strong performance and one that paved the way for Bates' most rewarding period, when he appeared for Schlesinger in *Far from the Madding Crowd*, Ken Russell in *Women in Love* and Joe Losey in *The Go-Between*.

Kathy Bates

Born Memphis, Tennessee, USA, 28 June 1948

Oscars (1): Best Actress for Annie Wilkes in *Misery* (Castle Rock/ Columbia, 1990)

Few performers win Oscars for enjoying themselves in a piece of Grand Guignol. In *Misery*, Kathy Bates proved the exception to the rule with an all-the-stops-pulled-out portrait of a psychopath who rescues author James Caan from a car wreck, reveals she is his greatest fan, breaks his ankles and then keeps him chained up until he brings back to life the popular heroine he has just killed off in his latest novel. In the 'Golden Age' the role probably wouldn't have rated even a nomination, but Hollywood was in a quirky mood in the early nineties (*The Silence of the Lambs* was on the horizon), and Kathy Bates – swinging, yelling and clubbing – carried all before her, often with a smile!

Anne Baxter

Born Michigan City, Indiana, USA, 7 May 1923; died 1985

Oscars (1): Best Supporting Actress for Sophie Nelson in *The Razor's Edge* (20th Century-Fox, 1946)

Oscar Nominations (1): Best Actress for Eve Harrington in *All About Eve* (20th Century-Fox, 1950)

Zanuck thought she had no sex appeal and was suitable only for playing librarians. Anne Baxter proved him wrong by winning an Oscar at the age of twenty-three for her alcoholic Sophie in *The Razor's Edge* and then match-ing Bette Davis' Margo Channing line for line as the scheming understudy in *All About Eve*. That was that as far as Oscar was concerned, although *All About Eve* refused to leave her. She replaced Lauren Bacall (this time playing Margo) in the musical stage production *Applause* and had plans to work with Joe Mankiewicz on a sequel depicting what happened to Eve after she had left the stage. Her only major film role in her later years was as the wife of the Pharaoh in DeMille's *The Ten Commandments*. Her dialogue wasn't exactly up to the standard of Joe Mankiewicz. In one scene she was required to make believable the line: 'Oh Moses, Moses, you stubborn, splendid, adorable fool!' She failed.

Warner Baxter

Born Columbus, Ohio, USA, 29 March 1891; died 1951

Oscars (1): Best Actor for the Cisco Kid in *In Old Arizona* (Fox, 1928/29)

An Oscar-winner for his happy-go-lucky Cisco Kid – a kind of Western Robin Hood with a six-shooter and a guitar – Warner Baxter enjoyed another claim to fame in the thirties as the harassed Broadway producer in *42nd Street* who pushes Ruby Keeler from the wings to instant stardom with the words: 'Sawyer, you're going out a youngster but you've got to come back a star!' Among the most popular and best-paid leading men of the pre-war period (he twice more played the Cisco Kid), he was mostly a B-movie player later in his career, featuring in the forties series *The Crime Doctor*. His Oscar-winning role came about by accident. Actor-director Raoul Walsh had originally been assigned the part but had to bow out when he lost an eye in a car accident.

Ned Beatty

Born Louisville, Kentucky, USA, 6 July 1937

Oscar Nominations (1): Best Supporting Actor for Arthur Jensen in *Network* (United Artists, 1976)

Chubby, round-faced and with a sly grin that often betrays the fact that he is not always a man to be trusted, Ned Beatty has a penchant for characters who are non too bright and aren't quite sure of what's going on around them. Surprisingly nominated just the once in his twenty-five-year career – for his megalomaniac head of the United Broadcasting System in Lumet's satirical *Network* – he came in behind Jason Robards, who won on Oscar night for his portrayal of Ben Bradlee in *All the President's Men*. A veteran of more than sixty films and TV movies, he made his début as one of the four city guys who spend a traumatic weekend on a canoeing trip in John Boorman's *Deliverance*.

Warren Beatty

Born Richmond, Virginia, USA, 30 March 1937

Oscar Nominations (4): Best Actor for Clyde Barrow in *Bonnie and Clyde* (Warner Bros, 1967), Joe Pendleton in *Heaven Can Wait* (Paramount, 1978), John Reed in *Reds* (Paramount, 1981) and Bugsy Siegel in *Bugsy* (TriStar, 1991)

Give him something to rail against and he's in his element. At least that's how it seems. The Academy has so far thought him worthy of four acting nominations but not the award itself, preferring his work behind the cameras – he won as best director for *Reds* – to his maladjusted on-screen heroes, most of whom have seemed more than a little out of synch with society. His Academy mentions: for his Depression gangster trying to make a living out of robbing banks in the Midwest, his young footballer berating the heavenly powers for killing him off before his time, his Communist journalist John Reed, and his psychotic Bugsy Siegel, a man up against just about everything other than his dream of building the glittering desert town of Las Vegas. All though may not be lost in the acting department. The top award might still come Beatty's way if he gets the chance to put his long-awaited biography of Howard Hughes before the cameras.

Note: Beatty has also received Academy nominations for producing, co-directing and writing *Heaven Can Wait*, co-scripting *Shampoo* (1975), producing and co-scripting *Reds* and producing the nominated best pictures *Bonnie and Clyde* and *Bugsy*.

Wallace Beery

Born Kansas City, Missouri, USA, 1 April 1885; died 1949

Oscars (1): Best Actor for Andy 'Champ' Purcell in *The Champ* (MGM, 1931/32)

Oscar Nominations (1): Best Actor for Machine Gun Butch Schmidt in *The Big House* (Cosmopolitan/MGM, 1929/30)

'My mug is my fortune,' Wallace Beery would say, relishing in his beaten-up, wrinkled and frequently mischievous features. It was also his passport to Oscar success, making him perfect for the washed-up prizefighter idolised by his young son in *The Champ* and the rebellious prison thug in *The Big House*. A notoriously difficult actor to work with – he upstaged his fellow actors, refused to rehearse and changed his dialogue at the last minute – he won his Oscar for *The Champ*, sharing the award with Fredric March (*Dr Jekyll and Mr Hyde*), the Academy rules of the time stating that if two performers were within three votes of one another, the result would be a tie. March polled one more vote. The double award still remains the only best actor tie in Oscar history.

Ed Begley

Born Hartford, Connecticut, USA, 25 March 1901; died 1970

Oscars (1): Best Supporting Actor for 'Boss' Finley in *Sweet Bird of Youth* (MGM, 1962)

A wide grin that could be both nervous and anxious, and at times deadly, a heavy frame and a voice that could rise from a whisper to a roar in just a matter of seconds! Just some of the characteristics of Ed Begley, who featured in over forty movies in the post-war years, making his mark as the alcoholic businessman in *Patterns* and the bigoted juror in *12 Angry Men*, and winning the Academy Award for his malevolent redneck political boss in *Sweet Bird of Youth*. 'I'm the laziest man in the world in everything except acting,' he would say. A quick tally of his work rate bears out his claim: 12,000 radio programmes, more than 250 TV appearances and a dozen or so plays – plus the films!

Barbara Bel Geddes

Born New York City, USA, 31 October 1922

Oscar Nominations (1): Best Supporting Actress for Katrin in *I Remember Mama* (RKO, 1948)

One of those unlucky actresses whose career never quite took off on the big screen (despite an Oscar nomination for her exquisite rendering of Irene Dunne's young writer-daughter in *I Remember Mama*), Barbara Bel Geddes eventually enjoyed success on television in the long-running soap opera *Dallas*, in which she played the somewhat less demanding but rather better-known role of Miss Ellie Ewing! Thirty-two years after being nominated for an Oscar at the age of twenty-six, she received an Emmy – not quite the same thing, but all things considered a fair enough reward. Hitchcock (who featured her in his classic *Vertigo*) also offered her a tasty morsel on the small screen, casting her in one of his thirty-minute TV films, *Lamb to the Slaughter*, in which she murders her husband with a frozen leg of lamb and then serves it up to the cops investigating the killing.

Ralph Bellamy

Born Chicago, USA, 17 June 1904; died 1991

Oscar Nominations (1): Best Supporting Actor for Daniel Leeson in *The Awful Truth* (Columbia, 1937)

For an actor of Ralph Bellamy's stature, to be constantly referred to in Hollywood as 'the man who never got the girl' was demeaning, even though it did, on one occasion, bring him a nomination for his slow-witted Oklahoma boyfriend of Irene Dunne in *The Awful Truth*. The Oscar itself never came his way (except for a deserved honorary award in 1986), although once he had passed the age when not getting the girl ceased to matter, his roles increased in interest. His unluckiest miss at nominations time occurred in 1960 when he was overlooked for repeating his Broadway portrayal of President Roosevelt in *Sunrise at Campobello*, an account of Roosevelt's early years in politics when he was fighting against polio.

William Bendix

Born New York City, USA, 4 January 1906; died 1964

Oscar Nominations (1): Best Supporting Actor for Aloysius (Smacksie) Randall in *Wake Island* (Paramount, 1942)

Audiences liked Bill Bendix as a barman or taxi driver or someone dumb, a guy who was none too bright but who they could relate to. If he had a few jokes along the way so much the better. And if he starred as a sidekick alongside Alan Ladd, the evening's entertainment was assured. A nominee for his Marine sergeant in Paramount's wartime production *Wake Island*, he enjoyed his most satisfying screen moment in 1948 when he got to play his childhood hero Babe Ruth, to whom he had rushed hot dogs when working as a bat boy with the New York Giants. A tough New Yorker, he had no pretensions about his fame. His credo was simple: 'Save a buck or two and keep on acting – that's all there is to it.'

Annette Bening

Born Topeka, Kansas, USA, 29 May 1958

Oscar Nominations (1): Best Supporting Actress for Myra Langtree in *The Grifters* (Miramax, 1990)

'The lady or the loot?' coos a giggling and tantalisingly naked Annette Bening as she lies provocatively on the couch in her room. Not surprisingly, the landlord, who had only come for the rent, takes the lady. The film was *The Grifters* and earned Bening her only Oscar nomination to date, as the delectable con artist who uses her body to wend her precarious way through life and pays for it in a most horrific way. Famous in real life as the lady who persuaded Warren Beatty that marriage might be a good idea, she was originally cast as Cat Woman in *Batman Returns* but was replaced by Michelle Pfeiffer when she conceived Beatty's child.

Tom Berenger

Born Chicago, USA, 31 May 1950

Oscar Nominations (1): Best Supporting Actor for Sgt Barnes in *Platoon* (Hemdale, 1986)

None of the actors won any awards for *Platoon*, although a case could be made that they should have done so. Willem Dafoe missed out for his saintly sergeant, so too did Tom Berenger for his battle-scarred veteran in charge of the platoon that massacres the inhabitants of a native village. Little of Academy Award quality has come his way since, just thrillers and crime movies that have helped exploit his dark, handsome masculinity. His best moment in movies? Not from *Platoon* but from his earlier *The Big Chill*, when his popular TV star agrees to demonstrate how he leaps into the driving seat of his car during the credits of his weekly cop show and then finds to his discomfort that it's beyond him!

Candice Bergen

Born Beverly Hills, California, USA, 8 May 1946

Oscar Nominations (1): Best Supporting Actress for Jessica Potter in *Starting Over* (Paramount, 1979)

Always a girl with more than one string to her bow – she has long been a photojournalist whose work has been used in magazines and exhibited at galleries – Candice Bergen found herself among the 1979 nominees for her slinky former wife of Burt Reynolds who takes to writing hideous pop songs and, to everyone's chagrin, starts singing them as well. Meryl Streep, though, was doing her damnedest to 'find her space' in *Kramer vs. Kramer*, which meant that it was 'let's forget it' time for the remaining nominees. Best known these days as the star of the award-winning TV show, *Murphy Brown*, Bergen was married to French film-maker Louis Malle until his death in 1995. She is the daughter of ventriloquist Edgar Bergen.

Ingrid Bergman

Born Stockholm, Sweden, 29 August 1915; died 1982

Oscars (3): Best Actress for Paula Alquist in *Gaslight* (MGM, 1944) and the title role in *Anastasia* (20th Century-Fox, 1956); Best Supporting Actress for Greta Ohlsson in *Murder on the Orient Express* (Paramount, 1974)

Oscar Nominations (4): Best Actress for Maria in *For Whom the Bell Tolls* (Paramount, 1943), Sister Benedict in *The Bells of St Mary's* (RKO, 1945), the title role in *Joan of Arc* (Wanger, RKO, 1948) and Charlotte in *Autumn Sonata* (ITC/Sweden, 1978)

'I was loved by people and hated by them. I was perhaps loved too much and hated too cruelly.' Ingrid Bergman's melancholy summing-up of her turbulent private life was probably all too accurate. On screen, however, she never failed to mesmerise, even during the years away from Hollywood with Roberto Rossellini. An Oscar-winner in the forties when she was sent almost insane by the scheming Charles Boyer, in the fifties when she returned in triumph as the amnesiac refugee Anastasia, and then later for her repressed missionary in *Murder on the Orient Express*, she also made the lists for her Spanish peasant girl ('I would kiss you but where do the noses go?'), her Sister Superior teamed with Crosby's Father O'Malley, her Joan of Arc and her concert pianist at odds with daughter Liv Ullmann in *Autumn Sonata* – the only occasion that Bergman (Ingrid) worked with Bergman (Ingmar).

Elisabeth Bergner

Born Drohobycz, Poland (now Russia), 27 August 1897; died 1986

Oscar Nominations (1): Best Actress for Gemma Jones in *Escape Me Never* (Wilcox, United Artists, 1935)

Coming up with the name of an Elisabeth Bergner film is not the easiest job in the world these days. At best, most people remember just two – *Catherine the Great*, which she made for Korda at about the same time Dietrich was filming *The Scarlet Empress* in Hollywood, and the weepie *Escape Me Never*, about an unmarried waif with a child who finds happiness (and misery) with a musician. Nominated, rather surprisingly, for the latter role, she came in third behind the year's winner, Bette Davis for *Dangerous*, and

Katharine Hepburn for *Alice Adams*. A frail blonde whose girlish personality resulted in her frequently being cast in waif-like roles, she settled in England with her husband, director Paul Czinner, after fleeing from the Nazis in the thirties. A highly regarded stage actress both in Europe and on Broadway, she was the star of several German silent films of the twenties.

Jeannie Berlin

Born Los Angeles, USA, 1 November 1949

Oscar Nominations (1): Best Supporting Actress for Lila Kolodny in *The Heartbreak Kid* (20th Century-Fox, 1972)

A bit like Anne Bancroft, a bit like Ingrid Bergman, with a touch of Tiny Tim thrown in for good measure! That was how Jeannie Berlin described herself when she found she was in line for an Oscar for her irritating young Jewish bride, dumped on honeymoon by husband Charles Grodin in favour of golden girl Cybill Shepherd. In the end, she didn't quite make it, although the New York Critics thought her worthy of the award, naming her as the year's best female support. The daughter of the film's director, Elaine May, she informed the press that the role was not hers for the taking; her mother made her test for the part. The 1972 Supporting Oscar went to Eileen Heckart for *Butterflies Are Free*.

Charles Bickford

Born Cambridge, Massachusetts, USA, 1 January 1889; died 1967

Oscar Nominations (3): Best Supporting Actor for Peyremaie in *The Song of Bernadette* (20th Century-Fox, 1943), Clancy in *The Farmer's Daughter* (RKO, 1947) and Black McDonald in *Johnny Belinda* (Warner Bros, 1948)

Three nominations in just six years! Such riches should have resulted in an Oscar. Not, unfortunately, in the case of the crinkly-haired, gruff-voiced Charles Bickford, who could play just about anyone convincingly on screen but finished up with no prizes, just nomination certificates for his understanding priest in *The Song of Bernadette*, family butler in *The Farmer's*

Daughter and martinet fisherman father of Jane Wyman's mute heroine in *Johnny Belinda*. Lucky to be around to be even a nominee – he was badly mauled and had his throat torn close to the jugular by a 400lb lion during the making of the 1935 actioner *East of Java* – he had originally intended to be an engineer but after a date with a burlesque queen and a subsequent interview with the show's impresario, decided that showbiz held more attractions.

Theodore Bikel

Born Vienna, Austria, 2 May 1924

Oscar Nominations (1): Best Supporting Actor for Sheriff Man Muller in *The Defiant Ones* (United Artists, 1958)

Remembered by many as 'that guy chasing those two escaped cons' in Stanley Kramer's *The Defiant Ones*, Theodore Bikel's film career never reached much above minor roles and run-of-the-mill parts. His sheriff in Kramer's film offered him his one gem – a man who knows his job is on the line if he doesn't bring in the two men but who refuses to be caught up in the lynch-mob psychology of the rest of the posse. An established folk singer and guitarist as well as an actor, he lost 1958's supporting prize to another folk-singer-guitarist-actor, Burl Ives, for *The Big Country*.

Karen Black

Born Park Ridge, Illinois, USA, 1 July 1942

Oscar Nominations (1): Best Supporting Actress for Rayette Dipesto in *Five Easy Pieces* (Columbia/BBS, 1970)

Too often cast as the floozie from the wrong side of the tracks, Karen Black did at least profit from the fact that Hollywood was awash with floozie roles in the early seventies, and she took full advantage. Oscar-nominated for her warm-hearted waitress girlfriend of Jack Nicholson in *Five Easy Pieces*, she was even better as the Hollywood extra Faye Greener in Schlesinger's *Day of the Locust* and as the desperate, sex-hungry wife of garage owner Scott Wilson in *The Great Gatsby*. She lost in 1970 to Helen Hayes' impish stowaway in *Airport* but enjoyed her moment of triumph five years later when she was cast as a stewardess in *Airport '75*, took over the controls of a Boeing 747 and single-handedly navigated it through the mountains!

Betsy Blair

Born New York City, USA, 11 December 1923

Oscar Nominations (1): Best Supporting Actress for Clara in *Marty* (United Artists, 1955)

The question 'When is a leading role a supporting role?' is one that has been asked many times when the Oscar nominations have been announced. Betsy Blair, the shy young schoolteacher who meets Bronx butcher Ernest Borgnine at a Saturday-night dance in *Marty*, was one performer who certainly must have puzzled over things in 1955. A winner of the best actress prize at the Cannes Film Festival, she was relegated to supporting status at Oscar time and, worse still, to loser status on awards night, Jo Van Fleet picking up the award for *East of Eden*. Unlucky? To say the least, especially when just about everyone else connected with the film – Borgnine, writer Paddy Chayefsky and director Delbert Mann – enjoyed the fruits of its success.

Linda Blair

Born St Louis, Missouri, USA, 22 January 1959

Oscar Nominations (1): Best Supporting Actress for Regan MacNeil in *The Exorcist* (Warner Bros, 1973)

Portraying someone possessed by the Devil was by no means new to cinema screens in 1973, but a fourteen-year-old playing a demonic child most certainly was, and on Oscar night it came down to a battle of the kids in the supporting actress category – Linda Blair, complete with swivelling head, green bile and a lurid vocabulary for *The Exorcist*, and the nine-year-old Tatum O'Neal as the Depression con artist travelling the Midwest with her father in *Paper Moon*. O'Neal took the award and Blair was left with a subsequently disappointing career that included repeating her role in an innocuous *Exorcist* sequel and appearing in a long line of low-budget exploitation movies.

Ronee Blakley

Born Stanley, Idaho, USA, 1946

Oscar Nominations (1): Best Supporting Actress for Barbara Jean in *Nashville* (Paramount, 1975)

Just how the Academy voters decided who to nominate and why in Robert Altman's multi-starred *Nashville* remains a mystery, but the two they did choose from the pack were Lily Tomlin and, for her neurotic country singer who is wounded by gunfire, Ronee Blakley. Neither won, and any number of actresses in the cast could just as easily have been nominated in their place, but at least Blakley (primarily a singer-songwriter) managed her acting breakthrough and has since become one of the few stars to write her own songs for the movies in which she appears.

Joan Blondell

Born New York City, USA, 30 August 1909; died 1979

Oscar Nominations (1): Best Supporting Actress for Annie in *The Blue Veil* (RKO, 1951)

Every Hollywood studio had its 'wisecracking broad' and in Joan Blondell, Warners had the best, a veritable warhorse who in the thirties sometimes churned out as many as ten films a year. Embellishing put-downs of the 'aren't men cute but creeps' variety, she eventually earned an Oscar nomination (although regrettably never the award itself) for her fading musical actress who hires nanny Jane Wyman in the 1951 tear-jerker *The Blue Veil*. Memorable when singing 'My Forgotten Man' in *Gold Diggers of 1933*, and for her many verbal sparrings with James Cagney, she later excelled as the card dealer 'Ladyfingers' in *The Cincinnati Kid*.

Ann Blyth

Born Mt Kisco, New York, USA, 16 August 1928

Oscar Nominations (1): Best Supporting Actress for Veda Pierce in *Mildred Pierce* (Warner Bros, 1945)

She had some good lines, did Ann Blyth in *Mildred Pierce*, especially when they were directed at Joan Crawford: 'You think just because you made a little money you can get yourself a new hairdo and some expensive clothes and turn yourself into a lady, but you can't, because you'll never be anything but a common frump whose father lived over a grocery store and whose mother took in washing!' Her delivery and pout and juvenile bitchiness earned her a nomination, but it remained her only Oscar mention and she spent the rest of her career uttering somewhat less inflammatory dialogue and resting in the comforting arms of stars like Greg Peck and Robert Taylor. In the fifties she starred opposite Mario Lanza in *The Great Caruso* and sang the year's hit song, 'The Loveliest Night of the Year'.

Humphrey Bogart

Born New York City, USA, 23 January 1899; died 1957

Oscars (1): Best Actor for Charlie Allnut in *The African Queen* (Romulus, 1951)

Oscar Nominations (2): Best Actor for Rick Blaine in *Casablanca* (Warner Bros, 1943) and Captain Queeg in *The Caine Mutiny* (Columbia, 1954)

Bogart's recipe for Oscar success was unique: 'Once you've got your five nominees, the best way to pick the winner is to ask all of them to speak the soliloquy from *Hamlet*. When they've all had their say you'll be able to tell.' Not a bad idea all things considered, although if Bogie's own rule had been applied it's somewhat doubtful whether he would have won for his grizzled old tugboat skipper in *The African Queen*. Bogart saying 'To be or not to be' takes some swallowing. Nominated for his disillusioned Rick Blaine in *Casablanca* (he should have won, agree millions) and his neurotic Captain Queeg in *The Caine Mutiny*, he was four times married, lastly to Lauren Bacall with whom he starred in a quartet of movies.

Beulah Bondi

Born Chicago, USA, 3 May 1892; died 1981

Oscar Nominations (2): Best Supporting Actress for Rachel Jackson in *The Gorgeous Hussy* (MGM, 1936) and Mary Wilkins in *Of Human Hearts* (MGM, 1938)

Sweet old ladies, spinsters, grannies, pioneer women, high-class ladies, low-class mums, even mountain witches! They all came alike to Beulah Bondi who, although somewhat less well known than the French actress bearing the initials BB, was somewhat ahead of her when it came to subtle and sensitive acting. Sharp-featured and with a smile that could be either beguiling or lethal, she was up for an Oscar in the first year of the supporting actress award for her pipe-smoking backwoods mistress of Andrew Jackson, then again two years later for her sacrificing wife of a frontier preacher in *Of Human Hearts*. A regular performer for Frank Capra and George Stevens, she said of the art of acting: 'What distinguishes the real actor from the pseudo is the passionate desire to know what is going on in the hearts and minds of people.' She managed it in every one of her films, and also in 1977 on TV in *The Waltons*, for which she won an Emmy.

Shirley Booth

Born New York City, USA, 30 August 1907; died 1992

Oscars (1): Best Actress for Lola Delaney in *Come Back, Little Sheba* (Paramount, 1952)

One of those actresses Hollywood didn't quite know what to do with, Shirley Booth was never a major box-office star but amazed everyone by becoming a huge favourite in the sixties in the TV series *Hazel*, in which she played the inefficient maid of a well-heeled lawyer family. The show ran for several years, rather longer than Miss Booth's stay in Hollywood (1952–58), during which time she won her Oscar for repeating her Broadway role as the slatternly housewife living out a stale marriage with former alcoholic Burt Lancaster. A great performance but not what the public wanted to see; they preferred *Hazel*. Paramount executives simply shook their heads and said, 'Where did we go wrong?'

Ernest Borgnine

Born Hamden, Connecticut, USA, 24 January 1917

Oscars (1): Best Actor for the title role in *Marty* (United Artists, 1955)

'Ma, sooner or later there comes a point in a man's life when he's got to face some facts. And one fact I got to face is that whatever it is that women like, I ain't got it. I chased after enough girls in my life . . . I don't want to get hurt no more.' On live American television it had been Rod Steiger who uttered Paddy Chayefsky's lines; on screen it was Ernest Borgnine, who, as the fat, ugly, rejected Brooklyn butcher, cast aside his image as a heavy and stole the Oscar with one of the most heart-rending performances of the fifties. Thereafter he was never out of work, appearing in more than a hundred films but never again being offered a role of such depth and realistic conviction. Thirty-six before he made his screen début, he was best known in his pre-*Marty* days for his sadistic Sergeant Fatso Judson who beats Sinatra half to death in the stockade in *From Here to Eternity*.

Charles Boyer

Born Figeac, France, 28 August 1897; died 1978

Oscar Nominations (4): Best Actor for Napoleon in *Conquest* (MGM, 1937), Pepe Le Moko in *Algiers* (Universal, 1938), Gregory Anton in *Gaslight* (MGM, 1944) and Cesar in *Fanny* (Warner Bros, 1961)

Charles Boyer didn't, of course, actually say 'Come with me to the Casbah' (the line was uttered by a mimic in a nightclub routine), but then he didn't need to. His leading ladies, who included Garbo, Bergman, Dietrich and Hedy Lamarr, would have come anyway. Dismissed by many critics as being nothing more than just another suave French actor with bedroom eyes, he was Oscar-nominated four times – for his Napoleon, his fugitive thief trapped in Algiers, his sadistic husband of Ingrid Bergman and his waterfront café proprietor in *Fanny*. He never received the ultimate accolade, although in 1942 he was presented with a special Oscar for his progressive cultural achievement in establishing the French Research Foundation in Los Angeles. He would often make fun of his accent by joking that he could say 'wiz the' or 'with ze' but never 'with the'. Married to the former British actress Pat Paterson for forty-four years, he decided that life wasn't worth living without her. He committed suicide just two days after her death.

Lorraine Bracco

Born Brooklyn, New York, USA, 1955

Oscar Nominations (1): Best Supporting Actress for Karen Hill in *Goodfellas* (Warner Bros, 1990)

'Right down there . . . yeah, over there on the corner . . . right over there!' If ever an actress showed fear it was Lorraine Bracco as she hesitantly follows the psychotic Robert De Niro's advice and starts down a deserted alley in search of a warehouse full of free dresses. Wisely deciding that she can do without her freebies and that it might be better to hang on to her life, she makes a run for it. Just a moment from *Goodfellas*, but one good enough to demonstrate that Bracco was more than deserving of her supporting nod and belongs with the brightest young talents currently around in American cinema. She lost on Oscar night to Whoopi Goldberg in *Ghost*. Nothing as rewarding as *Goodfellas* has come her way since.

Alice Brady

Born New York City, USA, 2 November 1892; died 1939

Oscars (1): Best Supporting Actress for Molly O'Leary in *In Old Chicago* (20th Century-Fox, 1937)

Oscar Nominations (1): Best Supporting Actress for Angelica Bullock in *My Man Godfrey* (Universal, 1936)

Who stole Alice Brady's Academy Award? Nobody ever found out, for when she was named best supporting actress for her Irish pioneer mother in the Fox spectacular *In Old Chicago* she was unable to attend the ceremony because of a broken ankle. An unnamed representative accepted the statuette on her behalf, left the podium and was never heard of again. The perplexed Miss Brady was presented with a replacement Oscar at an informal ceremony two weeks later. Nominated the year before for her scatterbrained New York socialite in *My Man Godfrey*, she enlivened many screwball comedies, Deanna Durbin musicals and action movies of the thirties but died of cancer at the tragically early age of forty-seven after completing her role in John Ford's *Young Mr Lincoln*.

Kenneth Branagh

Born Belfast, Northern Ireland, 10 December 1960

Oscar Nominations (1): Best Actor for the title role of *Henry V* (Renaissance Films, 1989)

At his most effective when presenting Shakespeare on screen – by earning nominations for acting and directing *Henry V* he went one better than Olivier with his 1946 version – Kenneth Branagh has seemed less sure of himself when straying from the Bard, failing to convince either as an actor or director with his sub-standard thriller *Dead Again*, his cutesy *Peter's Friends* and the limp and overblown *Frankenstein*. *Much Ado About Nothing*, on the other hand, was lively and refreshing, and his Iago in Oliver Parker's *Othello* devious and deadly. Shakespeare, it seems, is with whom he should stay – for the moment anyway.

Note: Olivier was nominated as best actor at the 1946 awards and won a special Oscar for 'his outstanding achievement as actor, producer and director in bringing *Henry V* to the screen'.

Klaus Maria Brandauer

Born Altaussee, Austria, 22 June 1944

Oscar Nominations (1): Best Supporting Actor for Baron Bror Blixen-Finecke in *Out of Africa* (Universal, 1985)

By rights he should have made it to the Hollywood mainstream and stayed there. The world of movies, however, knows no logic, and despite picking up a nomination for Meryl Streep's womanising husband in *Out of Africa* and enjoying himself as a Bond villain (*Never Say Never Again*), Brandauer has generally fared better in Europe, where he made his name in *Colonel Redl* and as the actor who sells his soul to the Nazis in *Mephisto*. Unfortunately, as yet, they don't give Oscars for such things, although the latter film did pick up the award as the best foreign-language picture of 1981.

Marlon Brando

Born Omaha, Nebraska, USA, 3 April 1924

Oscars (2): Best Actor for Terry Malloy in *On the Waterfront* (Columbia, 1954) and Don Vito Corleone in *The Godfather* (Paramount, 1972)

Oscar Nominations (6): Best Actor for Stanley Kowalski in *A Streetcar Named Desire* (Warner Bros, 1951), Emiliano Zapata in *Viva Zapata!* (20th Century-Fox, 1952), Marc Antony in *Julius Caesar* (MGM, 1953), Major Lloyd Gruver in *Sayonara* (Warner Bros, 1957), and Paul in *Last Tango in Paris* (United Artists, 1973); Best Supporting Actor for Ian McKenzie in *A Dry White Season* (MGM/UA, 1989)

Only in recent times has Brando's greatness as an actor begun to be seriously questioned, rightly so, perhaps, for after five glorious years (1950–54) when he looked the best in the world, he has contributed little in the subsequent forty to equal his earlier achievements. The Academy hasn't distinguished between early Brando and late Brando, honouring him four times in a row (the only time an actor has been nominated thus for the main award) for his brutish rapist in *Streetcar*, Mexican revolutionary Zapata, Marc Antony, and broken-down boxer Terry Malloy, and then subsequently for his Korean War air ace in *Sayonara*, his mumbling Mafia boss Don Corleone, ageing American Lothario for Bertolucci, and his South African human rights lawyer in *A Dry White Season*. As to whether he was, in his prime, the greatest American actor of all time, the case for the defence usually rests on one scene in the back of a taxi in *On the Waterfront*. 'I coulda had class,' he says in anguish, blaming brother Rod Steiger. 'I coulda been a contender! I coulda been somebody! Instead of a bum which is what I am!'

Note: Brando refused his 1972 Oscar for *The Godfather* in protest against the industry's treatment of American Indians in films, on TV and in movie reruns.

Eileen Brennan

Born Los Angeles, USA, 3 September 1935

Oscar Nominations (1): Best Supporting Actress for Captain Doreen Lewis in *Private Benjamin* (Warner Bros, 1980)

Great at playing cynical, world-weary, 'take life as it comes'-type characters, Eileen Brennan achieved the unusual distinction of being Oscar-nominated for her tough army sergeant who knocks Goldie Hawn into shape in *Private Benjamin* and then winning an Emmy for repeating the role in the subsequent TV series of the early eighties. A favourite of director Peter Bogdanovich (*The Last Picture Show, Daisy Miller, At Long Last Love*), she was badly injured in a car accident in 1983 and confined to a wheelchair for a time, but has since recovered and made a comeback in lesser roles.

Walter Brennan

Born Swampscott, Massachusetts, USA, 25 July 1894; died 1974

Oscars (3): Best Supporting Actor for Swan Bostrum in *Come and Get It* (United Artists, 1936), Peter Goodwin in *Kentucky* (20th Century-Fox, 1938) and Judge Roy Bean in *The Westerner* (United Artists, 1940)

Oscar Nominations (1): Best Supporting Actor for Pastor Rosier Pile in *Sergeant York* (Warner Bros, 1941)

Prone to punctuating his scripts with high-pitched whoops, wheezing exclamations and grumbling annoyance, Walter Brennan was the first and, to date, only performer to win three supporting awards – for his Swedish lumberjack Swan Bostrum, his crotchety old Kentucky horse-breeder and the notorious Judge Roy Bean, the sole law west of the Pecos. He might have made it four for his village pastor/storekeeper in *Sergeant York* but he eventually tasted defeat when he lost to Donald Crisp for *How Green Was My Valley*. A favourite of director Howard Hawks, he proved that character acting could be a highly profitable business. In addition to his eleven-acre ranch in the San Fernando Valley he owned a somewhat larger spread in Oregon – 12,000 acres where he had a large herd of cattle. He also owned a hotel and a small movie house.

Jeff Bridges

Born Los Angeles, USA, 4 December 1949

Oscar Nominations (3): Best Supporting Actor for Duane Jackson in *The Last Picture Show* (Columbia, 1971) and Lightfoot in *Thunderbolt and Lightfoot* (United Artists, 1974); Best Actor for the title role in *Starman* (Columbia, 1984)

'Good as always,' wrote a critic when assessing one of Jeff Bridges' screen performances. Few would disagree with the use of the word 'always' or the fact that as far as Oscar is concerned, Bridges remains one of the unluckiest of contemporary American performers. Nominated for his unsettled fifties teenager growing up in a dying Texas town, his drifter on the run with Clint Eastwood and his alien ill at ease in an earthly environment, he somewhat surprisingly failed to make the 1989 short list for *The Fabulous Baker Boys*. The rugged cynicism, coupled with the occasional disillusionment that has become so much a part of his more recent roles, should put him among the winners before the decade is out. Neither his father Lloyd nor his older brother Beau has been nominated by the Academy.

☆

Albert Brooks

Born Los Angeles, USA, 22 July 1947

Oscar Nominations (1): Best Supporting Actor for Aaron Altman in *Broadcast News* (20th Century-Fox, 1987)

There may have been funnier scenes in American movies of the eighties but it's difficult to come up with anything that equals poor Albert Brooks' valiant attempts to make his breakthrough as a TV anchor man in *Broadcast News*. Covered in sweat, unable to focus properly on the autocue and with a set that is literally collapsing around him, he could have earned his nomination for the one scene alone. Cold-shouldered on Oscar night when *Broadcast News* failed to capitalise on any of its seven nominations, he has been an infrequent screen performer (and occasional writer-director) over the years and has appeared in only a handful of films in his twenty-year career. The son of comedian Harry Einstein, a former sidekick to Eddie Cantor, he made his name on *Saturday Night Live*. His real name is Albert Einstein.

Leslie Browne

Born New York City, USA, 1958

Oscar Nominations (1): Best Supporting Actress for Emilia Rodgers in *The Turning Point* (20th Century-Fox, 1977)

A nineteen-year-old dancer whose lucky break occurred when ballerina Gelsey Kirkland fell ill, Leslie Browne made it to the Academy short list for her portrayal of Shirley MacLaine's teenage daughter who gets her chance to become a star in Anne Bancroft's ballet company and seizes it with both feet. The film was based in part on Browne's own family, who twenty-five years earlier had left New York and the American Ballet Theatre to go west and found their own ballet school. Vanessa Redgrave won the year's supporting award for *Julia*. No contest really.

Yul Brynner

Born Sakhalin (an island east of Siberia and north of Japan), 12 July 1915; died 1985

Oscars (1): Best Actor for King Tut in *The King and I* (20th Century-Fox, 1956)

Described by one critic as 'more of a sex symbol than an actor and the personification of untameable masculinity', Yul Brynner remained untamed for some forty-three films, although governess Deborah Kerr came close to managing it in *The King and I*. His Mongolian countenance, fierce stare and shaven head were at their most effective for DeMille as the Pharaoh Rameses in *The Ten Commandments*, and as the sardonic, cheroot-smoking leader of *The Magnificent Seven*. The son of a Swiss-born mining engineer and a gypsy mother, he was estimated at the time of his death to have played his Oriental monarch in *The King and I* some 4,625 times over a period of thirty-four years.

Genevieve Bujold

Born Montreal, Canada, 1 July 1942

Oscar Nominations (1): Best Actress for Anne Boleyn in *Anne of the Thousand Days* (Universal, 1969)

Perhaps her start was just too good, but Genevieve Bujold has never again come close to equalling her Anne Boleyn. A shade too delicate and sensitive for most modern tastes, she nonetheless revealed another side to her nature as the masochistic actress who sleeps with a pair of Jeremy Irons twins in *Dead Ringers*. No Oscar for that, although she deserved consideration for her earlier Hitchcock-type role as the wife and (or) daughter of Cliff Robertson in Brian De Palma's *Obsession*.

Victor Buono

Born San Diego, USA, 1938; died 1982

Oscar Nominations (1): Best Supporting Actor for Edwin Flagg in *What Ever Happened to Baby Jane?* (Warner Bros, 1962)

A kind of sixties version of Sydney Greenstreet – he weighed in at 300lb – Victor Buono was cast as Bette Davis' piano accompanist after director Robert Aldrich had seen him as a character called Mr Moon in an episode of *The Untouchables*. Just twenty-four when he appeared in *Baby Jane*, he was named as one of the year's best supporting nominees, not least because of his facial expression as he waits at the piano and watches aghast as Davis launches into her comeback routine. Disliked at first by Davis, who found him grotesque, he later received from her an apology for her attitude and a letter stating how much she admired his talent. They later appeared together in another Aldrich chiller, *Hush . . . Hush, Sweet Charlotte*, in which he appeared in the prologue and at the age of twenty-six played Davis' father!

☆

Billie Burke

Born Washington, DC, USA, 7 August 1885; died 1970

Oscar Nominations (1): Best Supporting Actress for Mrs Emily Kilbourne in *Merrily We Live* (Roach/MGM, 1938)

The perfect actress for any role that required a female to be dithery, empty-headed and completely endearing, Billie Burke is remembered these days mainly for her Glinda, the Good Witch in *The Wizard of Oz*. Back in the thirties and forties, however, she was a regular in all kinds of movies, earning her Oscar nomination for her eccentric who rehabilitates tramps and employs a writer as her chauffeur by mistake. A great Broadway beauty at the beginning of the century, she was married to Florenz Ziegfeld and acted as adviser on MGM's lavish 1936 tribute *The Great Ziegfeld*, in which she was played by Myrna Loy. She tried television towards the end of her career but gave up, complaining that 'television directors had no patience with little old ladies'!

Catherine Burns

Born New York City, USA, 25 September 1945

Oscar Nominations (1): Best Supporting Actress for Rhoda in *Last Summer* (Perry-Alsid/Allied Artists, 1969)

The problems of adolescence are not the easiest to convey convincingly on screen; the four youngsters in Frank Perry's *Last Summer* managed it superbly, however, especially the plumpish Catherine Burns whose loneliness and a hoped-for happy summer by the sea turn into a nightmare of violence and disillusionment. Terrific performances from all four, with Burns the sole nominee in the acting department. Goldie Hawn won the award for the rather less strenuous exercise of playing herself in *Cactus Flower*.

George Burns

Born New York City, USA, 20 January 1896; died 1996

Oscars (1): Best Supporting Actor for Al Lewis in *The Sunshine Boys* (MGM, 1975)

No performer has yet managed to make a comeback after thirty-five years and win an Oscar for starting anew at eighty. Other than George Burns, of course, who managed it with consummate ease in 1975 when he was tempted out of retirement to play one of two cantankerous vaudevillians who haven't spoken to each other for years but are reunited for a TV special. Walter Matthau played the other one and found himself up for a best actor award for more or less the same amount of screen time. He lost, Burns won, although Matthau perhaps shaded his co-star when it came to Neil Simon's best lines, especially when he summed up Burns' character: 'As an actor no one could touch him. As a human being, no one wanted to!'

Ellen Burstyn

Born, Detroit, USA, 7 December 1932

Oscars (1): Best Actress for Alice Hyatt in *Alice Doesn't Live Here Anymore* (Warner Bros, 1974)

Oscar Nominations (4): Best Supporting Actress for Lois Farrow in *The Last Picture Show* (Columbia, 1971); Best Actress for Mrs MacNeil in *The Exorcist* (Warner Bros, 1973), Doris in *Same Time, Next Year* (Universal, 1978) and Edna Mae McCauley in *Resurrection* (Universal, 1980)

Too old at forty? Many actresses would say so, but not Ellen Burstyn, who had a field day in her forties, winning an Oscar for her wandering mother trying to rekindle her youthful dream of becoming a singer, and then adding nominations for raising a child possessed by the Devil, meeting Alan Alda for a once-a-year affair, and discovering that she has healing powers in *Resurrection*. At thirty-nine she also made it into the supporting category as Cybill Shepherd's disillusioned mother in *The Last Picture Show*. A lot of mothers in there, but it mattered little. Burstyn proved what could be done given half the chance and a varied range of intelligent scripts. A member of the Actor's Studio, she became co-director of the studio with Al Pacino after the death of Lee Strasberg in 1982.

Richard Burton

Born Pontrhydfen, South Wales, 10 November 1925; died 1984

Oscar Nominations (7): Best Supporting Actor for Philip Ashley in *My Cousin Rachel* (20th Century-Fox, 1952); Best Actor for Marcellus Gallio in *The Robe* (20th Century-Fox, 1953), the title role in *Becket* (Paramount, 1964), Alec Leamas in *The Spy Who Came in from the Cold* (Paramount, 1965), George in *Who's Afraid of Virginia Woolf?* (Warner Bros, 1966), Henry VIII in *Anne of the Thousand Days* (Universal, 1969) and Dr Martin Dysart in *Equus* (United Artists, 1977)

Richard Burton blamed cash for his lack of Hollywood stature. 'Too many zeros,' he said. 'I've done the most unutterable rubbish because of cash. I didn't need it but the lure was just too great.' The rubbish was there all right, but so too was the quality, and also seven Oscar nominations. Had he won first time out for his young aristocrat obsessed with his cousin Rachel, things might have turned out differently. As it was, Anthony Quinn took the award that night, and after that it was one long haul as nomination followed nomination with no reward at the end of things: a Roman tribune, the Archbishop Thomas Becket, a disillusioned agent (arguably his finest screen performance), an alcoholic university professor, a boisterous Henry VIII, and a psychiatrist. He laughed off the charge that he had thrown it all away on drink and the good things of life. 'I rather like my reputation,' he said. 'That of a spoiled genius from the Welsh gutter, a drunk, a womaniser. It's rather an attractive image.' It all ended in August of 1984 when he died of a cerebral haemorrhage.

Note: Together with Peter O'Toole, Burton remains the most nominated actor never to win the Academy Award.

Gary Busey

Born Goose Creek, Texas, USA, 29 June 1944

Oscar Nominations (1): Best Actor for the title role in *The Buddy Holly Story* (Innovasions-ECA, 1978)

For sheer energy and versatility, Gary Busey deserved the 1978 Academy Award more than any of the year's other nominees – his Buddy Holly make-up, the glasses and the brilliant singing (he performed all of Holly's songs) gave him the edge, even if he was the year's surprise candidate. No luck, of course, portraits of rock'n'rollers, jazzmen and the like rarely win prizes, and in the end Busey contented himself with just the nomination. Jon Voight took the top award for his embittered Vietnam paraplegic in one of the year's heavyweight contenders, *Coming Home*.

Red Buttons

Born New York City, USA, 5 February 1919

Oscars (1): Best Supporting Actor for Sergeant Joe Kelly in *Sayonara* (Warner Bros, 1957)

No one outside the States knew anything about Red Buttons until *Sayonara*, when he revealed himself to be a small, red-headed character actor who looked a bit like Mr Everyman and who specialised in playing the little guy who has had to struggle to make it through life. An Oscar-winner for his American soldier who joins his Japanese wife in a suicide pact rather than be parted from her, he deserved another for his desperate sailor who fails to make it through one of Hollywood's dance marathons in *They Shoot Horses, Don't They?* The stage name Red Buttons was adopted in his early days when he appeared as a bellboy-singer in a Bronx tavern.

Spring Byington

Born Colorado Springs, Colorado, USA, 17 October 1886; died 1971

Oscar Nominations (1): Best Supporting Actress for Penny Sycamore in *You Can't Take It With You* (Columbia, 1938)

The kind of woman who brought a homely warmth to just about every movie in which she appeared, Spring Byington came closest to winning an Oscar when Frank Capra cast her as the pixieish moonstruck mother who is always writing unfinished plays, in *You Can't Take It With You*. Expert at persuading audiences that the world wasn't such a bad place after all and that small-town America – Hollywood style – really did exist, she was just about everyone's favourite mother or aunt, sometimes scatterbrained, sometimes normal, but always pleasantly maternal. A star of over a hundred films, she made her début as Marmee in the 1933 version of *Little Women*. She later appeared as a regular in the TV western series, *Laramie*.

C

James Caan

Born the Bronx, New York, USA, 26 March 1939

Oscar Nominations (1): Best Supporting Actor for Sonny Corleone in *The Godfather* (Paramount, 1972)

They were a pretty malevolent bunch, the three supporting nominees for *The Godfather*: James Caan's headstrong Sonny, Robert Duvall's family lawyer, and heir apparent Al Pacino, although even they might have had trouble in knowing how to dispose of the year's winner – Joel Grey's decadent and cunning Master Of Ceremonies in *Cabaret*. Caan's nomination for his Sonny, mown down by machine-gun fire at a tollgate, has remained his only Academy mention, proving, if nothing else, that death by a thousand bullets has been as good a way as any of getting a nomination over the years, Brando's Emiliano Zapata being massacred at the end of Kazan's *Viva Zapata!* and Beatty and Dunaway meeting a similar fate in *Bonnie and Clyde*.

Adolph Caesar

Born Harlem, New York, USA, 1934; died 1986

Oscar Nominations (1): Best Supporting Actor for Master Sergeant Vernon C. Waters in *A Soldier's Story* (Columbia, 1984)

Just the one nomination for Adolph Caesar, but for a quite remarkable role – that of a tough black sergeant who is shot dead on a country road in 1944 Louisiana when returning drunkenly to his all-black unit and whose life and the events leading to his murder are slowly pieced together by the black army attorney investigating the case. Already fifty years old at the time, he lost to the year's favourite, Haing Ngor for *The Killing Fields*, but seemed assured of a late-flowering screen career. His mini-stardom lasted for just two years. In 1986 he was felled by a heart attack after only one day's filming on the Kirk Douglas/Burt Lancaster movie *Tough Guys*.

A remarkable performance in an all but forgotten film. Alan Bates earning his only Oscar nomination as the Russian peasant accused of murder in John Frankenheimer's *The Fixer* (MGM, 1968)

'Here's looking at you, kid!' Everyone did of course but it was Bogie not Bergman who won the Oscar nomination. The year 1943; the film *Casablanca* (Warner Bros)

Surviving a hell on earth. Battle-scarred Tom Berenger, Oscar nominated for his Vietnam veteran Sergeant Barnes in Oliver Stone's *Platoon* (Hemdale/Orion, 1986)

The many faces of Brando. His Oscar-winning roles: (*bottom left*) Terry Malloy in *On the Waterfront* (Columbia, 1954) and (*top, second left*) Don Vito Corleone in *The Godfather* (Paramount, 1972)

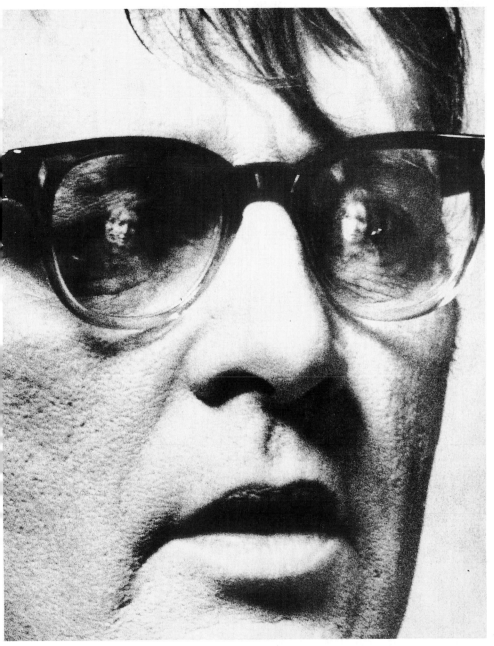

Visions of Liz. Richard Burton, nominated in 1966 for his alcoholic history professor in *Who's Afraid of Virginia Woolf?* (Warner Bros). Liz won, he lost!

Another one on the way down! A defeated Nicolas Cage drinking himself to death in his Oscar-winning role in Mike Figgis' *Leaving Las Vegas* (Lumiere Pictures/United Artists, 1995)

Chaplin's last chance of a best actor Oscar in the dual role of the Jewish barber and the dictator Adenoid Hynkel in his 1940 production *The Great Dictator* (United Artists). Sharing things with him in this scene: co-star and real-life partner Paulette Goddard

Oscar nominated Montgomery Clift (seen here with a young Elizabeth Taylor) as the social climbing George Eastman in *A Place in the Sun* (Paramount, 1951). A four-time Oscar nominee between 1948 and 1961, he never won the prized statuette

Too much to handle! Oscar nominee Glenn Close giving Michael Douglas a permanently hard time in the 1987 thriller *Fatal Attraction* (Paramount)

Bette Davis (*centre*) in perhaps her most celebrated role as fading actress Margo Channing in *All About Eve* (20th Century-Fox, 1950). Putting up with her moods: fellow Oscar nominee Celeste Holm and Hugh Marlowe

En route to the Marabar caves and disaster. Oscar nominated Judy Davis and Victor Banerjee in David Lean's *A Passage to India* (GW Films, 1984)

Vito Corleone before he became a Don. Oscar-winning Robert De Niro as the Brando character in younger years in Coppola's 1974 sequel *The Godfather Part II* (Paramount). De Niro's role was spoken throughout in Italian

Texas rich! James Dean (*second right*) about to inherit the land that will make him a multi-millionaire in George Stevens' *Giant* (Warner Bros, 1956). An Oscar nominee for his Jett Rink, he was joined in the best actor lists by Rock Hudson (*left*). Neither won. Yul Brynner was the year's winner for *The King and I*

Jane Fonda and Jason Robards in tender mood in Fred Zinnemann's *Julia* (20th Century-Fox, 1977). Both were Oscar nominated. Who won the award? Robards for his portrait of novelist Dashiell Hammett

City cop Harrison Ford learning from child Lucas Haas that one of his colleagues is a killer in Peter Weir's *Witness* (Paramount, 1985). Ford's best actor nomination remains his only Academy mention to date

Before the assault: Jodie Foster, best actress of 1988, plays pinball before becoming a gang rape victim in the harrowing *The Accused* (Paramount)

Nicolas Cage

Born Long Beach, California, USA, 7 January 1964

Oscars (1): Best Actor for Ben in *Leaving Las Vegas* (Lumiere Pictures/ MGM-UA, 1995)

Vegas hasn't exactly been the happiest of settings for Nicolas Cage. In *Honeymoon in Vegas* he lost his bride to big-time gangster James Caan in a poker game; in *Leaving Las Vegas* he lost out for good as the failed Hollywood scriptwriter who burns all his possessions and heads for the desert town with one objective in mind – to drink himself to death. The run-up to the Oscars saw him win every critical award in sight. Scarcely surprising then that the Oscar came his way as well. A nephew of Francis Ford Coppola (he changed his name to Cage in 1982), he won his award in March 1996, exactly fifty years after Ray Milland had been named for his failed novelist struggling with the bottle in *The Lost Weekend*.

Note: Although Cage earned deserved acclaim for his performance in *Leaving Las Vegas* he was somewhat upstaged on Oscar night by Mel Gibson, an actor who has yet to be nominated for his acting prowess but who picked up two of the main awards of the evening – best director and co-producer of 1995's best film, *Braveheart*.

James Cagney

Born New York City, USA, 17 July 1899; died 1986

Oscars (1): Best Actor for George M. Cohan in *Yankee Doodle Dandy* (Warner Bros, 1942)

Oscar Nominations (2): Best Actor for Rocky Sullivan in *Angels with Dirty Faces* (Warner Bros, 1938) and Martin 'the Gimp' Snyder in *Love Me or Leave Me* (MGM, 1955)

He said he packed it in when 'movies ceased to be fun and when all the effort that had gone into making them never looked as though it had been worthwhile on screen'. As good a reason as any, but with his retirement a little bit of magic went out of the movies, and filmgoers could no longer count on a man who could strut, talk and dance like no one else on screen. Shoving a grapefruit into the face of Mae Clarke in *Public Enemy* didn't bring him Academy recognition; singing and dancing his way through *Yankee Doodle Dandy* did! Two of his gangster roles – the convicted killer who feigns cowardice as he goes to the electric chair in *Angels with Dirty Faces*, and the racketeer obsessed with singer Ruth Etting in *Love Me or Leave Me* – brought him additional nominations, although there was nothing for what many regard as his finest portrayal: Cody Jarrett, the killer with the mother-fixation in *White Heat*.

Michael Caine

Born London, England, 14 March 1933

Oscars (1): Best Supporting Actor for Elliot in *Hannah and Her Sisters* (Orion, 1986)

Oscar Nominations (3): Best Actor for the title role in *Alfie* (Paramount, 1966), Milo Tindle in *Sleuth* (20th Century-Fox, 1972) and Dr Frank Bryant in *Educating Rita* (Acorn/Rank, 1983)

By far the cheekiest of the British working-class actors to emerge in the sixties, Michael Caine might have been a winner three times over – for his Cockney seducer Alfie, his victim of fun-and-games aristocrat Laurence Olivier, or his alcoholic university professor in *Educating Rita*. Things didn't work out, for one reason or another, and in the end, he was named best support for his fifty-something husband suffering a mid-life crisis in Woody Allen's *Hannah and Her Sisters*. Not quite the same, but better than nothing. His chance of the top prize may have gone, although one can never be sure in the Oscar business.

Louis Calhern

Born New York City, USA, 16 February 1895; died 1956

Oscar Nominations (1): Best Actor for Oliver Wendell Holmes in *The Magnificent Yankee* (MGM, 1950)

One of the surprise best actor nominees of the early fifties for his Judge Wendell Holmes, Louis Calhern was usually at his best in roguish parts, constantly looking as though he was 'on the make', with his mischievous smile and twinkling eyes, and bringing an urbane treachery to many of his roles. Memorable as the crooked lawyer Emmerich (the 'uncle' of Marilyn Monroe in *The Asphalt Jungle*), he spent his final years at MGM signing his seven-year contract without ever reading it. He enjoyed one of his most delightful screen moments in *High Society* when, arriving for the wedding with a monstrous hangover, he winces as the early-morning silence is broken by a bird chirping on a nearby branch. Glaring with contempt at the offending culprit, he says: 'Shut up, you fool!'

Dyan Cannon

Born Tacoma, Washington, USA, 4 January 1937

Oscar Nominations (2): Best Supporting Actress for Alice in *Bob and Carol and Ted and Alice* (Columbia, 1969) and Julia Farnsworth in *Heaven Can Wait* (Paramount, 1978)

No Oscars, just nominations all the way along the line for Dyan Cannon, but at least they proved she amounted to rather more than what the tabloids kept calling her – the young woman who mothered Cary Grant's only child! The nominations proved she could play spiteful – as one of the partner-swapping quartet in *Bob and Carol and Ted and Alice* – and also hysterical – as she and lover Charles Grodin keep failing to bump off hubby Warren Beatty in *Heaven Can Wait*. They also proved she was something of a dab hand behind the cameras when she was nominated for writing, producing, directing and co-editing the 1976 documentary, *Number One*. The post-seventies period has, unfortunately, been less rewarding.

Harry Carey

Born the Bronx, New York, USA, 16 January 1878; died 1947

Oscar Nominations (1): Best Supporting Actor for the President of the Senate in *Mr Smith Goes to Washington* (Columbia, 1939)

An Oscar nomination for Harry Carey? The odds were against it in the thirties. Stars of westerns and action movies just didn't rate. Frank Capra changed all that by casting the veteran actor as the warm, dignified vice-president and presiding officer of the Senate in *Mr Smith Goes to Washington*. Thomas Mitchell snatched things for his Doc Boone but the nomination alone was reward enough for a star who had begun back in the silent days with D. W. Griffith at Biograph, and who, a year after his death in 1947, earned perhaps the most affectionate of all on-screen movie tributes in John Ford's *Three Godfathers*: 'To the memory of Harry Carey – bright star of the early western sky.'

Lynn Carlin

Born 1930

Oscar Nominations (1): Best Supporting Actress for Maria Forst in *Faces* (Cassavetes/Reade-Continental, 1968)

A former secretary to Robert Altman, Lynn Carlin suddenly found herself in Oscar contention when director John Cassavetes sank his $140,000 acting fee for *Rosemary's Baby* into his cheap, quickly made, improvisational little movie, *Faces*. Carlin's role? That of a Los Angeles wife whose world is collapsing around her and who is trapped in a dull, colourless marriage. The film premiered in November, some five months after *Rosemary's Baby*, earning nods for both Carlin and Ruth Gordon (as the witch with all them 'erbs) in the supporting category. It was really no contest, Gordon coming out an easy winner for *Baby*, but for Carlin it was, to say the least, a most unusual way to win a nomination.

Art Carney

Born Mount Vernon, New York, USA, 4 November 1918

Oscars (1): Best Actor for Harry Coombs in *Harry and Tonto* (20th Century-Fox, 1974)

The advice given to Art Carney by one newspaper prior to Oscar night in 1975 was 'don't bother to turn up'. Jack Nicholson, it was suggested, was the odds-on winner for *Chinatown*. What the pundits overlooked was that actors playing private eyes – no matter how dextrous they are with the wisecracks (even Nicholson) – don't win Oscars, and so it proved yet again in 1975. Carney, whose film experience prior to *Harry and Tonto* was limited to just a couple of movie parts, walked off with the award for his role as an old widower who hitch-hikes across America with his pet cat. A dramatic and comedy performer on Broadway and a six-time Emmy winner for his TV work, he said in his acceptance speech that he hadn't been sure about the role but had taken the advice of his agent who had told him: 'Do it – you are *old*!'

Leslie Caron

Born Boulogne-Billancourt, near Paris, France, 1 July 1931

Oscar Nominations (2): Best Actress for Lili Daurier in *Lili* (MGM, 1953) and Jane Fosset in *The L-Shaped Room* (Romulus, 1963)

With her wide-eyed smile and gamine personality, the most unusual of all MGM's post-war musical stars, Leslie Caron was given the once-over by Gene Kelly in *An American in Paris* and told: 'With a binding like you've got, people are going to want to know what's in the book.' What was in the book was not only a sublimely talented Roland Petit-trained dancer but an actress of some quality, one that earned Academy Award nominations for her French waif entranced by Mel Ferrer's puppets in *Lili* and her pregnant French girl finding life not so swinging in sixties London in *The L-Shaped Room*. She missed out on the Oscars but there were compensations. She got to dance with Gene Kelly and Fred Astaire. No awards for that, but then none were needed!

Diahann Carroll

Born the Bronx, New York, USA, 17 July 1935

Oscar Nominations (1): Best Actress for Claudine Price in *Claudine* (Third World Cinema-Selznick-Pine/20th Century-Fox, 1974)

An outsider in the 1974 Oscar race, Diahann Carroll at least found herself the kind of role for which she had been searching, not for months but for years – that of a thirty-six-year-old woman struggling to bring up her six children on welfare and who enjoys a romance with cheerful garbage collector James Earl Jones. One critic described the film as a kind of black version (with the gloss removed) of a Doris Day–Rock Hudson-type comedy; another described it as 'sentimental tosh'. One thing about which they all agreed was that Carroll deserved her nomination. Ellen Burstyn achieved rather more, winning the best actress award for *Alice Doesn't Live Here Anymore*.

Nancy Carroll

Born New York City, USA, 19 November 1904; died 1965

Oscar Nominations (1): Best Actress for Hallie Hobart in *The Devil's Holiday* (Paramount, 1929/30)

Scarcely remembered these days other than by a loyal, ageing band of devotees, the vivacious, red-headed musical star Nancy Carroll could do a bit of everything on screen and was a boon to Paramount in the thirties, even though her films rarely amounted to anything more than routine vehicles. An exception was the film that earned her her nomination, *The Devil's Holiday*, in which she played a gold-digging manicurist transformed by love. MGM's Norma Shearer was the year's favourite and duly won for *The Divorcee*.

Peggy Cass

Born Boston, Massachusetts, USA, 21 May 1924

Oscar Nominations (1): Best Supporting Actress for Agnes Gooch in *Auntie Mame* (Warner Bros, 1958)

Another in the long line of distinguished stage performers who have dabbled in films from time to time, comedy star Peggy Cass earned her Academy nomination for repeating her Tony-winning Broadway role in *Auntie Mame* – as Mame's plain-Jane secretary who finds herself unwed and pregnant when she throws off the shackles and takes her eccentric employer's advice to 'live a little'. Beatrice Arthur, who reprised Agnes in the subsequent musical film version, *Mame*, failed to make the nominations.

John Cassavetes

Born New York City, USA, 9 December 1929; died 1989

Oscar Nominations (1): Best Supporting Actor for Victor Franko in *The Dirty Dozen* (MGM, 1967)

The Academy nominated him for being one of Robert Altman's misfits in *The Dirty Dozen*, overlooked him for lending his wife to the Devil in *Rosemary's Baby*, but honoured him with additional nominations for his work as a writer (*Faces*) and director (*A Woman Under the Influence*). Orson Welles he was not, but as an actor who could write, a writer who could direct, and a director who made some absorbing semi-improvisational dramas in the sixties and seventies, he was a film-maker of some distinction. Faltering relationships and nervous breakdowns were his speciality. Not, however, his own. His thirty-year marriage to actress Gene Rowlands lasted until his death in 1989.

Seymour Cassel

Born Detroit, USA, 22 January 1935

Oscar Nominations (1): Best Supporting Actor for Chet in *Faces* (Cassavetes/Reade Continental, 1968)

Another of the surprise nominees for John Cassavetes' *Faces*, Seymour Cassel made the honoured five for his sexy but ageing beach bum who makes a night of it with disillusioned wife Lynn Carlin and then has to rescue her from a sleeping pill overdose the next morning. A moving, imaginative and quite subtle little cameo but nothing on Oscar night, nor anything for Carlin, or indeed Cassavetes, who was up for an award in one of the writing categories. Times, though, they were a-changing. For a cheaply made improvised movie like *Faces* to make the Academy lists was something of a breakthrough, and *Easy Rider* was just a year away.

Richard Castellano

Born the Bronx, New York, USA, 4 September 1933; died 1988

Oscar Nominations (1): Best Supporting Actor for Frank Vecchio in *Lovers and Other Strangers* (ABC Pictures/Cinerama, 1970)

Moviegoers probably remember Richard Castellano best as the burly Corleone assassin Clemenza who arranged for Pacino's gun to be taped inside the toilet cistern in *The Godfather*. His Oscar nomination, however, was earned for repeating his Broadway role in *Lovers and Other Strangers* as a father trying to get to grips with all kinds of family problems at his son's wedding and not really solving any of them. A fine performance, in that it ranged from comedy to seriousness and back, it tended to get a bit lost on Oscar night among all the antics of John Mills' Irish halfwit Michael in *Ryan's Daughter*.

George Chakiris

Born Norwood, Ohio, USA, 16 September 1933

Oscars (1): Best Supporting Actor for Bernardo in *West Side Story* (United Artists, 1961)

Not a star for whom the Oscar did a great deal, the dark, handsome George Chakiris burned brightly for one movie – *West Side Story*, in which he played the leader of the Puerto Rican gang the Sharks – then disappeared into routine assignments and eventually TV soap opera. Pre-*West Side Story* he was a dancer in such films as *Gentlemen Prefer Blondes*, *White Christmas* and *Brigadoon*. Post-*West Side* it was stuff like *The Big Cube*, *Jekyll and Hyde...* *Together Again*, and *Dallas*.

Jeff Chandler

Born Brooklyn, New York, USA, 15 December 1918; died 1961

Oscar Nominations (1): Best Supporting Actor for Cochise in *Broken Arrow* (20th Century-Fox, 1950)

Pretty good with the 'white man talk with forked tongue' type dialogue so beloved of Hollywood's western screenwriters, Jeff Chandler brought a kind of dignity to such lingo with his performance as the peace-loving Cochise in Delmer Daves' distinguished pro-Indian western *Broken Arrow*. Unlucky to be nominated in a year when it was more or less all over bar the shouting (George Sanders won for *All About Eve*), Chandler repeated his role twice more in a couple of Universal actioners of the early fifties but never again came within shouting distance of an Oscar. Highly popular with female audiences, with his distinctive grey curly hair and rugged physique, he was approaching maturity as an actor when he died at the early age of forty-two from blood poisoning following spinal surgery.

Carol Channing

Born Seattle, USA, 31 January 1921

Oscar Nominations (1): Best Supporting Actress for Muzzy Van Hossmere in *Thoroughly Modern Millie* (Universal, 1967)

Carol Channing's wide smile, saucer eyes and inimitable squeaky voice have belonged more to the musical theatre (*Gentlemen Prefer Blondes, Hello Dolly*) than to the cinema. Her comedic gifts and exuberant personality were, however, allowed to blossom in at least one of her half-dozen movies, *Thoroughly Modern Millie*, a satire of the flapper age in which she played the fun-loving Long Island widow Muzzy Van Hossmere. Her rendering of the numbers 'Do It Again' and the dynamic 'Jazz Baby' went some way to earning her her Academy Award nomination. Estelle Parsons, for her portrait of a somewhat less happy lady – Gene Hackman's terrified wife in *Bonnie and Clyde* – took the award.

Stockard Channing

Born New York City, USA, 13 February 1944

Oscar Nominations (1): Best Actress for Ouisa Kittredge in *Six Degrees of Separation* (MGM/New Regency Productions, 1993)

She's still remembered for her leader of the high school 'Pink Ladies' in *Grease* (she was thirty-three at the time!), but her Oscar nomination was for something very different, for her chic Fifth Avenue wife married to art dealer Donald Sutherland who finds her life changed forever when a young black man bleeding from a knife wound arrives at her door and is taken in for the night. The film (adapted from the play by John Guare) was acted to within an inch of its life but Stockard had to be content with just the nomination, Holly Hunter being the year's best actress for keeping things to herself in *The Piano*.

Charles Chaplin

Born London, England, 16 April 1889; died 1977

Oscar Nominations (2): Best Actor for Charlie, a tramp, in *The Circus* (United Artists, 1927/28) and Adenoid Hynkel, Dictator of Tomania, and a Jewish barber in *The Great Dictator* (United Artists, 1940)

Charlie never won a competitive Oscar for his acting (or for his writing or direction, for that matter), although he might have done so had the Academy not overlooked his best actor and comedy direction nominations in the first year of the ceremonies and incorporated them in a special award 'for writing, acting, directing and producing *The Circus*', adding that the collective accomplishments put him in a class by himself. Whether he would have been quite so pleased about things if he'd known there was nothing more to come in the years ahead is unlikely. Nothing for his memorable little tramp in *City Lights* or *Modern Times*, just a nomination for his dual role (Hitler take-off and Jewish barber) in *The Great Dictator*, and a couple of writing mentions. Then political troubles and exile. The honorary award ('for the incalculable effect he has had in making motion pictures the art form of this century') arrived amid emotion in April 1972 when Jack Lemmon presented him with the tramp's bowler and cane and the entire audience rose as one.

Note: In 1972 Chaplin did eventually earn a competitive Oscar – for his music of *Limelight*. The award was presented twenty years late, the film not having played in Los Angeles (primarily because of Chaplin's political trouble) – where a picture has to be shown in order to qualify for Oscar consideration – until two decades after its initial American release.

Ruth Chatterton

Born New York City, USA, 24 December 1893; died 1961

Oscar Nominations (2): Best Actress for Jacqueline in *Madame X* (MGM, 1928/29) and Sarah Storm in *Sarah and Son* (Paramount, 1929/30)

A pound to a penny would get you that Ruth Chatterton earned a nomination for Walter Huston's social-climbing wife in *Dodsworth*. Not so. Walter Huston got the nod for having to put up with her. Chatterton's mentions were limited to two of her early screen sufferers: the self-sacrificing wife and mother in *Madame X*, and her impoverished singer turned opera star searching for her lost child in *Sarah and Son*. On screen for just ten years, she later enjoyed a successful career as a novelist but had to bow to the talents of first Mary Pickford (1928/29) and then Norma Shearer (1929/30) when the awards were handed out.

Michael Chekhov

Born Leningrad, Russia, 29 August 1891; died 1955

Oscar Nominations (1): Best Supporting Actor for Dr Alex Brulow in *Spellbound* (United Artists, 1945)

Any nephew of playwright Anton Chekhov should amount to something, and Michael certainly didn't disappoint, acting in Russian films as early as 1913 and forming distinguished drama schools in both London and the United States. His moment of Oscar glory occurred in 1945 when he appeared for Hitchcock in *Spellbound* and sat well into the night waiting for Gregory Peck to confront him with an open cut-throat razor. He also had some 'classic' Ben Hecht dialogue to deliver. Aware that psychiatrist Ingrid Bergman has fallen in love with the disturbed Mr Peck, he casts doubts on her ability to analyse his problems: 'What is there for you to say? We both know that the mind of a woman in love is operating on the lowest level of the intellect.' For Chekhov a nomination but no Oscar. That went to James Dunn for *A Tree Grows in Brooklyn*.

Cher

Born El Centro, California, USA, 20 May 1946

Oscars (1): Best Actress for Loretta Castorini in *Moonstruck* (MGM, 1987)

Oscar Nominations (1): Best Supporting Actress for Dolly Pelliker in *Silkwood* (20th Century-Fox, 1983)

'Snap out of it!' yells an infuriated Cher in *Moonstruck* as she slaps the face of her lover of the night before, the still groggy Nicolas Cage. He did but he got her in the end, although it was Cher who deservedly took the Oscar for her delightful performance as the Brooklyn widow who can't quite make up her mind as to whether she wants to take another husband or stay single. Famed for her colourful and outrageous outfits, she earned an earlier nomination for her lesbian friend of Meryl Streep in *Silkwood* but has generally played down her film career in favour of her musical one. A pity, for up until now she hasn't really given a dud performance.

Maurice Chevalier

Born Paris, France, 12 September 1888; died 1972

Oscar Nominations (2): Best Actor for Count Alfred in *The Love Parade* and Pierre Mirande in *The Big Pond* (both Paramount, 1929/30)

A cheery smile, a suave manner and a debonair persona; Maurice Chevalier could do no wrong in the early thirties when his charm carried all before him and helped him win two Oscar nominations in the same year – for his amorous count in Lubitsch's *The Love Parade* and his young Frenchman with his heart set on Claudette Colbert in *The Big Pond*. No wins but a special award in 1958 when many felt he should have been up for the supporting Oscar for his ageing ladies' man in *Gigi*. Not everyone was taken in by his roguish smile and twinkle-eyed charm. Co-star Jeanette MacDonald found him self-centred and once remarked: 'I could never say that working with him was anything more than agreeable. All he cared about was his career and his mother.'

Julie Christie

Born Chukua, Assam, India, 14 April 1941

Oscars (1): Best Actress for Diana Scott in *Darling* (Warner-Pathe-Anglo-Amalgamated, 1965)

Oscar Nominations (1): Best Actress for Constance Miller in *McCabe and Mrs Miller* (Warner Bros, 1971)

For much of the time in British movies of the sixties, actresses were busily getting pregnant. Not Julie Christie, who as the ambitious fashion model Diana Scott in *Darling* experienced all the excitement and sex of swinging London only to end up alone after three bitter romances and to be accused by Dirk Bogarde: 'Your idea of fidelity is not having more than one man in bed at the same time!' The role won her an Oscar and ushered in a period when she could do little wrong, either as Lara in *Doctor Zhivago*, Bathsheba in *Far from the Madding Crowd* or the aristocratic and destructive Marian Maudsley in *The Go-Between*. She won her second nomination for Altman's *McCabe and Mrs Miller*, in which she played a feisty, opium-addicted brothel madam, which is conceivably what Diana Scott might have become had she lived in another time and another place.

Diane Cilento

Born Brisbane, Australia, 5 October 1933

Oscar Nominations (1): Best Supporting Actress for Molly Seagrim in *Tom Jones* (United Artists, 1963)

The only trouble with Diane Cilento's performance in *Tom Jones* was that it was over too quickly. Once she had risen from the night grass, whispered, 'Aah, Tom . . . a wicked l-a-a-d', and seduced a grateful hero, her part in things was more or less done, other than to defy the local rustics with her pregnancy. Still, she was around long enough to qualify for a supporting nomination, along with the equally sexy Joyce Redman and the formidable

Edith Evans. Sex had nothing to do with it at Oscar time. Margaret Rutherford won for *The VIPs*.

Candy Clark

Born Norman, Oklahoma, USA, 20 June 1947

Oscar Nominations (1): Best Supporting Actress for Debbie in *American Graffiti* (Universal, 1973)

Candy Clark was the one who came out of the pack in the sixties 'coming of age' movie *American Graffiti*, although any one of the film's young performers (they included Richard Dreyfuss, Harrison Ford and Ron Howard) could easily have made the lists. Named for her blonde swinger who finds herself the object of some very clumsy seduction ideas, all of them in a borrowed Chevy, she found herself, like the year's other supporting nominees, to be no match for little Tatum O'Neal who stole the award, just as she had stolen every scene, as her junior con artist in *Paper Moon*.

Jill Clayburgh

Born New York City, USA, 30 April 1944

Oscar Nominations (2): Best Actress for Erica Benton in *An Unmarried Woman* (20th Century-Fox, 1978) and Marilyn Homberg in *Starting Over* (Paramount, 1979)

'Not quite up to expectations' must be the verdict on Jill Clayburgh, who in the late seventies looked for a while as though she was going to be the dominant actress of the American cinema for the next decade. That honour went to Meryl Streep; Clayburgh had to be content with a couple of Oscar nominations – for her wife deserted by her husband for a younger woman in *An Unmarried Woman* and, in a somewhat lighter vein, her schoolteacher involved with a divorced Burt Reynolds in *Starting Over*. Otherwise, it was a gradual fall from grace and the lack of suitable scripts to accommodate her talents – an all too familiar story.

Montgomery Clift

Born Omaha, Nebraska, USA, 17 October 1920; died 1966

Oscar Nominations (4): Best Actor for Ralph Stevenson in *The Search* (MGM, 1948), George Eastman in *A Place in the Sun* (Paramount, 1951) and Robert E. Lee Prewitt in *From Here to Eternity* (Columbia, 1953); Best Supporting Actor for Rudolf Petersen in *Judgment at Nuremberg* (United Artists, 1961)

Arguably the most intelligent and sensitive screen actor of his generation, and for many superior to Brando in the fifties, Montgomery Clift should, by rights, have won several Academy Awards. Instead, he finished up with just a list of nominations for his work with Fred Zinnemann (as the GI who cares for a displaced Czech boy in post-war Germany in *The Search* and the defiant army bugler in *From Here to Eternity*), George Stevens (as the doomed social climber in *A Place in the Sun*) and Stanley Kramer (as the pathetic sterilised Nazi victim in *Judgment at Nuremberg*). A man who loathed Hollywood and all it stood for, but like so many before him was drawn to it time and time again, he was badly injured in a car accident in 1957, which resulted in surgery that drastically altered his looks. He made just seventeen films in his twenty-year career. When working on a Hollywood movie and writing to his friends in New York he would sign his letters, 'Vomit, California'.

Glenn Close

Born Greenwich, Connecticut, USA, 19 March 1947

Oscar Nominations (5): Best Supporting Actress for Jenny Fields in *The World According to Garp* (Warner Bros, 1982), Sarah Cooper in *The Big Chill* (Columbia, 1983) and Iris in *The Natural* (Tri-Star, 1984); Best Actress for Alex Forrest in *Fatal Attraction* (Paramount, 1987) and the Marquise de Merteuil in *Dangerous Liaisons* (Warner Bros, 1988)

So far she's been the ultimate in feminist mothers, a former college radical, a virginal good girl for Robert Redford, a bad gal to Michael Douglas in *Fatal Attraction* ('I *won't* be ignored!') and schemed her way to self-destruction as a French aristocrat in *Dangerous Liaisons*. As far as the Oscar is concerned, however, it's all been to no avail and Glenn Close (a late starter in movies at the age of thirty-five) remains another of those contemporary American actresses whose obvious talent has yet to go rewarded. Perhaps if they film the musical version of *Sunset Boulevard* – she has played Norma Desmond both in Los Angeles and on Broadway – it will do the trick.

Lee J. Cobb

Born New York City, USA, 8 December 1911; died 1976

Oscar Nominations (2): Best Supporting Actor for Johnny Friendly in *On the Waterfront* (Columbia, 1954) and Fyodor Karamazov in *The Brothers Karamazov* (MGM, 1958)

Few performers are unlucky enough to lose their hair at twenty but such a fate befell Lee J. Cobb, and, not surprisingly, it somewhat limited him. 'We all want to play romantic figures,' he said ruefully. 'But because I lost my hair I was stuck playing butchers and crooks.' For audiences, at least, it was a good thing he did, for without the premature hair loss there would have been no mobsters, reporters, cops and loud-voiced patriarchs to savour and, on stage, no Willy Loman in *Death of a Salesman*. Nominated twice for Oscars, for his union racketeer in *On the Waterfront* and his Fyodor Karamazov, he later achieved fame as Judge Garth in the TV series *The Virginian*. It made him a wealthy man, although he later referred to it as 'a rather routine life on the TV range'.

Charles Coburn

Born Savannah, Georgia, USA, 19 June 1877; died 1961

Oscars (1): Best Supporting Actor for Benjamin Dingle in *The More the Merrier* (Columbia, 1943)

Oscar Nominations (2): Best Supporting Actor for Merrick in *The Devil and Miss Jones* (RKO, 1941) and Alexander Gow in *The Green Years* (MGM, 1946)

Perfect as eccentric millionaires, wealthy businessmen, and uncles and grandfathers most moviegoers would dearly have loved to call their own, Charles Coburn won his Oscar for doing what he did best, playing comedy, as the daffy old gent who shares an apartment with Jean Arthur and Joel McCrea in *The More the Merrier*. Nominated twice more – for his store-owner masquerading as an employee in *The Devil and Miss Jones* and his salty great-grandfather of Dean Stockwell in *The Green Years*, he turned to movies in his sixties (after forty years in the theatre), joining what he liked to call the cinema's 'ageing newcomers'. A big sports enthusiast, he enjoyed attending live events and ran his own stable of racehorses, which, in 1937, cost him $21,000 a year. The monocle he always wore was not an affectation but was used to combat a stigmatism.

James Coco

Born New York City, USA, 21 March 1929; died 1987

Oscar Nominations (1): Best Supporting Actor for Jimmy Perino in *Only When I Laugh* (Columbia, 1981)

At his most amusing when delivering the smart lines of Neil Simon, James Coco earned his Oscar nomination for his gay, unemployed actor friend of Marsha Mason in *Only When I Laugh*, making the most of and even, at times it seemed, improving on the author's original dialogue. A star of two original screen spoofs by Simon – *Murder by Death* and *The Cheap Detective* – he demonstrated his versatility with his performance as the silent film star Jolly Grimm (modelled closely on Fatty Arbuckle) in James Ivory's *The Wild Party*. A regular in films, the theatre and on TV, he authored the *James Coco Diet Book* in which he demonstrated how he had reduced his weight from 25 to 18 stone. Sadly, he eventually lost his life-long battle with obesity, dying from a heart attack at the age of fifty-seven.

Claudette Colbert

Born Paris, France, 13 September 1905

Oscars (1): Best Actress for Ellie Andrews in *It Happened One Night* (Columbia, 1934)

Oscar Nominations (2): Best Actress for Dr Jane Everest in *Private Worlds* (Paramount, 1935) and Annie Hilton in *Since You Went Away* (United Artists, 1944)

The story goes that Claudette Colbert was so certain she wouldn't win the Academy Award of 1934 that she decided to leave Los Angeles by train on the night of the awards, only to be rushed back to the ceremony with a motorcycle escort when it was revealed that she had won after all. She accepted her Oscar dressed in a travelling suit and a brown felt hat! A winner for her runaway heiress in *It Happened One Night*, she was subsequently nominated for her psychiatrist in the dramatic *Private Worlds* and the mother who keeps the home flag flying in wartime in *Since You Went Away*. Mostly a Paramount star during her career, she was seen by DeMille as the wickedest woman in the world when he cast her as Poppaea in *The Sign of the Cross*. Most, though, preferred her in sophisticated comedy, at which she excelled, bringing her warm, merry laugh and all-knowing wisecracks to the films of Lubitsch and Leisen and many of those scripted by Wilder and Brackett. Such days!

Patricia Collinge

Born Dublin, Ireland, 20 September 1894; died 1974

Oscar Nominations (1): Best Supporting Actress for Birdie Hubbard in *The Little Foxes* (RKO, 1941)

Frail, cultivated and with a slight fussiness and nervous edge about her, Patricia Collinge appeared before the film cameras just seven times, preferring to display her delicate talents on the Broadway stage rather than the screen. Nominated for reprising her Broadway role as the dipsomaniac faded flower Aunt Birdie in Lillian Hellman's *The Little Foxes*, she was unlucky to miss a second mention two years later for her role in Hitchcock's *Shadow of a Doubt*, as the doting, elderly sister, innocent (or was she?) of the fact that her outwardly civilised brother, Joseph Cotten, is a mass murderer. Twice used by Fred Zinnemann (*Teresa, The Nun's Story*), she was also a talented writer, authoring a play, several books and many short stories.

Pauline Collins

Born Devon, England, 3 September 1940

Oscar Nominations (1): Best Actress for the title role in *Shirley Valentine* (Paramount, 1989)

A Liverpool housewife, fed up with her arrogant, bullying husband, opts for a spell in Greece, where she embarks on an affair with Greek waiter Tom

Conti who loves her despite her stretch marks. Most middle-aged actresses would have given their eye teeth for such a role. Pauline Collins – star of the TV series *Upstairs, Downstairs* and *Forever Green* – was the lucky one and made the most of it, winning an Oscar nomination at her first big-screen attempt. The only snag was that it was 1989 and Jessica Tandy was ready and waiting to be rewarded for *Driving Miss Daisy*. Mostly a stage and TV performer, Pauline Collins has been seen recently in *City of Joy* with Patrick Swayze.

Ronald Colman

Born Richmond, Surrey, England, 9 February 1891; died 1958

Oscars (1): Best Actor for Anthony John in *A Double Life* (Universal–International, 1947)

Oscar Nominations (3): Best Actor for the title role in *Bulldog Drummond* (Goldwyn, United Artists 1929/30), Michel Oban in *Condemned* (Goldwyn, United Artists 1929/30) and Charles Rainier in *Random Harvest* (MGM, 1942)

Ronald Colman arrived in the States in 1915 with just '37 dollars, three clean collars and two letters of introduction'. Thirty-five years later, he tied in second place (after Chaplin) with Laurence Olivier in *The Daily Variety*'s poll as 'best actor of the century'. In between, his rich voice and debonair charm embellished dramas, comedies, swashbucklers and romances, and earned four Oscar nominations – for his suave adventurer-detective Bulldog Drummond, escaped prisoner in *Condemned*, aristocratic amnesiac in *Random Harvest*, and the Shakespearean actor who commits murder when he believes he is Othello in real life. The last-named brought him his belated Academy Award at the age of fifty-seven. He was described by one critic as being 'possessed of integrity, inner strength, reliability and gentleness – in fact everything a woman could want'. Few women disagreed with the assessment.

Betty Compson

Born Beaver, Utah, USA, 18 March 1897; died 1974

Oscar Nominations (1): Best Actress for Carrie in *The Barker* (First National, 1928/29)

Many of today's top stars have difficulty in reaching thirty movies in their careers; in years to come it may be even fewer with the time they take to agree salaries between roles. The vivacious blonde Betty Compson, a 1928/29 nominee for her carnival hula dancer in *The Barker*, managed more than 180, most of them silent but a goodly number as a character actress in the first two decades of sound. Somewhere along the line she also found time to marry Hollywood director James Cruze, who directed her opposite Von Stroheim's crazed ventriloquist in *The Great Gabbo*.

Sean Connery

Born Edinburgh, Scotland, 25 August 1930

Oscars (1): Best Supporting Actor for Jim Malone in *The Untouchables* (Paramount, 1987)

They took their time but they gave it to him in the end – for his seasoned Irish beat cop who joins up with Eliot Ness against Al Capone in *The Untouchables*. It wasn't his most accomplished portrayal by any means, but the prize went some way to making amends for his being overlooked for his acerbic policeman near to breaking point in *The Offence*, his POW in a military camp in Africa in *The Hill*, and Rudyard Kipling's soldier-adventurer Daniel Dravot in Huston's *The Man Who Would Be King*. Nothing for James Bond, of course, but then no performer in a Bond film, not even those leering supervillains of Wiseman, Froebe, Donald Pleasence and co., has ever come close to an Academy statuette.

Tom Conti

Born Paisley, Scotland, 22 November 1941

Oscar Nominations (1): Best Actor for Gowan McGland in *Reuben, Reuben* (20th Century-Fox, 1983)

For many, something of an Al Pacino lookalike, the handsome, dark-haired Tom Conti's sorties into movies have generally been unremarkable, although he made the most of his POW in *Merry Christmas, Mr Lawrence* and his attractive but somewhat unlikely Greek waiter/lover of Pauline Collins in *Shirley Valentine*. His Oscar nomination came out of the blue for his boozy Scots poet residing in New England who enjoys womanising rather than writing and then falls for a beautiful young student. It was a year when three other Brits were also up for the award – Albert Finney and Tom Courtenay for *The Dresser*, and Michael Caine for *Educating Rita*. The sole American nominee, Robert Duvall, won for *Tender Mercies*.

Gary Cooper

Born Helena, Montana, USA, 7 May 1901; died 1961

Oscars (2): Best Actor for Alvin C. York in *Sergeant York* (Warner Bros, 1941) and Marshal Will Kane in *High Noon* (United Artists, 1952)

Oscar Nominations (3): Best Actor for Longfellow Deeds in *Mr Deeds Goes to Town* (Columbia, 1936), Lou Gehrig in *The Pride of the Yankees* (Goldwyn/RKO, 1942) and Robert Jordan in *For Whom the Bell Tolls* (Paramount, 1943)

Coop's theory about movie success was that 'if you hit the mark with two out of every five movies you'll keep the wheels of the cycle turning'. His own ratio was probably nearer three out of five and, at his peak, four out of five. His Oscars were for his World War I hero Alvin York, who single-handedly captured an entire German battalion, and his small-town marshal who had rather more trouble with a vengeful killer arriving on the noon train. Tall, lean, shy and hesitant of speech, he attributed his success to the fact that he looked like 'the guy down the street', which had more than a grain of truth to it although many women would have dearly loved to have found the street he was talking about! Nominated also for his tuba-playing country boy Longfellow Deeds, baseball star Lou Gehrig and Hemingway's

Spanish Civil War hero Robert Jordan, he was awarded a special Oscar in April 1961. It was accepted by a tearful James Stewart who, in an emotional tribute, revealed that Cooper had only weeks to live.

Gladys Cooper

Born Lewisham, London, England, 18 December 1888; died 1971

Oscar Nominations (3): Best Supporting Actress for Mrs Henry Windle Vale in *Now Voyager* (Warner Bros, 1942), Sister Vauzous in *The Song of Bernadette* (20th Century-Fox, 1943) and Mrs Higgins in *My Fair Lady* (Warner Bros, 1964)

A strikingly beautiful woman even in late middle age, Gladys Cooper was described by Bette Davis as 'one of the few actresses I felt privileged to play a scene with'. The Academy acknowledged her three times, honouring her icy cruelty as Davis' domineering mother in *Now Voyager*, the Sister who doubts the visions of Bernadette Soubirous in *The Song of Bernadette*, and, much later, the haughty mother who treats with total disdain son Henry Higgins in *My Fair Lady*. The end result, however, was nominations three, awards nil, which many felt was something of an injustice. Gladys Cooper's kindly side was perhaps best illustrated in *Rebecca* when she played the tweedy sister of Laurence Olivier and Joan Fontaine's ally against the machinations of the evil Mrs Danvers.

Jackie Cooper

Born Los Angeles, USA, 15 September 1921

Oscar Nominations (1): Best Actor for Skippy Skinner in *Skippy* (Paramount, 1930/31)

The only child performer to be nominated as best actor (all subsequent child nominees have been in the supporting categories), the ten-year-old Jackie Cooper won his nomination for bringing to life the cartoon strip hero Skippy. A nephew of the film's director, Norman Taurog, and a veteran of Hal Roach's *Our Gang* comedy shorts, he received no favours from his uncle during filming. Somewhat peeved because Cooper refused to cry in a scene, Taurog opted for terror by threatening to shoot Jackie's dog if he didn't do as he was told. When he began to howl the cameras began to roll. Taurog won the director's award, Cooper missed out, spending most of the evening asleep on Marie Dressler's arm. It mattered little. He went on to become one of the most popular child stars of the thirties and later became an actor and director on TV. He appeared as Perry White in the *Superman* films of the seventies and eighties.

Ellen Corby

Born Racine, Wisconsin, USA, 3 June 1913

Oscar Nominations (1): Best Supporting Actress for Aunt Trina in *I Remember Mama* (RKO, 1948)

Forever bustling around as fussy spinsters and teachers, Ellen Corby was in Oscar contention just the once, for her twittering Norwegian aunt in *I Remember Mama*. Nineteen forty-eight, however, was the year of John Huston, not only for *The Treasure of the Sierra Madre* but also *Key Largo*, and Claire Trevor walked off with the supporting award for her alcoholic floozie of Edward G. Robinson. A script girl for twelve years before becoming an actress, Corby wrote a couple of Hopalong Cassidy westerns and also contributed to the dialogue of the Raymond Chandler thriller *Farewell My Lovely*. Despite her scores of films she became best known for her TV role as Grandma in *The Waltons* (1972–79), for which she won three Emmys.

Valentina Cortese

Born Milan, Italy, 1 January 1924

Oscar Nominations (1): Best Supporting Actress for Severine in *Day for Night* (Les Films Du Carosse-PECF-PIC, France/Italy, 1974)

Quite how she missed the Oscar remains a mystery. Every other critical body seemed to name her except the Academy, who preferred Ingrid Bergman in *Murder on the Orient Express*. The role? That of a fading actress in turmoil over her private life who can't get to grips with her new movie, taking to the bottle, forgetting her lines and making unscheduled exits through set doors that lead to nowhere. Funny and tragic in turn, it belongs with the best performances of the seventies, just as the movie from which it comes, *Day for Night*, belongs with the best-ever films about the making of a film. Alas, no Oscar for Miss Cortese, although Truffaut's film did make it to the best foreign-language award.

Kevin Costner

Born Compton, near Los Angeles, USA, 18 January 1955

Oscar Nominations (1): Best Actor for Lt John Dunbar in *Dances With Wolves* (Tig/Orion, 1990)

For many, the modern cinema's answer to James Stewart, for others a 'What do people see in him?' kind of actor, Kevin Costner built his reputation on a couple of intriguing baseball movies, *Field of Dreams* and *Bull Durham*, and Brian De Palma's gangster flick *The Untouchables*. One of the most bankable American stars of the nineties, he has been nominated just the once for his acting, for his Union officer who sets out to 'see the frontier' in his massive western *Dances With Wolves*. He missed out on the acting prize but made amends by winning the two top awards of the evening – best director and best producer. Some recent inflated productions, among them *Wyatt Earp* and *Waterworld*, have suggested that he may have peaked at the box office.

Tom Courtenay

Born Hull, England, 25 February 1937

Oscar Nominations (2): Best Supporting Actor for Pasha/Streinikoff in *Doctor Zhivago* (MGM, 1965); Best Actor for Norman in *The Dresser* (Goldcrest/Columbia, 1983)

Unconvincing as a Russian revolutionary in *Doctor Zhivago* (a miscalculation by the usually meticulous David Lean), but nigh on perfect as the camp aide of flamboyant actor-manager Albert Finney in *The Dresser*, Tom Courtenay found himself Oscar-nominated for both roles but not for the part for which he is still best remembered, daydreamer supreme *Billy Liar*. The mythical kingdom of Ambrosia, the wild imaginings, the machine-gunning of parents, etc. do not therefore belong in the Academy record books – just Pasha and Norman. Martin Balsam won in the supporting category in the *Zhivago* year; Robert Duvall took the actor's prize in 1983.

Jeanne Crain

Born Barstow, California, USA, 25 May 1925

Oscar Nominations (1): Best Actress for Pinky/Patricia Johnson in *Pinky* (20th Century-Fox, 1949)

Just about the perfect 'girl-next-door', the brown-haired, hazel-eyed Jeanne Crain was, for the most part, required to do little more than gaze adoringly at her leading men. *Pinky*, in which she was directed by Elia Kazan and played a black nurse who passes for white, proved she could act as well as look beautiful and earned her an Oscar nomination. Had she not become pregnant and had to cancel one of her subsequent roles, she might well have had another. The movie was initially called *Best Performance*. It was retitled and Anne Baxter took the vacant part. The film: *All About Eve*.

Broderick Crawford

Born Philadelphia, USA, 9 December 1911; died 1986

Oscars (1): Best Actor for Willie Stark in *All the King's Men* (Columbia, 1949)

A run-of-the-mill performer (usually as a heavy) in westerns and low-budget actioners early in his career, Broderick Crawford seemed to come from nowhere to deliver two classic performances before returning to the routine and the mundane. The roles that brought him fame and keep his name firmly etched in the history books were his 'hick' politician Willie Stark (closely modelled on Louisiana governor Huey Long), which earned him an Academy Award for *All the King's Men*, and his bad-tempered junk tycoon Harry Brock, saddled in *Born Yesterday* with the dumbest of dumb mistresses, Judy Holliday. No award for the latter, although he perhaps deserved a mention, if only in the supporting category. Remembered for his heavy bulk, staccato delivery and brute force, Crawford later became popular on TV in the series *Highway Patrol*.

☆

Joan Crawford

Born San Antonio, Texas, USA, 23 March 1904; died 1977

Oscars (1): Best Actress for the title role of *Mildred Pierce* (Warner Bros, 1945)

Oscar Nominations (2): Best Actress for Louise Howell in *Possessed* (Warner Bros, 1947) and Myra Hudson in *Sudden Fear* (RKO, 1952)

'I love to play bitches,' said Joan Crawford, and a quick glance at her credits proved that she got her way for much of the time. Her Oscar, though, came for a model of self-sacrifice, a former waitress made good who spoils one of the most insufferable brat-daughters ever to grace the screen, even to the point of trying to take a murder rap on her behalf! Luckily she wised up. Ann Blyth got what was coming to her and Crawford got what was coming to her, a gold-plated Academy statuette as best actress of the year. Nominated twice more – for her murdering schizophrenic in *Possessed* and her playwright-wife married to a lethal younger husband in *Sudden Fear* – she earned nothing for her most outrageous role (in *Humoresque*) when, distraught that she can't have violinist John Garfield, she walks to her death into the Pacific Ocean, clad in a black sequined dress and with the strains of Wagner's *Tristan and Isolde* coming over the radio. No wonder director Clarence Brown regarded her as one of Hollywood's all-time superstars and said of her appeal: 'A star is when someone says, "to hell with it, let's leave the dishes in the sink and go see Joan Crawford in a movie".'

Donald Crisp

Born Aberfeddy, Scotland, 27 July 1880; died 1974

Oscars (1): Best Supporting Actor for Mr Morgan in *How Green Was My Valley* (20th Century-Fox, 1941)

Whenever Donald Crisp was around it seemed that to cross him would mean trouble and that his word counted for all, whether he be a western patriarch, priest, politician, military man or just plain family head, which he was on several occasions, most memorably as the stern father of the struggling Welsh mining family in *How Green Was My Valley*. An Academy Award-winner just the once, he began in films when Oscars were but a pipe dream as assistant to D. W. Griffith on *The Birth of a Nation* (1915) and *Broken Blossoms* (1919), graduating to both actor and director and guiding many of the films of John Barrymore and swashbuckler Douglas Fairbanks. He lived to be ninety-four and made his last appearance at the grand old age of eighty-three as the grandfather of Henry Fonda in *Spencer's Mountain*.

James Cromwell

Oscar Nominations (1): Best Supporting Actor for Arthur Hoggett in *Babe* (Universal, 1995)

'Never act with animals' has been a maxim with actors since time immemorial; to act with animals who 'talk' and push you down to eleventh place in the cast list would seem to be asking for trouble. James Cromwell, though, didn't seem to mind in the least, treating the events in *Babe* with the seriousness that they deserved and helping to make sure that the film's message – that all animal species deserve to be treated with respect – got across with some style. The story? About a sweet-tempered piglet won at a fair by farmer Cromwell and who finds a calling as a sheepdog. None of the other critical bodies named Cromwell in their lists of top supports. It was to the Academy's credit that they went their own way and did so.

Hume Cronyn

Born London, Ontario, Canada, 18 July 1911

Oscar Nominations (1): Best Supporting Actor for Paul Roeder in *The Seventh Cross* (MGM, 1944)

Worried, anxious and nervous-looking, Hume Cronyn was one of those character actors who frequently caused audiences to sit up and ask: 'Who *is* that little guy?' The answer was that he was a distinguished stage actor who occasionally made movies, often with his wife Jessica Tandy. Nominated just the once – for his German factory worker coming face to face with Fascism in

Fred Zinnemann's *The Seventh Cross* – he was unlucky to miss out for a subsequent role as the sadistic prison officer in Dassin's *Brute Force*, one of the most chilling portrayals of evil seen in post-war American cinema. The year though was 1947, and with Richard Widmark (*Kiss of Death*) and Robert Ryan (*Crossfire*) both in the running for the supporting award, the Academy probably felt that they had enough evil to be going on with.

Bing Crosby

Born Tacoma, Washington, USA, 2 May 1903; died 1977

Oscars (1): Best Actor for Father O'Malley in *Going My Way* (Paramount, 1944)

Oscar Nominations (2): Best Actor for Father O'Malley in *The Bells of St Mary's* (RKO, 1945) and Frank Elgin in *The Country Girl* (Paramount, 1954)

When asked to name the kind of movie in which he would most like to appear, Bing Crosby replied: 'It would open with me in a rocking chair on a veranda. The rest of the film would be what I saw.' The answer was typical of his laid-back attitude towards his acting career, which he regarded both as an enjoyable way of spending a day and a profitable adjunct to his enormous success as a crooner. His singing priest in *Going My Way* was hardly of Oscar calibre but was welcomed by an industry in wartime, not least for his rendering of the hit song 'When You Wish Upon a Star'. Easy-going, charming, some say at his best with Hope and Lamour in the *Road* films, Crosby had two more bites at the Oscar cherry – in 1945 for reprising his Father O'Malley in *The Bells of St Mary's* and in 1954 for his failed alcoholic actor in *The Country Girl*. A Paramount star for more than twenty years, he sang more Academy Award-winning songs (4) than any other performer: 'Sweet Leilani' in *Waikiki Wedding* (1937), 'White Christmas' in *Holiday Inn* (1942), 'When You Wish Upon a Star' in *Going My Way* (1944) and 'In the Cool, Cool, Cool of the Evening' in *Here Comes the Groom* (1951). His fortune from singing, films and TV was estimated to have been between $200 and $400 million.

Rupert Crosse

Born 1927; died 1973

Oscar Nominations (1): Best Supporting Actor for Ned McClaslin in *The Reivers* (National General Pictures, 1969)

The name of the first black actor to earn a supporting nomination has long since disappeared into the Oscar files of yesteryear but for the record it was Rupert Crosse who, in *The Reivers*, joined Steve McQueen and eleven-year-old Mitch Vogel on a colourful automobile trip to Memphis in the early years of the century. Nominated for his dude sidekick of McQueen, Crosse was described by one critic as 'making the screen more interesting whenever he was on it', which is as good a reason as any for being nominated. He would almost certainly have achieved much more had not cancer claimed him four years later at the tragically early age of forty-five.

Lindsay Crouse

Born New York City, USA, 12 May 1948

Oscar Nominations (1): Best Supporting Actress for Margaret Lomax in *Places in the Heart* (Tri-Star, 1984)

One of those fighting for small-town survival in Depression Texas in Robert Benton's *Places in the Heart*, Lindsay Crouse might well have stolen the film from star Sally Field had her role been a little more developed. Nominated for her home hairdresser whose marriage is fraying round the edges, she was unlucky in that she was up against Peggy Ashcroft in *A Passage to India*, and in 1984 there was really only one winner. The daughter of playwright-librettist-screenwriter Russell Crouse and the wife of playwright David Mamet, she has not been nominated since, although her psychologist turned con artist in Mamet's remarkable début film, *House of Games*, was more than deserving of mention in 1987.

Tom Cruise

Born Syracuse, New York, USA, 3 July 1962

Oscar Nominations (1): Best Actor for Ron Kovic in *Born on the Fourth of July* (Universal, 1989)

He's really only convinced as brash, shallow, hustler-type figures – the young pool player in *The Color of Money*, barman in *Cocktail*, brother of Dustin Hoffman in *Rain Man* – except the once, when Oliver Stone cast him as the real-life paraplegic Vietnam vet Ron Kovic, and then the Oscar looked to be his. A Golden Globe in one hand, an Oscar in the other, prophesied one movie magazine. Then along came Daniel Day-Lewis to snatch the award for his playing of cerebral palsy victim Christy Brown, and the chance was gone. It hasn't re-emerged and seven years have now elapsed.

Quinn Cummings

Born Hollywood, California, USA, 13 August 1967

Oscar Nominations (1): Best Supporting Actress for Lucy McFadden in *The Goodbye Girl* (MGM/Warner Bros, 1977)

Kids on screen can be either unbearable and a turn-off or charming and entertaining. Quinn Cummings fell into the latter category in *The Goodbye Girl*, always in the way when the battles were raging between mum Marsha Mason and actor/lodger Richard Dreyfuss and equally underfoot when things were thawing out. Neil Simon's lines helped her towards her nomination, although she failed to emulate Tatum O'Neal's win for *Paper Moon* some four years earlier. The somewhat taller Vanessa Redgrave was the one who stopped her in her tracks. She won for *Julia*, the only time in Academy history that a supporting Oscar has been awarded to an actress playing a title role.

☆

Tony Curtis

Born the Bronx, New York, USA, 3 June 1925

Oscar Nominations (1): Best Actor for John Jackson in *The Defiant Ones* (United Artists, 1958)

A solitary nomination is all he's received, and that's not really enough for an actor who used to be mocked for his 'Yonda lies the castle of my fadda' in *The Black Shield of Falworth* but who in the fifties and sixties essayed a range of roles as effectively as any actor in Hollywood. His nomination was for his runaway prisoner chained by the wrist to Sidney Poitier in *The Defiant Ones*. The roles the Academy overlooked included his seedy little press agent forever snapping at the heels of Burt Lancaster in *The Sweet Smell of Success*, his memorable jazz saxophonist in drag in *Some Like It Hot* (Jack Lemmon made it, he didn't), and his notorious mass murderer in *The Boston Strangler*.

Joan Cusack

Born Evanston, Illinois, USA, 11 October 1962

Oscar Nominations (1) Best Supporting Actress for Cyn in *Working Girl* (20th Century-Fox, 1988)

If Hollywood made more intelligent comedies, the name of Joan Cusack would almost certainly have attracted greater attention than it has so far received. They don't, so she has had to make the most of what have generally been slim pickings. The two exceptions have been *Working Girl* ('Can I get you anything?' she coyly asks Harrison Ford. 'Tea . . . coffee . . . me!') and *Broadcast News*, in which she says to Holly Hunter without a hint of malice: 'You're my perfect role model, except in your private life.' Nominated for the former film, she came in some way behind Geena Davis, who walked off with William Hurt's dog and the Oscar for *The Accidental Tourist*.

𝒟

Willem Dafoe

Born Appleton, Wisconsin, USA, 22 July 1955

Oscar Nominations (1): Best Supporting Actor for Sgt Elias in *Platoon* (Hemdale, 1986)

The only trouble with appearing in Oliver Stone's pictures is that (Michael Douglas apart) the actors get the nominations and Stone gets the awards. To date he's claimed three (for writing and direction), whilst his actors gaze adoringly at their nomination certificates. Willem Dafoe was one who must have thought his chance had come when Stone cast him against type as the humane and compassionate sergeant in *Platoon*. No such luck. Michael Caine took the award for worrying about women in *Hannah and Her Sisters*, and Dafoe and Tom Berenger (also nominated for *Platoon*) went back to their certificates.

Dan Dailey

Born New York City, USA, 14 December 1914; died 1978

Oscar Nominations (1): Best Actor for Skid in *When My Baby Smiles at Me* (20th Century-Fox, 1948)

That it was possible to win an Oscar nomination for a performance in a Betty Grable film was proved in 1948 when Dan Dailey entered the lists for his alcoholic burlesque comedian in *When My Baby Smiles at Me*. Had he picked a better year – Laurence Olivier was an obvious shoo-in for *Hamlet* – who knows? A genial song-and-dance man who was also a more than capable straight actor, Dailey partnered Grable in four of her later films at Fox, many of them reflecting his own musical background in vaudeville and burlesque. His last major musical was at MGM when he joined Gene Kelly and Michael Kidd in *It's Always Fair Weather* and in one exhilarating sequence danced with a dustbin lid on his foot!

John Dall

Born New York City, USA, 1918; died 1971

Oscar Nominations (1): Best Supporting Actor for Morgan Evans in *The Corn Is Green* (Warner Bros, 1945)

He'll best be remembered as one of the two Leopold-Loeb-type killers who murder a young student just for the fun of it in Hitchcock's *Rope*; his Oscar nomination, though, was won for a rather less violent character, a Welsh mining boy who comes under the guidance of teacher Bette Davis, who sees in him university potential. An affair with a young village girl and an unexpected pregnancy almost put paid to things, but Bette, being what she is, adopts the child and Dall goes on to bigger and better things at Oxford. Not on screen, though. His film career was only sporadic and a sudden heart attack brought it to an end when he was just fifty-two. James Dunn took the supporting award in 1945 for *A Tree Grows in Brooklyn*.

Dorothy Dandridge

Born Cleveland, Ohio, USA, 9 November 1923; died 1965

Oscar Nominations (1): Best Actress for the title role of *Carmen Jones* (20th Century-Fox, 1954)

'*Carmen Jones* was the best break I've ever had,' said Dorothy Dandridge. 'But no producer ever knocked on my door. There just aren't that many parts for a black actress.' She made the remark in the fifties but she might just as well have been saying it in the nineties, for no black performer (Dandridge was the first nominee) has yet won the best actress award and Oscar is heading for his seventieth birthday. A nightclub singer whose sensuous delivery and gold lamé costumes left audiences breathless and goggle-eyed, Dandridge appeared in other movies of the fifties (she had been a Hollywood bit-player as a kid) but featured to advantage in only one, Sam Goldwyn's *Porgy and Bess*. Declared bankrupt in 1962, she was found dead in her Hollywood apartment from an overdose of sleeping tablets mixed with alcohol.

Bobby Darin

Born New York City, USA, 14 May 1936; died 1973

Oscar Nominations (1): Best Supporting Actor for Corporal Jim Tompkins in *Captain Newman MD* (Universal, 1963)

A highly popular singing star and nightclub entertainer whose version of 'Mack the Knife' sold two million copies, Bobby Darin tried in the sixties to emulate the success of other singers turned actors, notably Crosby and Sinatra. Despite earning an Oscar nomination for his troubled and ill-fated corporal in *Captain Newman MD*, things didn't quite work out as he had hoped, and his post-nomination films were few and disappointing. His most accomplished role, and one that showed just what he was capable of, was his young Nazi racist in Hubert Cornfield's *Pressure Point*. Troubled with heart problems for many years, he met an early death after undergoing heart surgery.

Jane Darwell

Born Palmyra, Missouri, USA, 15 October 1879; died 1967

Oscars (1): Best Supporting Actress for Ma Joad in *The Grapes of Wrath* (20th Century-Fox, 1940)

A bit grumpy on Oscar night (she kept complaining that she hadn't worked in seven months), Jane Darwell had her ruffled feathers smoothed somewhat when the Academy announced her as the year's top female support for her portrayal of Steinbeck's doughty Depression ma who, with her family, journeys west in a battered old Ford to start a new life in California. A favourite of director John Ford and frequent co-star of Henry Fonda, she really had no right to be out of sorts at the ceremony. During her sound career she appeared in more than 170 movies. Her last film role was as the Bird Woman in *Mary Poppins*.

Jaye Davidson

Oscar Nominations (1): Best Supporting Actor for Dil in *The Crying Game* (Palace, 1992)

The Academy were up against it in 1992. They either overlooked Jaye Davidson completely and thus deprived him of his Oscar chance, or they let the cat out of the bag by nominating him as best supporting actor for a role in which for 75 per cent of the time he appeared as a secret and seductive transvestite. They opted for the latter and Davidson became one of the surprise nominees of the nineties for his petulant hairdresser Dil who first bewitches and then astonishes IRA volunteer Stephen Rea. An audacious performance, somewhat more controversial than the year's winner, the western sheriff of Gene Hackman in *Unforgiven*.

Bette Davis

Born Lowell, Massachusetts, USA, 5 April 1908; died 1989

Oscars (2): Best Actress for Joyce Heath in *Dangerous* (Warner Bros, 1935) and Julie Marston in *Jezebel* (Warner Bros, 1938)

Oscar Nominations (8): Best Actress for Judith Traherne in *Dark Victory* (Warner Bros, 1939), Leslie Crosbie in *The Letter* (Warner Bros, 1940), Regina Giddens in *The Little Foxes* (RKO, 1941), Charlotte Vale in *Now Voyager* (Warner Bros, 1942), Fanny Trellis in *Mr Skeffington* (Warner Bros, 1944), Margo Channing in *All About Eve* (20th Century-Fox, 1950), Margaret Elliot in *The Star* (20th Century-Fox, 1952) and Jane Hudson in *What Ever Happened to Baby Jane?* (Warner Bros, 1962)

She was always one to know her own mind, was Bette Davis, especially when it came to Oscars: 'I should have won for *Jane*,' she said defiantly, 'but they gave it to someone who had already played her role on stage. I never thought that was fair. Oscars should be for original screen work!' Like the inimitable fading actress Margo Channing, for instance, or the murdering planter's wife in *The Letter* or that most repressed of young spinsters, Charlotte Vale, in *Now Voyager*. In any event, the grand total of wins remained just two – for her fallen Broadway actress in *Dangerous* and her tempestuous Southern belle in *Jezebel* – and she never achieved her ambition of becoming the first actress to win three Academy Awards. Her other nominations: for her dying heiress in *Dark Victory*, her scheming Southern vixen in *The Little Foxes*, the selfish wife of a blind Claude Rains' Mr Skeffington, the former Hollywood award-winner in *The Star* and the precocious vaudeville child star turned grotesque in *Baby Jane*. 'Fasten your seatbelts, it's going to be a bumpy night' remains her most famous line; the moment when she serves a dead rat to Joan Crawford (in *Baby Jane*) her most outrageous scene!

Geena Davis

Born Wareham, Massachusetts, USA, 21 January 1957

Oscars (1): Best Supporting Actress for Muriel Pritchett in *The Accidental Tourist* (Warner Bros, 1988)

Oscar Nominations (1): Best Actress for Thelma in *Thelma and Louise* (MGM, 1991)

From the moment she gave a wide-eyed William Hurt (and his unruly little dog) the once-over and demolished him with her 'come-on' repartee, the short-skirted, high-heeled Geena Davis had 1988's supporting actress Oscar in the bag. Some felt she should have added to her laurels for her bored housewife who, with Susan Sarandon, wreaks havoc and carnage as they plough their way across the States in *Thelma and Louise*. Proving that women can be just as brainless as men seemed a somewhat pointless exercise, however, and she lost to the young Jodie Foster for her rape victim in *The Accused*. Married at one time to actor Jeff Goldblum and now to director Renny Harlin, she has also appeared as the luckless wife of *The Fly* and played women's baseball in *A League of Their Own*.

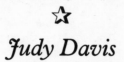

Judy Davis

Born Perth, Australia, 1955

Oscar Nominations (2): Best Actress for Adela Quested in *A Passage to India* (GW Films/Home Box Office, 1984); Best Supporting Actress for Sally in *Husbands and Wives* (TriStar, 1992)

Somehow, Judy Davis has managed to pull off a quite unique Oscar double, earning nominations for roles directed by two film-makers as far apart in style and method as it is possible to get – the late David Lean, who guided her to the best actress lists for her repressed (and allegedly raped) Adela in *A Passage to India*, and Woody Allen, who brought out her more neurotic side as the edgy New York wife suffering painful withdrawal symptoms following her mutual break-up from husband Sydney Pollack. She lost on both occasions. One suspects that she enjoyed herself rather more in New York than in India. But perhaps not.

Bruce Davison

Born Philadelphia, USA, 28 June 1946

Oscar Nominations (1): Best Supporting Actor for David in *Longtime Companion* (American Playhouse/Samuel Goldwyn, 1990)

Tom Hanks may have been the first actor to win an Oscar for playing an Aids victim but Bruce Davison was on the scene three years earlier for his moving performance as the lover of a TV scriptwriter who cares for his friend as he gradually deteriorates in the beach house where they and their companions have gathered over the years. Joe Pesci was the year's winner for his certifiable mobster in *Goodfellas*; in retrospect the sensitive Davison perhaps deserved the award more. The Golden Globe and New York Critics Circle awards offered some compensation.

Doris Day

Born Cincinnati, Ohio, USA, 3 April 1924

Oscar Nominations (1): Best Actress for Jan Morrow in *Pillow Talk* (Universal-International, 1959)

Huffing and puffing, going cross-eyed in anger and stamping her foot in exasperation, Doris Day would generally get the better of her leading men but always fell short at Oscar time, having to make do with a solitary nomination for her interior designer sharing a telephone party line with Rock Hudson. Had she accepted the role of Mrs Robinson in *The Graduate* things might have turned out differently. The butt of many Hollywood jokes ('I knew Doris Day before she was a virgin,' quipped Oscar Levant with relish), she warbled two Academy Award-winning songs in the fifties, first in Warner's *Calamity Jane* ('Secret Love') and then in Hitchcock's *The Man Who Knew Too Much*, in which she frequently held up the action by singing 'Que sera, sera'!

Daniel Day-Lewis

Born London, England, 29 April 1957

Oscars (1): Best Actor for Christy Brown in *My Left Foot* (Ferndale Films, 1989)

Oscar Nominations (1): Best Actor for Gerald Conlon in *In the Name of the Father* (Hell's Kitchen/Universal, 1993)

The label 'the most accomplished actor of his generation' is not the easiest to live up to, especially as the same accolade has been conferred on Anthony Hopkins. Still, all things considered, Daniel Day-Lewis isn't doing too badly for himself – an Oscar for his cerebral palsy victim in *My Left Foot*, a nomination for his wrongly imprisoned Gerald Conlon, and a splendid Hawkeye (no nomination but who cared) in Michael Mann's *The Last of the Mohicans*. His most accomplished role to date? Debatable, although many would plump for his nineteenth-century New York lawyer Newland Archer who in *The Age of Innocence* finds himself hopelessly entranced by the seductive countess of Michelle Pfeiffer and unable to break free from the conventions of society. The nomination for 1993 (the year of *In the Name of the Father*) may well have been awarded for the wrong performance.

James Dean

Born Marion, Indiana, USA, 8 February 1931; died 1955

Oscar Nominations (2): Best Actor for Cal Trask in *East of Eden* (Warner Bros, 1955) and Jett Rink in *Giant* (Warner Bros, 1956)

The only one of the rebels not to be nominated for *Rebel Without a Cause* (supporting players Natalie Wood and Sal Mineo were both honoured), James Dean reputedly spoke for a generation when he cried in anguish at his parents: 'You're tearing me *apart!*' Whether he would have become a great actor had he lived beyond his twenty-four years will forever be debated, but the Academy thought highly enough of him to award him two posthumous nominations – the first for his rebellious Cal in Kazan's version of *East of Eden* and the second for his oil-rich Jett Rink in George Stevens' *Giant*. The star of just the three movies, he was killed in a car crash near Cholame, California, while driving his Porsche Spyder at an estimated 86 miles an hour.

Olivia de Havilland

Born Tokyo, Japan, 1 July 1916

Oscars (2): Best Actress for Josephine Norris in *To Each His Own* (Paramount, 1946) and Catherine Sloper in *The Heiress* (Paramount, 1949)

Oscar Nominations (3): Best Supporting Actress for Melanie Hamilton in *Gone with the Wind* (Selznick/MGM, 1939); Best Actress for Emmy Brown in *Hold Back the Dawn* (Paramount, 1941) and Virginia Cunningham in *The Snake Pit* (20th Century-Fox, 1948)

'He came twice . . . I shall see to it he never comes a third time,' said Olivia de Havilland, suddenly cruel and heartless as she takes her lamp and ascends the stairs at the close of *The Heiress*, leaving Montgomery Clift hammering frantically at the door outside. She didn't know it then but the film marked the high spot of a career that had taken in romance with Errol Flynn, battles with Jack Warner over the seven-year contract (which she won) and five Oscar nominations in ten years. A winner in 1946 for her self-sacrificing mother in the soap opera *To Each His Own*, and then again for *The Heiress*, she also made the lists for her frail Melanie, her teacher in love with gigolo Charles Boyer, and her mentally ill frustrated writer confined to an asylum in *The Snake Pit*. The New York Critics and the National Board of Review voted her best of the year for the last-named role. On Oscar night the Academy chose Jane Wyman for *Johnny Belinda* but it must have been a close-run thing. Had she won she would have become the first actress to receive three Academy Awards. Katharine Hepburn achieved the feat some twenty years later, when she added her Eleanor of Aquitaine in *The Lion in Winter* to her previous wins for *Morning Glory* and *Guess Who's Coming to Dinner?*

William Demarest

Born St Paul, Minnesota, USA, 27 February 1892; died 1983

Oscar Nominations (1): Best Supporting Actor for Steve Martin in *The Jolson Story* (Columbia, 1946)

The Paramount index file on Bill Demarest in the forties read: 'suitable for loud-mouthed, not too bright characters. In a class by himself as prohibition bootleggers, marine sergeants, dumb cops and racetrack touts.' All of which writer-director Preston Sturges duly took note of when he cast him in all eight of the sparkling comedies he filmed at Paramount in the early forties. It was at Columbia, though, that Demarest earned his Oscar recognition, when Harry Cohn chose him for Al Jolson's long-suffering friend and mentor in *The Jolson Story*. The only surprise was that he didn't make the lists more often. Best described as cranky, peppery and a bit of a sourpuss, he also made his mark on TV in the sixties hit *My Three Sons*, in which he co-starred with Fred MacMurray.

Catherine Deneuve

Born Paris, France, 22 October 1943

Oscar Nominations (1): Best Actress for Eliane Devries in *Indochine* (Sony Pictures Classics, 1992)

The fact that such an astonishingly beautiful woman can be so accomplished an actress (and retain her looks past fifty) must be galling to those actresses who are attractive but can't act and those who are not exactly breathtaking but are among the best performers in the business. Her one nomination was for her French plantation-owner in love with the same man as her daughter in *Indochine*, a far less deserving role than her wife who hides her husband from the Nazis in Truffaut's *The Last Metro* and her daytime prostitute who discovers just what is in the Japanese man's little box in *Belle de Jour*. The answer, according to the film's director Luis Bunuel, was: 'What was in it was what *you* thought was in it!'

☆

Robert De Niro

Born New York City, USA, 17 August 1943

Oscars (2): Best Supporting Actor for Vito Corleone in *The Godfather Part II* (Paramount, 1974); Best Actor for Jake LaMotta in *Raging Bull* (United Artists, 1980)

Oscar Nominations (4): Best Actor for Travis Bickle in *Taxi Driver* (Columbia, 1976), Michael Vronsky in *The Deer Hunter* (EMI/Universal, 1978), Leonard Lowe in *Awakenings* (Columbia, 1990) and Max Cady in *Cape Fear* (Universal, 1991)

He is for many the best there is – intense, inarticulate, with a dangerous smile and a capacity for brooding silence – and when he comes to life and stabs the finger and says 'I want him *dead*!' you tend to believe him. A winner for his portrayal of middleweight boxing champ Jake LaMotta and for his young Vito Corleone (a remarkable performance spoken throughout in Italian), he has also made the lists for his psychotic cabbie driving through the New York streets at night in *Taxi Driver*, his war-shattered Vietnam veteran in *The Deer Hunter*, revived catatonic patient in *Awakenings* and demented ex-con in pursuit of Nick Nolte in *Cape Fear*. One of the greatest living exponents of the Method, he has been quoted as saying that 'a grunt can do more than a paragraph of script'.

Sandy Dennis

Born Hastings, Nebraska, USA, 27 April 1937; died 1992

Oscars (1): Best Supporting Actress for Honey in *Who's Afraid of Virginia Woolf?* (Warner Bros, 1966)

Always on the wrong side of an anxiety attack, Sandy Dennis was rather unkindly referred to by one critic as 'the walking nervous breakdown'. Unkind, but not far from the truth, when her gallery of spinsters, mistresses, teachers and kooks is taken into account. She won her Oscar for her fragile young faculty wife who, along with hubby George Segal, manages to survive one of Liz Taylor and Richard Burton's evenings of alcoholic fun and games. She also had some desperate, if rather more humorous, moments in Neil Simon's *The Out-of-Towners*, as she battles with husband Jack Lemmon to reach a seemingly forever distant New York.

Gerard Depardieu

Born Chateauroux, France 27 December 1948

Oscar Nominations (1): Best Actor for the title role in *Cyrano de Bergerac* (Orion Classics, 1990)

Regarded by many as the French cinema's modern equivalent to Jean Gabin, the earthy, sensual and powerful Gerard Depardieu hasn't really enjoyed the best of times during his sporadic visits to Hollywood. His one Oscar nomination was for his celebrated portrayal of the long-nosed swordsman-poet Cyrano, a role which almost but not quite earned him 1990's best actor award. Had he managed it, he would have become the first actor to win an Oscar for a role that had already been played in Academy Award-winning style by a previous performer – Jose Ferrer in the 1950 Stanley Kramer production, directed by Michael Gordon. The somewhat less passionate Jeremy Irons won the 1990 Oscar for his Claus Von Bulow in *Reversal of Fortune*.

Bruce Dern

Born Winnetka, near Chicago, USA, 4 June 1936

Oscar Nominations (1): Best Supporting Actor for Captain Bob Hyde in *Coming Home* (United Artists, 1978)

A nominee for his dangerously tortured Vietnam vet husband of Jane Fonda, Bruce Dern has found it difficult to escape the eye-rolling psychotics and menacing, slightly off-centre individuals that have been his bread and butter from the beginning of his career. More of an amiable crook for Hitchcock in the director's last film, *Family Plot*, he was at his best as the arrogant, rich and insufferable Tom Buchanan in Jack Clayton's version of *The Great Gatsby*. An award deserved, none received!

☆

Laura Dern

Born Los Angeles, USA, 10 February 1967

Oscar Nominations (1): Best Actress for Rose in *Rambling Rose* (Carolco, 1991)

Creating sexual havoc in a small town where nothing ever happens and nothing ever will is by no means new to American cinema, but in *Rambling Rose* Laura Dern breathed new life into the theme when she played the oversexed nineteen-year-old who is taken into a Southern family home in Georgia during the Depression thirties. Described by one critic as 'combining a childish gullibility with womanly voluptuousness', she earned her place among the year's five best actress nominees but found that Jodie Foster's efforts to keep up with the evil machinations of Hannibal Lecter were unassailable. Diane Ladd (Laura's real-life mom) was nominated in the supporting category for her genteel family matriarch (see p. 201).

Vittorio De Sica

Born Sora, Italy, 7 July 1902; died 1974

Oscar Nominations (1): Best Supporting Actor for Major Rinaldi in *A Farewell to Arms* (Selznick/20th Century-Fox, 1957)

Probably the best-looking director in the business, the tall, handsome Vittorio De Sica was lucky in that he had two strings to his bow – he was a fine, cultured actor of some 150 films and a director of a string of neo-realist masterpieces that reflected life and poverty in post-war Italy. A winner of four Academy Awards for best foreign-language film – *Shoe Shine*, *The Bicycle Thief*, *Yesterday, Today and Tomorrow*, and *The Garden of the Finzi Continis* – he guided Sophia Loren to her Oscar in *Two Women* and was himself nominated for an acting award for his cynical Major Rinaldi in Selznick's remake of *A Farewell to Arms*. Renowned as an art collector and a heavy gambler (he regularly lost $10,000 a night at Monte Carlo), he said of his neo-realist films: 'I love poor people. It is in their lives that drama can be found. After all, if you exclude adultery, what drama is there in the bourgeoisie?'

Brandon De Wilde

Born Brooklyn, New York, USA, 9 April 1942; died 1972

Oscar Nominations (1): Best Supporting Actor for Joey Starrett in *Shane* (Paramount, 1953)

Immortalised forever as the hero-worshipping rancher's son who, in the final scene of *Shane*, cries out to Alan Ladd and the echoing mountains, 'Shane . . . come back, Shane . . . SHANE!', Brandon De Wilde earned an Oscar nomination at the age of ten after being acclaimed on Broadway for his performance as the cousin of Julie Harris in Carson McCuller's *Member of the Wedding*. A loser on Oscar night to 'Ole Blue Eyes', who was making a comeback just as De Wilde was starting out, he later developed into one of America's finest young actors, being especially effective as another hero-worshipper – the nephew of arrogant Paul Newman in *Hud*. His career was brought to a tragic end when he was killed in a car crash near Denver at the age of thirty.

Leonardo DiCaprio

Born Hollywood, California, USA, 11 November 1974

Oscar Nominations (1): Best Supporting Actor for Arnie Grape in *What's Eating Gilbert Grape?* (Paramount, 1993)

Yet another young actor acclaimed as the 'new James Dean', DiCaprio deserves, like all the other performers who have been likened to the fifties rebel, to be judged in his own right. If director James Toback is anything to go by he has quite a future. 'The best sheer actor of his generation' is how he's described him. Time will tell. In the meantime he already has an Oscar nomination to his credit (earned when he was just nineteen) for his mentally impaired teenage brother of Johnny Depp in *Gilbert Grape*, and a list of rave reviews claiming that he matched De Niro scene for scene when they appeared together in *This Boy's Life*. That should be enough to be going on with.

Marlene Dietrich

Born Berlin, Germany, 27 December 1901; died 1992

Oscar Nominations (1): Best Actress for Amy Jolly in *Morocco* (Paramount, 1930/31)

A sophisticate, a legend, a fabulous star! But an actress? Possibly, although for many the jury is still out and probably always will be as far as Marlene Dietrich is concerned. Cosseted and brilliantly photographed in a series of Josef Von Sternberg extravaganzas at Paramount in the thirties, she was Oscar-nominated just the once – for her German cabaret singer who sets her cap at legionnaire Gary Cooper and in a celebrated (and somewhat ludicrous) final scene removes her three-inch high heels and trails after him into the desert. Startlingly effective for Billy Wilder in *Witness for the Prosecution* ('Do you want to kiss me, ducky?'), she was possessed of a unique, low, husky singing voice and the best legs of any superstar, the former being used to great effect in *Destry Rides Again*, the latter being seen at their most sensuous in *A Foreign Affair*.

Melinda Dillon

Born Hope, Arkansas, USA, 13 October 1939

Oscar Nominations (2): Best Supporting Actress for Jillian Guiler in *Close Encounters of the Third Kind* (Columbia, 1977) and Teresa in *Absence of Malice* (Columbia, 1981)

One of those sweet, reassuring, gentle-faced ladies who offer up a kind of serenity on screen, Melinda Dillon found favour with the Academy for searching for the *Close Encounters* mountain with Richard Dreyfuss and for her portrait of an emotionally disturbed woman driven to suicide by the reckless reporting of Sally Fields in *Absence of Malice*. An enjoyable performance in the first film; a beautifully crafted one in the second. Unfortunately, on both occasions she was up against two formidable contenders – Vanessa Redgrave (*Julia*) in 1977 and Maureen Stapleton (*Reds*) in 1981 – and the opportunities since have been few and far between.

Richard Dix

Born St Paul, Minnesota, USA, 18 July 1894; died 1949

Oscar Nominations (1): Best Actor for Yancey Cravat in *Cimarron* (RKO, 1930/31)

A celebrated stardom at Paramount in the twenties, a gradual falling-off in the early sound years, and B-movies in the forties! Richard Dix's film career followed the familiar pattern of many actors who were unable to sustain the popularity they had enjoyed in the silent days. His Oscar nomination was earned in the early thirties for his pioneer hero in the epic western *Cimarron* but was unable to halt his decline. Tall, rugged and dependable, he appeared in numerous westerns and played both Wild Bill Hickok and Wyatt Earp. He finished up in a series of sixty-minute programmers featuring a character called *The Whistler*.

Robert Donat

Born Manchester, England, 18 March 1905; died 1958

Oscars (1): Best Actor for Charles Chipping in *Goodbye, Mr Chips* (MGM, 1939)

Oscar Nominations (1): Best Actor for Andrew Manson in *The Citadel* (MGM, 1938)

Anyone shackled by the wrist to Madeleine Carroll and trying desperately to look sexually unmoved as his hand follows hers as she unrolls her stockings didn't really need an Oscar. The experience was a reward in itself. Still, Donat did eventually finish up among the winners, not for *The 39 Steps*, nor for his idealistic young doctor in *The Citadel*, but for his placid old schoolmaster Mr Chips who beat out Clark Gable on Oscar night and became one of the few non-*Gone with the Wind* winners of the evening. Recurring bouts of severe asthma restricted his screen appearances to a handful of roles which included the British film pioneer William Friese-Greene in *The Magic Box*. His last part was as the Mandarin in *The Inn of the Sixth Happiness*. He collapsed a week after filming had ended and died shortly afterwards in a London hospital.

Brian Donlevy

Born Portadown, Ireland, 9 February 1899; died 1972

Oscar Nominations (1): Best Supporting Actor for Sergeant Markoff in *Beau Geste* (Paramount, 1939)

A 'hard-boiled sentimentalist' is how one critic summed up the muscular Brian Donlevy, whose range of cops, hoods and military men adorned screens in the forties and fifties. He made most of his early films at Paramount, where he worked for DeMille on the railway epic *Union Pacific*, Preston Sturges in the political satire *The Great McGinty* and William Wellman, who in *Beau Geste* guided him to his only Oscar nomination, as the sadistic Sergeant Markoff who kills and is killed by the hero in a duel to the death over a family diamond. A rather softer and more cheerful performance, that of Thomas Mitchell as the drunken Doc Boone in *Stagecoach*, took the award in 1939. Donlevy averaged some three films a year during his heyday. He twice played Professor Quatermass in the British film adaptations of Nigel Kneale's science fiction TV series. He retired in the late sixties to live in Palm Springs and write short stories.

Kirk Douglas

Born Amsterdam, New York, USA, 9 December 1916

Oscar Nominations (3): Best Actor for Midge Kelly in *Champion* (United Artists, 1949), Jonathan Shields in *The Bad and the Beautiful* (MGM, 1952) and Vincent Van Gogh in *Lust for Life* (MGM, 1956)

Kirk should have won, of course. The thrusting, dimpled chin, fierce grin, and voice rising to a hoarse threat when roused have enhanced so many outstanding films that it seems incredible that no one has ever made the announcement on Oscar night: 'And the winner is Kirk Douglas for . . .' The problem is completing the sentence. Should it have been for one of his Oscar-nominated roles – the ferocious boxer Midge Kelly, the Selznick-type Hollywood producer in *The Bad and the Beautiful*, or his intensely moving portrait of Van Gogh? Or should it have been for roles for which he was not even mentioned – the ruthless newspaperman Chuck Tatum (probably the choice of most devotees) in *Ace in the Hole*, the tough cop in *Detective Story*, the World War I officer desperately trying to save his men from a firing squad in *Paths of Glory*? The question remains unanswerable but there's no doubt that Kirk Douglas ranks among the unluckiest of all Oscar contenders. The honorary award (presented by Steven Spielberg) duly arrived in the spring of 1996.

Melvyn Douglas

Born Macon, Georgia, USA, 5 April 1901; died 1981

Oscars (2): Best Supporting Actor for Homer Bannon in *Hud* (Paramount, 1963) and Benjamin Rand in *Being There* (Lorimar, 1979)

Oscar Nominations (1): Best Actor for Tom Garrison in *I Never Sang for My Father* (Columbia, 1970)

A winner only when he'd become a crusty old-timer, Melvyn Douglas should by rights have been in the frame in his pre-war days when he romanced such stars as Myrna Loy, Claudette Colbert, Irene Dunne, Joan Crawford and, most memorably, Garbo in *Ninotchka*, when he played the flippant Parisian who gradually thaws her Russian commissar. A winner in the supporting categories for his rancher father of Paul Newman's *Hud* and his wily presidential aide in *Being There*, he missed out on the best actor award despite being nominated for his manipulative old parent forever on the conscience of son Gene Hackman in *I Never Sang for My Father*.

Michael Douglas

Born New Brunswick, New Jersey, USA, 25 September 1944

Oscars (1): Best Actor for Gordon Gekko in *Wall Street* (20th Century-Fox, 1987)

'Greed is good! Greed is right! Greed works! Greed will save the USA!' purred amoral insider trader Michael Douglas in Oliver Stone's *Wall Street*. Douglas received many such lines in Stone's film ('Lunch is for wimps' has now entered the vernacular) and thoroughly deserved his award, although at the final count, one was still left with the impression that his father, in his younger years, would have made even more of the unscrupulous and manipulative Gordon Gekko. In recent years mostly a star of two-dimensional sexual thrillers – *Fatal Attraction, Basic Instinct, Disclosure* – Douglas was the recipient of an earlier Academy Award for co-producing, with Saul Zaentz, the best picture of 1975, *One Flew Over the Cuckoo's Nest.*

Brad Dourif

Born Huntington, West Virginia, USA, 18 March 1950

Oscar Nominations (1): Best Supporting Actor for Billy Bibbit in *One Flew Over the Cuckoo's Nest* (United Artists, 1975)

Tormented and disturbed characters have tended to have been Brad Dourif's forte over the years, notably his fanatical young evangelist in Huston's *Wise Blood* and brutal deputy sheriff in *Mississippi Burning*. Nominated for his suicidal mental patient in *One Flew Over the Cuckoo's Nest*, he looked to be part of the film's successful Oscar roll but was unlucky in that, after awarding the picture all of the five top awards – best film, director, actor, actress and screenplay – the Academy cried 'Enough!' and opted for some humour in the supporting category: George Burns in *The Sunshine Boys*.

Robert Downey Jr.

Born New York City, USA, 5 April 1965

Oscar Nominations (1): Best Actor for Charlie Chaplin in *Chaplin* (Carolco, 1992)

A role of a lifetime at twenty-seven! A real bonus when you're filming, but what happens afterwards? The problem has been facing Robert Downey ever since he played Chaplin in Richard Attenborough's lengthy biopic, and to date, the answer has to be 'not much', even though only a few years have passed since the film's release. An Oscar rather than just a nomination (the 1992 award went to Al Pacino for *Scent of a Woman*) would have helped Downey's cause considerably. His womaniser pursuing Molly Ringwald in *The Pick-up Artist* and his reincarnated husband of Cybill Shepherd in

Chances Are were among the roles that persuaded Attenborough that he had the skill and talent to portray the screen's greatest-ever comedy star.

Louise Dresser

Born Evansville, Indiana, USA, 5 October 1878; died 1965

Oscar Nominations (1): Best Actress for Mamma Pleznick in *A Ship Comes In* (Pathe-RKO Radio, 1927/28)

The surprises were there even in the first year of the awards, and Louise Dresser was one of them, a character actress nominated for her role as a Polish immigrant and pitted against two of the silent screen's most formidable stars – Gloria Swanson and Janet Gaynor. No chance, of course, but she enjoyed the first-ever banquet, at Hollywood's Roosevelt Hotel, went on with her career for a few more years and then retired in 1937 to work for the Motion Picture Country House and Hospital and savour memories of appearing opposite Rudolph Valentino in the silent days.

Marie Dressler

Born Coburg, Canada, 9 November 1869; died 1934

Oscars (1): Best Actress for Min in *Min and Bill* (MGM, 1930/31)

Oscar Nominations (1): Best Actress for Emma (Thatcher Smith) in *Emma* (MGM, 1931/32)

One critic once referred to Marie Dressler as 'having an ample figure like a rain barrel and a face that fell into folds like those of a St Bernard'. It was an accurate summing-up; in fact, at MGM in the early thirties, she was a kind of female Wallace Beery, short on looks but high in popularity, and it was perhaps fitting that she should receive her Oscar for a film in which she co-starred with the lovable old rogue – as a hard-boiled proprietress of a waterfront hotel who brings up a young girl deserted by her mother in infancy. Nominated again the following year for her faithful housekeeper of Jean Hersholt in *Emma*, she enjoyed her phenomenal success in the last four years of her life when she was voted the most popular movie star in

America. She was teamed with Wallace Beery on three occasions, most famously when she played the salty sea captain *Tugboat Annie* and said 'lovingly' of hubby Beery: 'He never struck me, except in self-defence.'

Richard Dreyfuss

Born Brooklyn, New York, USA, 29 October 1947

Oscars (1): Best Actor for Elliot Garfield in *The Goodbye Girl* (MGM/ Warner Bros, 1977)

Oscar Nominations (1): Best Actor for Glenn Holland in *Mr Holland's Opus* (Buena Vista/Hollywood Pictures, 1995)

He was one of the three men in a boat chasing after 'the Great White' in *Jaws*, and he moved heaven and earth to find that black mountain in Wyoming in *Close Encounters of the Third Kind*, but it was for his somewhat less strenuous efforts as the aspiring actor who shacks up with Marsha Mason and daughter in Neil Simon's *The Goodbye Girl* that Richard Dreyfuss won Oscar acclaim. Deservedly, too, especially for his crackling scenes with Mason and those in which he is persuaded by an off-Broadway director to play Shakespeare's Richard III as a ridiculously over-the-top gay. Chubby, short and curly-haired, and with a somewhat unusual persona for a leading man, he has recently added to his nominations tally with his moving performance as a composer who finds that teaching rather than writing music is his true role in life.

Olympia Dukakis

Born Lowell, Massachusetts, USA, 20 June 1931

Oscars (1): Best Supporting Actress for Rose Castorini in *Moonstruck* (MGM, 1987)

No one knew very much about Olympia Dukakis before *Moonstruck* and no one has seen an awful lot of her since but in the spring of 1988 she was riding high, taking the Oscar for her gently bewildered Italian-American mother trying to fathom out just what's going on among the various members of her family, and why older men always seem to run after sex. No one could really give her an answer. Not that anyone cared all that much; romantic comedies were thin on the ground in Hollywood in the late eighties and it was simply good to have a movie like *Moonstruck* around.

Patty Duke

Born Elmhurst, New York, USA, 14 December 1946

Oscars (1): Best Supporting Actress for Helen Keller in *The Miracle Worker* (United Artists, 1962)

A number of performers have appeared in the same screen story at different times in their careers – Jean Simmons, for instance, played the young Estella and later, on TV, Miss Havisham in *Great Expectations*. Few though have pulled off the achievement with such stunning brilliance as Patty Duke, who won her Oscar for repeating her Broadway role as the blind deaf mute Helen Keller in *The Miracle Worker*, and then seventeen years later recreated Anne Bancroft's original role of Keller's dedicated teacher Annie Sullivan in a 1979 TV version. A notable double, although much of the rest of Duke's screen output has tended to be on the undistinguished side.

Faye Dunaway

Born Bascom, Florida, USA, 14 January 1941

Oscars (1): Best Actress for Diana Christensen in *Network* (United Artists, 1976)

Oscar Nominations (2): Best Actress for Bonnie Parker in *Bonnie and Clyde* (Warner Bros, 1967) and Evelyn Mulwray in *Chinatown* (Paramount, 1974)

Green-eyed, sexually provocative and usually at her best as coldly ambitious, neurotic types who are dangerous to know, Faye Dunaway was twice nominated by the Academy – for her Depression gangster murdering her way across the Midwest with Warren Beatty and her *femme fatale* with the dark secret in *Chinatown* – before finally landing the award for her power-hungry TV programming executive in *Network*. Since then the pickings have been somewhat meagre, although her portrait of Joan Crawford in

Mommie Dearest has its admirers, and there can rarely have been a more dangerous Milady DeWinter! Sadly her long, lingering and highly seductive chess game with an increasingly uncomfortable Steve McQueen in *The Thomas Crown Affair* failed to rate a nomination.

James Dunn

Born New York City, USA, 2 November 1905; died 1967

Oscars (1): Best Supporting Actor for Johnny Nolan in *A Tree Grows in Brooklyn* (20th Century-Fox, 1945)

Not exactly a performer who left an indelible mark on Hollywood history, the amiable James Dunn nonetheless did emerge as one of Oscar's winners in the mid-forties for his genial alcoholic father adored by daughter Peggy Ann Garner in Betty Smith's turn-of-the-century tale of tenement life, *A Tree Grows in Brooklyn*. Popular in the early thirties for his début film *Bad Girl* and his song-and-dance routines with Shirley Temple, his later years were marred when he filed for bankruptcy in 1951, describing himself as unemployable after losing $40,000 in a stage production that failed to reach Broadway. He became an occasional character actor in the sixties, appearing as a conscience-stricken alcoholic in *The Bramble Bush* and a telegrapher in *Hemingway's Adventures of a Young Man*.

Michael Dunn

Born Shattuck, Oklahoma, USA, 20 October 1934; died 1973

Oscar Nominations (1): Best Supporting Actor for Glocken in *Ship of Fools* (Columbia, 1965)

By far the most versatile of the screen's dwarf actors, Michael Dunn managed to transcend the obvious freak roles to make his mark in a series of bizarre and rewarding parts – bookies, private eyes, writers and even, in Joseph Losey's *Boom*, a bodyguard, complete with a pack of vicious dogs, of ageing million-airess Elizabeth Taylor. He earned his Oscar nomination for his role in Stanley Kramer's *Ship of Fools* as the philosophising dwarf travelling with a doomed cargo of passengers from Mexico to Nazi Germany in 1933. A regular performer on stage and TV, he appeared on Broadway in the Carson McCullers play *The Ballad of the Sad Café*. He was found dead in his London hotel room during the filming of *The Abdication*.

Irene Dunne

Born Louisville, Kentucky, USA, 20 December 1898; died 1990

Oscar Nominations (5): Best Actress for Sabra Cravat in *Cimarron* (RKO, 1930/31), Theodora Lynn in *Theodora Goes Wild* (Columbia, 1936), Lucy Warriner in *The Awful Truth* (Columbia, 1937), Terry McKay in *Love Affair* (RKO, 1939) and Mama in *I Remember Mama* (RKO, 1948)

For critic James Agate, Irene Dunne's sweetness and noble self-sacrifice were enough to 'make his flesh crawl'. Cary Grant, on the other hand, thought: 'her timing was marvellous. She was so good that she made comedy look easy. If she'd made it look as difficult as it really is, she would have won her Oscar.' Her two comedy nominations were for *Theodora Goes Wild*, in which she played an author who writes a steamy best-seller about a small American town, and *The Awful Truth*, in which she co-starred with Grant as a husband and wife on the brink of divorce. She was also remembered for her pioneer wife in *Cimarron*, ill-fated lover of Charles Boyer in *Love Affair*, and Norwegian mother in George Stevens' *I Remember Mama*. A talented musical star (*Showboat, Roberta*) as well as a comedy and dramatic actress, she balanced all facets of her career with ease until her retirement at the age of fifty-one. The Oscar, though, proved elusive, even an honorary one, which the Academy, for reasons best known to itself, failed to present.

Mildred Dunnock

Born Baltimore, Maryland, USA, 25 January 1904; died 1991

Oscar Nominations (2): Best Supporting Actress for Linda Loman in *Death of a Salesman* (Columbia, 1951) and Aunt Rose Comfort in *Baby Doll* (Warner Bros, 1956)

A frail, delicate performer whose timid, bird-like personality enhanced some twenty-five films as well as any number of distinguished Broadway plays, Mildred Dunnock invested her spinsters, wives and aunts with a subtle intensity, especially the two that brought her Oscar nominations – the wife of Willy Loman in *Death of a Salesman* and the ancient, abused aunt of Carroll Baker's teenage bride in *Baby Doll*. 'I like to play parts that are not at all like myself,' she used to say. 'I'm not the least bit exciting.' She made her last film, the comedy *The Pick-up Artist*, in 1987, a somewhat less violent movie than one of those with which she began her career, *Kiss of Death*, in which she played an old woman confined to a wheelchair who is propelled to her death down a long flight of stairs by Richard Widmark's vicious thug, Tommy Udo.

Charles Durning

Born Highland Falls, New York, USA, 28 February 1923

Oscar Nominations (2): Best Supporting Actor for 'The Governor' in *The Best Little Whorehouse in Texas* (Universal, 1982) and Colonel Ehrhardt in *To Be or Not To Be* (Brooksfilm/20th Century-Fox, 1983)

An actor who for years interpreted on screen a succession of dumb, frustrated or just plain corrupt cops, the heavily built Charles Durning brought with him a non-too-believable smile that, as often as not, was followed by a quick left to the solar plexus. His Oscar nominations were for something completely different – the Governor who tries to close down *The Best Little Whorehouse in Texas* (his 'Sidestep' was one of the musical highlights of the year), and his recreation of Sig Rumann's old role, Concentration Camp Ehrhardt in Mel Brooks' remake of *To Be or Not To Be*. Louis Gossett Jr. (*An Officer and a Gentleman*) and Jack Nicholson (*Terms of Endearment*) saw to it that he remained only a nominee on the respective Oscar nights.

Robert Duvall

Born San Diego, California, USA, 5 January 1931

Oscars (1): Best Actor for Mac Sledge in *Tender Mercies* (EMI/Universal/AFD, 1983)

Oscar Nominations (3): Best Supporting Actor for Tom Hagen in *The Godfather* (Paramount, 1972) and Lt-Col Kilgore in *Apocalypse Now* (United Artists, 1979); Best Actor for Bull Meechum in *The Great Santini* (Orion, 1980)

'I love the smell of napalm in the morning . . . it smells like victory,' said Robert Duvall's half-crazy commander in *Apocalypse Now*. An Oscar nomination for that and also one for his earlier portrayal of lawyer Tom Hagen in the first of the *Godfather* films. Then a third for his tyrannical Marine pilot in *The Great Santini*, and finally a nomination *and* the award for taking things a bit more gently as the destitute country and western singer who finds a new life with Vietnam war widow Tess Harper in *Tender Mercies*. Now if he'd been a little bit nicer along the way he might have won the award even earlier! Nothing since – rather surprisingly, for he remains one of the finest character actors working in American movies.

E

Jeanne Eagels

Born Kansas City, Missouri, USA, 26 June 1894; died 1929

Oscar Nominations (1): Best Actress for Leslie Crosbie in *The Letter* (Paramount, 1928/29)

Notorious not so much for her movies (she made just a handful) but for her colourful lifestyle, which was often as outrageous as anything dreamed up for her by twenties playwrights, Jeanne Eagels earned her place in the Oscar record books by becoming the first posthumous nominee in the history of the awards. Her nomination was for her murdering planter's wife in Somerset Maugham's *The Letter*, a role which has never proved successful at Oscar time, Bette Davis also losing out in William Wyler's 1940 remake. Eagels died of a heroin overdose in October 1929, just four weeks before her nomination was announced. Kim Novak played her on screen in the sanitised 1957 biopic of George Sidney.

Clint Eastwood

Born San Francisco, USA, 31 May 1930

Oscar Nominations (1): Best Actor for William Munny in *Unforgiven* (Warner Bros, 1992)

He wasn't really in with much of a shout for the acting award – Al Pacino's time had come for *Scent of a Woman* – but at least his nomination for his outlaw turned farmer in *Unforgiven* was some reward for the thirty years he'd toiled before the cameras. Not that he shed many tears when he lost; the direction and best film awards climaxed the evening and he picked up both, just as Kevin Costner had done two years earlier for *Dances With Wolves*. No acting nominations since. Not that it matters a great deal, for he remains the world's most famous movie star since John Wayne.

Note: In 1995 Eastwood was presented with the Irving G. Thalberg Memorial Award, a distinguished award for 'outstanding motion picture production' and one of the most coveted of the Academy prizes.

Samantha Eggar

Born London, England, 5 March 1938

Oscar Nominations (1): Best Actress for Miranda Grey in *The Collector* (Columbia, 1965)

An English beauty who made her name as the art student kidnapped by psychotic young bank clerk Terence Stamp in *The Collector*, Samantha Eggar might have been better served had she débuted in Hollywood in the studio days when they knew how to handle attractive young starlets. Unfortunately, the sixties saw the break-up of the studio system and after a few minor frolics with Cary Grant in Tokyo in *Walk, Don't Run* and Rex Harrison and the Giant Sea Snail in *Doctor Dolittle*, her career went into freefall and schlock horror with *The Brood*, *The Exterminator* and *Demonoid*. Named best actress for *The Collector* at the 1965 Cannes Film Festival, she lost on Oscar night to another British newcomer, Julie Christie in *Darling*.

Denholm Elliott

Born London, England, 31 May 1922; died 1992

Oscar Nominations (1): Best Supporting Actor for Mr Emerson in *A Room with a View* (Merchant Ivory/Cinecom, 1986)

Considering his reputation as a scene-stealer *par excellence* ('Never work with children, animals or Denholm Elliott' was the maxim in film and stage circles), it was surprising that Elliott received just the one Oscar nomination and then for a performance that was some way from being his best – the genial, working-class intellectual in *A Room with a View*. He would perhaps have been better represented by his dissolute aristocratic black sheep in *Nothing but the Best*, seedy, down-at-heel journalist in *Defence of the Realm*, or his haughty but eminently bribeable butler in *Trading Places*. Weary-looking and with somewhat ravaged, lived-in features in later middle age, he once revealed how he went about accepting a script. 'I open it halfway through,' he said. 'Then if I find a few characters I wouldn't mind having a drink with in a pub I go back to the beginning'!

Hope Emerson

Born Hawarden, Iowa, USA, 27 October 1897; died 1960

Oscar Nominations (1): Best Supporting Actress for Evelyn Harper in *Caged* (Warner Bros, 1950)

Any woman weighing in at 230lb and standing 6ft 2in is either going to provoke laughter or instil a nasty dose of terror. Hope Emerson won her Oscar nomination when she was in the latter mode as the sadistic prison matron who puts poor Eleanor Parker through the wringer in Warner's powerful prison drama, *Caged*. That she did have her lighter moments was demonstrated in Cukor's classic Tracy-Hepburn comedy *Adam's Rib*, when she was called by Katie as a vital witness and lifted up poor old Spence with one hand! Laughter in court. No further Oscar nominations. Josephine Hull won in 1950 for *Harvey*.

Stuart Erwin

Born Squaw Valley, California, USA, 14 February 1902; died 1967

Oscar Nominations (1): Best Supporting Actor for Amos Dodd in *Pigskin Parade* (20th Century-Fox, 1936)

Anyone winning an Oscar nomination for playing a country bumpkin who can throw a water melon farther than anyone else, thus becoming the hero of a football team, must by the sheer nature of the story have earned his mention in the early days of the awards. Stuart Erwin received his in 1936 for a film which was memorable not only for its melon-throwing but also for the fact that it was Judy Garland's first feature and included Betty Grable in its cast. A bumbling, rather hapless character on screen, Erwin was married to actress June Collyer and was one of the first performers to profit from appearing on television in the post-war years. He made over a hundred films.

Edith Evans

Born London, England, 8 February 1888; died 1976

Oscar Nominations (3): Best Supporting Actress for Miss Western in *Tom Jones* (Woodfall, 1963) and Mrs St Maugham in *The Chalk Garden* (Universal, 1964); Best Actress for Mrs Ross in *The Whisperers* (Seven Pine Productions, 1967)

The kind of actress who could strike fear with a single sentence, most memorably as Oscar Wilde's Lady Bracknell ('A . . . ha . . . and . . . baag!'), Edith Evans enjoyed some golden screen moments in the sixties when the Academy looked on her favourably on three occasions but never quite got round to handing her its main award. Nominated first for her meddlesome aunt in *Tom Jones* ('Wake up, you country stewpot! Rouse yourself from this pastoral torpor!' she cries at Hugh Griffith), then for her elderly grandmother in *The Chalk Garden*, she was named finally for her lonely old lady who no one wants and who has nowhere to go in *The Whisperers*. The role won her awards all over the world, in Berlin, New York and London. Only Hollywood opted for someone different – Katharine Hepburn in *Guess Who's Coming to Dinner?*

ℱ

Peter Falk

Born New York City, USA, 16 September 1927

Oscar Nominations (2): Best Supporting Actor for Abe Reles in *Murder Inc.* (20th Century-Fox, 1960) and Joy Boy in *Pocketful of Miracles* (United Artists, 1961)

Peter Falk's constant shuffling about on TV as Columbo tends to obscure the fact that he enjoyed an acting life before television, one that brought him two Oscar nominations – the first for his lethal killer in *Murder Inc.* in 1960, the second a year later for his slightly more affable bodyguard of Dave the Dude in Capra's *Pocketful of Miracles*. Never a major star in the movies, he was nonetheless a regular in gangster films, detective thrillers and comedies before Columbo finally took him by the scruff of the neck and refused to let go. His famous squinty gaze is the result of a tumour he suffered at the age of three and which cost him an eye.

Richard Farnsworth

Born Los Angeles, USA, 1 September 1920

Oscar Nominations (1): Best Supporting Actor for Dodger in *Comes a Horseman* (United Artists, 1978)

No one in modern movies has quite such creased, weatherbeaten features as lean old-timer Richard Farnsworth, and no one is ever surprised when he reveals that in the old days he used to be a stunt man and double for Roy Rogers and other western stars. His Oscar nomination was earned for his ranch foreman of Jane Fonda in Alan Pakula's *Comes a Horseman*, although by far his best role to date has been that of the real-life stagecoach- turned train-robber Bill Miner in *The Grey Fox*. It won him no Oscars but earned him wide acclaim in Canada, where he was voted best actor of 1982. A performer in bit-parts and minor roles since the sixties, his recent films have included *The Two Jakes*, *Misery* and the remake of *The Getaway*.

Jose Ferrer

Born Santurce, Puerto Rico, 8 January 1909; died 1992

Oscars (1): Best Actor for the title role in *Cyrano de Bergerac* (United Artists, 1950)

Oscar Nominations (2): Best Supporting Actor for the Dauphin in *Joan of Arc* (RKO, 1948); Best Actor for Henri de Toulouse-Lautrec in *Moulin Rouge* (Romulus, 1952)

Jose Ferrer never had any illusions about his film career. 'The truth is, I made a few good movies in the fifties then went into freefall,' he said. Not quite true (there was always his Turkish Bey in Lean's *Lawrence of Arabia* to consider), but close. The peak years were when he was nominated for his Dauphin and his crippled painter Toulouse-Lautrec, and when he won for his triumphant rendering of the long-nosed swordsman-poet Cyrano de Bergerac. After that things were complicated by the Un-American Activities Committee, who grilled him about his alleged Communist past and accused him of attending Communist fund-raising events during the war. Ferrer declared that yes, he had attended the meetings and also that during the long run of Paul Robeson's *Othello* (in which he played Iago) he had failed to notice that Mr Robeson was a Communist or, indeed, even black!

Sally Field

Born Pasadena, California, USA, 6 November 1946

Oscars (2): Best Actress for the title role in *Norma Rae* (20th Century-Fox, 1979) and Edna Spalding in *Places in the Heart* (Tri-Star, 1984)

'You like me, you really like me!' Poor Sally Field will forever be remembered for that part of her overexuberant Oscar acceptance speech for *Norma Rae*. It tends to overshadow her prowess as an actress and her talent for bringing to life on screen brave, self-reliant women who fight for a cause, whether it be trade union rights in a Southern textile mill in Martin Ritt's *Norma Rae* or trying to save a farm from closure in the Depression in *Places in the Heart*. Add to that her performances opposite Paul Newman in

Absence of Malice and James Garner in *Murphy's Romance* and you have a formidable actress. Difficult to believe that she was once known as 'the Flying Nun' in the popular TV series of the sixties.

Ralph Fiennes

Born Suffolk, England, 22 December 1962

Oscar Nominations (1): Best Supporting Actor for Amon Goeth in *Schindler's List* (Amblin/Universal, 1993)

A star of the future, or a 'here today, gone tomorrow' movie actor whose fame will be mostly reserved for the stage? Only time will tell, although Ralph Fiennes already has one Oscar nomination under his belt for his demonic SS officer in command of the slave labour camp in Plaszow in *Schindler's List*. He lost (unluckily in many people's view) to Tommy Lee Jones for his hard-bitten cop chasing Harrison Ford in *The Fugitive*, and also failed to make the 1994 nominees for his personable young intellectual yet ultimately crooked contestant in Robert Redford's *Quiz Show*. The future, it seems, is in the balance.

Peter Finch

Born London, England, 28 September 1916; died 1977

Oscars (1): Best Actor for Howard Beale in *Network* (United Artists, 1976)

Oscar Nominations (1): Best Actor for Dr Daniel Hirsh in *Sunday Bloody Sunday* (United Artists, 1971)

Admirably summed up by one American critic as 'a suave, literate man who exuded an air of worldly grace', Peter Finch appeared in films for more than a quarter of a century, enhancing many that were sub-standard and adding immeasurably to those of quality. Felled by a massive heart attack three months before the 1977 ceremony, he was awarded a posthumous Oscar for his performance as the demented TV news commentator who threatens to kill himself on air in order to increase the ratings. Nominated previously for his homosexual doctor in *Sunday Bloody Sunday*, he was at his most effective in roles that allowed him to underplay his quiet sincerity – his Hans Langsdorff in *The Battle of the River Plate*, his cultivated arch-criminal Flambeau in *Father Brown* and his Congo doctor in *The Nun's Story*. When asked why he had chosen such a hazardous profession as acting he replied: 'If I was going to be broke I decided I might as well be with actors as anyone else. They were cheerful idiots and seemed to take it better.'

Frank Finlay

Born Farnworth, Lancashire, England, 6 August 1926

Oscar Nominations (1): Best Supporting Actor for Iago in *Othello* (BHE/Warner Bros, 1965)

No one can really make a mess of Shakespeare's scheming Iago and Frank Finlay duly cruised in as one of 1965's top supporting players for his portrayal in Olivier's film of his National Theatre production. None of the cast came out a winner (Olivier, Maggie Smith and Joyce Redman were also nominees), and Finlay returned to doing what he did best on screen, bringing a touch of melancholy to his characters, among them the convict who unintentionally causes the downfall of the great train robbers in *Robbery*, and the dim, incompetent Inspector Lestrade in a couple of Sherlock Holmes films. His Porthos in the Musketeer swashbucklers of Dick Lester showed him in a more boisterous mood.

Albert Finney

Born Salford, Lancashire, England, 9 May 1936

Oscar Nominations (4): Best Actor for the title role in *Tom Jones* (United Artists, 1963), Hercule Poirot in *Murder on the Orient Express* (EMI, 1974), 'Sir' in *The Dresser* (Goldcrest/Columbia, 1983) and Geoffrey Firmin in *Under the Volcano* (Universal, 1984)

Hollywood mostly didn't give a hoot about Britain's army of angry young men of the sixties but they did rather take to the lustful sexual appetites of the seventeenth-century rebel Tom Jones, brought vividly to life in 1963 by Albert Finney. Not vividly enough, unfortunately, at least as far as the

Academy was concerned. Albert lost to Sidney Poitier for *Lilies of the Field*, and despite three subsequent nominations – for the fussy Belgian sleuth Hercule Poirot, the flamboyant actor-manager in *The Dresser* and the alcoholic diplomat in *Under the Volcano* – he has never really come close again. Had he accepted the title role in *Lawrence of Arabia* (he was tested and offered the part by David Lean) things might have been different.

Peter Firth

Born Bradford, Yorkshire, England, 27 October 1953

Oscar Nominations (1): Best Supporting Actor for Alan Strang in *Equus* (United Artists, 1977)

Considered something of a star in the making when he appeared in the National Theatre production of Peter Shaffer's *Equus*, the boyish-looking Peter Firth seemed as though he would build on his initial success when director Sidney Lumet chose him to repeat his role on screen. The role was tough and challenging (that of a disturbed stable boy who undergoes psychiatric treatment after blinding the horses in his care), the execution dramatically flawless and the Oscar nomination gratifying, but that's as far as it went. Jason Robards won it in 1977 for his grizzled portrait of Dashiell Hammett, and Firth has never made the lists again.

Laurence Fishburne

Born Augusta, Georgia, USA, 30 July 1961

Oscar Nominations (1): Best Actor for Ike Turner in *What's Love Got to Do With It?* (Touchstone, 1993)

Mentioned these days in the same breath as Morgan Freeman and Denzel Washington, Larry Fishburne adds fuel to the belief that the nineties are fast becoming something of a golden age for black actors. Glimpsed early in his career in numerous Coppola movies – *Apocalypse Now, Rumble Fish, The Cotton Club* – he made a big impression as the fatherly figure in *Boyz N the Hood* and an even bigger one as the promoter/husband of Tina Turner in *What's Love Got to Do With It?* He earned a deserved Oscar nomination for

Ike (he and Angela Bassett were the first two black performers to be nominated for lead roles in the same film) but was somewhat disappointingly overlooked for his recent rendering of the noble Moor opposite Kenneth Branagh's Iago in *Othello*.

Barry Fitzgerald

Born Dublin, Ireland, 10 March 1888; died 1961

Oscars (1): Best Supporting Actor for Father Fitzgibbon in *Going My Way* (Paramount, 1944)

Oscar Nominations (1): Best Actor for the same role in the same film (see below)

An actor who brought a wrinkly-faced craftiness and a twinkling smile to every movie in which he appeared, Barry Fitzgerald earned a place in movie history by becoming the first actor to be nominated in both the leading and supporting categories for the same role – Father Fitzgibbon in *Going My Way*. He won in the supporting category (his co-star Bing Crosby taking the major award), the rules being changed shortly thereafter so that such a situation could not occur again. Memorable in whimsical roles as country doctors, gardeners, bookies and the like, he seemed at times to be operating in a kind of Hollywood never-never land, 'stuffing', as one critic noted, 'the English language down the back of his throat'. A winner for just the one movie he was at his best as the pipe-smoking cop tracking down a New York killer in *The Naked City*, and when showing his less than lovable side as the lethal little judge in Rene Clair's *And Then There Were None*.

Geraldine Fitzgerald

Born Dublin, Ireland, 24 November 1912

Oscar Nominations (1): Best Supporting Actress for Isabella Linton in *Wuthering Heights* (Goldwyn/United Artists, 1939)

'Fitz acted brilliantly . . . *Dark Victory* would have been only half the film without her,' said Bette Davis, remembering one of her most famous films.

Warners, however, didn't seem to share Davis' enthusiasm, and after a handful of roles at the studio (she turned down Mary Astor's *femme fatale* in *The Maltese Falcon*), Geraldine Fitzgerald tended to look elsewhere for parts, which never amounted to major roles, just juicy character ones. She was nominated only the once – for her luckless Isabella in *Wuthering Heights* who finds herself married to Heathcliff because he has been spurned by Cathy. Fitzgerald deserved more but that, in the end, was all there was.

Louise Fletcher

Born Birmingham, Alabama, USA, July 1934

Oscars (1): Best Actress for Nurse Ratched in *One Flew Over the Cuckoo's Nest* (United Artists, 1975)

Of all the mean characters in American cinema of the seventies, Louise Fletcher's asylum nurse – cool, calculating, finally lethal – comes close to the top of the list, enduring Jack Nicholson's rebelliousness for just so long but finally putting an end to his mischief in the most brutal way she knows how – through a lobotomy! An Oscar, of course (*One Flew Over the Cuckoo's Nest* won all four of the main awards), and although there have been no nominations since, her win remains one of the best remembered of the decade, not least for the chill factor. The daughter of totally deaf parents, she spoke to them at their Alabama home via sign language during her acceptance speech.

Nina Foch

Born Leyden, Holland, 20 April 1924

Oscar Nominations (1): Best Supporting Actress for Erica Martin in *Executive Suite* (MGM, 1954)

Blonde, sophisticated and with a slightly cool persona, Nina Foch never quite got the opportunities she deserved at Metro in the early fifties, making the most of the generally inferior roles that came her way and coping with the disappointment of being tested and rejected for Lina Lamont in *Singin' in the Rain*. Elegant and bitchy as Gene Kelly's wealthy patron and would-be lover in *An American in Paris*, she was rather more emotional in the role for which she earned her sole nomination – the grief-stricken secretary of a recently deceased company boss in *Executive Suite*. She subsequently appeared for Kubrick in *Spartacus*, displaying just the right amount of decadence as a Roman noblewoman who casts a lascivious eye over a row of husky slaves and then selects those she wishes to fight to the death. In recent years she has put such things behind her and concentrated mainly on work in the theatre and on TV.

Henry Fonda

Born Grand Island, Nebraska, USA, 16 May 1905; died 1982

Oscars (1): Best Actor for Norman Thayer, Jr. in *On Golden Pond* (ITC/IPC, 1981)

Oscar Nominations (1): Best Actor for Tom Joad in *The Grapes of Wrath* (20th Century-Fox, 1940)

It took the Academy nearly fifty years to acknowledge the quiet genius of Henry Fonda. When eventually it did, it was for his portrait of a cantankerous eighty-year-old former college professor struggling to come to terms with old age. The role they should have honoured, of course, was his Tom Joad, Steinbeck's tragic dustbowl victim of the Depression. All they could manage was a nomination. A man who came to symbolise decent, liberal-minded integrity, Fonda was married five times and 'goddamned ashamed of it'. He disliked the awe in which he was held. 'I'm not that pristine pure,' he commented. 'I guess I've broken as many rules as the next feller. But I reckon my face looks honest enough and if people buy it, Hallelujah.' He received nothing for one of his favourite roles, his juror in *12 Angry Men*; Robert Redford presented him with an honorary award for his screen accomplishments in March 1981.

Note: Fonda enjoyed some compensation for missing out on an acting nomination for *12 Angry Men* by receiving a mention as one of the film's co-producers when it was named as one of the five best pictures of 1957.

Jane Fonda

Born New York City, USA, 21 December 1937

Oscars (2): Best Actress for Bree Daniels in *Klute* (Warner Bros, 1971) and Sally Hyde in *Coming Home* (United Artists, 1978)

Oscar Nominations (5): Best Actress for Gloria Beatty in *They Shoot Horses, Don't They?* (Palomar-Cinerama, 1969), Lillian Hellman in *Julia* (20th Century-Fox, 1977), Kimberly Wells in *The China Syndrome* (Columbia, 1979); Best Supporting Actress for Chelsea Thayer Wayne in *On Golden Pond* (ITC/IPC, 1981); Best Actress for Alex Sternbergen in *The Morning After* (20th Century-Fox, 1986)

Some French frolics for Vadim, a few nice-girl roles in Hollywood and a dash of Neil Simon (*Barefoot in the Park*) was just about the sum of Jane Fonda's achievements before she hit the Oscar trail in the seventies, when she looked for a while as though she might become the first performer to win three best actress awards in a decade. In the end she had to make do with two, the first for her New York hooker terrified by an unseen insanity in *Klute*, the second for her Vietnam war wife in love with a paraplegic in *Coming Home*. She missed out on her portrait of playwright Lillian Hellman, embroiled in personal tragedy in thirties Europe in *Julia*. Nominated on four other occasions, she brought her resolute, often cynical persona to her desperate marathon dancer in *They Shoot Horses, Don't They?*, TV news reporter in *The China Syndrome*, aggressive daughter in *On Golden Pond* and alcoholic actress in *The Morning After*. In 1982 she accepted the best actor award on behalf of her ailing father (for *On Golden Pond*) and immediately left the ceremony to present the Oscar to him at his bedside.

Joan Fontaine

Born Tokyo, Japan, 22 October 1917

Oscars (1): Best Actress for Lina McLaidlaw in *Suspicion* (RKO, 1941)

Oscar Nominations (2): Best Actress for Mrs de Winter in *Rebecca* (United Artists, 1940) and Tessa Sanger in *The Constant Nymph* (Warner Bros, 1943)

Anyone who had put up with Mrs Danvers deserved some kind of recognition, and Joan Fontaine duly received hers when she was nominated for her timid heroine in Hitchcock's *Rebecca*. Passed over in favour of Ginger Rogers' *Kitty Foyle*, she had to wait but a year for the award to arrive on her mantelpiece, this time for another Hitchcock thriller, in which she believed that hubby Cary Grant was trying to poison her with a glass of milk. He was, too, but RKO instructed Hitch to change the ending on the grounds that *no one* would believe that Cary was a killer! Nominated a third time for her young girl in love with composer Charles Boyer in *The Constant Nymph*, Fontaine eventually finished up one Oscar short of sister Olivia de Havilland, who won for *To Each His Own* and *The Heiress*. De Havilland also won more nominations, five to Fontaine's three.

Lynn Fontanne

Born Woodford, Essex, England, 6 December 1892; died 1982

Oscar Nominations (1): Best Actress for 'The Actress' in *The Guardsman* (MGM, 1931/32)

Like her husband and co-star Alfred Lunt a 1932 Oscar nominee, the British-born Lynn Fontanne dabbled briefly with the notion of becoming a Hollywood star, repeated her role in Molnar's *The Guardsman* (as the wife who is seduced by her own heavily disguised uniformed husband) and then said 'Thanks but no thanks' to Louis B. Mayer when he suggested that her future lay at MGM. Quite why he suggested it remains something of a mystery. The pair made no impact at the box office and quickly took their light, gay sophistication back to Broadway.

Harrison Ford

Born Chicago, USA, 13 July 1942

Oscar Nominations (1): Best Actor for John Book in *Witness* (Paramount, 1985)

Whether Harrison Ford will ever find time to settle down and give an Oscar-winning performance is doubtful, considering he has been 'on the go' in the *Star Wars* trilogy, the *Indiana Jones* adventures and the Jack Ryan movies since the mid-seventies. One of the few occasions he did stop for breath was for *Witness*, when he was nominated for his cop in hiding with the Amish after discovering, through the testimony of a young boy, that there is corruption among his colleagues. His sensitive playing revealed depths that have not been reached since, even in films such as *The Mosquito Coast* and *Presumed Innocent*. The Oscar still awaits.

Frederic Forrest

Born Waxahachie, Texas, USA, 23 December 1936

Oscar Nominations (1): Best Supporting Actor for Houston Dyer in *The Rose* (20th Century-Fox, 1979)

Poor Frederic Forrest was one of those who embarked on the river trip to hell in Coppola's *Apocalypse Now*. He was also the one whose head was severed from his body by an insane Brando and carried through the teeming rain for a ground-level inspection by Martin Sheen. No Oscar nomination for losing one's head; that came for his young army deserter shacked up with rock star Bette Midler in *The Rose*. Wily old Melvyn Douglas ensured that he remained a nominee by taking the year's supporting nod for *Being There*.

Jodie Foster

Born Los Angeles, USA, 19 November 1962

Oscars (2): Best Actress for Sarah Tobias in *The Accused* (Paramount, 1988) and Clarice Starling in *The Silence of the Lambs* (Orion, 1991)

Oscar Nominations (2): Best Supporting Actress for Iris Steensman in *Taxi Driver* (Columbia, 1976); Best Actress for the title role in *Nell* (20th Century-Fox, 1994)

A double Oscar winner by the time she was thirty, Jodie Foster has been attending awards ceremonies now for some twenty years, since she was nominated for her drug-addicted child prostitute in Scorsese's controversial *Taxi Driver*. Nothing came of her first nomination ('Kids talk like sailors now, adults don't want to know,' she said later), but she's more than made up for things since, with her tough portraits of the gang-rape victim in *The Accused* and the courageous FBI agent who enlists the help of Dr Hannibal Lecter as she searches for a serial killer in *The Silence of the Lambs*. Two awards in just three years and a subsequent nomination for her Nell, a wild child raised outside civilisation! It's difficult to believe that there isn't more to come.

Anthony Franciosa

Born New York City, USA, 28 October 1928

Oscar Nominations (1): Best Actor for Polo in *A Hatful of Rain* (20th Century-Fox, 1957)

Perhaps the start was too good – a repeat of his Broadway role in *A Hatful of Rain* and an Oscar nomination for his caring brother of the drug-addicted Don Murray – but Anthony Franciosa never really built on his early Hollywood promise, and instead of joining the band of young, forceful actors who were making a name for themselves in the fifties, he settled for a career that was solid and respectable rather than exciting, and which boasted only the occasional movie of class – *Let No Man Write My Epitaph*, *Career*, *Period of Adjustment*. TV took up much of his time in the seventies and eighties; his unprincipled agent/manager of Andy Griffith in Kazan's biting TV satire *A Face in the Crowd* was further indication of a promise not quite fulfilled.

Morgan Freeman

Born Memphis, Tennessee, USA, 1 June 1937

Oscar Nominations (3): Best Supporting Actor for Fast Black in *Street Smart* (Golan/Globus, 1987); Best Actor for Hoke Colburn in *Driving Miss Daisy* (Warner Bros, 1989) and Ellis Boyd 'Red' Redding in *The Shawshank Redemption* (Columbia/Castle Rock, 1994)

In many people's view the next black winner of the best actor award, Morgan Freeman was so depressed about his career in the early eighties that he thought of throwing it all up and becoming a taxi driver. Luckily he had second thoughts and the result has been a string of notable performances that have included a mercurial pimp, the grey-haired chauffeur of Southern matron Jessica Tandy and an affable lifer in the prison movie *The Shawshank Redemption*. Nominations for all three, but not the award. The time must surely come – and soon!

Leonard Frey

Born Brooklyn, New York, USA, 4 September 1938; died 1988

Oscar Nominations (1): Best Supporting Actor for Motel in *Fiddler on the Roof* (United Artists, 1971)

The relatively brief film career of Leonard Frey contrasted sharply with his extensive work on Broadway, in opera and as a character actor for the Repertory Theatre of Lincoln Center. He earned his Oscar nomination for his portrayal of Motel, the timid tailor seeking a wife in Norman Jewison's screen version of the musical *Fiddler on the Roof*. Well known for his flamboyant performances, he first gained prominence as Harold the birthday boy in *The Boys in the Band*, a role he subsequently repeated with relish on screen, being described by one critic as 'queening it over the whole pack like Bette Davis in *All About Eve*'!

Brenda Fricker

Born Dublin, Ireland, 17 February 1944

Oscars (1): Best Supporting Actress for Mrs Brown in *My Left Foot* (Ferndale Films, 1989)

Homely, kindly, honest, warm, plain-speaking: Brenda Fricker is and has been all these things, especially as the remarkable mother of cerebral palsy victim Christy Brown in *My Left Foot*. A former star of the long-running British TV series *Casualty*, she has been seen mostly in America since her Oscar win, although the quality of her Hollywood films has been somewhat less than inspiring: *Hook, Home Alone II: Lost in New York, Angels in the Outfield* and *So I Married an Axe Murderer*.

G

Clark Gable

Born Cadiz, Ohio, USA, 1 February 1901; died 1960

Oscars (1): Best Actor for Peter Warne in *It Happened One Night* (Columbia, 1934)

Oscar Nominations (2): Best Actor for Fletcher Christian in *Mutiny on the Bounty* (MGM, 1935) and Rhett Butler in *Gone with the Wind* (Selznick, MGM, 1939)

'Frankly, my dear, I don't give a damn,' said Clark Gable's Rhett Butler as he bid his famous farewell to Vivien Leigh in *Gone with the Wind*. On Oscar night in 1940, however, Gable most certainly did give a damn, for by then he was the only actor capable of equalling Spencer Tracy's record of winning two Oscars in the Academy's first decade. He lost to Robert Donat's gentle schoolmaster in *Goodbye, Mr Chips*, and that was that as far as Gable and the Oscars were concerned – one win for his journalist trying to get the lowdown on runaway heiress Claudette Colbert, and two nominations, for his rebellious Fletcher Christian and blockade runner Rhett Butler. Modest about his fame, he would frequently quip that they'd write on his tombstone 'He was lucky and he knew it'. The writers of the Raoul Walsh western *The Tall Men*, in which he co-starred with Robert Ryan, put it rather more poetically when Ryan summed him up thus: 'He's what every boy thinks he's going to be when he grows up and wishes he had been when he's an old man.'

Greta Garbo

Born Stockholm, Sweden, 18 September 1905; died 1990

Oscar Nominations (4): Best Actress for the title role in *Anna Christie* (MGM, 1929/30), Rita Cavallini in *Romance* (MGM 1929/30), Marguerite in *Camille* (MGM, 1937) and Lena Yakushova 'Ninotchka' in *Ninotchka* (MGM, 1939)

She never won, of course, although she might have done had they known she was going to call it a day at thirty-six and never return. For her waterfront streetwalker Anna Christie, perhaps, or her dying courtesan in *Camille*. Or best of all for her Russian commissar in *Ninotchka*, which was billed with the slogan 'Garbo Laughs' and allowed her to deliver, courtesy of writers Brackett, Wilder and Reisch, the wittiest dialogue of her career. 'Why should you carry other people's bags?' she asks a Parisian porter. 'Well, that's my business, madam,' he replies. 'That's no business,' she retorts. 'That's social injustice.' Comes the payoff. 'That depends on the tip.' Presented with an honorary award in 1954 (she failed to turn up), she retreated into a quiet retirement in 1941, refusing all offers of a comeback and leaving her fragile beauty to history.

Andy Garcia

Born Havana, Cuba, 12 April 1956

Oscar Nominations (1): Best Supporting Actor for Vincent Mancini in *The Godfather Part III* (Paramount, 1990)

The early *Godfather* movies could be counted on to produce a host of Oscar nominations in both the major and the supporting categories. Unfortunately, by the time the third and last film in the series came round, the appeal of the Corleones had worn off a little, and only the Cuban-born Andy Garcia made it to the lists, for his illegitimate son of Sonny and heir apparent to Al Pacino. Voters were more impressed with the less handsome and considerably more vicious Joe Pesci, who operated on a somewhat lower Mafia level in Scorsese's *Goodfellas*.

Vincent Gardenia

Born Naples, Italy, 7 January 1922; died 1992

Oscar Nominations (2): Best Supporting Actor for Dutch Schnell in *Bang the Drum Slowly* (Paramount, 1973) and Cosmo Castorini in *Moonstruck* (MGM, 1987)

Cops and hustlers, urban men who have lived in the tenements and known poverty and who have usually grown up to be tough but honest. Too simplistic a summing-up of the kind of men played on screen by Vincent Gardenia? Perhaps, but he played many like them, and the roles for which he was Oscar-nominated were made for him – the down-to-earth manager of the baseball team in *Bang the Drum Slowly* and Cher's straying, middle-aged father in *Moonstruck,* who in one memorably awkward moment comes face to face with his daughter when accompanying his new lady friend to a night at the opera!

Ava Gardner

Born Grabton, near Smithfield, North Carolina, USA, 24 December 1922; died 1990

Oscar Nominations (1): Best Actress for Eloise 'Honey Bear' Kelly in *Mogambo* (MGM, 1953)

Quite what MGM boss Louis B. Mayer would have said had he viewed today's Sharon Stone or Demi Moore takes a bit of figuring, but he certainly knew what he liked and he liked Ava Gardner. Legend has it that after watching her screen test he said: 'She can't act. She don't talk. She's sensational. She's hired!' She went on to become one of his biggest stars, earn the label 'the world's most beautiful animal' and even an Oscar nomination for her wisecracking showgirl stranded in the African jungle with Clark Gable. No luck, though, in March 1954: showgirls were out, Roman princesses were in. Never a fan of her own acting, she would look at herself on screen and comment resignedly: 'Something was missing.' Her cynicism continued into her later years. When a reporter asked her what her screen career had amounted to, she replied: 'Nothing very much, honey. Not very much at all really.'

John Garfield

Born New York City, USA, 4 March 1913; died 1952

Oscar Nominations (2): Best Supporting Actor for Mickey Borden in *Four Daughters* (Warner Bros, 1938); Best Actor for Charlie Davis in *Body and Soul* (Enterprise/UA, 1947)

'Screen acting is my business but I get my kicks from Broadway,' said John Garfield, a trifle condescendingly, about his movie career. The remark was made during his contract days at Warners. Had he waited until his post-war independent years he might have been more appreciative of his screen potential, especially after his Oscar nomination for his young boxer owned by the mob in *Body and Soul*. Nominated some nine years earlier for his cynical young songwriter who disrupts the life of a small-town American family in *Four Daughters*, he was regarded by many as one of America's most formidable talents of the forties, but his left-wing views led to clashes with the House Un-American Activities Committee and a restriction on his screen performances. He died of a heart attack in 1952, aged thirty-nine – a rebel and role model for stars like James Dean who were just on the horizon.

William Gargan

Born Brooklyn, New York, USA, 17 July 1905; died 1979

Oscar Nominations (1): Best Supporting Actor for Joe in *They Knew What They Wanted* (RKO, 1940)

Mostly a B-movie actor who thrived in low-budget programmers of the forties, William Gargan got his one bite at the Oscar cherry when he found himself among the supporting nominees for his womanising foreman who loves and takes the wife of Italian farmer Charles Laughton in *They Knew What They Wanted*. Never in with much of a chance (Walter Brennan was busy making it three wins in five years for *The Westerner*), he later turned his B-movie talents to TV, where he played the popular private eye Martin Kane. A victim of cancer in his fifties, he was forced to abandon acting when his larynx was removed but later learned to speak again through a voice box. He regularly toured the country for the American Cancer Society.

Judy Garland

Born Grand Rapids, Minnesota, USA, 10 June 1922; died 1969

Oscar Nominations (2): Best Actress for Vicki Lester in *A Star Is Born* (Warner Bros, 1954); Best Supporting Actress for Irene Hoffman in *Judgment at Nuremberg* (United Artists, 1961)

In the end it seemed to come down to who could cope with their alcoholic screen partners the best: Garland and the inebriated James Mason in *A Star Is Born* or Grace Kelly and her boozy old Bing Crosby in *The Country Girl*. The voters decided in favour of Grace, although in retrospect it was Judy who gave the most complete performance – musical, emotional, vibrant. Nominated again in 1961 for her brilliant cameo as the pathetic German *hausfrau* in *Judgment at Nuremberg*, she finished up with just the one Oscar on her shelf – the special one presented to her in 1940 for 'her outstanding performance as a screen juvenile during the past year'. She sang two Academy Award-winning songs during her years at MGM – 'Over the Rainbow' from *The Wizard of Oz* (1939) and 'On the Atchison, Topeka and Santa Fe' from *The Harvey Girls* (1946).

☆

James Garner

Born Norman, Oklahoma, USA, 7 April 1928

Oscar Nominations (1): Best Actor for Murphy Jones in *Murphy's Romance* (Columbia, 1985)

One of those performers who has never once looked as though he was acting, either on the big screen or on TV in *The Rockford Files*, James Garner's chances of reaching the Oscar lists seemed remote until director Martin Ritt said he wanted him for *Murphy's Romance*. Then things changed for the better. Wonderfully laid-back as the small-town widowed pharmacist who finds himself attracted to young divorcee and mother Sally Field, he was among the most deserving of the year's nominees, thanks not only to Ritt's direction but also the script of Ravetch and Frank, which constantly probed beneath the surface of Murphy's earlier life. Showy things well above the surface helped William Hurt (*Kiss of the Spider Woman*) defeat the pack as the best of the year.

Teri Garr

Born Lakewood, Ohio, USA, 11 December 1949

Oscar Nominations (1): Best Supporting Actress for Sandy in *Tootsie* (Columbia, 1982)

Nominated for one of the most unrewarding roles in *Tootsie* – that of the failed actress and forgotten lover of Dustin Hoffman (she lost to the leggy Jessica Lange), Teri Garr looked for a moment as though she might be one of the movies' bright new comediennes. Critic Pauline Kael went so far as to call her 'the funniest neurotic, dizzy dame on the screen'. The comedy is still there on occasion but she has finished up as more of a Gloria Grahame kind of actress, proving just how talented a dramatic performer she is as the Kroeger-type spy wife in the TV film *Pack of Lies*. As yet, there have been no signs of any further Oscar nominations.

Greer Garson

Born County Down, Ireland, 29 September 1903; died 1996

Oscars (1): Best Actress for Kay Miniver in *Mrs Miniver* (MGM, 1942)

Oscar Nominations (6): Best Actress for Katherine Ellis in *Goodbye, Mr Chips* (MGM, 1939), Edna Gladney in *Blossoms in the Dust* (MGM, 1941), the title role in *Madame Curie* (MGM, 1943), Susie Parkington in *Mrs Parkington* (MGM, 1944), Mary Rafferty in *Valley of Decision* (MGM, 1945) and Eleanor Roosevelt in *Sunrise at Campobello* (Warner Bros, 1960)

If nobility, self-sacrifice and dedication were the order of the day (as they frequently were at MGM during the war years), Greer Garson was always the first choice of Louis B. Mayer. In an incredible run of six nominations between 1939 and 1945, her sweet serenity and reassuring personality helped entrance Robert Donat's schoolmaster Mr Chips, run a Texas orphanage, discover radium, rule as a glamorous matriarch and play a Pittsburgh servant girl who falls in love with Gregory Peck. Best of all it helped defy Hitler as the British housewife Mrs Miniver, the role that finally won her the award. A Metro star until the mid-fifties, she made a brief comeback in the sixties, earning her seventh Academy Award nomination for her Eleanor Roosevelt in *Sunrise at Campobello*, arguably her finest screen performance. Her acceptance speech for *Mrs Miniver* was reputedly clocked at five and a half minutes.

Janet Gaynor

Born Philadelphia, USA, 6 October 1906; died 1984

Oscars (1): Best Actress for Diane in *Seventh Heaven*, Angela in *Street Angel* and 'The Wife' in *Sunrise* (all Fox, 1927/28)

Oscar Nominations (1): Best Actress for Vicki Lester in *A Star Is Born* (Selznick/United Artists, 1937)

Waifs and diminutive heroines with large, sad eyes and a charm born of innocence. Only Janet Gaynor could play them to perfection in the late twenties and the Academy were only too well aware of the fact, handing out their first best actress award for her young farmer's wife in Murnau's *Sunrise*, Neapolitan girl in *Street Angel* and Parisian waif in *Seventh Heaven*. Nothing, sadly, for any of her films with her long-time romantic screen partner, Charles Farrell (they were known as 'America's favourite love birds'), but another nomination just prior to her retirement for her young star on the rise in the first official version of *A Star Is Born*. Some brief roles on radio and TV and as a mother in *Bernadine* were followed in 1977 by a special Academy Award for 'her truly immeasurable contribution to the art of motion pictures'.

Michael V. Gazzo

Born 1923; died 1995

Oscar Nominations (1): Best Supporting Actor for Frank Pentangeli in *The Godfather Part II* (Paramount, 1974)

Michael Gazzo's voice was hoarse even before all *The Godfather II* violence began; once he had been all but garrotted in a gang brawl in a New York bar he could barely manage anything above a whisper and finally exited the scene through a cut wrist suicide in his bath. A nomination, of course (the first two *Godfather* films each had three cast members honoured in the supporting category), but no award at the end of it, just the privilege of taking on Michael Corleone and losing! A noted playwright, Gazzo authored the much-acclaimed Broadway play about drug addiction, *A Hatful of Rain*, brought to the screen in 1957 by Fred Zinnemann.

Leo Genn

Born London, England, 9 August 1905; died 1978

Oscar Nominations (1): Best Supporting Actor for Petronius in *Quo Vadis?* (MGM, 1951)

The rich, aristocratic voice gave him an edge over other post-war British actors; unfortunately the personality, a touch on the dull side, didn't quite measure up to the tones, and for the most part Leo Genn found himself languishing in British films (and occasional American ones) as doctors, lawyers, teachers and assorted army officers. His two most accomplished roles were his caring doctor treating the mental illness of Olivia de Havilland in the harrowing *The Snake Pit* and his Roman nobleman involved with an even greater madness, that of Peter Ustinov's Nero, in *Quo Vadis?* Nominated for an Oscar for the latter performance, he was somewhat outclassed on awards night by Karl Malden in *A Streetcar Named Desire*. A barrister by profession, he served as assistant prosecutor at the Belsen trial at the end of World War II.

Chief Dan George

Born British Columbia, Canada, 1899; died 1981

Oscar Nominations (1): Best Supporting Actor for Old Lodge Skins in *Little Big Man* (National General, 1970)

A bit ancient for the stereotype Indian who falls with a shriek from his horse and into the camera, Chief Dan George brought a dignity to his Hollywood roles in the seventies, earning a nomination for his Cheyenne father of Dustin Hoffman in *Little Big Man* and enjoying himself as one of the strays picked up by Clint Eastwood in *The Outlaw Josey Wales*. An active campaigner for environmental causes, he was also a pioneer in lobbying for Native Americans to be played by Native Americans and not Hollywood extras with greasepaint on their faces. A New York Critics winner for *Little Big Man*, he turned up at the presentations in full ceremonial dress and had the time of his life!

Gladys George

Born Patten, Maine, USA, 13 September 1904; died 1954

Oscar Nominations (1): Best Actress for Carrie Snyder in *Valiant Is the Word for Carrie* (Paramount, 1936)

Invariably cast as a girl from the wrong side of the tracks, Gladys George's brassy blonde with a heart of gold enhanced films with Cagney, Bogart, Garfield and any number of screen tough men. Her nomination, though, was for a film in which she took centre stage as a good-hearted dame from the Bayou country who takes on a couple of kids and gains self-respect. Tear-jerking nonsense, but Gladys showed what she could do when given the chance and might well have won as best actress had not Luise Rainer been on hand at MGM in *The Great Ziegfeld*. Her most famous line in movies was at the close of *The Roaring Twenties* when she kneels on the church steps, cradles a dead James Cagney in her arms and says to a cop: 'He used to be a big shot.'

Giancarlo Giannini

Born Spezia, Italy, 1 August 1942

Oscar Nominations (1): Best Actor for Pasqualino Settebellezze in *Seven Beauties* (Medusa/Italy, 1976)

Known for his extraordinarily sad eyes (director Lina Wertmuller has said that he can scream, curse, plead, argue and make love with them), Giancarlo Giannini earned his nomination for one of the most remarkable performances of the seventies – as a small-time hoodlum cum Casanova who in *Seven Beauties* chooses to suffer humiliation and degradation in order to survive – at any cost – in a German concentration camp in World War II. Nineteen seventy-six was Peter Finch's year for *Network*, but Giannini's was the performance to remember. No Italian actor has yet won the best actor Academy Award; Giannini, Mastroianni (nominated on three occasions) and Troisi are the only Italian actors to win nominations for their roles in Italian films.

John Gielgud

Born London, England, 14 April 1904

Oscars (1): Best Supporting Actor for Hobson in *Arthur* (Warner Bros, 1981)

Oscar Nominations (1): Best Supporting Actor for King Louis VII in *Becket* (Paramount, 1964)

'I'll alert the media,' says haughty manservant John Gielgud as Dudley Moore's Arthur informs him he is going to take a bath. With lines such as these, and a delivery close to sarcastic perfection, the Oscar was his for the taking, and he took it (although not personally) on 29 March 1982. Nominated earlier for the somewhat forgotten role of King Louis VII in *Becket*, his eighty film roles have been mostly walk-ons and cameos in recent times, although some of his earlier cinematic work had more stature, notably his fine Cassius in *Julius Caesar* and Lord Cardigan in *The Charge of the Light Brigade* and, in a somewhat lighter vein, the rather more lethal valet in *Murder on the Orient Express*.

Jack Gilford

Born New York City, USA, 25 July 1907; died 1990

Oscar Nominations (1): Best Supporting Actor for Phil Greene in *Save the Tiger* (Paramount, 1973)

The Un-American Activities did for him, otherwise the name of Jack Gilford might have figured more prominently in the annals of Hollywood history. Still, he did manage a nomination once the blacklist was over, for his world-weary, soft-spoken businessman partner of Jack Lemmon in *Save the Tiger*. Lemmon (best actor) won, Gilford didn't, and he's best remembered nowadays for his role as the sad-eyed Roman slave Hysterium in *A Funny Thing Happened on the Way to the Forum*. The film offered him some good lines, although they didn't quite live up to his own when he was asked by the House Un-American Activities Committee if he believed in the overthrow of the United States government by force and violence and replied: 'No, just gently.'

Lillian Gish

Born Springfield, Ohio, USA, 14 October 1896; died 1993

Oscar Nominations (1): Best Supporting Actress for Laura Belle McCanles in *Duel in the Sun* (Selznick International, 1946)

If Oscars had been presented in the silent days it's more than likely that Lillian Gish would have been a winner several times over and established a record that would never be beaten. They weren't, and Miss Gish had to be content with a 1970 honorary award and a solitary nomination for her frail wife of cattle baron Lionel Barrymore in *Duel in the Sun*, dying beautifully as always whilst he sits at her bedside muttering about what an ornery old bastard he'd been all his life. The role she *should* have been nominated for (and won) was her kindly little matron who gives shelter to the two children on the run from mad preacher Robert Mitchum in *The Night of the Hunter*. The scenes of her sitting silently on the porch, a rifle across her lap, while he lurks by the gate outside, belong with the memorable cinematic moments of the fifties.

Jackie Gleason

Born Brooklyn, New York, USA, 26 February 1916; died 1987

Oscar Nominations (1): Best Supporting Actor for Minnesota Fats in *The Hustler* (20th Century-Fox, 1961)

Very few people outside America knew much about Jackie Gleason until *The Hustler*, but once he'd played those two marathon games of pool with Paul Newman, *everyone* knew him, not so much under his own name but by that of his character in the movie, the legendary Minnesota Fats, immaculately clad in smart suit and waistcoat, white shirt and tie, and a flower in his buttonhole. Only a whisker away from winning as the year's top supporting actor (George Chakiris won as part of the *West Side Story* bandwagon), Gleason later created a second notable movie character, the apoplectic red-necked sheriff forever in pursuit of Burt Reynolds in the *Smokey and the Bandit* films. A long-time favourite on American TV, he was raised in Brooklyn, spending much of his youth in and around pool rooms. Newman's admiring comment: 'Fat man, you shoot a great game of pool', was thus not inappropriate.

James Gleason

Born New York City, USA, 23 May 1886; died 1959

Oscar Nominations (1): Best Supporting Actor for Max Corkle in *Here Comes Mr Jordan* (Columbia, 1941)

Everyone's favourite cop on the beat, milkman, taxi driver, reporter, gambler, janitor (you name him, he played him), the slim-faced, bald-headed James Gleason was one of Hollywood's *real* characters, worldly-wise, rough around the edges and with a heart of gold. Frequently referred to on screen as 'Pop', he appeared in more than 150 movies, collaborating on the scripts and writing additional dialogue for many of his early talkies. He was nominated just the once, for his manager of boxer Robert Montgomery who is mistakenly taken to heaven before his time. Jack Warden also made the Oscar lists (this time as a football coach) when he reprised the role in Warren Beatty's retitled remake of 1978, *Heaven Can Wait*. Neither Gleason nor Warden won. Whoever plays the role when they get round to making it for a third time may be luckier.

Paulette Goddard

Born Whitestone Landing, New York, USA, 3 June 1905; died 1990

Oscar Nominations (1): Best Supporting Actress for Lt Jean O'Doul in *So Proudly We Hail* (Paramount, 1943)

A nomination (and a supporting one at that!) for a flip combat nurse serving in Bataan in World War II seemed scant reward for an actress who had twice played memorable waifs for Charlie Chaplin (*Modern Times*, *The Great Dictator*) and come within a whisker of landing the role of Scarlett O'Hara in *Gone with the Wind*, but that was indeed the extent of Paulette Goddard's involvement with Oscar. Vivacious, blue-eyed and strikingly attractive in the early years of Technicolor, she was a tempestuous three-time heroine for DeMille at Paramount, and in 1939 enjoyed a memorable loan-out to MGM in *The Women*. As the predatory chorus girl Miriam, she offers to do battle with Joan Crawford on behalf of Norma Shearer. 'Shall I spit in Crystal's eye for you?' she asks. 'You're passing up a swell chance, honey. Where *I* spit, *no* grass grows.' Married to Chaplin, actor Burgess Meredith and author Erich Maria Remarque, she retired in the fifties to live in luxury in Europe. She left $20 million and one of the most famous jewellery collections in the world.

Whoopi Goldberg

Born New York, USA, 13 November 1949

Oscars (1): Best Supporting Actress for Oda Mae Brown in *Ghost* (Paramount, 1990)

Oscar Nominations (1): Best Actress for Celie in *The Color Purple* (Warner Bros, 1985)

The unheard-of almost happened in 1985 when pundits began saying that Whoopi Goldberg might become the first black actress to win the top award, for her Celie in Spielberg's *The Color Purple*. It didn't happen (the film missed out on everything despite eleven nominations) and Whoopi had to wait another five years for Academy recognition for her role in *Ghost* as the storefront medium who discovers to her surprise that she really does have psychic powers after all. It wasn't the major award, alas, but she was still the first black performer to win as supporting actress since Hattie McDaniel fifty years earlier. A riot in the *Sister Act* films, she has also made more than her fair share of junk in the nineties but has saved most of it by employing to full advantage the widest grin in movies.

Thomas Gomez

Born New York City, USA, 10 July 1905; died 1971

Oscar Nominations (1): Best Supporting Actor for Pancho in *Ride the Pink Horse* (Universal-International, 1947)

An actor whose physical presence – oily, chubby, gum-chewing – could evoke a cunning menace, Thomas Gomez should by rights have gone on to become one of the most successful of Hollywood's post-war heavies, but apart from the occasional quality role in the late forties his career subsequently foundered in a morass of big-studio mediocrity. Nominated in 1947 for his small-town carousel proprietor in the thriller *Ride the Pink Horse*, he was also memorable the following year in Polonsky's *Force of Evil* as a small-time operator of a numbers racket who is rubbed out by gangsters who want to remove all competition. Carol Reed perhaps drew the best performance from him in the fifties as the Parisian circus manager in *Trapeze*.

Dexter Gordon

Born Los Angeles, USA, 27 February 1923; died 1990

Oscar Nominations (1): Best Actor for Dale Turner in *'Round Midnight* (Warner Bros, 1986)

For a jazz performer to reach the Academy short list of five best actor nominees was remarkable enough; to look as though, at one time, he might actually win the award was even more impressive. Unfortunately for Dexter Gordon it was Paul Newman's year for *The Color of Money*, and despite all kinds of shufflings, gruntings and mutterings, he was always on the outside looking in. Still, the jazz was marvellous, as was his performance as the burned-out saxophonist ruined by booze and drugs who tries for one last comeback.

Ruth Gordon

Born Wollaston (Quincy), Massachusetts, USA, 30 October 1896;
died 1985

Oscars (1): Best Supporting Actress for Minnie Castevet in *Rosemary's Baby* (Paramount, 1968)

Oscar Nominations (1): Best Supporting Actress for 'The Dealer' in *Inside Daisy Clover* (Warner Bros, 1965)

No one in their right mind would have drunk the concoction served up by Ruth Gordon to Mia Farrow in *Rosemary's Baby*, but as Roman Polanski later remarked: 'Was Farrow in her right mind or was she imagining the whole thing?' Either way, it didn't matter as far as Gordon was concerned, for she took the supporting Oscar for her Manhattan witch Minnie Castevet whose other peculiarities included making sure her victims wore a 'charm' of evil-smelling tannis root around their necks at all times. In Hollywood parlance, a multi-talented artist – actress, playwright, novelist, screenwriter – she was also nominated in 1965 for her aged mother of rising young film star Natalie Wood in *Inside Daisy Clover*. She shared Academy Award nominations with her husband Garson Kanin for the screenplays of *A Double Life*, *Adam's Rib* and *Pat and Mike*.

Louis Gossett Jr.

Born Brooklyn, New York, USA, 27 May 1936

Oscars (1): Best Supporting Actor for Sgt Emil Fowley in *An Officer and a Gentleman* (Paramount, 1982)

'No one can make anything out of a role like this' was the general consensus of opinion among actors approached to play the tough Marine sergeant who puts Richard Gere through his paces in *An Officer and a Gentleman*. Many white actors turned it down; Louis Gossett didn't, making the most of his opportunities and earning the plaudits of *Newsweek*, who commented: 'Gossett's whiplike edge manages to make a hackneyed character seem almost fresh.' The Academy certainly thought so. In April 1983 Gossett became the first black actor to be named in the supporting category. The supporting actress award has gone (to Hattie and Whoopi), so too has the best actor nod (to Sidney Poitier). The best actress Oscar is still up for grabs.

Elliott Gould

Born Brooklyn, New York, USA, 29 August 1938

Oscar Nominations (1): Best Supporting Actor for Ted Henderson in *Bob and Carol and Ted and Alice* (Columbia, 1969)

Something of a hot property in the early seventies, Elliott Gould earned his Oscar nomination not, as one might suppose, for his irreverent army surgeon Trapper John in Robert Altman's *M·A·S·H* (Donald Sutherland, never an Oscar nominee, also missed out for his Hawkeye), but for his lawyer Ted Henderson, by far the most amusing of the partner-swapping quartet in *Bob and Carol and Ted and Alice*. Oscar success proved elusive, however, as did enduring stardom, and Gould's doleful personality and self-deprecating humour that had so endeared him to the young post-sixties generation quickly lost its appeal. By the end of the decade he had become yet another 'nearly man' of contemporary American cinema. The best of his most recent roles has been that of the dumb gangster in *Bugsy* who becomes such a nuisance that he is taken to some railway sidings and quickly disposed of.

Gloria Grahame

Born Los Angeles, California, USA, 28 November 1924; died 1981

Oscars (1): Best Supporting Actress for Rosemary Bartlow in *The Bad and the Beautiful* (MGM, 1952)

Oscar Nominations (1): Best Supporting Actress for Ginny Tremaine in *Crossfire* (RKO, 1947)

A pout (her top lip seemed twice as large as her lower one) and a thin, flirtatious voice were enough to see Gloria Grahame comfortably through her early career as one of the screen's most durable bad girls. Her Oscar in 1952 for her Southern trollop wife of writer Dick Powell was perhaps a fortunate one (see Jean Hagen, p. 149), although she thoroughly deserved her earlier nomination for her 'brazen and bathetic' floozie in *Crossfire*, which perfectly illustrated her penchant for smart-talking girls who had grown up the hard way and took life day by day, usually pessimistically. Married four times (director Nicholas Ray was one of her husbands), she remains perhaps best known for risking her face beneath an elephant's foot in DeMille's *The Greatest Show on Earth* and as the gangster's moll disfigured by boiling coffee thrown by Lee Marvin in Fritz Lang's brutal gangster movie *The Big Heat*.

Cary Grant

Born Bristol, England, 18 January 1904; died 1986

Oscar Nominations (2): Best Actor for Roger Adams in *Penny Serenade* (Columbia, 1941) and Ernie Mott in *None But the Lonely Heart* (RKO, 1944)

He had his dark side (brought out most effectively by Hitchcock in *Notorious*, when he cast him as an American intelligence officer who sends the woman he desires into the bed of a Nazi agent) but most people preferred the casual, romantic image that served him so well for more than thirty years. Had his forte been other than sophisticated comedy and escapist thrillers he might have accumulated rather more than his two nominations – for his newspaperman father in *Penny Serenade* and his Cockney drifter in *None But the Lonely Heart* – but two it remained until he received an honorary award in 1970. It was presented by Frank Sinatra, who said: 'Cary has so much skill he makes it all look easy.' That he did, although in his private life things were never quite so smooth – five marriages, depression and insecurity. Little wonder that when a reporter asked him what it was like to be Cary Grant, he replied: 'I wish I knew. *I'd* like to know what it's like to be Cary Grant.'

Lee Grant

Born New York City, USA, 31 October 1927

Oscars (1): Best Supporting Actress for Felicia Carr in *Shampoo* (Columbia, 1975)

Oscar Nominations (3): Best Supporting Actress for 'The Shoplifter' in *Detective Story* (Paramount, 1951), Mrs Enders in *The Landlord* (United Artists, 1970) and Lili Rosen in *Voyage of the Damned* (ITC/Avco Embassy, 1976)

She seems to have been around forever, does Lee Grant, even though she was missing from the screen for a decade when she refused to testify against her playwright husband before the House Un-American Activities Committee. For a former blacklisted performer she has done pretty well out of the Oscars, earning a nomination for her first film role, as an *ingénue* shoplifter in Wyler's *Detective Story* and adding to her laurels in the seventies with three more nominations – for her campy, predatory mother in *The Landlord*, her bored wife in *Shampoo* and her Jewish refugee in *Voyage of the Damned*. No surprise that she won for *Shampoo*. A bored wife will take it any time. Also a distinguished documentary film-maker, she shared the 1986 feature documentary Oscar for directing and narrating *Down and Out in America*, an exposé of mass unemployment.

Bonita Granville

Born New York City, USA, 2 February 1923; died 1988

Oscar Nominations (1): Best Supporting Actress for Mary Tilford in *These Three* (United Artists, 1936)

An actress who relished playing spiteful, mischievous girls, Bonita Granville was the first child performer to earn a nomination in the then newly formed supporting actress category. Nominated just the once – for her lethal child who almost causes tragedy with her vicious lies – she went on to star as the fictional girl detective Nancy Drew and in a few Hollywood mainstream pictures before retiring in 1947 to marry Texas entrepreneur Jack Wrather. She later produced several programmes in her husband's long-running *Lassie* TV series of the fifties and sixties.

Graham Greene

Born Six Nations Reserve, Ontario, Canada

Oscar Nominations (1): Best Supporting Actor for Kicking Bird in *Dances With Wolves* (Tig/Orion, 1990)

The second Native American to find his way into the Oscar lists (Chief Dan George was the first, see p. 133), Graham Greene was among the seventeen individuals mentioned for their work before and behind the cameras on *Dances With Wolves*. Nominated for his Sioux Indian who befriends Kevin Costner's Union officer Lt John Dunbar, he lost to Joe Pesci for his somewhat less noble mobster Tommy DeVito in Scorsese's *Goodfellas*. The defeat doesn't seem to have done him any harm. His career has flourished in the nineties, with key roles in such films as *Thunderheart*, *Maverick* and *North*.

Sydney Greenstreet

Born Sandwich, Kent, England, 27 December 1879; died 1954

Oscar Nominations (1): Best Supporting Actor for Casper Gutman in *The Maltese Falcon* (Warner Bros, 1941)

A heavy in every sense of the word (he weighed in at 280lb), Greenstreet was sixty-two before he made his movie début in *The Maltese Falcon* in 1941, some forty years after first treading the boards in the theatre. His role of Casper Gutman, the chuckling, sinister crook obsessed with 'the black bird', brought him immediate acclaim, although not the Oscar, the supporting award that year going to Donald Crisp for *How Green Was My Valley*. Greenstreet remained in front of the cameras for another ten years, appearing mostly at Warners in a variety of roles, often with his diminutive partner in crime, Peter Lorre. Always remembered as 'the Fat Man', he died in 1954 of Bright's disease. At the time of his death he was said to know more than 1,200 lines of Shakespeare.

Joel Grey

Born Cleveland, Ohio, USA, 11 April 1932

Oscars (1): Best Supporting Actor for 'The Master of Ceremonies' in *Cabaret* (Allied Artists, 1972)

Joel Grey's malevolent Master of Ceremonies in Berlin's pre-war Kit Kat Klub was described by Pauline Kael as being 'every tantalisingly disgusting showbiz creep one has ever seen'. She had it about right. Grey won a Tony and an Oscar for bringing him to life on stage and screen, but like so many actors associated with one famous part has lived to regret it. Some minor roles for Altman, Herbert Ross and Steven Soderbergh have been his chief pickings since *Cabaret*. Nearly a quarter of a century on he is still remembered best for 'Welcome . . . leave your troubles behind. Outside life is disappointing? Forget it. In here life is beautiful, the girls are beautiful, even the orchestra is beautiful!' Quite an illusion!

Hugh Griffith

Born Marian Glas, Anglesey, North Wales, 30 May 1912; died 1980

Oscars (1): Best Supporting Actor for Sheik Ilderim in *Ben-Hur* (MGM, 1959)

Oscar Nominations (1): Best Supporting Actor for Squire Western in *Tom Jones* (Woodfall/United Artists, 1963)

Director William Wyler made a point of stressing that in his epic *Ben-Hur* all the Romans were played by British performers and all the Jews by American actors. He failed, however, to mention that for the mischievous Arab sheik he opted for a Welshman, Hugh Griffith. He chose well. The rascally Griffith brought a sparkle and a glint in the eye to his horse-loving sheik and took the supporting award with ease in *Ben-Hur*'s eleven-Oscar triumph. Four years later he almost made it a double with his lusty squire in *Tom Jones*, but quiet dignity rather than bawdiness ruled in 1963 and Melvyn Douglas was named for his aged rancher in *Hud*.

Melanie Griffith

Born New York City, USA, 9 August 1957

Oscar Nominations (1): Best Actress for Tess McGill in *Working Girl* (20th Century-Fox, 1988)

As the bright young secretary of a New York brokerage firm who is double-crossed by her foxy boss, Melanie Griffith illustrated that her years at Stella Adler's acting classes in the early eighties had not been wasted. Her Oscar nomination for the role didn't exactly open up a brilliant new career, but she made a brave attempt to follow Judy Holliday in the remake of *Born Yesterday* and was effective as Bruce Willis' downtrodden wife who almost, but not quite, skips town with ageing Paul Newman (he's the one who refuses!) in Robert Benton's *Nobody's Fool*. Cast in sexy nymphet roles early in her career, she is the daughter of Hitchcock actress Tippi Hedren.

Alec Guinness

Born London, England, 2 April 1914

Oscars (1): Best Actor for Colonel Nicholson in *The Bridge on the River Kwai* (Columbia, 1957)

Oscar Nominations (3): Best Actor for Henry Holland in *The Lavender Hill Mob* (Ealing, 1952); Best Supporting Actor for Ben (Obi-Wan) Kenobi in *Star Wars* (20th Century-Fox, 1977) and William Dorrit in *Little Dorrit* (Sands Films, 1988)

The ability of Alec Guinness to hide his features behind the art of the make-up man led critic Kenneth Tynan to write that 'were Guinness to commit murder I have no doubt that the number of false arrests following the circulation of his description would break all records'. His real features were much more apparent in his Oscar-winning role of Colonel Nicholson in *The Bridge on the River Kwai*, just as they were in his three nominated roles – as the meek little Lavender Hill bank clerk who plans a bullion robbery, the old Jedi knight Obi-Wan Kenobi, and the debtor condemned to the Marshalsea in *Little Dorrit*. The two glaring omissions from his nominations list (perhaps the figure should be nine) are his eight members of the D'Ascoyne family bumped off by Dennis Price in *Kind Hearts and Coronets* and his brilliant portrait of Fagin in *Oliver Twist*. A quiet, subtle actor who at times does not appear to be acting at all, he was a long-time favourite of director David Lean. He earned a best screenplay nomination for his 1958 adaptation of *The Horse's Mouth* and in 1979 was awarded an honorary Oscar for 'advancing the art of screen acting'.

Edmund Gwenn

Born Glamorgan, Wales, 26 September 1875; died 1959

Oscars (1): Best Supporting Actor for Kris Kringle in *The Miracle on 34th Street* (20th Century-Fox, 1947)

Oscar Nominations (1): Best Supporting Actor for Skipper in *Mister 880* (20th Century-Fox, 1950)

Everyone's favourite Santa Claus, Edmund Gwenn won his Oscar for teasing his audience into believing that he might in fact be the real thing and not just a hired hand for Macy's department store at Christmas time. Most of his competitors in the 1947 Oscar race were tough guys – newcomer Richard Widmark, Robert Ryan, Thomas Gomez. None, though, was a match for Gwenn, who added to his laurels three years later with another nomination, this time for his benevolent little forger *Mister 880*. Mostly a genial old man in movies (he was often seen as quietly spoken college professors and clergymen), he also had his nastier side. A more cold, calculating little villain than his assassin in Hitchcock's *Foreign Correspondent* would be hard to find. The fact that he plunged to his death from Westminster Cathedral troubled no one.

H

Joan Hackett

Born New York City, USA, 1 May 1942; died 1983

Oscar Nominations (1): Best Supporting Actress for Toby Landau in *Only When I Laugh* (Columbia, 1981)

More of a stage actress than a movie star, the cool, intelligent Joan Hackett never really seemed at home in movies, even though she got off to a good start as the young Bostonian Dottie, one of Mary McCarthy's *The Group*. Neil Simon's reworking of his play *The Gingerbread Man* did the trick as far as the Academy was concerned, earning her some of the author's best lines and a nomination for her tart-tongued, determined-to-be-glamorous best friend of Marsha Mason. No Oscar, though, which was a pity. That went to veteran Maureen Stapleton for *Reds*. A former fashion model who subsequently studied with Lee Strasberg, Joan Hackett died of cancer just a year after the Oscar ceremony at the age of forty-one.

Gene Hackman

Born San Bernardino, California, USA, 30 January 1931

Oscars (2): Best Actor for Jimmy 'Popeye' Doyle in *The French Connection* (20th Century-Fox, 1971); Best Supporting Actor for Sheriff 'Little Bill' Daggett in *Unforgiven* (Warner Bros, 1992)

Oscar Nominations (3): Best Supporting Actor for Buck Barrow in *Bonnie and Clyde* (Warner Bros, 1967) and Gene Garrison in *I Never Sang for My Father* (Columbia, 1970); Best Actor for Rupert Anderson in *Mississippi Burning* (Orion, 1988)

No one has yet quite managed to put a finger on what it is that makes Gene Hackman such a distinguished and dependable actor. Versatility is probably the answer, for he's as effective as western villains and shady lawyers as

Fredric March as fading movie star Norman Maine and Janet Gaynor – in her last screen role before her retirement – as rising young hopeful Vicki Lester in the 1937 version of *A Star Is Born* (United Artists). Both were nominated, neither won

The inimitable Judy in Warner's 1954 *A Star Is Born* remake. Like her predecessor a loser for her Vicki Lester, she was nominated twice by the Academy but never won a competitive Oscar

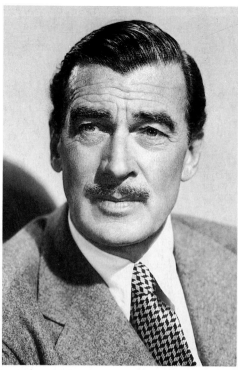

MGM's 'A' team of the 1940s: Greer Garson and Walter Pidgeon, who appeared in eight movies together at the studio. Seven-time nominee Garson was named best actress for her Mrs Miniver; Pidgeon was nominated for his roles in *Mrs Miniver* and *Madame Curie*

Raw recruit Richard Gere gets the treatment in *An Officer and a Gentleman* (Paramount, 1982). No Oscar for him but reward for the guy doing the hosing down, Louis Gossett Jr., who won as best supporting actor of the year

The search for the black bird. Elisha Cook, Sydney Greenstreet and Bogie at odds in John Huston's *The Maltese Falcon* (Warner Bros, 1941). The Oscar nominee from the trio? The untrustworthy man in the centre, outwardly civilised, inwardly obsessed

Stubbornness versus insanity: Sessue Hayakawa as the Japanese PoW commandant and Oscar-winner Alec Guinness as Colonel Nicholson in David Lean's 1957 epic *The Bridge on the River Kwai* (Columbia)

Girl gets cake! Gene Kelly (*left*), Donald O'Connor (*right*) and behind the mess in the centre – Jean Hagen, nominated but not a winner for her squeaky voiced silent movie queen Lina Lamont. The film, of course, *Singin' in the Rain* (MGM, 1952)

Tom Hanks on the way to his second consecutive Oscar as much-loved simple guy Forrest Gump (Paramount, 1994). With him in this scene: supporting nominee Gary Sinise whose life is saved by Gump in Vietnam

George III on an off day. Nigel Hawthorne repeating his stage portrayal in the film version of *The Madness of King George* (Close Call Films Production/ Samuel Goldwyn/ Channel Four). Alas no Oscar: 1994 was Tom Hanks' year

And to think Truman Capote wanted Marilyn Monroe for the part! Audrey Hepburn in one of her five Oscar nominated roles as 'super-tramp' Holly Golightly in *Breakfast at Tiffany's* (Paramount, 1961)

Judy Holliday, one of the few comediennes to win as best actress at Oscar time. The year, 1950; the film, *Born Yesterday* (Columbia); her co-star, William Holden

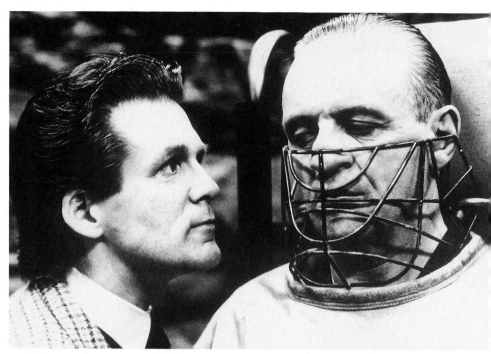

Not the man to taunt too much: Oscar-winner Anthony Hopkins waits his turn as Hannibal Lecter in *The Silence of the Lambs* (Orion, 1991)

Oscar winners both: Holly Hunter as determined Scottish mother Ada McGrath and eleven-year-old Anna Paquin as her daughter finding a new life in nineteenth century New Zealand in *The Piano* (Miramax, 1993)

Best actor Jeremy Irons, ice cool as European aristocrat Claus Von Bulow accused of murder in *Reversal of Fortune* (Reversal Films/Warner Bros, 1990). Pictured with him here, Christine Baranski as Bulow's mistress Andrea Reynolds

Unforgettable! Sally Kellerman as Major 'Hot Lips' Houlihan, the luckless butt of all the male jokes in Robert Altman's *M·A·S·H* (20th Century-Fox, 1970). A best supporting actress nominee, she lost to Helen Hayes' little stowaway in *Airport*

Six nominations but no awards for Deborah Kerr although she came close for her promiscuous wife in the 1953 hit *From Here to Eternity* (Columbia). Pursuing her in this famous scene, fellow *Eternity* nominee Burt Lancaster

Partners in crime. Jamie Lee Curtis, who promised the sexual attractions, and Oscar-winner Kevin Kline, who provided the maniacal jealousy in the zany heist romp *A Fish Called Wanda* (MGM, 1988)

he is with cops, family men, rejected lovers and surveillance men about to come apart at the seams. Twice an Oscar-winner, first for his tough New York cop forever chasing Frog One and then for his sadistic western sheriff 'Little Bill' Daggett, he has also been up for his FBI man investigating the disappearance of three civil rights workers in *Mississippi Burning* and for two earlier supporting roles – Warren Beatty's reckless brother in *Bonnie and Clyde* and the forty-year-old son trying to care for his elderly parent in *I Never Sang for My Father*. Still only in his sixties, he might yet take his Oscar tally to three, something no actor has yet accomplished. Not without a sense of humour, he once replied to the question 'Why did you want to play the villain in *Superman*?' with 'You mean besides the two million dollars?'

Jean Hagen

Born Chicago, USA, 3 August 1923; died 1977

Oscar Nominations (1): Best Supporting Actress for Lina Lamont in *Singin' in the Rain* (MGM, 1952)

Just how did she lose? It's a question that often arises when people get round to discussing the unluckiest Oscar nominees of all time. But lose Hagen did, and her classic, squeaky-voiced silent movie queen Lina Lamont went unrecognised apart from a nomination. Her famous line, 'What do you think I am, dumb or something?' applied more to the Academy voters of 1952, who opted instead for Gloria Grahame's twittery Southern belle in *The Bad and the Beautiful*. An unlucky performer throughout her career, Hagen was also overlooked (not even a nomination) for her devoted gangster's moll in Huston's *The Asphalt Jungle*. The best of her later roles were her two-timing Hollywood wife in Aldrich's *The Big Knife* and her secretary of President Franklin Roosevelt in *Sunrise at Campobello*. She made just nineteen films in her career which ended in 1964. She died from throat cancer in 1977 at the age of fifty-four.

Grayson Hall

Born 1927; died 1985

Oscar Nominations (1): Best Supporting Actress for Judith Fellowes in *The Night of the Iguana* (Seven Arts, 1964)

The cast of *The Night of the Iguana* included Richard Burton, Ava Gardner and Deborah Kerr, but it was one of the film's lesser-known players, stage actress Grayson Hall, who took the Academy honours for her vindictive schoolteacher who determines to bring defrocked priest Richard Burton to book for dallying too long with young schoolmarm Sue Lyon, either because she wants Mr B for herself or because she wants Miss Lyon. All the spite and repression didn't pay dividends on Oscar night; Lila Kedrova won the year's supporting nod for her tender portrait of the ageing French prostitute in *Zorba the Greek*.

Tom Hanks

Born Concord, California, USA, 9 July 1956

Oscars (2): Best Actor for Andrew Beckett in *Philadelphia* (TriStar, 1993) and for the title role in *Forrest Gump* (Paramount, 1994)

Oscar Nominations (1): Best Actor for Josh Baskin in *Big* (20th Century-Fox, 1988)

You have to be a good picker as well as a good actor to stay on top of the precarious world of modern-day film-making. In recent years Tom Hanks has been just that, becoming the first actor since Spencer Tracy (see p. 348) to win the major award in consecutive years. Despite the quality of his Oscar-winning performances as the Aids victim in *Philadelphia* and the good-hearted simpleton Forrest Gump, it was his earlier nominated role in *Big* – as the thirteen-year-old kid who suddenly finds himself in the body of a thirty-five-year-old man – that best demonstrated his versatility as a performer. Most recently seen as astronaut Jim Lovell in *Apollo 13*, he has overcome such earlier 'bad picks' as *Joe Versus the Volcano* and *Bonfire of the Vanities*.

☆

Ann Harding

Born Fort Sam Houston, Texas, USA, 7 August 1901; died 1981

Oscar Nominations (1): Best Actress for Linda Seton in *Holiday* (Pathe, 1930/31)

Too many tear-jerkers and too many gentle, noble ladies was the verdict of many on Ann Harding's screen career, which was a little unfair in that in the thirties movie stars did what they were told and played the roles for which they were most suited, in both looks and demeanour. Her one Oscar chance came in *Holiday* when she broke the mould for once as the unconventional sister of Mary Astor, stealing Astor's would-be husband and making the most of all the opportunities that came her way. Katie Hepburn reprised the role in the more famous remake of 1938; the more down-to-earth Marie Dressler won the 1930/31 Oscar for *Min and Bill*.

Tess Harper

Born Mammoth Springs, Arkansas, USA, 1952

Oscar Nominations (1): Best Supporting Actress for Chick Boyle in *Crimes of the Heart* (De Laurentiis Entertainment Group, 1986)

If you're showing how three sisters try to come to terms with themselves and get rid of a few pent-up emotions and resentments during a family reunion, you need a little bit of humour to brighten things up every now and then. Tess Harper provided it in *Crimes of the Heart* as the nosy neighbour and family cousin Chick Boyle. It earned her a nomination but she lost to Dianne Wiest who in *Hannah and Her Sisters* was trying to come to terms with herself and rid herself of a few pent-up emotions and resentments, etc. etc. Ah well. No nominations for Harper since, although she was unlucky to miss out for her Vietnam war widow in Bruce Beresford's earlier *Tender Mercies*.

Barbara Harris

Born Evanston, Illinois, USA, 25 July 1935

Oscar Nominations (1): Best Supporting Actress for Allison in *Who Is Harry Kellerman and Why Is He Saying Those Terrible Things About Me?* (Cinema Centre/National General, 1971)

It comes as a bit of a surprise to learn that Barbara Harris earned a nomination at Oscar time. The mind searches for the name of the movie. Hitchcock's *Family Plot*, in which she played a fake medium? Altman's *Nashville*, in which she was a scatterbrained country girl on the run from marriage? Coppola's *Peggy Sue Got Married?* None of these. Instead a film that is now almost (some would say totally) forgotten, *Who Is Harry Kellerman and Why Is He, etc. etc.* Dustin Hoffman starred as a not-quite-right-in-the-head rock composer. Barbara Harris played his would-be singer girlfriend. She didn't win the award. It made absolutely no difference to her subsequent career.

Ed Harris

Born Tenafly, New Jersey, USA, 28 November 1950

Oscar Nominations (1): Best Supporting Actor for Gene Kranz in *Apollo 13* (Universal, 1995)

He received nothing for his portrait of John Glenn in *The Right Stuff* but he did manage a nomination more than a decade later for his chain-smoking flight director whose job it was to bring back alive the three astronauts marooned in outer space in *Apollo 13*. He managed it, of course, as history relates; on Oscar night, however, no one seemed to appreciate his sterling efforts, preferring crime to heroism and Kevin Spacey in *The Usual Suspects*. Perhaps a role in a third space movie sometime in the next ten years might eventually do the trick.

☆

Julie Harris

Born Grosse Pointe, Michigan, USA, 2 December 1925

Oscar Nominations (1): Best Actress for Frankie Adams in *The Member of the Wedding* (Columbia, 1952)

Seemingly born to play sensitive, subtle roles and characters in various stages of anguish, neurosis and almost total breakdown, the thin, sad-faced Julie Harris entered the Oscar lists just the once – for repeating her remarkable Broadway portrayal of a twelve-year-old girl approaching adolescence and growing up in the deep South in *The Member of the Wedding*. Her complex role as the troubled lover of both Dean and Richard Davalos in *East of Eden*, her all-but-forgotten straight portrayal of Sally Bowles in *I Am a Camera* and her terrified spinster in *The Haunting* were followed during the eighties by a somewhat less demanding supporting part in the long-running TV soap opera, *Knots Landing*.

Richard Harris

Born Limerick, Ireland, 1 October 1930

Oscar Nominations (2): Best Actor for Frank Machin in *This Sporting Life* (Independent Artists, British, 1963) and 'Bull' McCabe in *The Field* (Granada/Avenue Pictures, 1990)

A hellraiser who made the front pages as much for his off-screen exploits as for his film appearances, Richard Harris was by far the most explosive of the British new-wave actors of the sixties. Nominated for his ex-colliery worker in torment over his relationship with passionless widow Rachel Roberts, he reached the Academy lists again some twenty-seven years later for his stubborn Irish farmer in *The Field*. He lost on both occasions; worse, he didn't even rate a nomination for arguably his most moving role, that of the melancholy King Arthur, who for four enchanting minutes in *Camelot* sings wistfully: 'How to Handle a Woman'.

Rosemary Harris

Born Ashby, Suffolk, England, 19 September 1930

Oscar Nominations (1): Best Supporting Actress for Rose Haigh-Wood in *Tom and Viv* (Miramax, 1994)

The Academy has tended to shower the Brits with nominations in recent years, not least those stage actresses whose roles fall into the supporting categories and who appear on screen only occasionally. Rosemary Harris deservedly found her way into 1994's nominated five for her quiet, understanding mother of disturbed socialite Vivienne Haigh-Wood in *Tom and Viv*. She enjoyed just a scene or two at the film's beginning, and the same at its close, but they made all the difference to a picture that had more than its fair share of pallid moments. Dianne Wiest made it to the podium in March 1995 for her *grande dame* leading lady in *Bullets Over Broadway*.

Rex Harrison

Born Huyton, Merseyside, England, 5 March 1908; died 1990

Oscars (1): Best Actor for Professor Henry Higgins in *My Fair Lady* (Warner Bros, 1964)

Oscar Nominations (1): Best Actor for Julius Caesar in *Cleopatra* (20th Century-Fox, 1963)

Often referred to in the gossip columns as 'sexy Rexy', Rex Harrison was not only close to perfection as the debonair, silver-tongued charmer, he was also near to being as selfish and bad-tempered in real life as he was on stage and screen. Margaret Lockwood had it about right in Carol Reed's *Night Train to Munich* when she tells him: 'If you ever loved a woman the way you love yourself it would be one of the great romances of history.' A winner (inevitably) for his Professor Higgins in *My Fair Lady*, he was also nominated a year earlier for his Caesar in Joe Mankiewicz's *Cleopatra*. Described by one critic as 'the tweedy sophisticate with just a dash of the misogynist to intrigue and challenge women', he was married six times. His early Hollywood career in the late forties was ruined when he became involved with Fox starlet Carole Landis, who committed suicide because of their affair.

Elizabeth Hartman

Born Youngstown, Ohio, USA, 23 December 1941; died 1987

Oscar Nominations (1): Best Actress for Selina D'Arcey in *A Patch of Blue* (MGM, 1965)

Acclaimed as one of the more interesting new faces of the sixties, the frail, sensitive Elizabeth Hartman earned an Oscar nomination for her very first film role – as the eighteen-year-old blind girl in love with Sidney Poitier in *A Patch of Blue*. Had she won the award rather than just a nomination it might just have made a difference to her subsequent career which, although it included roles for Lumet in *The Group* and Coppola in *You're a Big Boy Now*, failed to build on her early promise. Fragile and highly strung, and depressed over the lack of film offers, she underwent psychiatric treatment in Pittsburgh, where she did voluntary work at the Carnegie Museum. She died in 1987 when she fell from her fifth-floor apartment, an apparent suicide.

Laurence Harvey

Born Yomishkis, Lithuania, 1 October 1928; died 1973

Oscar Nominations (1): Best Actor for Joe Lampton in *Room at the Top* (Romulus, 1959)

At his best as a smarmy louse with charm, Laurence Harvey could either be reptilian among the decadent élite, as in John Schlesinger's *Darling*, or ruthless among the working class, as the social-climbing Joe Lampton in *Room at the Top*. Oscar-nominated for the latter role – but somewhat dwarfed on awards night by the physical size of Charlton Heston's three-hour forty-minute job as Ben-Hur – he was a regular in Hollywood during the sixties, even though his arrogant manner did not always go down too well with his colleagues. After starring with him in the steamy Southern drama *A Walk on the Wild Side*, Jane Fonda remarked: 'There are actors and actors – and then there are the Laurence Harveys. With them it's like acting by yourself.' None of which upset Harvey in any way. He said: 'Someone once asked me, "Why is it so many people hate you?" and I said, "Do they?

How super. I'm really quite pleased about it." ' Of Jewish Lithuanian parentage, Harvey appeared in more than forty films. He was at his most effective as the brainwashed assassin in *The Manchurian Candidate*.

Goldie Hawn

Born Washington, DC, USA, 21 November 1945

Oscars (1): Best Supporting Actress for Toni Simmons in *Cactus Flower* (Columbia, 1969)

Oscar Nominations (1): Best Actress for Judy Benjamin in *Private Benjamin* (Warner Bros, 1980)

Terrific on TV in the zany *Laugh-In*, when she donned a bikini and demonstrated a giggling sense of humour and a quite unique talent for scatterbrained comedy, Goldie Hawn hasn't been quite so terrific in the years that have followed, despite winning an Oscar for just her second role – as Walter Matthau's young mistress in *Cactus Flower*. Still, there's no denying there have been plenty of laughs along the way, some goodish but not great comedies and another nomination for her well-to-do Jewish girl who joins the army in *Private Benjamin*. If only Billy Wilder had written and directed a film especially for her, as he promised to do, things might have been even better.

Nigel Hawthorne

Born Coventry, England, 5 April 1929

Oscar Nominations (1): Best Actor for King George III in *The Madness of King George* (Close Call Films/Samuel Goldwyn Company/Channel Four, 1994)

Nineteen ninety-four was Gumpy year, and anyone who was up against Tom Hanks' likeable simpleton was really on a hiding to nothing, as Nigel Hawthorne discovered when he reprised for the screen his stage role of George III, the British monarch who fell victim to a terrible illness that rendered him irrational. Early in the decade, British actors could do no wrong, winning the best actor award in three consecutive years. In 1994 the luck ran out, and for Hawthorne it was back to the stage and the telly and memories of starring opposite Sylvester Stallone in *Demolition Man*.

Sessue Hayakawa

Born Nanaura, Chiba, Japan, 10 June 1889; died 1973

Oscar Nominations (1): Best Supporting Actor for Colonel Saito in *The Bridge on the River Kwai* (Columbia, 1957)

A new face to younger filmgoers in the fifties when he was Oscar-nominated for his Japanese prison camp commandant in *The Bridge on the River Kwai*, Sessue Hayakawa hailed back to the silent days, when he was an exotic leading man in over a hundred films, lived in the Hollywood fast lane, and earned $7,500 a week, gambling regularly at Monte Carlo, where it was said he once lost $965,000 in one night! His career declined with the coming of sound but revived briefly in the fifties when he appeared with Bogart in *Tokyo Joe* and Claudette Colbert in *Three Came Home*. He ended his days in a modest five-room bungalow in an unfashionable suburb of Tokyo, where he taught acting and devoted his time to Zen Buddhism.

Helen Hayes

Born Washington, DC, USA, 10 October 1900; died 1993

Oscars (2): Best Actress for the title role in *The Sin of Madelon Claudet* (MGM, 1931/32); Best Supporting Actress for Ada Quonsett in *Airport* (Universal, 1970)

Helen Hayes had two goes at Hollywood; the first, despite an Academy Award for her self-sacrificing mother with an illegitimate son, was a disaster, and she returned to Broadway with the MGM verdict 'no sex appeal' around her neck. The second, when she was in her seventies, was rather more fun, bringing with it yet another Oscar for her aged stowaway in *Airport* and a long line of mischievous, diminutive old ladies who got up to all kinds of tricks at the Disney studio. Married to playwright-screenwriter Charles MacArthur, her career spanned more than eighty years. In addition to her Oscars, she won two Tony awards and an Emmy for her TV work.

Susan Hayward

Born Brooklyn, New York, USA, 30 June 1918; died 1975

Oscars (1): Best Actress for Barbara Graham in *I Want to Live* (United Artists, 1958)

Oscar Nominations (4): Best Actress for Angie Evans in *Smash Up – The Story of a Woman* (Universal International, 1947), Eloise Winters in *My Foolish Heart* (Goldwyn, RKO, 1949), Jane Froman in *With a Song in My Heart* (20th Century-Fox, 1952) and Lillian Roth in *I'll Cry Tomorrow* (MGM, 1955)

My, how she suffered, but she got there in the end – on 6 April 1959 to be precise – when she at last clutched her Oscar for her remarkable portrait of the petty criminal Barbara Graham, executed in the gas chamber in *I Want to Live*. It was a fitting climax to a fiery career that had included four earlier nominations, all of them for sufferers of one kind or another – her alcoholic in *Smash Up*, unmarried mother in *My Foolish Heart*, crippled singer Jane Froman and on-the-skids entertainer Lillian Roth. Described by one critic as 'not so much an actress, more a Stanwyck-like star who was good, gutsy, entertaining fun', she enjoyed (and endured) a private life that at times was every bit as dramatic as those she played on screen – two husbands, a custody battle over twin boys and a suicide attempt. A seizure resulting from a brain tumour from which she had been suffering for two years led to her early death at the age of fifty-seven.

Eileen Heckart

Born Columbus, Ohio, USA, 29 March 1919

Oscars (1): Best Supporting Actress for Mrs Baker in *Butterflies Are Free* (Columbia, 1972)

Oscar Nominations (1): Best Supporting Actress for Mrs Daigle in *The Bad Seed* (Warner Bros, 1956)

An award a decade seemed to be Eileen Heckart's way of going about things as far as acting honours were concerned: the Drama Critics Award in the fifties for her role in *The Dark at the Top of the Stairs*, a TV Emmy in the sixties for *Win Me a Place at Forest Lawn*, and the Oscar in the seventies for her possessive mother of blind musician Edward Albert, determined to make a go of it on his own and without Heckart's help in *Butterflies Are Free*. She might have won back in 1956 for her alcoholic mother of one of Patty McCormack's victims in *The Bad Seed*, but that was the year when Dorothy Malone was flouncing about all over the place as a nymphomaniac in *Written on the Wind* and when sexual need won out over alcoholism and murder!

Van Heflin

Born Walters, Oklahoma, USA, 13 December 1910; died 1971

Oscars (1): Best Supporting Actor for Jeff Hartnett in *Johnny Eager* (MGM, 1942)

Self-deprecating about his acting and the way he appeared on screen ('I just didn't have the looks and if I didn't do a good acting job I looked terrible'), Van Heflin nonetheless won an Academy Award early in his career for his scholarly, Shakespeare-quoting sidekick of racketeer Robert Taylor in *Johnny Eager*. Later, the shy, slightly crooked smile, hesitant speech and determined personality were seen to rather better effect, especially as the crooked cop in Losey's *The Prowler* and homesteader Joe Starrett in the epic western *Shane*. Never again close to an Oscar nomination, he died after being found unconscious, clinging to the ladder of his swimming pool. He never recovered from his coma, which lasted for several weeks.

Mariel Hemingway

Born Ketchum, Idaho, USA, 22 November 1961

Oscar Nominations (1): Best Supporting Actress for Tracy in *Manhattan* (United Artists, 1979)

Get yourself a role in a Woody Allen movie and you have about a one-in-three chance of an Oscar nomination. Not Allen's own assessment (his antipathy towards the awards is well known) but, in general, the way things have worked out over the years. Mariel Hemingway was among the first of the Allen nominees, earning a supporting nod for her teenage drama student living with Woody's fed-up TV comedy writer in *Manhattan*. Appealing though she was, her luck was out on Oscar night, Meryl Streep taking the award for her battles with Dustin Hoffman and son in *Kramer vs. Kramer*. A granddaughter of Ernest Hemingway, she is most famous for her portrayal of *Playboy* centrefold Dorothy Stratten in Bob Fosse's *Star 80*.

Justin Henry

Born Rye, New York, USA, 25 May 1971

Oscar Nominations (1): Best Supporting Actor for Billy Kramer in *Kramer vs. Kramer* (Columbia, 1979)

Memorable in the scene when he does everything Dustin Hoffman tells him not to do ('If you touch that you're in *big* trouble') and gets away with it – almost – Justin Henry proved himself one of the most appealing child actors of the seventies. Had he won in the supporting category (he was just eight years old at the time) he would have become the youngest-ever Oscar winner. As it was, Melvyn Douglas, at seventy-nine ten times his age, won for *Being There*, and Meryl Streep and Hoffman took the *Kramer* awards for playing Justin's screen mom and dad.

Audrey Hepburn

Born near Brussels, Belgium, 4 May 1929; died 1993

Oscars (1): Best Actress for Princess Anne in *Roman Holiday* (Paramount, 1953)

Oscar Nominations (4): Best Actress for Sabrina Fairchild in *Sabrina* (Paramount, 1954); Sister Luke in *The Nun's Story* (Warner Bros, 1959); Holly Golightly in *Breakfast at Tiffany's* (Paramount, 1961) and Susy Hendrix in *Wait Until Dark* (Warner Bros, 1967)

As the runaway princess who enjoys the eternal city with journalist Gregory Peck, Audrey Hepburn earned her Oscar (at the age of twenty-three) for her very first starring role. Thereafter she was never far from Academy consideration, earning mentions for her chauffeur's daughter in love with William Holden, her novice nun who renounces her vows, and her New York 'supertramp' Holly Golightly. She won her final nomination for her blind woman terrorised by thieves in Terence Young's edge-of-the-seat thriller *Wait Until Dark*. Her waif-like vulnerability, huge dark eyes and elfin smile attracted her to many of Hollywood's leading directors, several of whom worked with her on more than one occasion – William Wyler (three times), Stanley Donen (three), Billy Wilder (twice). A long-serving goodwill ambassador for the United Nations Children's Fund, she received a posthumous Academy Award on behalf of the children of the world. Her last role, perhaps appropriately, was that of an angel in Spielberg's *Always*.

Katharine Hepburn

Born Hartford, Connecticut, USA, 9 November 1907

Oscars (4): Best Actress for Eva Lovelace in *Morning Glory* (RKO, 1932/33), Christina Drayton in *Guess Who's Coming to Dinner?* (Columbia, 1967), Eleanor of Aquitaine in *The Lion in Winter* (Avco Embassy, 1968), and Ethel Thayer in *On Golden Pond* (IPC Films/ITC/Universal, 1981)

Oscar Nominations (8): Best Actress for the title role of *Alice Adams* (RKO, 1935), Tracy Lord in *The Philadelphia Story* (MGM, 1940), Tess Harding in *Woman of the Year* (MGM, 1942), Rose Sayer in *The African Queen* (Horizon/United Artists, 1951), Jane Hudson in *Summertime* (United Artists, 1955), Lizzie Curry in *The Rainmaker* (Paramount, 1956), Mrs Venable in *Suddenly, Last Summer* (Columbia, 1959) and Mary Tyrone in *Long Day's Journey into Night* (Landau/Embassy, 1962)

'Box-office poison!' cried exhibitors whenever Katie Hepburn's name shone out above the marquee. 'Oscar delight,' chorused the Academy voters, who honoured her four times as the year's best and then nominated her on a further eight occasions, making her the most honoured Oscar actress of all time. Her best roles? Ironically, those for which she was nominated but not victorious – her spoiled heiress in *The Philadelphia Story*, international correspondent Tess Harding, missionary helping Bogie navigate the rapids in *The African Queen* and lonely spinster who finds love in Venice in David Lean's *Summertime*. Partnered in real life (and nine times on screen) by Spencer Tracy, she received her second Oscar, for *Guess Who's Coming to Dinner?*, some ten months after Tracy's death. 'Did Mr Tracy get one too?' she asked when told the news. 'No, Miss Hepburn,' said the journalist. 'That's all right,' she replied. 'Mine's for both of us.' Her winning roles: the stagestruck young actress in *Morning Glory*, her liberal-minded wife of Spence in *Guess Who's Coming to Dinner?*, the squabbling Eleanor of Aquitaine, and the wife of retired professor Henry Fonda in *On Golden Pond*. Her remaining nominations: the ambitious, social climbing Alice Adams, the spinster charmed by a con man in *The Rainmaker*, the devouring mother anxious for Elizabeth Taylor to have a lobotomy (and for good reason) in *Suddenly, Last Summer*, and her tortured, drug-addicted mother in O'Neill's *Long Day's Journey into Night*.

Charlton Heston

Born Evanston, Illinois, USA, 4 October 1923

Oscars (1): Best Actor for Judah Ben-Hur in *Ben-Hur* (MGM, 1959)

'The epic is the easiest kind of film to make badly,' said Charlton Heston of the genre that helped make him an international star. It also helped earn him his only Oscar, as Judah Ben-Hur, the Jewish prince who vows revenge on the boyhood friend who has wronged him and ultimately battles it out to the death in the chariot race in the Circus Maximus. A star of more epics than any other actor, he appeared as Moses for DeMille, spent *55 Days at Peking*, was murdered as Gordon in Khartoum, painted the ceiling of the Sistine Chapel and rode into legend in *El Cid*. A fine raconteur, he enjoys recalling how he broke into the big time at Paramount by waving at Cecil B. DeMille (whom he had never met) as he drove out of the studio gates. DeMille asked his secretary: 'Who is that young man?' She checked her notebook and replied: 'A young actor named Charlton Heston. He made a test. You didn't like it.' 'No,' mused DeMille, 'but I liked the way he waved.' A star was born!

William Hickey

Born Brooklyn, New York, USA, 1928

Oscar Nominations (1): Best Supporting Actor for Don Corrado Prizzi in *Prizzi's Honor* (ABC/20th Century-Fox, 1985)

A thin, almost skeletal character actor who has popped up briefly in the odd scene or two in such recent films as *Sea of Love* and *The Name of the Rose*,

William Hickey scored a bull's-eye in 1985 with his portrait of the devilish octogenarian head of a Sicilian Mafia family. The film was *Prizzi's Honor*, the director was John Huston. The New York Critics loved it, the Academy less so. Only Anjelica Huston (see p. 177) took anything from its eight nominations. Hickey came in behind Don Ameche's rejuvenated crumbly in *Cocoon*.

Wendy Hiller

Born Bramshall, Cheshire, England, 15 August 1912

Oscars (1): Best Supporting Actress for Miss Pat Cooper in *Separate Tables* (United Artists, 1958)

Oscar Nominations (2): Best Actress for Eliza Doolittle in *Pygmalion* (MGM, British, 1938); Best Supporting Actress for Alice More in *A Man for All Seasons* (Columbia, 1966)

Eliza Doolittle has never been a lucky role as far as the Oscars are concerned. The captivating Wendy Hiller – the first British actress to be nominated for a performance in a British film – came in behind Bette Davis' *Jezebel* in 1938, and a quarter of a century later Audrey Hepburn didn't even rate a nomination for *My Fair Lady*. Justice was eventually done in Hiller's case when she earned a supporting award for her moving performance as the lonely proprietress of an English seaside hotel in *Separate Tables*. She was also nominated in 1966 for her portrait of the wife of Sir Thomas More. No mentions, though, for her Salvation Army lass *Major Barbara* or her young socialite who finds romance on an island in the Hebrides in the Powell/Pressburger classic *I Know Where I'm Going*.

Judd Hirsch

Born New York City, USA, 15 March 1935

Oscar Nominations (1): Best Supporting Actor for Dr Tyrone Berger in *Ordinary People* (Paramount, 1980)

If *Taxi* had been made into a movie, Judd Hirsch would probably have been trotting up to the podium to receive an Oscar as best actor of the year. TV adaptations, however, were less popular back in the late seventies, and Hirsch has so far had to be content with just the one Academy nod for his psychiatrist treating troubled teenager Timothy Hutton in Redford's *Ordinary People*. He completed the role during a ten-day break between episodes of *Taxi* when Gene Hackman had to call off at the last minute. He lost in March 1981 to his screen patient Hutton! Primarily a television performer – in both comedy series and TV movies – he was unlucky to miss out on a second nomination, for his sixties radical on the run with his family from the FBI in Lumet's *Running on Empty*.

Dustin Hoffman

Born Los Angeles, USA, 8 August 1937

Oscars (2): Best Actor for Ted Kramer in *Kramer vs. Kramer* (Columbia, 1979) and Raymond Babbitt in *Rain Man* (United Artists, 1988)

Oscar Nominations (4): Best Actor for Ben Braddock in *The Graduate* (Embassy, 1967), Enrico 'Ratso' Rizzo in *Midnight Cowboy* (United Artists, 1969), Lenny Bruce in *Lenny* (United Artists, 1974) and Michael Dorsey/Dorothy Michaels in *Tootsie* (Columbia, 1982)

Perhaps the most startling statistic about Dustin Hoffman's early career is that he was thirty and Anne Bancroft thirty-six when she seduced him in *The Graduate*; the biggest surprise is that he didn't make it to the Oscar podium until 1979, having earned additional nominations for his shuffling little tubercular hustler 'Ratso' Rizzo and his no-holds-barred portrait of stand-up comedian Lenny Bruce. A winner for his workaholic father left by Meryl Streep to care for his young son in *Kramer vs. Kramer* and subsequently for his autistic savant in *Rain Man*, he was nominated but overlooked for what many regard as their favourite Hoffman role; the out-of-work actor who takes to women's clothing and becomes the TV soap superstar, *Tootsie*.

William Holden

Born O'Fallon, Illinois, USA, 17 April 1918; died 1981

Oscars (1): Best Actor for Sefton in *Stalag 17* (Paramount, 1953)

Oscar Nominations (2): Best Actor for Joe Gillis in *Sunset Boulevard* (Paramount, 1950) and Max Schumacher in *Network* (United Artists, 1976)

When visited on the set by a journalist, Bill Holden revealed that he had cured his sleeping problem. 'I've found the greatest sleeping pill in the world,' he laughed, 'this script!' The name of the film remains unknown. The only certainty is that it wasn't one by writer-director Billy Wilder, whose casting of Holden as Gloria Swanson's gigolo (after Montgomery Clift had turned down the role at the last minute) in *Sunset Boulevard* paved the way for Holden's stardom and eventually his Oscar as the cynical PoW in Wilder's *Stalag 17*. His similar role in David Lean's subsequent *The Bridge on the River Kwai* brought him one of the best deals in movies: a $300,000 fee plus 10 per cent of the gross, paid at a maximum rate of $50,000 a year for the rest of his life. Twice more a star for Wilder (*Sabrina*, *Fedora*), he earned his last nomination for his TV news executive involved with Faye Dunaway in *Network*. He died in his Santa Monica apartment after slipping and striking his head on a bedroom table. He was not found for four days.

Judy Holliday

Born New York City, USA, 21 June 1922; died 1965

Oscars (1): Best Actress for Billie Dawn in *Born Yesterday* (Columbia, 1950)

'Do me a favour, will ya, Harry? Drop dead!' The words still bring a smile, even though they were first uttered nearly fifty years ago, by one of the most delightful and intelligent dumb blondes ever to make it to the screen. Her film career lasted for just ten years (during which time her Columbia boss Harry Cohn didn't know what to do with her), beginning with her Oscar and ending with the musical *Bells Are Ringing*. A star of just seven movies, she always maintained that she was not 'the Hollywood type' and returned to New York whenever the first plane was available. As for being dumb? Her IQ was 172. She died of cancer at the much too early age of forty-two.

Stanley Holloway

Born London, England, 1 October 1890; died 1982

Oscar Nominations (1): Best Supporting Actor for Alfred Doolittle in *My Fair Lady* (Warner Bros, 1964)

'Wiv a Little Bit of Luck' he might have made it! Alas, the competition was too strong (literally) in the form of Peter Ustinov, who won the 1964 award for his strong-armed Arthur Simpson in the light-hearted heist movie, *Topkapi*. Instead, Stanley Holloway had to be content with just a nomination for his Alfred Doolittle, which although not the ultimate reward was at least rather more than Wilfrid Lawson achieved for the same role in the straight version of *Pygmalion* in 1938. Long a favourite of the British stage and music halls, the always genial and hearty Stan featured in more than seventy films and was nominated just the once, although the Academy should perhaps have looked more closely at his jovial station attendant constantly chatting up the haughty Joyce Carey in *Brief Encounter*, and Alec Guinness' partner in crime in *The Lavender Hill Mob*.

Celeste Holm

Born New York City, USA, 29 April 1919

Oscars (1): Best Supporting Actress for Anne Detrie in *Gentleman's Agreement* (20th Century-Fox, 1947)

Oscar Nominations (2): Best Supporting Actress for Sister Scolastica in *Come to the Stable* (20th Century-Fox, 1949) and Karen Richards in *All About Eve* (20th Century-Fox, 1950)

'You see, girls, I've run off with one of your husbands,' coos the off-screen voice of Celeste Holm as the small-town vamp Addie Ross in *A Letter to Three Wives*. No Oscar mentions for that (she was only heard in the movie, never seen), but plenty of other Academy honours during the period – the award itself for her vivacious magazine editor in *Gentleman's Agreement*, and a couple of nominations, for her French nun with a penchant for tennis in *Come to the Stable* and her friend and ally of Bette Davis in *All About Eve*, all within the space of four years. Much loved by male audiences for her wisecracking smart girls, she is quick to disillusion journalists whenever questioned about her image. 'I hated that,' she says. 'It's stereotyped. I only played that kind of a role in two pictures and that was enough, thank you. It's not *me*.' A pity!

Ian Holm

Born Goodmayes, Essex, England, 12 September 1931

Oscar Nominations (1): Best Supporting Actor for Sam Mussabini in *Chariots of Fire* (Enigma, 1981)

Rightly described as an actor who has never given a bad performance, Ian Holm has been a robot in outer space, an explorer in darkest Africa, the repressed would-be lover of Ruth Ellis, and dallied with young girls on the banks of the Thames as Lewis Carroll. He has also played Prince John, Napoleon, Polonius and Fluellen. His Oscar nomination was earned for his richly embroidered performance as the athletics coach who trains the up-and-coming Harold Abrahams to an Olympic medal in *Chariots of Fire*. The medal may have gone to Abrahams, the Oscar sadly didn't go to Holm, who lost to another Brit – John Gielgud's uppercrust butler in *Arthur*. No offence to Sir John, but it may have been the wrong choice.

Oscar Homolka

Born Vienna, Austria, 12 August 1898; died 1978

Oscar Nominations (1): Best Supporting Actor for Uncle Chris in *I Remember Mama* (RKO, 1948)

Memorable as the anarchist-saboteur Verloc in Hitchcock's *Sabotage*, the heavily accented Oscar Homolka was often involved in espionage during his long screen career, frequently turning up 'against our side' as a spymaster, Russian general or something mysterious in the KGB. Equally adept at comedy (he was one of the seven professors enamoured with Barbara Stanwyck's burlesque stripper in *Ball of Fire*), he earned his Oscar nomination for repeating his Broadway role in *I Remember Mama* – as the bombastic and mischievous Uncle Chris, one of the more colourful members of a Norwegian family living in San Francisco at the turn of the century. Good as he was, he lost to another old-timer – the toothless, gold-struck Walter Huston in *The Treasure of the Sierra Madre*.

Anthony Hopkins

Born Port Talbot, South Wales, 31 December 1937

Oscars (1): Best Actor for Dr Hannibal Lecter in *The Silence of the Lambs* (Orion, 1991)

Oscar Nominations (2): Best Actor for Stevens in *The Remains of the Day* (Merchant Ivory/Columbia, 1993) and Richard M. Nixon in *Nixon* (Buena Vista/Hollywood Pictures, 1995)

'I have to go now, Clarice, I'm having an old friend for dinner,' said Anthony Hopkins as he signed off as Hannibal the Cannibal at the close of *The Silence of the Lambs*. Twelve months later he was clutching his Oscar, and although compared with Jodie Foster's FBI agent in the same film his was essentially a supporting performance – one touched throughout with quiet menace and a lip-quivering insanity – few begrudged him the award, following as it did a long line of memorable performances in such films as *The Bounty* (as Captain Bligh), *The Elephant Man* and *84 Charing Cross Rd*. He has subsequently been nominated for his faithful manservant in *The Remains of the Day* and his portrayal of Richard Nixon in Oliver Stone's controversial three-hour biopic of the late American President.

Miriam Hopkins

Born Savannah, Georgia, USA, 18 October 1902; died 1972

Oscar Nominations (1): Best Actress for the title role in *Becky Sharp* (Pioneer/RKO, 1935)

A glamorous and seductive actress who was equally at home in Lubitsch comedies or as a good-hearted floozie (most notably the barmaid who suffers at the hands of the bestial Fredric March in *Dr Jekyll and Mr Hyde*), Miriam Hopkins somehow never quite hit the mark as far as the Oscars were concerned. Nominated for her portrayal of Thackeray's unscrupulous social climber Becky Sharp in the year that Bette Davis won the first of her awards, she never again came close, and by the time the thirties had ended, so too, more or less, had her screen career. A warm, witty, intellectual woman who enjoyed giving elegant New York parties, she felt her lack of Oscar success was partly her own fault: 'I'm a bad judge of a play or film,' she recalled. 'I turned down the movie *It Happened One Night*. It won Claudette Colbert an Oscar. I said it was just a silly comedy.'

Dennis Hopper

Born Dodge City, Kansas, USA, 17 May 1936

Oscar Nominations (1): Best Supporting Actor for Shooter in *Hoosiers* (Hemdale, 1986)

Just mention of his name conjurs up frenzied psychos, killers, mad bombers and the like, so it comes as something of a surprise to find that Dennis Hopper's only acting nomination to date has been for someone who was relatively normal, a small-town drunk who used to be a top basketball star and who comes to the aid of Gene Hackman's high-school basketball team in *Hoosiers*. Always a bit of a rebel (as both an actor and a sometime director), he worked with James Dean at Warners on both *Rebel Without a Cause* and *Giant*. He earned notoriety during the filming of the Fox western *From Hell to Texas* when he took more than seventy takes over one scene – much to the ire of short-fused director Henry Hathaway. In 1969 he earned a writing nomination with Peter Fonda and Terry Southern for *Easy Rider*.

Bob Hoskins

Born Bury St Edmunds, Suffolk, England, 26 October 1942

Oscar Nominations (1): Best Actor for George in *Mona Lisa* (Palace Pictures, 1986)

When an actor has won just about every prize for a performance, he is entitled to feel just a little aggrieved if he fails to carry off the Oscar as well, especially when the guy who steals it from under his nose is Paul Newman for reprising a role he had first given twenty-five years earlier (see p. 256). Not Bob Hoskins. 'We all knew Paul was going to win,' he said later. 'We toasted him in the bar before and afterwards!' Still, Hoskins *was* unfortunate to miss out for his small-time ex-con who gradually falls for the black call girl he chauffeurs from client to client for wealthy crook Michael Caine. Enjoyable as the down-to-earth shopkeeper lover of Cher in *Mermaids* and memorable as the gruff, ageing Irish-American involved with spinster Maggie Smith in *The Lonely Passion of Judith Hearne*, he has shown a remarkable versatility over the last decade but still awaits a second nomination.

John Houseman

Born Bucharest, Romania, 22 September 1902; died 1988

Oscars (1): Best Supporting Actor for Professor Kingsfield in *The Paper Chase* (20th Century-Fox, 1973)

Effective as aloof, authoritarian figures, John Houseman emerged as a regular screen actor by accident when James Mason decided against the role of the stern Harvard law professor in *The Paper Chase* and had to be replaced at short notice. Director James Bridges wanted Houseman, Houseman suggested Edward G. Robinson, Robinson was too ill, Houseman gave way, and at the age of seventy suddenly found himself on his way to an acting career and an Oscar. Known primarily for his distinguished work as a film producer and as story editor on *Citizen Kane*, he subsequently portrayed, among others, a crusty old sea salt and teller of tales in *The Fog*, the ailing father of Gena Rowlands in Woody Allen's *Another Woman*, and the Fat Man, Jasper Blubber, in the Neil Simon parody *The Cheap Detective*. He also reprised his Professor Kingsfield in the popular TV series derived from the 1973 film.

Leslie Howard

Born London, England, 24 April 1893; died 1943

Oscar Nominations (2): Best Actor for Peter Standish in *Berkeley Square* (Fox, 1932/33) and Professor Henry Higgins in *Pygmalion* (MGM/British, 1938)

Tall, slim and fragile-looking, Leslie Howard pushed his Oscar claims twice in the thirties – for his wealthy American suddenly transported back to eighteenth-century England in *Berkeley Square*, and for his superb Professor Higgins in *Pygmalion*. There never was a better Higgins, but Tracy was riding high at Metro (he won for the second year running, for *Boys' Town*), and that was that. Never much enamoured with one of his most famous roles, Ashley Wilkes in *Gone with the Wind* (he only agreed to play the part on the condition that Selznick did not make him read the book), Howard was regarded by many as the embodiment of the perfect Englishman but was, in fact, the son of Hungarian immigrant parents. He was killed when the plane on which he was returning from Lisbon – he was on a government mission at the time – was shot down by the Germans, who mistakenly believed that Winston Churchill was on board.

Trevor Howard

Born Cliftonville, Margate, Kent, England, 29 September 1916; died 1988

Oscar Nominations (1): Best Actor for Walter Morel in *Sons and Lovers* (20th Century-Fox, 1960)

Neither of the two *Brief Encounter* stars won Oscars for their performances, although Celia Johnson did at least earn a nomination. Poor Trevor Howard had to wait another fifteen years for his, for his drunken coal-miner father of Dean Stockwell in *Sons and Lovers*. He enjoyed no luck on Oscar night (it was Burt Lancaster's year), not that that worried him a great deal. The latest cricket score was more his mark, and one of his cardinal rules was that he never allowed himself to be filming when a Test match was in progress. At his peak for Carol Reed in the golden years of post-war British cinema (*The Third Man*, *Outcast of the Islands*), he was a heavy drinker but preferred the term 'lover of life' to 'hellraiser'! He once ordered champagne for the entire orchestra when carousing in a European nightclub, and later ruefully reflected: 'When I discovered I hadn't the money to pay for it I spent the night in jail, but that often happens'!

Rock Hudson

Born Winnetka, Illinois, USA, 17 November 1925; died 1985

Oscar Nominations (1): Best Actor for Bick Benedict in *Giant* (Warner Bros, 1956)

Anyone who could survive an early billing as 'The Baron of Beefcake' deserved some sort of reward for staying the course; Rock Hudson earned his in 1956 when he was nominated for his Texas cattle rancher in George Stevens' *Giant*. It was his only mention and also his own favourite film, but his talent for comedy (opposite Doris Day) and emotional melodrama (*Magnificent Obsession*, *Written on the Wind*) proved him to be a good all-rounder and among the most reliable of Hollywood actors. Except, that is, in the film in which he made his screen début, *Fighter Squadron*, directed by Raoul Walsh. His one line in the movie was 'You'd better get a bigger blackboard.' He fluffed it thirty-seven times. His Oscar nomination arrived eight years later.

Tom Hulce

Born White Water, Wisconsin, USA, 6 December 1953

Oscar Nominations (1): Best Actor for Wolfgang Amadeus Mozart in *Amadeus* (Orion, 1984)

Squealing and giggling and proving to everyone who came in contact with him that Mozart was an insufferable prat as well as a musical genius, Tom Hulce seemed destined for a long and profitable Hollywood career once an Oscar nomination came his way. Alas, it didn't happen. The Oscar went to his co-star F. Murray Abraham (for his Salieri), and Hulce's subsequent roles have generally been in indifferent and uncommercial films that have done little to help him build on his *Amadeus* stardom. Had he won the Oscar would things have been different? Possibly, but it's always a question that's highly debatable. Sadly, one of the eighties' forgotten stars.

Josephine Hull

Born Newton, Massachusetts, USA, 3 January 1886; died 1957

Oscars (1): Best Supporting Actress for Veta Louise Simmons in *Harvey* (Universal International, 1950)

Bewilderment and eccentricity were the key ingredients in Josephine Hull's brief excursions into movies (she made only five), most notably as the sister who never quite knows whether she's coming or going and has to put up with a permanently inebriated James Stewart and his invisible white rabbit Harvey. A deserved winner of the supporting award, she was unlucky not to have been on the winner's podium five years earlier for *Arsenic and Old Lace*, in which, together with sister Jean Adair and much to the horror of nephew Cary Grant, she poisons a dozen old gents and buries their bodies in the basement. Little wonder that, during the movie, Grant utters: 'Insanity runs in my family . . . It practically gallops!'

Arthur Hunnicutt

Born Gravelly, Arkansas, USA, 17 February 1911; died 1979

Oscar Nominations (1): Best Supporting Actor for Uncle Zeb in *The Big Sky* (RKO, 1952)

The personification of the grizzled western old-timer, Arthur Hunnicutt (clad usually in buckskin) tended to lean on his rifle, chew on his tobacco and then spit before telling everyone just what they didn't want to know: that Indians were thereabouts! Tall, lean and usually bearded, he was a frontiersman in innumerable westerns for more than three decades. He won his Oscar nomination for his drawling Uncle Zeb, who helps take a keelboat expedition up the Missouri in the 1830s. Arkansas-born, he fought Indians for many directors, including Raoul Walsh and Delmer Daves, served in the Union army for John Huston in *The Red Badge of Courage*, and was a more than serviceable Davy Crockett in Frank Lloyd's undervalued account of the Alamo, *The Last Command*. He lost on Oscar night to Anthony Quinn for *Viva Zapata!*

Linda Hunt

Born Morristown, New Jersey, USA, 2 April 1945

Oscars (1): Best Supporting Actress for Billy Kwan in *The Year of Living Dangerously* (MGM/UA, 1983)

In many ways the most extraordinary winner of an Academy acting prize, Linda Hunt was cast as the Chinese-Australian press photographer in *The Year of Living Dangerously* because director Peter Weir couldn't find a man small enough or talented enough to play the part. Diminutive to say the least (she is just 4ft 9in), she made the most of the role, scene-stealing throughout the picture and outstripping her rivals with ease on Oscar night. Needless to say, she is the only woman playing a man to win an Academy Award, and is likely to remain so.

Holly Hunter

Born Conyers, Georgia, USA, 20 March 1958

Oscars (1): Best Actress for Ada McGrath in *The Piano* (Miramax, 1993)

Oscar Nominations (2): Best Actress for Jane Craig in *Broadcast News* (20th Century-Fox, 1987); Best Supporting Actress for Tammy Hemphill in *The Firm* (Paramount, 1993)

As the thrusting young TV news producer in *Broadcast News*, Holly Hunter never stopped talking; as the nineteenth-century Scottish mother living out a lonely, erotic life in the wilds of New Zealand in *The Piano*, she was mute. The first role earned her a nomination, the second the award itself, although many felt that the result should have been the other way round. No matter; together with Jodie Foster she remains one of the most interesting young actresses of the nineties, even if, at times, she is difficult to cast. She earned her third nomination in *The Piano* year for her secretary/lover of a murdered private eye in *The Firm*.

☆

Kim Hunter

Born Detroit, USA, 12 November 1922

Oscars (1): Best Supporting Actress for Stella Kowalski in *A Streetcar Named Desire* (Warner Bros, 1951)

An actress whose film career was badly damaged when she fell foul of the Un-American Activities Committee (her name found its way into the red scare pamphlet *Red Channels*, making her virtually unemployable for several years), Kim Hunter won her award before all the trouble began, for her brilliant performance as the wife of the brutish Marlon Brando in *Streetcar*. An occasional film performer in later years, she is perhaps most famous for a role that rendered unrecognisable her lovely features, chestnut hair and green eyes, that of the sympathetic chimpanzee Dr Zira in the *Planet of the Apes* films. In Britain she is fondly recalled for *A Matter of Life and Death*, in which she played the American radio operator who talks with pilot David Niven during what she believes are his last minutes on earth.

John Hurt

Born Chesterfield, Derbyshire, England, 22 January 1940

Oscar Nominations (2): Best Supporting Actor for Max in *Midnight Express* (Columbia, 1978); Best Actor for John Merrick in *The Elephant Man* (Brooksfilm, Paramount, 1980)

The only actor to win a nomination with his features completely hidden behind grotesque make-up, John Hurt won his best actor mention for his terribly disfigured nineteenth-century freak John Merrick in the very year that Robert De Niro was having his face battered to a pulp in *Raging Bull*. It was, unfortunately, no contest, although Hurt might justifiably have considered himself a little unlucky not to have won a couple of years earlier for his dissipated long-term prisoner in a Turkish jail in *Midnight Express*. Christopher Walken was 1978's supporting winner, for *The Deer Hunter*.

William Hurt

Born Washington, DC, USA, 20 March 1950

Oscars (1): Best Actor for Luis Molina in *Kiss of the Spider Woman* (HB Films for Island Alive, 1985)

Oscar Nominations (2): Best Actor for James Leeds in *Children of a Lesser God* (Paramount, 1986) and Tom Grunick in *Broadcast News* (20th Century-Fox, 1987)

In the eighties it seemed for a while as though William Hurt would become *the* big star of the future, as he essayed a whole range of withdrawn, complex and unemotional characters whose true feelings were simmering away just below the surface. The public weren't drawn to him but the Academy voters were, naming him best of the year for his homosexual sharing a cell with a political prisoner in a South American jail, and then nominating him in successive years for his teacher-lover of Marlee Matlin in *Children of a Lesser God* and his TV newscaster in *Broadcast News*. The chances of him equalling Brando's record of four straight best actor nominations on the trot rested on his 1988 role in *The Accidental Tourist*, as the jaded, grief-stricken travel writer still lamenting the loss of his son. All he needed was a nomination. It didn't happen, and he hasn't been named since.

Ruth Hussey

Born Providence, Rhode Island, USA, 30 October 1914

Oscar Nominations (1): Best Supporting Actress for Elizabeth Imbrie in *The Philadelphia Story* (MGM, 1940)

Celeste Holm sang about wanting to be a millionaire in *High Society*; Ruth Hussey, who essayed the same smart-talking magazine photographer in the original version, just wisecracked about it. The dialogue and the way she dished it out helped her gain an Academy nomination but didn't exactly do much for her career. Socialites, sophisticated wives and fiancées were the order of the day at MGM, and a career that had promised much simply petered out. 'I just stayed out of sight I guess,' recalled Hussey. 'I probably didn't seek work but then producers didn't seek me out either.' Celeste Holm was not nominated for her role in the musical remake.

Anjelica Huston

Born Los Angeles, USA, 1952

Oscars (1): Best Supporting Actress for Maerose Prizzi in *Prizzi's Honor* (20th Century-Fox, 1985)

Oscar Nominations (2): Best Supporting Actress for Tamara in *Enemies: A Love Story* (20th Century-Fox, 1989); Best Actress for Lilly Dillon in *The Grifters* (Cineplex, 1990)

'Come on, Chawley. Ya wanna do it? Let's do it right here on the Oriental,' purred Mafia gal Anjelica Huston to the slow-witted Jack Nicholson in *Prizzi's Honor*. The sexual delivery undeniably helped persuade the Academy membership that she was deserving of the year's supporting award, although she has subsequently earned only nominations for what many regard as superior performances – as the Jewish wife, long thought dead, who appears from the past in *Enemies: A Love Story*, and the bag lady working a racetrack scam for Baltimore racketeers in *The Grifters*. Deliciously flamboyant as the Grand High Witch with plans to turn all children into mice (alas, she fails) in *The Witches*, she has also appeared for Woody Allen in *Crimes and Misdemeanors* and *Manhattan Murder Mystery*.

John Huston

Born Nevada, Missouri, USA, 5 August 1906; died 1987

Oscar Nominations (1): Best Supporting Actor for Cardinal Glennon in *The Cardinal* (Columbia, 1963)

A director whose penchant for walk-on roles subsequently led to an Oscar nomination for his portrait of a crusty old Boston cardinal, John Huston employed his smooth, drawling voice and wicked grin in more than twenty films other than his own. At his most convincing as the loathsome Noah Cross, seducer of his own daughter, in Polanski's *Chinatown*, he also, on occasion, operated on a somewhat lower level, hiding his face behind a monkey mask as the Simian Law Giver in *Battle for the Planet of the Apes*. The only director to have guided both his father, Walter, and daughter,

Anjelica, to Academy Awards, he received his own statuettes for writing and directing *The Treasure of the Sierra Madre* in 1948. About his acting he commented: 'It's a nice way to make a buck. It's a lark and very well paid but I don't take it seriously.'

Note: Huston earned an additional twelve nominations, eight for writing achievements and four for direction – *The Asphalt Jungle* (1950), *The African Queen* (1952), *Moulin Rouge* (1953) and *Prizzi's Honor* (1985) – in the period 1940–85.

Walter Huston

Born Toronto, Canada, 6 April 1884; died 1950

Oscars (1): Best Supporting Actor for Howard in *The Treasure of the Sierra Madre* (Warner Bros, 1948)

Oscar Nominations (3): Best Actor for Sam Dodsworth in *Dodsworth* (United Artists, 1936) and Mr Scratch in *All That Money Can Buy* (RKO, 1941); Best Supporting Actor for Jerry Cohan in *Yankee Doodle Dandy* (Warner Bros, 1942)

The sight (and sound) of a toothless Walter Huston dancing and laughing as he calls Humphrey Bogart and Tim Holt a pair of jackasses, telling them that the gold they've been searching for for weeks is right there under their feet, belonged with the most enjoyable moments in post-war American movies. The Academy voters obviously agreed, naming Huston as the best male support of 1948 after having thrice nominated him and thrice overlooked him in previous years – for his dissatisfied middle-aged American Dodsworth who finds solace in Europe (a repeat of his Broadway role), the most mischievous of all screen devils, Mr Scratch, and the father of song and dance man George M. Cohan. First directed by his son John in an unbilled walk-on part in *The Maltese Falcon* (as a ship's captain who delivers the black bird to Bogie's office before dying of gunshot wounds), he was also famous for his rendition of the hit 'September Song' which he first sang on Broadway in 1938 in *Knickerbocker Holiday*.

Timothy Hutton

Born Malibu, California, USA, 16 August 1960

Oscars (1): Best Supporting Actor for Conrad Jarrett in *Ordinary People* (Paramount, 1980)

Collecting an Oscar for one's début film is not necessarily an advantage, as Timothy Hutton has discovered in recent years. A winner at the age of twenty for his performance in Robert Redford's *Ordinary People* (as the adolescent son in torment over his brother's death), he has since found it difficult to break through to star status, despite working with such directors as John Schlesinger and Alan Rudolph. Sidney Lumet perhaps drew the best from him as the young, idealist DA investigating police corruption in *Q&A*. A sensitive performer who studies intensely for his roles, he is still only in his mid-thirties and his second 'breakthrough' may yet materialise. The son of sixties comedy actor Jim Hutton, he married Debra Winger in 1986. They were divorced in 1990.

Martha Hyer

Born Fort Worth, Texas, USA, 10 August 1924

Oscar Nominations (1): Best Supporting Actress for Gwen French in *Some Came Running* (MGM, 1958)

Had she been a slightly more accomplished actress, Martha Hyer would have been perfect for Hitchcock. As it was she was most at ease in roles billed just below the title, often as bitchy socialites or well-bred career women. Her nomination for her icy college instructor in love with Frank Sinatra's aspiring writer in *Some Came Running* was her first and last, although her cool blonde Texas beauty continued to smoulder through any number of films in the sixties and seventies. Effective on occasion as women at the other end of the social scale – the call girl turned into a movie star by George Peppard's Howard Hughes-type mogul in *The Carpetbaggers* – she was married to the distinguished Hollywood producer Hal Wallis.

I

John Ireland

Born Vancouver, Canada, 30 January 1914; died 1992

Oscar Nominations (1): Best Supporting Actor for Jack Burden in *All the King's Men* (Columbia, 1949)

It must have been the thin eyes, lean, hunched frame and one-tone voice, but John Ireland never hit the front rank of Hollywood stars, even though he won an Oscar nomination for his reporter following the rise of Willie Stark in *All the King's Men*. Ill at ease in large-scale movies, he seemed more at home in smaller pics such as the western *Outlaw Territory* which he co-produced and co-directed with distinguished cameraman Lee Garmes. He also seemed to enjoy himself rather more off screen than on. A frequent headline-maker as a womaniser, he hit the front pages in 1959 for his affair with the sixteen-year-old Tuesday Weld. Then forty-five, he said: 'If there wasn't such a difference in our ages I'd ask her to marry me. That and her mother are the only things that stop me.'

Jeremy Irons

Born Isle of Wight, England, 19 September 1948

Oscars (1): Best Actor for Claus Von Bulow in *Reversal of Fortune* (Reversal Films/Warner Bros, 1990)

He was a star from the moment he appeared in and narrated *Brideshead Revisited,* and after his Oscar he could quite easily have 'gone Hollywood' and embarked on all that entailed. He preferred freedom, however, an English base and the opportunity to choose what he wanted to make rather than what others told him to do. Full marks to Jeremy Irons, who has been described as 'the great stylist among today's English actors' and whose slim, elegant frame and distinctive, velvety voice have embraced such films as *The French Lieutenant's Woman, Dead Ringers, Waterland* and *Kafka*. So far, though, only one Oscar role, that of the international playboy found not guilty of trying to murder his heiress wife Sunny. Another nomination is somewhat overdue.

Amy Irving

Born Palo Alto, California, USA, 10 September 1953

Oscar Nominations (1): Best Supporting Actress for Hadass in *Yentl* (MGM/UA, 1983)

A nomination for playing the 'wife' of Barbra Streisand sounds a mite complicated, but that's basically how it all turned out in Streisand's musical *Yentl*, which told of a young woman (Streisand) in turn-of-the-century Poland who disguises herself as a boy to become a Talmudic scholar. Irving was nominated for her Jewish girl who falls for Streisand thinking she's a man! She didn't win. Who did? Linda Hunt, a diminutive actress who played a Chinese-Australian *male* photographer working in Indonesia in *The Year of Living Dangerously*. A complicated year.

Burl Ives

Born Hunt, Illinois, USA, 14 June 1909; died 1995

Oscars (1): Best Supporting Actor for Rufus Hannassey in *The Big Country* (United Artists, 1958)

Most people think of him as the rotund, guitar-playing folk singer of such ditties as 'The Blue Tail Fly' and 'The Big Rock Candy Mountain'. Those who recall the movies of the fifties, however, will remember him best as a character actor of some power, especially in *Cat on a Hot Tin Roof* (no nomination for his bullying red-necked Big Daddy) and in the same year as the feuding cattle baron in Wyler's epic western *The Big Country* (a nomination and a win). Unlucky to miss out on another mention for his doomed refugee from Hitler in Carol Reed's *Our Man in Havana*, he was once described as being 'a man who likes his food, likes his drink, likes meeting people, and likes talking but who has not yet succumbed to the temptation of liking himself'.

J

Glenda Jackson

Born Birkenhead, Merseyside, England, 9 May 1936

Oscars (2): Best Actress for Gudrun Brangwen in *Women in Love* (United Artists, 1970) and Vicki Allessio in *A Touch of Class* (Avco Embassy, 1973)

Oscar Nominations (2): Best Actress for Alex Greville in *Sunday, Bloody Sunday* (United Artists, 1971) and the title role in *Hedda* (Brut Productions, 1975)

For a time it seemed as though Glenda Jackson would challenge Katharine Hepburn's Oscar record of four best actress awards, but with advancing years and less attractive roles, her nominations dried up by the mid-seventies and she had to be content with just two – for her brilliant portrayal of the emancipated artist in Ken Russell's *Women in Love* and, three later, in somewhat lighter vein, for her divorcee who embarks on an affair with George Segal in *A Touch of Class*. Nominated also for her lover of young designer Murray Head in *Sunday, Bloody Sunday* and her Hedda in Trevor Nunn's revised version of *Hedda Gabler*, she has never been overenthusiastic about her Oscars: 'My mother polishes them to within an inch of their lives until the metal shows. That sums up the Academy Awards – all glitter on the outside and base metal coming through. Nice presents for a day. But they don't make you any better.'

Samuel L. Jackson

Born 1949

Oscar Nominations (1): Best Supporting Actor for Jules in *Pulp Fiction* (Miramax, 1994)

Just about the only thing missing from Sam Jackson's portrayal of the 'hit man' Jules in *Pulp Fiction* were the words 'love' and 'hate' on his knuckles, so close was he in character to Robert Mitchum's preacher (a distant cousin, twice removed?) in *Night of the Hunter*. Spouting Ezekiel at his terrified victims before blowing them away, and enjoying his business with a bloody fervour, he lost to Martin Landau's portrait of spooky old Bela Lugosi in *Ed Wood*. A supporting award-winner at Cannes for his earlier Harlem crack addict in Spike Lee's *Jungle Fever*, he is the co-founder of the Atlanta-based 'Just Us Theatre Company'.

Richard Jaeckel

Born Long Beach, New York, USA, 10 October 1926

Oscar Nominations (1): Best Supporting Actor for Joe Ben Stamper in *Sometimes a Great Notion* (Universal, 1971)

One of those long-serving character actors who elicits the response: 'Who *is* that guy? I know the face but what the hell's his name?', Richard Jaeckel has also been one of those performers who has always remained young-looking even in advancing years. Frequently seen in cowardly and sadistic roles and only occasionally in sympathetic mode, he made it to the Academy lists just the once for his brother of Paul Newman in Newman's Oregon logging drama, *Sometimes a Great Notion*. Veteran Ben Johnson, who really was as old as he looked, took the prize for *The Last Picture Show*.

Sam Jaffe

Born New York City, USA, 8 March 1891; died 1984

Oscar Nominations (1): Best Supporting Actor for Doc Riedenschneider in *The Asphalt Jungle* (MGM, 1950)

Mad as a hatter as the Russian Grand Duke Peter in *The Scarlet Empress*, old and mysterious as the High Lama in *Lost Horizon*, heroic as the native water-carrier in *Gunga Din* . . . Sam Jaffe's wizened, frail versatility made quite an impression in Hollywood in the thirties, although it wasn't until the post-war years that he at last received Academy recognition. Nominated for his performance in *The Asphalt Jungle* as the criminal mastermind whose liking for young female flesh causes him to dally just that bit too long at a roadside diner and miss his escape route, he came in behind George Sanders' sophisticate in *All About Eve*. He received compensation by being named best actor (not best supporting actor) for his Doc at the 1950 Venice Film Festival.

Dean Jagger

Born Lima, Ohio, USA, 7 November 1903; died 1991

Oscars (1): Best Supporting Actor for Major Harvey Stovall in *Twelve O'Clock High* (20th Century-Fox, 1949)

An actor who had the misfortune never to look young, and who became well known for playing fathers, doting and otherwise, Dean Jagger didn't come into the Oscar reckoning until 1949 when he made the most of a gem of a part as the humane group adjutant holding together the frayed nerve ends of an American bomber group stationed in England during World War II. Never again an Oscar nominee, he liked to recall that his sound career almost ended before it began. His first film, *The Woman from Hell*, was a silent and starred Mary Astor. A week later the studios turned to sound. He said: 'With one film to my credit I was considered as part of that group of untouchables – silent film stars!'

Emil Jannings

Born Rorschach, Switzerland, 23 July 1884; died 1950

Oscars (1): Best Actor for August Schiller in *The Way of All Flesh* and General Dolgorucki (Grand Duke Sergius Alexander) in *The Last Command* (both Paramount, 1927/28)

Two roles earned Emil Jannings the first best actor Academy Award – a middle-aged cashier ruined by a *femme fatale* in *The Way of All Flesh* and a former Russian general reduced to a film extra in *The Last Command*. After that, it was goodbye Hollywood, hello Goebbels, as he lent his talents to the Fascist cinema of the thirties and worked exclusively for the Third Reich. Blacklisted by the Allied authorities after the war, he died a broken and disillusioned man in Vienna in 1950. Widely acclaimed before his political associations for his university professor destroyed by the physical charms of Marlene Dietrich in *The Blue Angel,* he also distinguished himself for Murnau, Dupont and other German directors in the silent twenties, most notably in *Waxworks, The Last Laugh, Variety,* and *Faust,* in which he appeared as Mephistopheles.

Glynis Johns

Born Pretoria, South Africa, 5 October 1923

Oscar Nominations (1): Best Supporting Actress for Mrs Firth in *The Sundowners* (Warner Bros, 1960)

A genuine screen original, with large eyes, a coquettish manner and a voice that was deliciously husky and squeaky at the same time, Glynis Johns picked up her Oscar nomination for her role in *The Sundowners* as the vivacious hotel-keeper in the Australian outback who moves heaven and earth to get English sea captain Peter Ustinov into her marriage bed. No luck there, nor on Oscar night, but the luck was running with her five years earlier when she was cast in *The Court Jester* and took part in a little piece of movie history as she and Mildred Natwick tried to help but ultimately confused would-be duellist Danny Kaye. The end result of their advice was that 'The pellet with the poison's in the flagon with the dragon. The vessel with the pestle has the brew that is true.' All of which sounds straightforward enough in the cold light of day. The fun was seeing how they arrived at that conclusion, especially after they'd 'broken the chalice from the palace'!

Ben Johnson

Born Foraker, near Pawhuska, Oklahoma, USA, 13 June 1918; died 1996

Oscars (1): Best Supporting Actor for 'Sam the Lion' in *The Last Picture Show* (Columbia, 1971)

For many, Ben Johnson's old-timer lamenting about the old days as he runs a pool hall and the local picture house in a small Texas town during the fifties was the logical extension of all the whoopin' westerners and cavalrymen he had played for John Ford when he seemed to ride a horse faster than anyone else in the movies. A champion rodeo performer who began in Hollywood as a wrangler for Howard Hughes on *The Outlaw*, he graduated from stunt man and double to a character actor in some of the best westerns ever made – *She Wore a Yellow Ribbon, Shane, One-Eyed Jacks, Will Penny, The Wild Bunch*. How he missed appearing in Zinnemann's *High Noon* remains a mystery. Possessed of a rich, slow, drawling voice, he appeared in more than thirty westerns, and later in his career became a regular performer for Sam Peckinpah. In 1973 he was a memorable Melvin Purvis in John Milius' *Dillinger*.

Celia Johnson

Born Richmond, Surrey, England, 18 December 1908; died 1982

Oscar Nominations (1): Best Actress for Laura Jesson in *Brief Encounter* (Rank, 1946)

Nominated just the once – for her most famous role as the refined suburban housewife who almost, but not quite, runs away with doctor Trevor Howard – Celia Johnson came close to becoming the first British performer to win as best actress in a British movie. The New York Critics voted her the year's best; not, unfortunately, the Academy, which preferred an American form of self-sacrifice supplied by Olivia de Havilland in the Paramount weepie, *To Each His Own*. Equally adept at playing working-class South London mums and refined English gentlewomen of the purest breeding, Celia Johnson appeared in just a dozen movies, among them *In Which We Serve, This Happy Breed* and *A Kid for Two Farthings*. Julie Christie eventually became the first British actress to win for a British film when she took the award for *Darling* some nineteen years later.

Carolyn Jones

Born Amarillo, Texas, USA, 28 April 1929; died 1983

Oscar Nominations (1): Best Supporting Actress for 'The Existentialist' in *The Bachelor Party* (United Artists, 1957)

Famous for her Morticia in *The Addams Family* TV series of the sixties, Carolyn Jones hung about in movies for something like twenty-five years without ever really getting anywhere. Mad old Vincent Price poured molten wax all over her in *House of Wax* and turned her into Joan of Arc, and she won an Oscar nomination for her five-minute spot as a Greenwich Village gal in *The Bachelor Party*. Still no fame – and no award. She was even one of those taken over in Siegel's *Invasion of the Body Snatchers*. Still no joy, and there never was – but at least there was always Morticia!

James Earl Jones

Born Arkabutla, Mississippi, USA, 17 January 1931

Oscar Nominations (1): Best Actor for Jack Jefferson in *The Great White Hope* (20th Century-Fox, 1970)

James Earl Jones should by now have won an Academy Award; indeed he might have claimed the top prize had his boxer Jack Jefferson (a thinly veiled portrait of the world's first black heavyweight champion Jack Johnson) not coincided with George C. Scott's Patton, but it did and that was that. Scott was named and said no, Jones was bypassed and would have said yes. Famous for his TV portrayal of Alex Haley in *Roots*, and for his marvellously menacing voice of Darth Vader in the *Star Wars* trilogy, he was a shade unlucky to miss a supporting nomination for his sixties writer who is brought back from his reclusive existence to meet Shoeless Joe Jackson in *Field of Dreams*.

Jennifer Jones

Born Tulsa, Oklahoma, USA, 2 March 1919

Oscars (1): Best Actress for Bernadette Soubirous in *The Song of Bernadette* (20th Century-Fox, 1943)

Oscar Nominations (4): Best Supporting Actress for Jane Hilton in *Since You Went Away* (Selznick/United Artists, 1944); Best Actress for Singleton in *Love Letters* (Paramount, 1945), Pearl Chavez in *Duel in the Sun* (Selznick International, 1946) and Han Suyin in *Love Is a Many-Splendored Thing* (20th Century-Fox, 1955)

The last of Fred Astaire's dancing partners – she glided with him around a crowded ballroom in *The Towering Inferno* – Jennifer Jones has tended to be dismissed as a somewhat limited actress. Few, though, have been able to convey with conviction both saintliness (she won her Oscar for her Maid of Lourdes who sees a vision of the Virgin Mary) and girls who were as bad as Bernadette was good. Of her bad girls, only the sensual half-breed in *Duel in the Sun* made it into the Oscar listings; on other occasions the Academy voters preferred her in less dangerous mood, as the daughter of Claudette Colbert in *Since You Went Away*, a lovely amnesiac in *Love Letters* and the Eurasian doctor Han Suyin in *Love Is a Many-Splendored Thing*. Married to producer David Selznick for sixteen years, she appeared as the tragic Catherine ('Too old,' roared Hemingway) in the ill-fated remake of *A Farewell to Arms*.

Shirley Jones

Born Smithton, Pennsylvania, USA, 31 March 1934

Oscars (1): Best Supporting Actress for Lulu Bains in *Elmer Gantry* (United Artists, 1960)

She sang Rodgers and Hammerstein so sweetly in *Oklahoma* and *Carousel*, and she was nigh on perfect as the librarian in *The Music Man*. Her Oscar, though, came for a role that was anything but wholesome – the seductive prostitute seeking revenge on Burt Lancaster's boozy, on-the-make salesman Elmer Gantry. It was the only time she reached the Oscar lists. In later years she preferred TV, reverting to her sweeter image, especially with stepson David Cassidy in *The Partridge Family*. Janet Leigh (*Psycho*) and Mary Ure (*Sons and Lovers*) were among the supporting nominees of 1960.

Tommy Lee Jones

Born San Saba, Texas, USA, 15 September 1946

Oscars (1): Best Supporting Actor for Deputy US Marshal Samuel Gerard in *The Fugitive* (Warner Bros, 1993)

Oscar Nominations (1): Best Supporting Actor for Clay Shaw in *JFK* (Warner Bros, 1991)

The role of a dogged, determined cop relentlessly pursuing someone on the run is by no means new to the cinema, or indeed TV, where *The Fugitive* first began in the sixties. Or was it in Hugo's *Les Misérables*? Nonetheless, Tommy Lee Jones made the most of his chances in Andrew Davis' film, bringing a cynicism and silent admiration to his part that at last won him an Oscar after more than twenty years on screen. Nominated two years earlier for his New Orleans businessman accused of complicity in the assassination of President Kennedy, he won an Emmy for his TV portrayal of controversial murderer Gary Gilmore in *The Executioner's Song*.

Katy Jurado

Born Guadalajara, Mexico, 16 January 1927

Oscar Nominations (1): Best Supporting Actress for Señora Devereaux in *Broken Lance* (20th Century-Fox, 1954)

Described by director Edward Dmytryk as a woman 'of sharp intelligence, sensitivity and great bawdy humour', Katy Jurado was one of the few Mexican actresses to break into mainstream American cinema in the post-war years. Dark-haired and sensuous, she smouldered her way through numerous Hollywood movies of the fifties, many of them westerns, including *High Noon*, in which she played the old flame of Marshal Gary Cooper (a role for which many felt she should have been nominated), and Brando's *One-Eyed Jacks*, as the Mexican wife of the sadistic Karl Malden. She eventually won her nomination for her Comanche wife of cattle baron Spencer Tracy in the Fox western *Broken Lance*. Legend has it that her great-great-grandfather once owned most of what is now Texas.

K

Madeline Kahn

Born Boston, USA, 29 September 1942

Oscar Nominations (2): Best Supporting Actress for Trixie Delight in *Paper Moon* (Paramount, 1973) and Lili Von Shtupp in *Blazing Saddles* (Warner Bros, 1974)

'Is that a ten-gallon hat or are you just enjoying the show?' rasped Madeline Kahn, Dietrich-style, as saloon singer Lili Von Shtupp in Mel Brooks' *Blazing Saddles*. The delivery and the rest of the performance brought her an Oscar nomination, following on from the one she had earned just the year before for her fading thirties floozie Trixie Delight. Two nominations in two years seemed to indicate a certain Oscar-winner of the future. It was not to be. Brooks allowed her to be ravished by Peter Boyle's monster in *Young Frankenstein*, but after that her comedy chances faded, as did the careers of the two directors – Brooks and Peter Bogdanovich – who had done much to establish her as one of the American cinema's brightest young comediennes.

Ida Kaminska

Born Odessa, Russia, 4 September 1899; died 1980

Oscar Nominations (1): Best Actress for Rozalie Lautmannova in *The Shop on Main Street* (Prominent Films, Czechoslovakia, 1966)

They didn't really come much better than Ida Kaminska, superb in *The Shop on Main Street* as the old Jewish woman who runs a button shop in occupied Czechoslovakia and for a while is protected from the Nazis and the gas chamber by the simple, good-natured carpenter who takes over the premises. It is to the Academy's credit that it saw fit to nominate the sixty-five-year-old Kaminska; the pity is that the voters opted for Liz Taylor's yelling, blowsy alcoholic in *Virginia Woolf*. Kaminska simply bowed to the inevitable and enjoyed the glamour of the evening. Russian-born, she appeared in Polish films in the twenties and thirties although nothing that equalled *Main Street*.

Carol Kane

Born Cleveland, Ohio, USA, 18 June 1952

Oscar Nominations (1): Best Actress for Gitl in *Hester Street* (Midwest Films, 1975)

One of the seventies' unsung Oscar nominees, Carol Kane's nomination is nowadays forgotten by most and remembered by only a few. The few are the lucky ones, for her portrayal of the young Jewish immigrant who joins her husband in the New World at the turn of the century, only to discover that he has forsaken the old ways and finds her something of an embarrassment, was one of the unexpected delights of 1975. She made the lists just the once; Louise Fletcher took the year's best actress prize for her ruthless nurse in *One Flew Over the Cuckoo's Nest*.

Diane Keaton

Born Los Angeles, USA, 5 January 1946

Oscars (1): Best Actress for the title role in *Annie Hall* (United Artists, 1977)

Oscar Nominations (1): Best Actress for Louise Bryant in *Reds* (Paramount, 1981)

Just as Bogie will forever be remembered as Rick Blaine and Vivien Leigh as Scarlett O'Hara, so will Diane Keaton always be Annie Hall, joking, enjoying and sharing with Woody Allen and the audience a sparkling New York romance that has already entered into movie legend. Woody even allowed her the occasional good line – 'Why do all the books you lend me have death in the title?' she complains, as well as plenty of 'Oh well, la-dee-dahs'. Deservedly voted best actress of 1977, she was also nominated four years later for her tempestuous feminist lover of American

Communist John Reed in Warren Beatty's *Reds*. To date she has appeared in eight movies for Woody Allen.

Lila Kedrova

Born Leningrad, Russia, 1918

Oscars (1): Best Supporting Actress for Madame Hortense in *Zorba the Greek* (20th Century-Fox, 1964)

An ageing French courtesan and ex-cabaret dancer who runs a hotel in Crete and is courted by the lusty, roguish Anthony Quinn! The opportunities were there and Lila Kedrova took them eagerly, winning for a performance that was humorous, pathetic and tragic by turn, and upsetting the odds when everyone believed that four-time nominee Agnes Moorehead (*Hush... Hush, Sweet Charlotte*) was going to be 1964's supporting winner. Based in Paris and a regular performer in European cinema over the years, Kedrova's occasional ventures into English-speaking cinema have invariably been lively and colourful, both Hitchcock (*Torn Curtain*) and Huston (*The Kremlin Letter*) making use of her during the sixties.

Harvey Keitel

Born Brooklyn, New York, USA, 13 May 1941

Oscar Nominations (1): Best Supporting Actor for Mickey Cohen in *Bugsy* (TriStar, 1991)

Anything low-budget, made by a first-time film-maker and with a halfway intelligent script often gets the nod from Harvey Keitel, especially if there's a hood or corrupt cop in there somewhere. Little wonder that he's one of the favourites among young American directors looking for their first break. Nominated just the once, ironically for one of his few mainstream pictures, in which he played the gangster associate of Warren Beatty's Bugsy Siegel, he lost to former heavy turned philosophical trail boss Jack Palance (*City Slickers*). He remains a more than likely Oscar winner of the future, probably the near future.

☆

Cecil Kellaway

Born Cape Town, South Africa, 22 August 1891; died 1973

Oscar Nominations (2): Best Supporting Actor for Horace in *The Luck of the Irish* (20th Century-Fox, 1948) and Monsignor Ryan in *Guess Who's Coming to Dinner?* (Columbia, 1967)

Jolly, plump, with twinkling eyes and a mischievous little smile, Cecil Kellaway seemed as though he was never out of work during his Hollywood career, even if his roles did sometimes only amount to some twenty minutes of screentime. A centuries-old warlock for Rene Clair in *I Married a Witch*, the doctor treating Jimmy Stewart in *Harvey* (and desperate to see the invisible rabbit for himself), the murdered hubby of Lana Turner in *The Postman Always Rings Twice* – any one of these roles could have brought him a nomination. As it was, Hollywood decided to honour him for his performance as a leprechaun in *The Luck of the Irish* and a priest in *Guess Who's Coming to Dinner?* How versatile can you get?

Sally Kellerman

Born Long Beach, California, USA, 2 June 1936

Oscar Nominations (1): Best Supporting Actress for Major 'Hot Lips' Houlihan in *M·A·S·H* (20th Century-Fox, 1970)

'Hot Lips' Houlihan was a hard act to follow for Sally Kellerman. Had she won the Oscar rather than the nomination things might have been different. Had she repeated the role on television they most certainly would have been. She didn't, and she didn't. Still, she *was* the only cast member of the *M·A·S·H.* team to reach the nominations list, and she still conjures up fond memories for her lovemaking session broadcast over the camp public-address system and her taking of a shower in a tent that collapses accidentally on purpose around her!

☆

Gene Kelly

Born Pittsburgh, USA, 23 August 1912; died 1996

Oscar Nominations (1): Best Actor for Joseph Brady in *Anchors Aweigh* (MGM, 1945)

'My style is strong, wide open, bravura. Fred's is intimate, cool, easy,' said Gene Kelly when comparing his dancing with that of Fred Astaire. He never passed comment on their respective acting abilities, although both managed Oscar nominations during their careers, Astaire for *The Towering Inferno* (see p. 13) and Kelly for his carefree sailor on shore leave in Hollywood with Frank Sinatra in *Anchors Aweigh*. Never considered to be in with much of a chance, he lost to the usually debonair Ray Milland who, courtesy of Billy Wilder, took a plunge into the alcoholic lower depths in *The Lost Weekend*. Kelly was honoured with a special Academy Award in 1951 'in appreciation of his versatility as actor, singer, director and dancer, and especially for his brilliant achievements in the art of choreography'.

☆

Grace Kelly

Born Philadelphia, USA, 12 November 1928; died 1982

Oscars (1): Best Actress for Georgie Elgin in *The Country Girl* (Paramount, 1954)

Oscar Nominations (1): Best Supporting Actress for Linda Nordley in *Mogambo* (MGM, 1953)

Scenes of Grace Kelly offering Cary Grant 'a leg or a breast' and previewing some silk night attire for James Stewart as 'forthcoming attractions' have tended to remain in filmgoers' minds rather longer than her Oscar-winning role as the dowdy, embittered wife of an alcoholic Bing Crosby in *The Country Girl*. None of which is too surprising, for she was invariably at her best for Hitchcock, who was taken with her 'sexual elegance' and always tried to expose the sexual heat he sensed lay beneath her cool exterior. Nominated also in the supporting category for her repressed wife with a yen for big white hunter Clark Gable in *Mogambo*, she lost to a cooler, more in control Donna Reed for *From Here to Eternity*. In Hollywood for just six years, she retired from the screen to become Princess Grace of Monaco. Almost tempted back by Hitchcock for *Marnie*, she died when she suffered a stroke while driving in the mountain roads above Monaco.

Nancy Kelly

Born Lowell, Massachusetts, USA, 25 March 1921; died 1995

Oscar Nominations (1): Best Actress for Christine in *The Bad Seed* (Warner Bros, 1956)

The closest Nancy Kelly came to an Oscar was in March 1955 when she accepted an honorary award in New York on behalf of Greta Garbo, who hadn't made a film since 1941. 'In this year of awards there's more than one Kelly,' she said (Grace had been named best actress for *The Country Girl*), 'but there's only one Garbo!' Her own nomination two years later was for her role as the horrified mother of the murdering little child monster Patty McCormack in *The Bad Seed*. The role had brought her a Tony on Broadway; the Oscar went elsewhere – to Ingrid Bergman, who was on the comeback trail in *Anastasia*.

Arthur Kennedy

Born Worcester, Massachusetts, USA, 17 February 1914; died 1990

Oscar Nominations (5): Best Supporting Actor for Connie Kelly in *Champion* (United Artists, 1949); Best Actor for Larry Nevins in *Bright Victory* (Universal-International, 1951); Best Supporting Actor for Barney Castle in *Trial* (MGM, 1955), Lucas Cross in *Peyton Place* (20th Century-Fox, 1957) and Frank Hirsh in *Some Came Running* (MGM, 1958)

A worrier . . . a brooding presence . . . at times warm and easy-going, at others cold and dangerous. Arthur Kennedy was all these things, earning five nominations in just nine years but never quite getting close enough to nudge into the number one spot. His nominated roles: the crippled brother of Kirk Douglas' boxing champion, a blinded World War II veteran, a Communist lawyer, Peyton Place's rapist father, and Sinatra's small-town social-climbing brother. His own favourite? None of those. He preferred the westerns he made with Jimmy Stewart (*Bend of the River*, *The Man from Laramie*), in which he was a baddie on both occasions.

George Kennedy

Born New York City, USA, 18 February 1925

Oscars (1): Best Supporting Actor for 'Dragline' in *Cool Hand Luke* (Warner Bros, 1967)

A 'one nomination, one win' man, the 6ft 4in, 230lb George Kennedy won his Oscar for his brutal leader of a Southern chain gang in *Cool Hand Luke* after enjoying a profitable decade as a second-string Hollywood heavy. Lethal as the steel-armed thug who almost does away with Cary Grant in *Charade,* and effective in numerous westerns, he later took on meatier co-starring roles, becoming firmly established in the *Airport* series as the cigar-chewing, no-nonsense maintenance chief Pat Patroni. He began his entertainment career as a technical adviser on the *Sergeant Bilko* TV series after serving sixteen years in the army, first in combat, then as an armed forces radio and TV officer.

Deborah Kerr

Born Helensburgh, Scotland, 30 September 1921

Oscar Nominations (6): Best Actress for Evelyn Boult in *Edward My Son* (MGM, 1949), Karen Holmes in *From Here to Eternity* (Columbia, 1953), Anna Leonowens in *The King and I* (20th Century-Fox, 1956), Sister Angela in *Heaven Knows, Mr Allison* (20th Century-Fox, 1957), Sybil Railton-Bell in *Separate Tables* (United Artists, 1958) and Ida Carmody in *The Sundowners* (Warner Bros, 1960)

'Hollywood moviemakers concluded I wasn't a woman but a lady; anaemic, prissy, frigid,' said Deborah Kerr. 'I yearned to sink my teeth into some roles I could chew on.' In the end, she got her chance, but as far as Oscar was concerned it made little difference; six nominations, six defeats, even though her characters ranged from an alcoholic wife to a promiscuous one, a governess to a nun, a boarding-house spinster to the down-to-earth spouse of an Australian sheep-herder. In the end (in 1994) the Academy's honorary award came her way when she was named as 'an artist of impeccable grace and beauty and a dedicated actress'. The only regret is that they didn't see fit to award her a competitive Oscar, either for one of the six roles for which she was nominated, or for the roles for which she wasn't even considered – namely the three women in different periods of the twentieth century in *The Life and Death of Colonel Blimp*. There indeed was grace and elegance, and a fragile, red-haired beauty.

Ben Kingsley

Born Snaiton, Yorkshire, England, 31 December 1943

Oscars (1): Best Actor for the title role in *Gandhi* (Columbia, 1982)

Oscar Nominations (1): Best Supporting Actor for Meyer Lansky in *Bugsy* (TriStar, 1991)

Brilliant as Gandhi – rarely can an acting award have been so richly deserved – Ben Kingsley showed the Academy his other side a decade later with his portrait of mobster Meyer Lansky in *Bugsy*. Another nomination but no award this time, just several other roles in similar mould, and nothing in the field he cherishes most, comedy. 'I would have loved to have played The Joker in *Batman*,' he said mournfully, 'but that part's gone.' Offers could be in the pipeline. His unluckiest movie: *Schindler's List*. His Jewish accountant Itzhak Stern was every bit as memorable as the nominated Liam Neeson's Schindler.

Sally Kirkland

Born New York City, USA, 31 October 1944

Oscar Nominations (1): Best Actress for the title role in *Anna* (Magnus Films, 1987)

When the 1987 nominations were announced, many voters asked: 'What is this film called *Anna*?' Some even enquired: 'Who's Sally Kirkland?' The answer was that *Anna* was an independent production made on a shoestring and given only a limited release, and that Sally Kirkland was a bit of an outsider from the Hollywood mainstream (she had formerly mixed with the Andy Warhol set) and was up for a quite stunning performance as a one-time famous Czech actress domiciled in New York who finds herself betrayed by the young protégée she takes under her wing. The opposition turned out to be too strong. Cher won at a canter for *Moonstruck*.

Kevin Kline

Born St Louis, Missouri, USA, 24 October 1947

Oscars (1): Best Supporting Actor for Otto in *A Fish Called Wanda* (Prominent Features/MGM, 1988)

It's easy to see how anyone could get obsessed with Jamie Lee Curtis, but to take it to the lengths of Kevin Kline's insanely jealous, super-active assassin in *A Fish Called Wanda* seemed a trifle excessive. It paid off, though, at Oscar time, Kevin picking up his only award (and nomination) to date and ensuring that the phrase 'Don't call me stupid!' entered into movie parlance. No really great roles as yet, although he made a highly effective Donald Woods in Richard Attenborough's *Cry Freedom* and has made several films (*The Big Chill, Silverado, Grand Canyon*) with distinguished writer-director Lawrence Kasdan.

Shirley Knight

Born Goessel, Kansas, USA, 5 July 1937

Oscar Nominations (2): Best Supporting Actress for Reenie in *The Dark at the Top of the Stairs*, (Warner Bros, 1960) and Heavenly Finley in *Sweet Bird of Youth* (MGM, 1962)

She never liked Hollywood very much, did the outspoken Shirley Knight, who much preferred the freedom of working in Europe, where she gave easily her finest film performance, in the British-made *Dutchman* as the sluttish and dangerous Lula who travels the New York subway with a knife in search of racial victims. The role won her the best actress award at the 1967 Venice Film Festival but nothing from the Academy; they favoured her for a couple of roles originally written for the New York stage – as the daughter of roving salesman Robert Preston in *The Dark at the Top of the Stairs* and as Paul Newman's childhood sweetheart in *Sweet Bird of Youth*. More recently she received an Emmy for her performance in the hit TV series *Thirtysomething*.

Alexander Knox

Born Strathroy, Ontario, Canada, 16 January 1907; died 1995

Oscar Nominations (1): Best Actor for Woodrow Wilson in *Wilson* (20th Century-Fox, 1944)

Authoritative, with a dignified demeanour, and a dry, academic tone that made him perfect for judges, schoolteachers and doctors, Alexander Knox had only the one shot at the Oscar, when Darryl Zanuck cast him as President Woodrow Wilson in his long and painstaking biography of the mid-forties. Bitterly disappointed at losing to a 'crooner' (Bing Crosby in *Going My Way*), he subsequently concentrated on mostly character roles and employing his talents, of which there were many, in co-writing a couple of his Hollywood films, stage plays, detective novels and also two highly praised documentary books on Native Americans. Director Joseph Losey, with whom he made several films when domiciled in Britain, claimed that he could build his own house if he had to! His last performance was as the ageing Control in *Tinker, Tailor, Soldier, Spy*.

☆

Susan Kohner

Born Los Angeles, USA, 11 November 1936

Oscar Nominations (1): Best Supporting Actress for Sarah Jane Johnson in *Imitation of Life* (Universal-International, 1959)

One of those young actresses about whom one asks: 'Whatever became of . . . ?' The answer is simple enough: in 1964 she married a fashion designer, gave up acting, became the hostess of a weekly radio show for the blind and also a member of the Board of Associates of the Juilliard School of Music. None of which pleased Universal overmuch, for they had high hopes for her as a future star after her performance as the black girl who passes for white in Douglas Sirk's remake of *Imitation of Life*. Just twenty-three when she was nominated, Kohner made only ten films in her ten-year career, among them *To Hell and Back*, *Freud* and *By Love Possessed*. She is the daughter of the Mexican-born actress Lupita Tovar and the Czech-born Hollywood agent Paul Kohner.

Miliza Korjus

Born Warsaw, Poland, 18 August 1900; died 1980

Oscar Nominations (1): Best Supporting Actress for Carla Donner in
The Great Waltz (MGM, 1938)

Among the least remembered of all Oscar nominees, Miliza Korjus earned
her mention for her one solitary film – MGM's *The Great Waltz*, a tribute to
the music of Johann Strauss in which she played 'the other woman', a
temptress who tries to entice poor Johann away from ever-loving wife Luise
Rainer. A voluptuous blonde soprano who appeared with many European
companies, including the Berlin Opera, before the war, Korjus' recordings
of such Strauss melodies as 'I'm in Love with Vienna' and 'One Day When
We Were Young' (lyrics by Oscar Hammerstein II) became bestsellers.
Films, however, seemed to hold no attractions for her, and she was content
with her singing career until her retirement in the early fifties.

Jack Kruschen

Born Winnipeg, Canada, 20 March 1922

Oscar Nominations (1): Best Supporting Actor for Dr Dreyfuss in *The
Apartment* (United Artists, 1960)

Not perhaps a name that immediately springs to mind, but a quick mention
of the doctor living next door to Jack Lemmon in *The Apartment*
('Mildred . . . he's at it again!') and you'll have him in one. Nominated as
best supporting actor for the scenes in which he saves would-be suicide
Shirley MacLaine from certain death, he was the third member of the cast
to be honoured, but like the film's leading players he came away empty-
handed. A burly Canadian-born actor who has essayed a long line of
professors, inventors, doctors, cops, saloon-keepers, etc., he has appeared
in more than seventy films. Peter Ustinov was named best supporting actor
of 1960 for his slave master in *Spartacus*.

L

Diane Ladd

Born Meridian, Mississippi, USA, 29 November 1932

Oscar Nominations (3): Best Supporting Actress for Flo in *Alice Doesn't Live Here Anymore* (Warner Bros, 1974), Marietta Pace in *Wild at Heart* (Polygram/Propaganda Films, 1990) and Mother Hillyer in *Rambling Rose* (Carolco Pictures, 1991)

Three nominations for a supporting performer isn't at all bad going in these non-studio days. Diane Ladd has managed it for her earthy bleached-blonde waitress friend of Ellen Burstyn, her insanely possessive mother in hot pursuit of daughter and Nicolas Cage, and her sensitive Southern matriarch (in *Rambling Rose*). The last-named film saw her achieve a place in the Oscar history books as she and her daughter Laura Dern became the only real life mother-daughter duo to be nominated in the same film. The award, though, would have been more welcome than the record.

Jocelyn LaGarde

Born 1922; died 1979

Oscar Nominations (1): Best Supporting Actress for the Alii Nui, Malama, in *Hawaii* (United Artists, 1966)

The tallest and heaviest actress ever to make it into the nominations lists, the Tahitian-born Jocelyn LaGarde stood 6ft tall, weighed in at 418lb and boasted vital statistics of 52-48-54 when she played the island queen in *Hawaii*. Add to that the fact that she had never acted before, couldn't speak a word of English and had to learn her part phonetically, and she must rank as the most unusual nominee in the history of the Academy. The somewhat slimmer Sandy Dennis took the award for *Virginia Woolf* but wasn't half as much fun on screen.

Christine Lahti

Born Birmingham, Michigan, USA, 14 April 1950

Oscar Nominations (1): Best Supporting Actress for Hazel Zanussi in *Swing Shift* (Warner Bros, 1984)

A best actress in the years ahead? A strong possibility in the case of Christine Lahti, who has already made the nominations lists for her former nightclub dancer turned World War II factory worker in *Swing Shift* and been undeservedly overlooked for her on-the-run wife of Judd Hirsch in *Running on Empty*, and her freewheeling vagabond aunt in charge of a couple of teenagers in Bill Forsyth's undervalued *Housekeeping*. Oscar success continues to elude her, although the Los Angeles Critics recognised her talents and named her best actress for *Running on Empty*. In 1996 the Academy at least recognised her work behind the cameras for co-producing and directing the year's live action short film, *Lieberman in Love*.

✩

Burt Lancaster

Born New York, USA, 2 November 1913; died 1994

Oscars (1): Best Actor for the title role in *Elmer Gantry* (United Artists, 1960)

Oscar Nominations (3): Best Actor for Sergeant Warden in *From Here to Eternity* (Columbia, 1953), Robert Stroud in *Birdman of Alcatraz* (United Artists, 1962), and 'Lou' in *Atlantic City USA* (Enterprise, 1981)

Burt Lancaster once said of himself: 'Most people seem to think I'm the kind of guy who shaves with a blowtorch. Actually I'm exactly the opposite. I'm bookish and worrisome.' His self-assessment went some way to explaining why he was later able to make the effortless change from the swashbuckling and action roles that had made him famous, to the quieter, more distinguished parts of his middle and later years. His Oscar for his gin-swigging fiery salesman turned evangelist Elmer Gantry was for a role he was born to play, although for many his chilling, all-powerful New York columnist J. J. Hunsecker (for which he was not even nominated) in *The*

Sweet Smell of Success is the superior performance. His independent company (formed with Harold Hecht) produced the year's best picture, *Marty*, in 1955. In later years he worked with distinction for such directors as Robert Aldrich, Luchino Visconti, Robert Altman and Louis Malle. He died, aged eighty, in the autumn of 1994.

Elsa Lanchester

Born Lewisham, London, England, 28 October 1902; died 1986

Oscar Nominations (2): Best Supporting Actress for Miss Potts in *Come to the Stable* (20th Century-Fox, 1949) and Miss Plimsoll in *Witness for the Prosecution* (United Artists, 1957)

A great big smile, a fussy manner and an eccentric nature – that was mostly Elsa Lanchester on screen. It was certainly her to the life as the peckish nurse taking care of real-life hubby Charles Laughton in *Witness for the Prosecution*. An Oscar favourite for the role, just ahead of Diane Varsi and Carolyn Jones, she had to watch as the Japanese actress Miyoshi Umeki confounded the pundits by taking the year's supporting nod for *Sayonara*. Nominated earlier for her religious artist who gives sanctuary to two nuns in *Come to the Stable*, she was perhaps a shade unlucky in that supporting awards had not been introduced when she played the screeching *Bride of Frankenstein* in 1935.

Martin Landau

Born Brooklyn, New York, USA, 20 June 1928

Oscars (1): Best Supporting Actor for Bela Lugosi in *Ed Wood* (Buena Vista, 1994)

Oscar Nominations (2): Best Supporting Actor for Abe Karatz in *Tucker – The Man and His Dream* (Paramount, 1988) and Judah Rosenthal in *Crimes and Misdemeanors* (Orion, 1989)

No one who treads on poor old Cary Grant's fingers as he hangs on to the edge of Mount Rushmore (with Eva Marie Saint holding on to him!)

deserves much sympathy, but for a while in the late eighties and early nineties, Martin Landau was certainly getting his fair share of 'he looks as though he'll never win it' kind of remarks at Oscar time. Until, that is, he played Bela Lugosi and the breakthrough was made. Nominated previously for his business partner of Jeff Bridges in Coppola's *Tucker* and his eminent doctor anxious to dispose of his mistress in Woody Allen's *Crimes and Misdemeanors*, he was a 'heavy' in movies until he became famous as one of the early heroes in the TV series *Mission Impossible*. He was a cartoonist with the *New York Daily News* before deciding on an acting career.

Hope Lange

Born Redding Ridge, Connecticut, USA, 28 November 1931

Oscar Nominations (1): Best Supporting Actress for Selena Cross in *Peyton Place* (20th Century-Fox, 1957)

A Fox hopeful of the late fifties who like several other starlets arrived at the studio when its great days were over, Hope Lange found that opportunities for young actresses to make a name for themselves were few and far between. The one opportunity that did come her way was the role of the Peyton Place girl raped by brutal stepfather Arthur Kennedy and who commits murder in self-defence. An Oscar nomination for that (what else!), but just about everyone in the film's cast seemed to be up for Oscars on awards night and Lange eventually found more rewarding opportunities on TV, where she won Emmys for her comedy talents in *The Ghost and Mrs Muir* and starred in *The New Dick Van Dyke Show*.

Jessica Lange

Born Cloquet, Minnesota, USA, 20 April 1949

Oscars (2): Best Supporting Actress for Julie in *Tootsie* (Columbia, 1982); Best Actress for Carly Marshall in *Blue Sky* (Orion, 1994)

Oscar Nominations (4): Best Actress for Frances Farmer in *Frances* (EMI/Universal, 1982), Jewell Ivy in *Country* (Touchstone, 1984), Patsy Cline in *Sweet Dreams* (HBO/TriStar, 1985) and Ann Talbot in *Music Box* (Carolco/TriStar, 1989)

There are ways and ways of winning an Academy Award, but Jessica Lange scored something of a first in 1995 when a film she had made three years earlier, and which had been shelved because its distributor had gone bankrupt, was dusted down, released in time for the Oscars and hey presto – she was best actress of the year! So much for the quality of the other female performers, and little wonder that Lange commented that good scripts are 'as rare as hen's teeth'. A supporting winner in the early eighties for her glamorous young TV soap star in *Tootsie*, she also made the lists for her performances in a couple of biopics – as the controversial thirties movie star Frances Farmer and the country singer Patsy Cline – plus her desperate farmer's wife in *Country* and her attorney who finds herself defending her father on a charge of war crimes in *Music Box*. Her win in 1995 was for her blowsy army wife in the late Tony Richardson's *Blue Sky*.

Angela Lansbury

Born London, England, 16 October 1925

Oscar Nominations (3): Best Supporting Actress for Nancy Oliver in *Gaslight* (MGM, 1944), Sybil Vane in *The Picture of Dorian Gray* (MGM, 1945) and 'Raymond's Mother' in *The Manchurian Candidate* (United Artists, 1962)

Twice nominated during her period at MGM – for her conniving maid who joins Charles Boyer in trying to drive Ingrid Bergman mad, and then as a victim herself as a fragile music-hall singer in *The Picture of Dorian Gray* – the pouting, slightly insolent looking Angela Lansbury enjoyed her most flamboyant screen role when she was cast as the monstrous, power-mad mother of Communist assassin Laurence Harvey in *The*

Manchurian Candidate. The National Board of Review voted her the year's best, but the Academy opted for Patty Duke in *The Miracle Worker*. She did, though, at least get a vote of confidence from President Kennedy. When asked for the go-ahead for a possibly dangerous film about political assassination, he agreed wholeheartedly to the project and asked, 'Who's going to play the mother?' When told Angela Lansbury, he replied: 'Perfect!'

Charles Laughton

Born Scarborough, Yorkshire, England, 1 July 1899; died 1962

Oscars (1): Best Actor for the title role in *The Private Life of Henry VIII* (London Films, British, 1932/33)

Oscar Nominations (2): Best Actor for Captain William Bligh in *Mutiny on the Bounty* (MGM, 1935) and Sir Wilfrid Robarts in *Witness for the Prosecution* (United Artists, 1957)

From the first burp the Oscar was his, and for a while it seemed as though British actors would challenge Hollywood stars as the most popular in the world. It didn't last, but Charles Laughton did, journeying to Hollywood once the Oscar was in his grasp and finding himself nominated again two years later for another British tyrant, Captain Bligh. Some twenty years later he was nominated for a third time for his ailing barrister who defends Tyrone Power in *Witness for the Prosecution* and makes devastating use of the word 'Liar!' when Marlene Dietrich is in the witness box. There should, perhaps, have been more nominations, even Oscars (his English valet, *Ruggles of Red Gap*, Javert in *Les Misérables*, *The Hunchback of Notre Dame*), and how he came to be overlooked for his direction of *The Night of the Hunter* belongs with the all-time mysteries of the Oscar awards. In shame, the voters should hang their heads.

Piper Laurie

Born Detroit, USA, 22 January 1932

Oscar Nominations (3): Best Actress for Sarah Packard in *The Hustler* (20th Century-Fox, 1961); Best Supporting Actress for Margaret White in *Carrie* (United Artists, 1976) and Mrs Norman in *Children of a Lesser God* (Paramount, 1986)

'Tits and sand' movies (often opposite Tony Curtis or Rock Hudson) were the kind of flicks on which Piper Laurie cut her teeth in the fifties. If things had stayed that way, no doubt she would have called it a day, but along came the alcoholic crippled girlfriend of hustler Paul Newman (plus an Oscar nomination), and suddenly all the Universal double features and conversing with Francis the Talking Mule seemed to have been worthwhile. A three-time nominee, she also made it to the lists for going over the top as Sissy Spacek's religious fanatic mom and for playing somewhat more reservedly as the mother of the deaf Marlee Matlin.

Cloris Leachman

Born Des Moines, Iowa, USA, 30 April 1926

Oscars (1): Best Supporting Actress for Ruth Popper in *The Last Picture Show* (Columbia, 1971)

Most people in the cast of *The Last Picture Show* were lonely, frustrated or disillusioned about one thing or another. Cloris Leachman's problem was one of neglect – by her football coach husband – one she eventually solved by embarking on an affair with eager high-school boy Timothy Bottoms. All the anguish and tenderness brought an Academy Award, making it a double for *Picture Show* in the supporting category, Ben Johnson also winning for his Sam the Lion. A sometime comedy performer for Mel Brooks (*Young Frankenstein, High Anxiety*), Leachman has won no fewer than six Emmys for her TV work.

Peggy Lee

Born Jamestown, North Dakota, USA, 26 May 1920

Oscar Nominations (1): Best Supporting Actress for Rose Hopkins in
Pete Kelly's Blues (Warner Bros, 1955)

A singer first, a lyricist second and an actress third, Peggy Lee featured in
only two movies in the fifties – in Warner's remake of *The Jazz Singer* (as the
wife of Danny Thomas) and in the same studio's *Pete Kelly's Blues*, a
twenties gangster movie notable for a superbly staged shootout in a
deserted ballroom and a finely judged performance from Lee as a fading
singer taken to the bottle. Jo Van Fleet, for her portrait of a brothel madam
in *East of Eden*, emerged victorious on Oscar night, but Lee enjoyed some
satisfaction during the year with her rendering of the hit movie song 'He's a
Tramp' (from Disney's feature cartoon *Lady and the Tramp*), for which she
also wrote the lyrics.

Andrea Leeds

Born Butte, Montana, USA, 18 August 1913; died 1984

Oscar Nominations (1): Best Supporting Actress for Kaye Hamilton in
Stage Door (RKO, 1937)

High on the list of now forgotten Academy nominees, Andrea Leeds
enjoyed only a four-year career in movies before deciding to marry a
millionaire and breed racehorses. Sounds like a Betty Grable Fox musical
come true! Her one nomination? For her tragic suicide in Gregory LaCava's
version of the Ferber/Kaufman Broadway hit, *Stage Door*, about the lives of
some aspiring young actresses living in a theatrical boarding house in New
York. Alice Brady won in 1937 for helping to destroy Chicago in the city's
great fire of 1871.

Eva Le Gallienne

Born London, England, 11 January 1899; died 1991

Oscar Nominations (1): Best Supporting Actress for Grandma Pearl in *Resurrection* (Universal, 1980)

'I would rather play Ibsen than eat and that's often what it amounts to,' lamented Eva Le Gallienne, whose theatrical ambitions of taking the classics to the masses might have earned a financial boost had she ventured into the cinema more often. She ventured just three times, playing the Queen opposite Richard Burton's Hamlet in *Prince of Players*, Mrs Dudgeon in *The Devil's Disciple* and, when she was in her eighties, the faith-healing Ellen Burstyn's grandmother in *Resurrection*. Oscar-nominated for the latter role, she was not the recipient of a sentimental win. Mary Steenburgen took the year's supporting award for *Melvin and Howard*.

Janet Leigh

Born Merced, California, USA, 6 July 1927

Oscar Nominations (1): Best Supporting Actress for Marion Crane in *Psycho* (Paramount, 1960)

She should have been worried the minute Anthony Perkins said softly, 'A boy's best friend is his mother', and by the stuffed birds adorning the motel office walls. But Janet Leigh ignored the warning signs and went right on in there and took her shower! Result: one of the nastiest deaths in movies (even Hitchcock movies) and an Academy Award nomination for forty minutes' worth of screen acting. No Oscar – Shirley Jones took that for *Elmer Gantry* – but a firm place in film history, for both her acting and her screen death, and for wearing possibly the most attractive white bra ever seen in movies.

Vivien Leigh

Born Darjeeling, India, 5 November 1913; died 1967

Oscars (2): Best Actress for Scarlett O'Hara in *Gone with the Wind* (Selznick/MGM, 1939) and Blanche DuBois in *A Streetcar Named Desire* (Warner Bros, 1951)

Olivier may have earned the nominations, but wife Vivien came out ahead as far as actual wins were concerned, two to his one, and both, rather incredibly, for portraits of Southern belles – the first for her flirtatious and spirited Scarlett, the second (when her own fragile beauty had faded a little) for the tragic Blanche DuBois, a woman lost in an illusory world of broken dreams. She made just nineteen films in her career, ten prior to *Gone with the Wind* and eight after; only Glenda Jackson and Elizabeth Taylor among British-born actresses have equalled her double win, although not for Southern belles!

Margaret Leighton

Born Barnt Green, near Birmingham, England, 26 February 1922; died 1976

Oscar Nominations (1): Best Supporting Actress for Mrs Maudsley in *The Go-Between* (MGM/EMI, 1971)

There may have been deadlier screen mothers in the seventies but it's difficult to find anything to rival the class-obsessed bitchiness of Margaret Leighton, who in *The Go-Between* snuffs out the romance between daughter Julie Christie and local farmer Alan Bates – with tragic results. The Oscar went elsewhere (to Cloris Leachman for her neglected wife in *The Last Picture Show*), but for Leighton the nomination was probably reward enough and due recognition for her screen roles, which although not large in number were always subtle and interesting. Married three times – to publisher Max Reinhardt and actors Laurence Harvey and Michael Wilding – she died of multiple sclerosis at the age of fifty-four.

☆

Jack Lemmon

Born Boston, USA, 8 February 1925

Oscars (2): Best Supporting Actor for Ensign Frank Thurlowe Pulver in *Mister Roberts* (Warner Bros, 1955); Best Actor for Harry Stoner in *Save the Tiger* (Paramount, 1973)

Oscar Nominations (6): Best Actor for Jerry/Daphne in *Some Like It Hot* (United Artists, 1959), C. C. Baxter in *The Apartment* (United Artists, 1960), Joe Clay in *Days of Wine and Roses* (Warner Bros, 1962), Jack Godell in *The China Syndrome* (Columbia, 1979), Scottie Templeton in *Tribute* (20th Century-Fox, 1980) and Ed Horman in *Missing* (Universal, 1982)

The most successful loser the screen has ever known tends to sound like a contradiction in terms, but it's what Jack Lemmon has been all about since he found his way into Harry Cohn's Columbia studio back in the fifties. Give him a man close to desperation and despairing of the values of the modern world and he's right in there at the centre of things. A double Oscar-winner for his ebullient misfit in *Mister Roberts* and his desperate garment manufacturer who considers arson to be the only way out of his financial troubles, he has made the nomination lists twice for Billy Wilder – for his bass-playing 'Daphne' and the insurance clerk with the most popular apartment in town – and on four other occasions: for his advertising executive brought down by alcoholism, conscience-stricken nuclear plant employee, ailing New York press agent and his father searching desperately for his missing son in Chile. The only strange thing about the list is the absence of *The Odd Couple*. Why no mention for his fussy Felix Ungar? There was nothing either for Walter Matthau for his all-time slob Oscar Madison. Odd indeed!

Lotte Lenya

Born Hitzing, Austria, 18 October 1900; died 1981

Oscar Nominations (1): Best Supporting Actress for the Contessa Magda Terribili-Gonzales in *The Roman Spring of Mrs Stone* (Warner Bros, 1961)

Famous around the world for her sadistic lesbian assassin Rosa Klebb, who in *From Russia With Love* lands a sickening blow to the solar plexus of muscular hood Robert Shaw, Lotte Lenya was for twenty years married to German composer Kurt Weill, devoting much of her musical career to becoming a brilliant exponent of his work. Her Oscar nomination was earned for one of her five film roles, as Tennessee Williams' corrupt and procuring Italian contessa who runs a stable of handsome boys and sells to the highest bidder, one of whom is the recently widowed fifty-year-old actress Vivien Leigh. Lenya lost the Oscar but loved the role: 'So wicked and stark and old, this Contessa,' she said. 'But she was not all that vicious. She split fifty-fifty with her call boys. That's not bad for an agent.'

Michael Lerner

Born Brooklyn, New York, USA, 22 June 1941

Oscar Nominations (1): Best Supporting Actor for Jack Lipnick in *Barton Fink* (Barton Circle Prods/20th Century-Fox, 1991)

Somewhere along the line Michael Lerner decided on an acting career rather than continuing as a professor of dramatic literature. The professor-ship might have offered more security but the acting has proved fruitful, especially after his nomination for his Louis B. Mayer-type studio head in the Coen brothers' *Barton Fink*. Jack Palance (for his trail boss in *City Slickers*) got the better of him on Oscar night, but he has continued to prosper in TV movies and on the big screen as tricky lawyers and mobsters.

Juliette Lewis

Born California, USA, 1972

Oscar Nominations (1): Best Supporting Actress for Danielle Bowden in *Cape Fear* (Universal, 1991)

Known nowadays as one of Oliver Stone's *Natural Born Killers*, Juliette Lewis has enjoyed herself in two of America's most popular cult movies of the nineties: Woody Allen's *Husbands and Wives*, in which she likened Woody's unpublished novel to *Triumph of the Will* and was put down as 'a twenty-year-old twit', and Scorsese's remake of *Cape Fear*, in which she came dangerously close to succumbing to the lethal power of a psychotic

Robert De Niro. She was nominated for the latter role, although there are those who feel she would have been better served had she been mentioned for the former.

John Lithgow

Born Rochester, New York, USA, 19 October 1945

Oscar Nominations (2): Best Supporting Actor for Roberta Muldoon in *The World According to Garp* (Warner Bros, 1982) and Sam Burns in *Terms of Endearment* (Paramount, 1983)

A list of today's ten most underrated American character actors would almost certainly include John Lithgow. Able to play just about anything in films, he has been into outer space to find out what happened to poor old HAL in *2010*, served in World War II for David Puttnam in *Memphis Belle* and come up against Sylvester Stallone in *Cliffhanger*. His Oscar nominations were won in consecutive years in the early eighties for his 6ft 4in transsexual former football player and his rather more orthodox bank employee infatuated with Debra Winger. Nothing since. Mr Lithgow, however, remains lurking in the wings.

Sondra Locke

Born Shelbyville, Tennessee, USA, 28 May 1947

Oscar Nominations (1): Best Supporting Actress for Mick Kelly in *The Heart Is a Lonely Hunter* (Warner Bros, 1968)

She won her Oscar nomination for her very first film, when she was just twenty-one, for her lonely, music-loving adolescent who befriends deaf mute Alan Arkin. After that came Clint Eastwood – in both her personal life and the movies, when she finished up having knives thrown at her in *Bronco Billy*, co-starring with an orang-utan in *Every Which Way But Loose* and even moving out West in *The Outlaw Josey Wales*. None of which did a great deal for her acting career but all of which kept her very much in the public eye. As yet, no more Oscar nominations, but she began directing in the mid-eighties so her future may lie in that direction.

Gene Lockhart

Born London, Ontario, Canada, 18 July 1891; died 1957

Oscar Nominations (1): Best Supporting Actor for Regis in *Algiers* (United Artists, 1938)

An absolute gift to Hollywood studios in that he was equally effective as a kindly American college professor or a Nazi spy, the chubby-faced Gene Lockhart earned his sole Oscar nomination for his 'slimy but humorous' police informer in Hollywood's remake of *Algiers*. He lost, as it seemed did most character actors in those days, to Walter Brennan, for *Kentucky*. Memorable as a Nazi collaborator in Fritz Lang's *Hangmen Also Die*, and a memory freak who aids a German spy ring in *The House on 92nd Street*, Lockhart spent many of his later years at the Fox studio sometimes popping up for just a scene or two in major productions. As well as acting in more than 120 films, he succeeded Lee J. Cobb on Broadway in *Death of a Salesman*, sang opera, wrote a newspaper column, authored theatrical sketches, and composed songs, the most famous of which was 'The World Is Waiting for the Sunrise' which he wrote with Deems Taylor.

Robert Loggia

Born Staten Island, New York, USA, 3 January 1930

Oscar Nominations (1): Best Supporting Actor for Sam Ransom in *Jagged Edge* (Columbia, 1985)

One of the most reliable 'urban men' of American movies, Robert Loggia has been a cop, a hood, a hit man, a private eye and a few other things besides since his screen début back in the mid-fifties. Oscar-nominated for his colourful, foul-mouthed gumshoe hired by lawyer Glenn Close in the acclaimed thriller *Jagged Edge*, he has been a regular performer for director Blake Edwards over the years, appearing in three *Pink Panther* movies as well as *S.O.B* and *That's Life*. Of Sicilian descent, he has also excelled as a crime boss in De Palma's *Scarface* and a Mafioso in Huston's *Prizzi's Honor*.

Carole Lombard

Born Fort Wayne, Indiana, USA, 6 October 1908; died 1942

Oscar Nominations (1): Best Actress for Irene Bullock in *My Man Godfrey* (Universal, 1936)

'Hollywood is the place where they write the alibis first, before they write the story,' quipped prankster-superstar Carole Lombard, who in the thirties was the queen of screwball comedy and easily as much fun off the screen as she was on. Nominated just the once, for her socialite who picks up a bum from the city dump and turns him into the family butler, she was one of twenty people killed in a plane crash near Las Vegas early in 1942. Just thirty-four (two years younger than Marilyn Monroe at the time of her death), she was returning from a US bond-selling tour and had completed her last film, Lubitsch's *To Be or Not to Be*, a week before. Married first to William Powell and then to Clark Gable, she was portrayed by Jill Clayburgh in an inferior biopic of 1975.

☆

Sophia Loren

Born Rome, Italy, 20 September 1934

Oscars (1): Best Actress for Cesira in *Two Women* (Ponti, Embassy-Italy, 1961)

Oscar Nominations (1): Best Actress for Filumena Marturano in *Marriage, Italian Style* (Champion-Concordia, Embassy-Italy, 1964)

The only actress to win an Oscar in a foreign-language film, Sophia Loren triumphed for her role in DeSica's harrowing tale of a mother and daughter victimised by soldiers in war-ravaged Italy in World War II. Her subsequent nomination for her comedy role as Marcello Mastroianni's long-time mistress was again for an Italian film, illustrating that Hollywood hadn't quite realised her potential when they brought her to the States in the mid-fifties and cast her in comedies, thrillers and ultimately epics. Still, she did get to star opposite Cary Grant, Paul Newman, Gregory Peck and others; not bad for an illegimate child who grew up in the slums of Naples and began as an extra in *Quo Vadis?*. In 1990 she was presented with an honorary award by the Academy, who named her as 'one of the genuine treasures of world cinema'.

Joan Lorring

Born 1926

Oscar Nominations (1): Best Supporting Actress for Bessie Watty in *The Corn Is Green* (Warner Bros, 1945)

Spiteful adolescence can offer great opportunities on screen, but once performers have passed the age limit they need something in reserve if they are going to make the transition to full stardom. Joan Lorring didn't quite make the transition but she did make the most of her young temptress who seduces and almost ruins the life of Welsh student John Dall. No prizes on Oscar night, nor any for another Warner Little Miss Nasty, Ann Blyth, in *Mildred Pierce*. Instead, for Lorring, a few more roles as troubled teenagers, some radio work and a career on Broadway.

Bessie Love

Born Midland, Texas, USA, 10 September 1898; died 1986

Oscar Nominations (1): Best Actress for 'Hank' Mahoney in *The Broadway Melody* (MGM, 1928/29)

A bit of everything, was Bessie Love – comedy star, dramatic actress, musical performer – and although she never quite hit the top, she did manage an Oscar nomination for her musical talents (as half of a vaudeville sister act) in MGM's award-winning *The Broadway Melody*. Mostly a star of the silent days (sixty films in sixteen years, including *Intolerance* for Griffith), she retired from the mainstream in 1931 and settled in England four years later. She subsequently popped up from time to time in bit-parts in several notable movies – *The Barefoot Contessa*, *Ragtime*, *Reds* and *Sunday, Bloody Sunday* (as a telephone operator) – just to keep her hand in.

☆

Paul Lukas

Born Budapest, Hungary, 26 May 1894; died 1971

Oscars (1): Best Actor for Kurt Muller in *Watch on the Rhine* (Warner Bros, 1943)

Frequently the first in line when studios were casting around for middle-European seducers and villains, the heavily accented Paul Lukas found it difficult to stay afloat with the coming of sound and only survived at Paramount because of a crash course in English. The money was well spent. The course paved the way for a sinister heavy for Hitchcock in *The Lady Vanishes*, and ultimately an Oscar for his anti-Nazi refugee seeking freedom in the United States in Lillian Hellman's *Watch on the Rhine*. Self-deprecating about his efforts in Hellman's work, which he had first played on Broadway, he said: 'The writing is so right you don't have to learn the part. It sticks to you. I amuse myself by changing a gesture occasionally.' Both Bogie (*Casablanca*) and Gary Cooper (*For Whom the Bell Tolls*) were Oscar contenders in 1943.

Alfred Lunt

Born Milwaukee, Wisconsin, USA, 19 August 1892; died 1977

Oscar Nominations (1): Best Actor for 'The Actor' in *The Guardsman* (MGM, 1931/32)

Anyone was fair game for the movies in the thirties, even the 'Royalty of Broadway', the Lunts (Alfred Lunt and Lynn Fontanne), whom Louis B. Mayer tried to sign to a long-term contract at Metro. No luck. Their first movie, *The Guardsman*, a repeat of their New York stage success, rang no box-office bells and it was back to the boards, where they carried on as before. Lunt's nominated role? That of an Austrian actor who goes to elaborate lengths to prove his wife's infidelity. Audiences weren't interested. They preferred the year's other nominees: Wallace Beery who made 'em cry in *The Champ*, and Fredric March who scared the hell out of them as *Dr Jekyll and Mr Hyde*.

M

Mercedes McCambridge

Born Joliet, Illinois, USA, 17 March 1918

Oscars (1): Best Supporting Actress for Sadie Burke in *All the King's Men* (Columbia, 1949)

Oscar Nominations (1): Best Supporting Actress for Luz Benedict in *Giant* (Warner Bros, 1956)

A tragic private life severely hindered McCambridge's career, which for a moment in the late forties – when she won her Oscar for Broderick Crawford's cynical, all-knowing political aide – looked as though it was really going to blossom. Nineteen films in some forty-five years tells its own story, although there have been some pearls along the way, especially her surly Texas rancher Luz Benedict, and the mother of a mentally ill Elizabeth Taylor in *Suddenly, Last Summer*. Originally a radio performer, she was at one time described by Orson Welles as 'the greatest radio actress in the world', which is probably why she made such a superb job of creating the rasping and unnerving voice of the Devil in *The Exorcist*.

Kevin McCarthy

Born Seattle, USA, 15 February 1914

Oscar Nominations (1): Best Supporting Actor for Biff in *Death of a Salesman* (Columbia, 1951)

One of Hollywood's young dependables of the early fifties (his sister was the writer Mary McCarthy), Kevin McCarthy won Academy recognition for repeating his Broadway role as the son of Willy Loman, although he perhaps deserved an additional nomination five years later for escaping in *Invasion of the Body Snatchers*. Running in desperation for most of the latter part of the film, and losing the real Dana Wynter to the pod Dana Wynter (the ultimate tragedy), he yells at the audience at the climax 'You're in danger. They're here already! You're next! You're next! You're next!' He survived to repeat his warning in Philip Kaufman's 1978 remake but met his end beneath the wheels of a car.

Patty McCormack

Born Brooklyn, New York, USA, 21 August 1945

Oscar Nominations (1): Best Supporting Actress for Rhoda in *The Bad Seed* (Warner Bros, 1956)

A model at four, a TV performer at seven and one of the screen's worst child monsters at eleven, Patty McCormack demonstrated her penchant for murder in her repeat of her Broadway role as a lethal little killer with an inbred talent for homicide who sets about trying to murder just about everyone in sight and scores close to a 50 per cent strike rate! No go on Oscar night, however. She lost in 1956 to Dorothy Malone, who in *Written on the Wind* slept with everyone instead of killing them.

Hattie McDaniel

Born Wichita, Kansas, USA, 10 June 1895; died 1952

Oscars (1): Best Supporting Actress for Mammy in *Gone with the Wind* (Selznick/MGM, 1939)

'Taint fittin' . . . taint fittin',' mumbled Hattie McDaniel as she wandered her way through *Gone with the Wind*, doing her best to keep tabs on Scarlett but invariably finishing up one step behind. Today, her image of maid or servant is something of an affront to black performers, although in McDaniel's case it is difficult to imagine her doing anything other than cooking or serving or even, in *Song of the South*, muttering her way through a Disney number as she rolls the pastry. The first black performer to be honoured with an Academy Award, she was memorable in an earlier role in George Stevens' *Alice Adams* as the down-to-earth maid who completely ruins social climber Katharine Hepburn's attempts to provide an elegant dinner for the rich young Fred MacMurray.

Mary McDonnell

Born Ithaca, New York, USA, 1952

Oscar Nominations (2): Best Supporting Actress for Stands With Fist in *Dances With Wolves* (Tig/Orion, 1990); Best Actress for Mary-Alice Culhane in *Passion Fish* (Miramax, 1992)

Natalie Wood didn't make the nominated five for her white girl raised by Indians in John Ford's *The Searchers*; Mary McDonnell, on the other hand, managed it with some ease for her performance, in *Dances With Wolves*, as the emotionally traumatised white woman adopted in childhood by the Sioux tribe. Hollywood opted for the more showy Whoopi Goldberg for *Ghost* on Oscar night but has since nominated McDonnell again, this time for a major performance as the TV soap star fighting her way back after being paralysed from the waist down in an accident. This time it was Emma Thompson (*Howards End*) who barred the way to the Oscar. Not for long, one suspects.

Frances McDormand

Born Illinois, USA, 1958

Oscar Nominations (1): Best Supporting Actress for Mrs Pell in *Mississippi Burning* (Orion, 1988)

She made the lists for her few but telling scenes with FBI man Gene Hackman, who slowly and flirtatiously persuades her to reveal just what happened to the three missing civil rights workers in *Mississippi Burning*. The result on screen was a dreadful beating at the hands of her sadistic deputy sheriff husband; off screen it was a nomination, and deservedly so. No Oscar, though. Geena Davis had that all sewn up for *The Accidental Tourist*, and McDormand has since gone back to doing what she does best – making films for the Coen Brothers – *Raising Arizona*, *Miller's Crossing* and *Fargo*.

Elizabeth McGovern

Born Evanston, Illinois, USA, 18 July 1961

Oscar Nominations (1): Best Supporting Actress for Evelyn Nesbit in *Ragtime* (Paramount, 1981)

Anyone playing the notorious 'girl in a cage' beauty Evelyn Nesbit has a head start on her fellow performers, for it's a role to savour. Joan Collins did pretty well, all things considered, back in 1955 in Fleischer's *The Girl in the Red Velvet Swing*; Elizabeth McGovern did even better in *Ragtime*, earning a nomination for her portrait of the ex-chorus girl whose lover – famed architect Stanford White – was shot dead by her insane hubby Harry Thaw in full view of everyone in the Madison Square Roof Garden in 1906. Lots of nudity, plenty of sullen looks and some intelligent playing from McGovern as the girl with more than one eye on the half-chance – but no Oscar.

Ali MacGraw

Born Pound Ridge, New York, USA, 1 April 1938

Oscar Nominations (1): Best Actress for Jenny Cavilleri in *Love Story* (Paramount, 1970)

Once she and Ryan O'Neal had exchanged the immortal phrase 'Love means never having to say you're sorry', Ali MacGraw was on her way to becoming one of the hottest properties in Hollywood, but despite an Oscar nomination for her terminally ill music student in *Love Story*, things didn't quite work out as she had hoped. Her love-hate relationship with Steve McQueen led to her becoming a virtual recluse for several years, and when she decided on a comeback her hot-property days were over. At her best in her first starring film, as the vacationing Jewish student giving Richard Benjamin the permanent 'come-on' in *Goodbye Columbus*, she teamed just once with McQueen on screen, in the Sam Peckinpah gangster thriller *The Getaway*.

Dorothy McGuire

Born Omaha, Nebraska, USA, 14 June 1918

Oscar Nominations (1): Best Actress for Kathy Lacey in *Gentleman's Agreement* (20th Century-Fox, 1947)

No actress before or since has quite managed to convey the quiet serenity and inner calmness so beautifully evoked on screen by Dorothy McGuire. Unique as an actress and a personality, she won her nomination for her supposedly liberal fiancée of crusading journalist Gregory Peck, although many would claim she deserved it more for her young mute woman terrorised by an unseen killer in the spooky old house movie, *The Spiral Staircase*, or in later years for Wyler's *Friendly Persuasion*, when she brought a charm and mature intelligence to her Quaker wife of Gary Cooper. Only twenty-six films all told, not many for the number of years she was making movies, but there were very few duds among them.

Victor McLaglen

Born Tunbridge Wells, Kent, England, 10 December 1886; died 1959

Oscars (1): Best Actor for Gypo Nolan in *The Informer* (RKO, 1935)

Oscar Nominations (1): Best Supporting Actor for Red Will Danaher in *The Quiet Man* (Republic, 1952)

An Oscar-winner for his tragic Gypo who betrays his friends to the police during the Sinn Fein rebellion, and a post-war nominee for his brutish brother of Maureen O'Hara, Victor McLaglen was for more than twenty-five years one of director John Ford's favourite actors, especially when he was seeking comedy relief for his series of cavalry westerns. Not that filming could have held much excitement for the muscular, 220lb actor. His pre-movie career seemed much more exhilarating – serving in the Boer War, prospecting for gold in Canada, boxing and wrestling his way across America, and diving for pearls in the South Seas. Legend has it that when he was working in a travelling carnival he allowed his chest to be used as an anvil for men to break rocks on.

Shirley MacLaine

Born Richmond, Virginia, USA, 24 April 1934

Oscars (1): Best Actress for Aurora Greenway in *Terms of Endearment* (Paramount, 1983)

Oscar Nominations (4): Best Actress for Ginny Moorhead in *Some Came Running* (MGM, 1958), Fran Kubelik in *The Apartment* (United Artists, 1960), the title role in *Irma La Douce* (United Artists, 1963) and Deedee Rodgers in *The Turning Point* (20th Century-Fox, 1977)

'I lost to a tracheotomy,' said Shirley MacLaine, managing one of her celebrated elfin smiles when the name of Elizabeth Taylor – almost a fatal casualty during the filming of *Cleopatra* in London – was announced for *Butterfield 8*. Had she realised that it would be another twenty-three years before she would finally claim the award, she might not have been so sanguine. Stopping a bullet for Frank Sinatra didn't do it. Neither did playing an elevator girl and a Parisian prostitute for Billy Wilder. Nor portraying a one-time ballerina. Living next door to and sleeping with boozy old astronaut Jack Nicholson did. When asked whether she thought she had won for her performance or her body of work she replied, 'Both – and for my body too!'

Note: MacLaine was also nominated in 1975 as the producer, writer and co-director of the feature documentary *The Other Half of the Sky: A China Memoir*.

Aline MacMahon

Born McKeesport, Pennsylvania, USA, 3 May 1899; died 1991

Oscar Nominations (1): Best Supporting Actress for Mrs Ling Tan in *Dragon Seed* (MGM, 1944)

One of Warner's 'in-between stars' of the thirties – she was never a top screen performer and was always a little more than a character actress – Aline MacMahon developed a nice line in worldly-wise secretaries always ready with a touch of cynicism and the arched eyebrow. Her Oscar nomination was won for the very opposite of her Warner image – for her restrained Chinese farmer's wife in MGM's version of Pearl Buck's *Dragon Seed*. Her sad eyes and somewhat melancholy countenance enhanced more than forty films, although her finest tribute came not from a movie critic but from one who saw her many times in the theatre. Said Walter Kerr in the *New York Times*: 'Always she has pleased me; sometimes more, sometimes less. Nevertheless, always.'

Maggie McNamara

Born New York City, USA, 18 June 1928; died 1978

Oscar Nominations (1): Best Actress for Patty O'Neill in *The Moon Is Blue* (United Artists, 1953)

Nowadays, the name of Maggie McNamara is all but forgotten, but briefly in the fifties it was on everyone's lips as *The Moon Is Blue* girl who dared to say on screen such then taboo words as 'mistress', 'virgin' and 'seduction'. The fame, such as it was, was short-lived, but at least it brought an Oscar nomination and a contract from Darryl Zanuck at Fox, although she completed only two films at the studio (*Three Coins in the Fountain* and *Prince of Players*) before disappearing from the scene as quickly as she had arrived. Troubled with mental illness for much of her life, she spent her later years working as a secretary in an insurance company. She appeared in one more film, *The Cardinal*, before committing suicide from an overdose of sleeping tablets.

Steve McQueen

Born Slater, Missouri, USA, 24 March 1930; died 1980

Oscar Nominations (1): Best Actor for Jake Holman in *The Sand Pebbles* (20th Century-Fox, 1966)

Steve McQueen brought his wrinkled, slightly bewildered expression to nearly thirty films in his tragically short career, enlivening nearly every one with what critics liked to call 'his inner strength' but what most moviegoers recognised as just old-fashioned screen charisma. The Academy voted him a nomination just the once – for his naval machinist who joins a gunboat patrolling the Yangtze River in the twenties. He lost to the somewhat more stately Paul Scofield in *A Man for All Seasons* but wasn't all that surprised: 'I'm not a serious actor,' he said. 'There's something about my shaggy dog eyes that makes people think I'm good. But really, I'm not all that good.' If stuntwork had been an Oscar category it might have been a different story. McQueen would have been home and dry for his car chase in *Bullitt* and his motorcycle escapades in *The Great Escape*.

Amy Madigan

Born Chicago, USA, 11 September 1950

Oscar Nominations (1): Best Supporting Actress for Sunny Mackenzie in *Twice in a Lifetime* (Bud Yorkins Productions, 1985)

Nominated just the once – for her angry young daughter of Seattle steel-worker Gene Hackman – Amy Madigan is one of those actresses who should perhaps have been honoured rather more times over the years. An earthy, no-nonsense kind of gal who was a rock musician for ten years before turning to acting, she had every reason to feel a little aggrieved that she was passed over for her 'stand-by-my-man' wife in *Field of Dreams*. Anyone who stayed with Kev when he started hearing voices, hocking the farm and building baseball pitches for the long-dead Shoeless Joe Jackson deserved some kind of reward. It may still come.

Anna Magnani

Born Rome, Italy, 7 March 1908; died 1973

Oscars (1): Best Actress for Serafina Delle Rose in *The Rose Tattoo* (Paramount, 1955)

Oscar Nominations (1): Best Actress for Gloria in *Wild Is the Wind* (Paramount, 1957)

A slum child from Rome, Anna Magnani brought to all her roles the manners and language of the gutter, plus a large abundance of tears, laughter and sex. The result was mesmerising, making her for many directors, notably DeSica and Rossellini, 'Italy's finest actress and one of the most interesting in the world'. She won her Oscar for her ardent Sicilian widow who finds in oafish truck driver Burt Lancaster a replacement for her late husband. Nominated again two years later for her Nevada rancher's bride, she found opportunities in Hollywood few and far between and finished up making Italian films for television.

Marjorie Main

Born Acton, Indiana, USA, 24 February 1890; died 1975

Oscar Nominations (1): Best Supporting Actress for Ma Kettle in *The Egg and I* (Universal-International, 1947)

Raucous and breezy, Marjorie Main was not only one of the best scene-stealers in the business, she was also among the loudest, shouting at the top of her voice and following up with a laugh that would send most people running for cover. Nominated for her Ma Kettle, the hillbilly mother of a tribe of unruly kids in *The Egg and I*, she missed out on her Oscar, but with Percy Kilbride went on to make a series of Ma and Pa Kettle films at Universal, none of which cost a dime but all of which made a small fortune at the box office. A minister's daughter who changed her name to avoid the family embarrassment when she decided to become an actress, she featured in more than a hundred films, appearing as cooks, maids, dance hall operators, rural and slum mothers and even, on one occasion, as a lady blacksmith.

Mako

Born Kobe, Japan, 10 December 1933

Oscar Nominations (1): Best Supporting Actor for Po-han in *The Sand Pebbles* (20th Century-Fox, 1966)

An Eskimo guide, magician, martial arts expert, even an undercover agent involved with the Munchkins (in *Under the Rainbow*) – the Japanese-American actor Mako has, over the years, been just about all things in all movies. His Oscar nomination came for his début role, in *The Sand Pebbles*, as the coolie who is mercifully executed by seaman Steve McQueen before he is forced to endure excessive torture at the hands of the Chinese. The setting was the River Yangtze in the twenties. The Academy voters preferred the Cleveland of the sixties and opted for Walter Matthau's shyster lawyer in *The Fortune Cookie*.

Karl Malden

Born Chicago, USA, 22 March 1913

Oscars (1): Best Supporting Actor for Mitch in *A Streetcar Named Desire* (Warner Bros, 1951)

Oscar Nominations (1): Best Supporting Actor for Father Barry in *On the Waterfront* (Columbia, 1954)

Usually at his best when working with director Elia Kazan, Karl Malden, of the impish smile, bulbous nose and edgy personality, won his Oscar for his kindly, lonely lover of Vivien Leigh in *A Streetcar Named Desire*, following it three years later with a nomination for his dockland priest who helps defy the racketeers in *On the Waterfront*. Memorable also as one of the nastiest western villains of all time, the sadistic Dad Longworth who beats Brando's gun hand to a pulp in *One-Eyed Jacks*, he remains best known to world audiences for his partnership with Michael Douglas in the TV police series, *The Streets of San Francisco*, which ran for five years in the seventies and made both of its stars household names.

John Malkovich

Born Christopher, Illinois, USA, 9 December 1953

Oscar Nominations (2): Best Supporting Actor for Mr Will in *Places in the Heart* (Tri-Star, 1984) and Mitch Leary in *In the Line of Fire* (Castle Rock, 1993)

A nominee for his screen début role as Sally Field's blind boarder, and again nine years later for his former CIA man gone bad and out to assassinate the President of the United States, John Malkovich belongs with the more serious breed of contemporary American actors, preferring the theatre to the cinema but bringing a brooding intensity to the screen whenever he makes an appearance, most memorably as the decadent seducer in *Dangerous Liaisons*. Cast as Biff in the 1984 stage revival of *Death of a Salesman* (in which Dustin Hoffman played Willy Loman), he was one of the founder members of Chicago's famous Steppenwolf Theatrical Company.

Dorothy Malone

Born Chicago, USA, 30 January 1925

Oscars (1): Best Supporting Actress for Marylee Hadley in *Written on the Wind* (Universal-International, 1956)

Sexually provocative, with sleepy bedroom eyes and an inviting smile, Dorothy Malone seemed to enjoy screen moments rather than screen roles. Delightful as the bespectacled bookshop assistant who tries to serve a fey Bogie in *The Big Sleep*, she was also in top form a decade later in *Battle Cry* as a San Diego wife who goes in for the art of seduction in a revealing bathing suit. Her Oscar was won for her showiest role, as a nymphomaniac ('I'm filthy, period') who sleeps with just about anyone she can find because she can't have Rock Hudson. The role didn't lead to better times in the movies but it did lead to more rewarding things on TV, where she came close to superstardom for her portrayal of Constance MacKenzie in the phenomenally successful *Peyton Place*.

Joe Mantell

Oscar Nominations (1): Best Supporting Actor for Angie in *Marty* (United Artists, 1955)

Who was it who sat with Ernest Borgnine in the Saturday-night bar in *Marty* and asked with monotonous and hopeless regularity: 'What do you feel like doing tonight?' always to receive the same reply: 'I don't know, Ange, what do *you* feel like doing?' Answer: Joe Mantell, one of those American character actors you know by sight but can never quite put a name to. In 1955 he earned a nomination for his possessive Angie, but unlike Borgnine, who took the major award, he lost to the bright young Jack Lemmon, just arriving on the scene in *Mister Roberts*. Only seen in minor roles in his subsequent screen career – e.g., a travelling salesman for Hitchcock in *The Birds* and a couple of bit-parts in *Chinatown* and *The Two Jakes* – Mantell has never again entered the Oscar lists.

Fredric March

Born Racine, Wisconsin, USA, 31 August 1897; died 1975

Oscars (2): Best Actor for Dr Henry Jekyll/Mr Hyde in *Dr Jekyll and Mr Hyde* (Paramount, 1931/32) and Al Stephenson in *The Best Years of Our Lives* (Goldwyn, RKO, 1946)

Oscar Nominations (3): Best Actor for Tony Cavendish in *The Royal Family of Broadway* (Paramount, 1930/31), Norman Maine in *A Star Is Born* (Selznick, United Artists, 1937) and Willy Loman in *Death of a Salesman* (Columbia, 1951)

Twice a winner of the best actor award, Fredric March might, had he so desired, have claimed that he was the only actor in Oscar history to have been named for three performances – for his sensitive Dr Jekyll *and* his fiendish Hyde, and later his war-weary veteran in *The Best Years of Our Lives*. He didn't claim any such thing, but his Oscar record over the years was as good as any of the more glamorous stars of the period and encompassed three more nominations for the top award: his 1931 spoof of John Barrymore, his alcoholic movie star on the skids, and his failed salesman Willy Loman. Married to actress Florence Eldridge, with whom he appeared on stage and screen, he tended towards crusty old veterans in his later years.

Colette Marchand

Oscar Nominations (1): Best Supporting Actress for Marie Charlet in *Moulin Rouge* (Romulus, 1952)

'Watch yourself, Toulouse, you didn't buy me with that hundred francs!' With dialogue such as that (authored by John Huston and Anthony Veiller), it says much for Colette Marchand's acting that she managed to convince the Academy she was worthy of a nomination as the streetwalker/mistress who almost destroys crippled painter Toulouse-Lautrec. She lost to Gloria Grahame (*The Bad and the Beautiful*), not that that seemed to worry her a great deal. More of a cabaret entertainer and revue artist (she was known as 'Les Legs'), she preferred to demonstrate her Roland Petite-trained talents in ballet and the live theatre rather than on the screen. A six-month option with RKO studios in Hollywood came to nothing.

John Marley

Born New York City, USA, 1907; died 1984

Oscar Nominations (1): Best Supporting Actor for Phil Cavilleri in *Love Story* (Paramount, 1970)

Poor John Marley will never be remembered for the role that earned him an Oscar nomination; his place in movie history will be for his overconfident Hollywood mogul in *The Godfather* who says 'no' to Don Corleone and who wakes up in bed one fine morning to find he's sharing the sheets with the severed head of his prize stallion. The role for which he was nominated? The somewhat more tender-hearted working-class father of student Ali MacGraw in *Love Story*. John Mills hopped about a bit for David Lean and won for *Ryan's Daughter*.

Lee Marvin

Born New York City, USA, 19 February 1924; died 1987

Oscars (1): Best Actor for Kid Shelleen/Tim Strawn in *Cat Ballou* (Columbia, 1965)

Only when he became silver-haired did Lee Marvin emerge as a true star. By then he'd earned moviegoers' contempt for throwing scalding coffee into the face of Gloria Grahame in *The Big Heat* and committed other heinous acts of screen villainy. His Oscar was for someone a shade less treacherous, an alcoholic, over-the-hill gunfighter who has trouble staying on his horse and who has a murderous twin brother with a tin nose! There were no nominations before or after, just a reputation as a heavy drinker, two marvellous performances for John Boorman in *Point Blank* and *Hell in the Pacific*, and an immortal recording of 'Wand'rin' Star' in the otherwise unsensational *Paint Your Wagon*.

James Mason

Born Huddersfield, Yorkshire, England, 15 May 1909; died 1984

Oscar Nominations (3): Best Actor for Norman Maine in *A Star Is Born* (Warner Bros, 1954); Best Supporting Actor for James Leamington in *Georgy Girl* (Columbia, 1966) and Ed Concannon in *The Verdict* (20th Century-Fox, 1982)

Had it been 1953 or 1955, things might have been different, but James Mason's fading alcoholic movie star Norman Maine came up in 1954, the year of Brando and *On the Waterfront*, and no one but Marlon was going to win that year. Two supporting nods – for his mischievous sugar daddy enamoured with the gawky Georgy Girl of Lynn Redgrave, and his venomous lawyer in *The Verdict* – were the most he could amass in his later years as a character actor. Quite where the voters were when he appeared in *Odd Man Out*, *Five Fingers*, *Julius Caesar* and his final film, *The Shooting Party*, is anybody's guess!

Marsha Mason

Born St Louis, Missouri, USA, 3 April 1942

Oscar Nominations (4): Best Actress for Maggie Paul in *Cinderella Liberty* (20th Century-Fox, 1973), Paula McFadden in *The Goodbye Girl* (MGM/Warner Bros, 1977), Jennie MacLaine in *Chapter Two* (Columbia, 1979) and Georgia Hines in *Only When I Laugh* (Columbia, 1981)

She had her chances, did Marsha Mason – three nominations in just five years, all for troubled thirtysomething actresses in Neil Simon comedies, and all for women with plenty of problems on their minds: as the former Broadway dancer who has to put up with intrusive boarder Richard Dreyfuss (he won, she didn't) in *The Goodbye Girl*, as herself reliving her own romance and how she became Mrs Simon in *Chapter Two*, and as the alcoholic actress, just dried out and trying for a fresh start in *Only When I Laugh*. Perhaps her best chance had been for her earlier, non-Simon role as the good-natured Seattle hooker who befriends sailor James Caan in *Cinderella Liberty*. Whatever, the score remains: nominations four, Oscars nil, and the last nomination was more than a dozen years ago. An engaging actress but at Oscar time, it seems, a permanently unlucky one.

Daniel Massey

Born London, England, 10 October 1933

Oscar Nominations (1): Best Supporting Actor for Noël Coward in *Star!* (20th Century-Fox, 1968)

Considering that Noël Coward was far from being the easiest of men to play on screen (as Coward himself would no doubt have agreed), Daniel Massey did a remarkable job in the Gertrude Lawrence biopic *Star!*, offering some finely shaded underplaying and several of Coward's hit songs in his delightfully wistful impersonation of the young maestro. Enough for an Oscar, one would have thought. Not so, just a nomination, Jack Albertson taking home the year's supporting award for *The Subject Was Roses*. The son of Raymond Massey and the brother of Anna, Daniel has enjoyed most of his success in the theatre. He also enjoyed a certain advantage when playing Coward on screen. Noël was his real-life godfather.

Raymond Massey

Born Toronto, Canada, 30 August 1896; died 1983

Oscar Nominations (1): Best Actor for Abraham Lincoln in *Abe Lincoln in Illinois* (RKO, 1940)

Raymond Massey gained such fame for his stage portrayals of Abraham Lincoln that it was said he 'took the face of Lincoln off the penny and put it into the hearts of millions of Americans'. Little wonder that when he transferred his portrayal to the cinema screen he was nominated for an Oscar, although in 1940 the voters preferred Jimmy Stewart's romantic dallyings with Katharine Hepburn in *The Philadelphia Story* to the political career of a remarkable president. Tall, slim, and with a wickedly crooked smile that often evoked menace (*The Prisoner of Zenda*, *Reap the Wild Wind*, *Arsenic and Old Lace*), Massey later repeated his screen Lincoln in a thirty-second cameo in *How the West Was Won*. A playwright as well as a distinguished stage actor, he reached his widest audience as the authoritarian Dr Gillespie in the *Dr Kildare* TV series of the sixties. He failed to make the list of best supporting actor nominees of 1955 for his puritanical father of James Dean in *East of Eden*.

Mary Elizabeth Mastrantonio

Born Oak Park, Illinois, USA, 17 November 1958

Oscar Nominations (1): Best Supporting Actress for Carmen in *The Color of Money* (Touchstone, 1986)

The girl who made her mark as the flirtatious girlfriend of Tom Cruise in *The Color of Money*, Mary Elizabeth Mastrantonio quickly discovered that for every Scorsese film there's an *Abyss* (literally!) and that there aren't that many roles around these days for young actresses to chew on. There have been some high spots, especially her incestuous sister of Al Pacino in *Scarface* and her San Francisco lawyer in the courtroom drama *Class Action*, but her Maid Marian was a little on the tepid side and of late the opportunities have been rather limited. Dianne Wiest won 1986's supporting award for *Hannah and Her Sisters*.

Marcello Mastroianni

Born Fontana, Liri, Italy, 28 September 1923

Oscar Nominations (3): Best Actor for Ferdinando in *Divorce, Italian Style* (Embassy Pictures, Italian, 1962), Gabriele in *A Special Day* (Canafox Films, Cinema 5, Italian, 1977) and Romano in *Dark Eyes* (Excelsior Island Pictures, Italian, 1987)

A lot of movies, a lot of Italian, a lot of laughter, a lot of romance, plus an abundance of tired, bored-with-life looks that at times have made him seem the most disturbed man in movies! That doesn't quite sum up the Latin lover persona of Marcello Mastroianni but it comes close. By now he should have become the first European actor in a European film to win the best actor award, but despite three nominations, spanning a quarter of a century – for his impoverished Sicilian nobleman trying to bump off his wife in *Divorce, Italian Style*, his homosexual drawn to housewife Sophia Loren in *A Special Day* and his ageing Italian roué in *Dark Eyes* – he's still waiting. His two most famous Fellini roles – the disillusioned journalist in *La Dolce Vita* and the director waiting for inspiration in *8½* – were both overlooked by the Academy.

Marlee Matlin

Born Morton Grove, Illinois, USA 24 August 1965

Oscars (1): Best Actress for Sarah in *Children of a Lesser God* (Paramount, 1986)

To achieve a kind of serenity of performance is quite an achievement in these days of crass overacting. Marlee Matlin, deaf before her second birthday, triumphed in 1986 by attaining just such a serenity and by imbuing her performance with all kinds of subtleties and nuances. Her role? That of a young deaf woman working as a domestic cleaner at the school where she was once taught, and who finds love and understanding with the unorthodox new speech teacher at the school. William Hurt shared her most affecting moments; Randa Haines found her way into the record books by becoming the first woman in Academy history to direct a performer to a leading-role Oscar. No nomination for direction, though; the picture apparently directed itself!

Walter Matthau

Born New York City, USA, 1 October 1920

Oscars (1): Best Supporting Actor for Willie Gingrich in *The Fortune Cookie* (United Artists, 1966)

Oscar Nominations (2): Best Actor for Joseph P. Kotcher in *Kotch* (ABC Pictures/Cinerama, 1971) and Willy Clark in *The Sunshine Boys* (MGM, 1975)

Who better for a shyster lawyer than Walter Matthau? Billy Wilder saw the potential, cast him in *The Fortune Cookie*, and the Oscar was half won before a camera even turned. When they did turn, Matthau's dialogue (aimed at an injured Jack Lemmon, out of whom he intends to make a million bucks) went something along these lines: 'You feel sorry for insurance companies? They've got so much money they don't know what to do with it. They've run out of storage space. They have to *microfilm* it. What's a quarter of a million to them? They take it out of petty cash!' Nominated also for his aged parent Kotch and for one of Neil Simon's *Sunshine Boys*, he somewhat surprisingly missed out for one of his most famous roles – the all-American slob Oscar Madison in *The Odd Couple*.

Kay Medford

Born New York City, USA, 14 September 1920; died 1980

Oscar Nominations (1): Best Supporting Actress for Rose Brice in *Funny Girl* (Rastar, 1968)

A knockout as Momma Fanny Brice, Kay Medford reprised on screen exactly what she had done on stage on Broadway, which is really all you could ask for under the circumstances. No stranger to films – she'd been at MGM in the forties and subsequently appeared in such movies as *The Rat Race*, *Butterfield 8* and *Bye Bye Birdie* – she found herself up against Ruth Gordon for *Rosemary's Baby*, a slightly more sinister infant (and a lot less musical) than the one she'd mothered and turned into Barbra Streisand in *Funny Girl*.

☆

Adolphe Menjou

Born Pittsburgh, USA, 18 February 1890; died 1963

Oscar Nominations (1): Best Actor for Walter Burns in *The Front Page* (United Artists, 1930/31)

Famous for his suave sophistication and neat waxed moustache, Adolphe Menjou was up for the Oscar just the once – for his fiery editor in *The Front Page*, a role he inherited when Louis Wolheim, the actor originally selected for the part, died after just ten days of rehearsal. A master at screen lovers, roués and elegant seducers, Menjou was regularly listed as one of the nation's best-dressed men, boasting that his wardrobe included some 2,000 items, among them fifteen overcoats and a hundred suits. Not surprisingly, perhaps, he was a notorious right-winger (he was a staunch member of the John Birch Society) who eagerly named alleged Communists in the Hollywood witch-hunts of 1947. The most remarkable of his later performances was as the corrupt World War I General Broulard in Kubrick's *Paths of Glory*. Of his career, he said: 'My success has been as full of luck as a crapshooter's dream.'

Vivien Merchant

Born Manchester, England, 22 July 1929; died 1982

Oscar Nominations (1): Best Supporting Actress for Lily in *Alfie* (Sheldrake Films/Paramount 1966)

Married to playwright Harold Pinter for nearly twenty-five years, and the leading lady in many of his TV and stage plays, Vivien Merchant's forays into the world of cinema were rare but effective. Deliciously suspicious as the pregnant wife of Dirk Bogarde, the Oxford don with the mid-life crisis in Losey's *Accident,* she was equally amusing at the other end of the scale in Hitchcock's *Frenzy* as the wife who continually serves up inedible gourmet specialities to her Scotland Yard inspector husband Alec McCowen. She earned her Oscar nomination as one of the unlucky ladies collected by Michael Caine's Alfie, ending up in Caine's flat in the hands of seedy abortionist Denholm Elliott. Divorced from Harold Pinter in 1980, she died at the age of fifty-three of cirrhosis of the liver.

Melina Mercouri

Born Athens, Greece, 18 October 1923; died 1994

Oscar Nominations (1): Best Actress for Ilya in *Never on Sunday* (United Artists, 1960)

The sight of earthy, life-embracing prostitute Melina Mercouri striding and laughing her way along the waterfront of Piraeus in *Never on Sunday* was enough to gladden the heart of any man in the sixties. There was no surprise at her Oscar nomination, just disappointment on awards night when the Oscar went to Elizabeth Taylor whose sullen, bitchy hooker Gloria Wandrous in *Butterfield 8* wasn't half so much fun. Married to the American expatriate director of *Never on Sunday*, Jules Dassin, with whom she subsequently worked on several more films (among them the enjoyable heist romp *Topkapi*), she was an ardent foe of the military regime that ruled her country from 1967 to 1974. She served as Culture Minister in the socialist government which came to power in 1981. She was serving in the same capacity in a new socialist administration at the time of her death. She was known as 'the Last Greek Goddess'.

Burgess Meredith

Born Cleveland, Ohio, USA, 16 November 1908

Oscar Nominations (2): Best Supporting Actor for Harry Greener in *The Day of the Locust* (Paramount, 1975) and Mickey in *Rocky* (United Artists, 1976)

Yet another character actor who seems to have been around forever, Burgess Meredith has continued acting well into his eighties (he was blacklisted for a short time during the McCarthy years), earning just two nominations in a career that has spanned fifty years and included more than seventy films. Par for the course compared with many others in this volume, although the award should have been his somewhere along the line, preferably for his portrait of World War II combat correspondent Ernie Pyle in Wellman's *The Story of GI Joe*. Nominated for his down-on-his-luck vaudevillian Harry Greener and his crotchety old manager of Sylvester Stallone's *Rocky*, he remains perhaps best known to the general public for his villainous 'Penguin' in the sixties TV series of *Batman*. He won an Emmy in 1977 for his performance as lawyer Joseph Welch in the Joe McCarthy biography *Tail Gunner Joe*.

Una Merkel

Born Covington, Kentucky, USA, 10 December 1903; died 1986

Oscar Nominations (1): Best Supporting Actress for Mrs Winemiller in *Summer and Smoke* (Paramount, 1961)

Remembered best for her tooth-and-nail saloon scrap with Marlene Dietrich in *Destry Rides Again*, Una Merkel received rather belated Academy recognition when she was Oscar-nominated at the age of fifty-nine for her mother of small-town spinster Geraldine Page in *Summer and Smoke*. Even then she didn't win (the prize going to the slightly more vivacious Rita Moreno in *West Side Story*), and she was left with memories of some hundred movies, many of them dating back to the silent days, and of her years at MGM in the thirties when she wisecracked and smart-talked with the best of them.

Bette Midler

Born Honolulu, Hawaii, 1 December 1945

Oscar Nominations (2): Best Actress for 'Rose' in *The Rose* (20th Century-Fox, 1979) and Dixie Leonard in *For the Boys* (20th Century-Fox, 1991)

The self-confessed epitome of the truly tacky woman, Bette Midler looked for a while as though she would be able to transfer her enormous stage presence to the screen. Her début role – that of a Janis Joplin-style singer on the way down because of booze and drugs – earned her an Oscar nomination first time out, but in more recent years her screen persona seems to have been that of a loud, often unfunny woman making a lot of noise in loud, unfunny comedies. Her second Oscar nomination was for *For the Boys*, the story of the ups and downs of a husband and wife showbiz team. Both of her Oscar-nominated films were directed by Mark Rydell. She lost in 1979 to Sally Field in *Norma Rae* and in 1991 to Jodie Foster in *The Silence of the Lambs*.

Sarah Miles

Born Ingatestone, Essex, England, 31 December 1941

Oscar Nominations (1): Best Actress for Rosy Ryan in *Ryan's Daughter* (MGM, 1970)

She seduced with gay abandon in the sixties, did Sarah Miles. No one was really safe, not even Laurence Olivier (his schoolmaster in *Term of Trial* succumbed when she was just twenty-one) or Robert Mitchum, another schoolteacher bewitched by her charms in *Ryan's Daughter*. She was in with a chance for her role in the latter movie but 1970 was the year when Glenda Jackson was up to a few sexual tricks of her own in *Women in Love*, and that was that – goodbye, Oscar! Married, divorced and remarried to playwright-screenwriter Robert Bolt, she was unlucky in her later years to miss out for her marvellous wartime mum in John Boorman's *Hope and Glory*.

Sylvia Miles

Born New York City, USA, 9 September 1932

Oscar Nominations (2): Best Supporting Actress for Cass in *Midnight Cowboy* (United Artists, 1969) and Jessie Florian in *Farewell My Lovely* (Avco-Embassy, 1975)

A bit outrageous (to say the least) in many of her roles, Sylvia Miles has essayed a remarkable range of floozies, has-beens, never-weres and vulgar eccentrics, many of them with a caustic sense of humour. Oscar-nominated for giving Jon Voight a turn in her New York apartment (he finishes up giving *her* money for a taxi fare), and for her alcoholic widow in the remake of *Farewell My Lovely*, she has often been part of a screen world that is sleazy, tough and disturbingly real. A former student at the Actor's Studio, she was at her most amusing as the Jewish marriage-broker always trying to 'fix-up' Amy Irving in *Crossing Delancey*.

Penelope Milford

Born Winnetka, Illinois, USA, 1949

Oscar Nominations (1): Best Supporting Actress for Viola Munson in *Coming Home* (United Artists, 1978)

Actors playing decent, ordinary, unglamorous folk tend to get a bit taken for granted by audiences, often merging into the background as they are overshadowed by the stars around them. It's to Penelope Milford's credit that she more than held her own with Jane Fonda in their scenes together as volunteer workers in a hospital for disabled Vietnam veterans in *Coming Home*. Fonda and Jon Voight won the year's top acting awards; Milford earned just a nomination for her lovely performance as a woman desperately trying to keep an eye on her disturbed and ultimately tragic brother.

Ray Milland

Born Neath, Wales, 3 January 1907; died 1986

Oscars (1): Best Actor for Don Birnam in *The Lost Weekend* (Paramount, 1945)

Ray Milland's sparkling eyes and roguish smile didn't really belong in the lower depths of New York and the murky world of the alcoholic. Writer-director Billy Wilder, however, thought otherwise, and his courageous casting against type earned Milland an Oscar when few in Hollywood regarded him as anything more than a lightweight leading man. Although he never reached such heights again, the film did allow him, on occasion, to explore his darker side, e.g., as the very devil of a Devil in the much underrated *Alias Nick Beal* and the scheming hubby determined to rid himself of wife Grace Kelly in Hitchcock's *Dial M for Murder*. A talented director of interesting, small-scale movies in the fifties, he also made the occasional appearance for Roger Corman, most memorably in *The Man with X-Ray Eyes* who, in an horrific final scene that could have come from a nightmare in *The Lost Weekend*, plucks his eyes from their sockets!

☆

Jason Miller

Born Long Island City, New York, USA, 22 April 1939

Oscar Nominations (1): Best Supporting Actor for Father Karras in *The Exorcist* (Warner Bros, 1973)

Who's Jason Miller? Not too many moviegoers remember nowadays, but back in 1973 just about everyone knew his name as, along with Max Von Sydow, he battled with the Devil within Linda Blair in *The Exorcist* and paid for it with his life. It was a powerful climactic scene and quite a performance, although on awards night the voters tended to prefer something a little more sedate and stately – John Houseman's stern law professor in *The Paper Chase*. A playwright first, an actor second, Miller won the Pulitzer Prize, the Tony Award and the New York Drama Critics Award for his play *That Championship Season* which he later directed for the screen.

John Mills

Born Felixstowe, Suffolk, England, 22 February 1908

Oscars (1): Best Supporting Actor for Michael in *Ryan's Daughter* (MGM, 1970)

The upper lip of John Mills had been stiff and unwavering for so long and in so many British military sagas of the fifties that it came as a surprise when he accepted the role of a grotesque in David Lean's Irish love story, *Ryan's Daughter*. The sixteen-minute make-up job – a nose stuck on, an ear pulled out, a set of hideous teeth clipped in – did the trick, ensuring that he resembled a close relation of Charles Laughton's Quasimodo in *The Hunchback of Notre Dame* and convincing voters that his village mute who utters only pathetic sounds was worthy of both a nomination and the award itself. His finest role, that of the martinet commanding officer on the verge of nervous collapse in Ronald Neame's *Tunes of Glory*, was passed over by the Academy despite being rewarded with a best actor prize at the 1960 Venice Festival.

Sal Mineo

Born the Bronx, New York, USA, 10 January 1939; died 1976

Oscar Nominations (2): Best Supporting Actor for Plato in *Rebel Without a Cause* (Warner Bros, 1955) and Dov Landau in *Exodus* (United Artists, 1960)

Referred to by one critic as 'the young star who rose to fame in switchblade dramas of the fifties', Sal Mineo managed two Oscar nominations in his short career – the first for the youngest of the rich kid rebels in Nicholas Ray's *Rebel Without a Cause*, the second for his Zionist terrorist in *Exodus*. A prominent member of a chic gay set, he was attacked and stabbed to death when returning to his West Hollywood apartment after a play rehearsal. By an unnerving coincidence, all three of the rebels in Ray's 1955 film met early deaths – Dean in a car crash, aged twenty-four, Natalie Wood from drowning aged forty-three.

Liza Minnelli

Born Los Angeles, USA, 12 March 1946

Oscars (1): Best Actress for Sally Bowles in *Cabaret* (Allied Artists, 1972)

Oscar Nominations (1): Best Actress for Pookie in *The Sterile Cuckoo* (Paramount, 1969)

The only thing wrong with the performance of Liza Minnelli in Bob Fosse's stunning *Cabaret* was that it was simply *too* good. No one with her abundance of talent would have been caught dead in a dump like the Kit Kat Klub, even if they were trapped in Hitler's Germany of the thirties. That said, there was no denying that of all the musical performances of the seventies, hers deserved an Oscar the most, being in turn vivacious, outrageous and, in the scenes when she returns in the early hours from an abortion, deeply moving. Never a major box-office star like her mother Judy Garland (although she might well have been had she been active in the studio days), Liza was also nominated for an earlier performance as a neurotic college girl in Alan Pakula's undervalued *The Sterile Cuckoo*. An Emmy Award-winner for her TV special *Liza With a Z*, and a double Tony winner, she made her screen début at the age of three in *In the Good Old Summertime*.

Helen Mirren

Born Leigh-on-Sea, Essex, England, 26 July 1945

Oscar Nominations (1): Best Supporting Actress for Queen Charlotte in *The Madness of King George* (Samuel Goldwyn Company, 1994)

It's been a bit of an up-and-down film career, has that of Helen Mirren. Now as popular as she's ever been in the series of *Prime Suspect* TV films, she's been in and out of her screen clothes so many times it's difficult to recall those of her films in which she hasn't been in at least a partial state of undress. Raunchy and highly erotic in her younger years, and quite outstanding as Morgana in John Boorman's 1981 film, *Excalibur*, she finally got the Academy's nod when she touched fifty for her devoted queen who tends her husband's illness in *The Madness of King George*.

Thomas Mitchell

Born Elizabeth, New Jersey, USA, 11 July 1892; died 1962

Oscars (1): Best Supporting Actor for Doc Boone in *Stagecoach* (United Artists, 1939)

Oscar Nominations (1): Best Supporting Actor for Dr Kersaint in *The Hurricane* (Goldwyn/United Artists, 1937)

A master of screen scallywags and with mischievous features that could hide either a practical joke or a lethal murder plan, Thomas Mitchell enjoyed a dazzling screen career and also one dazzling year (1939) when it seemed he could do no wrong and had Academy voters scratching their heads as to which role they should nominate him for. The father of Scarlett in *Gone with the Wind*? His newspaperman in Capra's *Mr Smith Goes to Washington*? His grounded flyer in Hawks' *Only Angels Have Wings*? The King of the Beggars in *The Hunchback of Notre Dame*? In the end they chose Doc Boone, the alcoholic doctor who goes for a ride on John Ford's celebrated *Stagecoach*, sobers up en route when he has to deliver a baby, and gets to utter Dudley Nichols' immortal line: 'Somewhere, sometime, there may be the right bullet or the wrong bottle waiting for Josiah Boone. Why worry when or where?' Two years earlier the voters had nominated but overlooked him for another medic in Goldwyn's South Seas spectacular *The Hurricane*. Not this time. The Oscar was his.

Robert Mitchum

Born Bridgeport, Connecticut, USA, 6 August 1917

Oscar Nominations (1): Best Supporting Actor for Lt Walker in *The Story of GI Joe* (United Artists, 1945)

Just twenty-eight when he earned his sole Oscar nomination – for his battle-hardened infantry commander serving in Italy in World War II – Mitchum has since featured in more than a hundred films without ever again coming close to another nomination. Not surprising, say his detractors, who believe he repeats his laconic, sleepy-eyed performance in every film. Not so, say his admirers, who cite his crazed preacher in *The Night of the Hunter*, Marine stranded in the South Pacific with nun Deborah Kerr in *Heaven Knows, Mr Allison*, and ageing small-time hood in *The Friends of Eddie Coyle* as just three roles for which he deserved a mention if not the award itself. Most of the directors with whom he has worked, among them Huston, Walsh, Preminger and Zinnemann, have tended to agree with the latter view.

Robert Montgomery

Born Beacon, New York, USA, 21 May 1904; died 1981

Oscar Nominations (2): Best Actor for Danny in *Night Must Fall* (MGM, 1937) and Joe Pendleton in *Here Comes Mr Jordan* (Columbia, 1941)

A psychotic murderer who keeps his victims' heads in hat boxes and a prizefighter who's sent to heaven before his time and returns to earth in another man's body! A rather unique nomination double for Robert Montgomery, who at Metro was looked on as a debonair romantic star ideal for frothy comedies but who would have much preferred to have been regarded as a serious actor. Constant rows with studio boss Louis B. Mayer

Arch plotters and double Oscar nominees Angela Lansbury and Charles Boyer planning to send Ingrid Bergman slowly insane in *Gaslight* (MGM). Bergman had the last laugh, at least on Oscar night, when she was named best actress of 1944

More proficient at cards than love! Charles Laughton (best actor, 1932/33) on his wedding night with Anne of Cleves – played by his real-life wife Elsa Lanchester – in *The Private Life of Henry VIII* (London Films)

Rhett and Scarlett. It should have been a double for Gable and Leigh in 1939 for *Gone with the Wind* (MGM). Leigh managed it with consummate ease; Robert Donat spoilt the party by winning for his dedicated schoolteacher in *Goodbye, Mr Chips*

A harassed Jack Lemmon near breaking point as the businessman close to ruin in *Save the Tiger* (Paramount). Lemmon was named best actor of 1973 by the Academy

The usually debonair Ray Milland as the alcoholic Don Birnam in *The Lost Weekend* (Paramount, 1945), the first serious study of the devastating effects of alcoholism. The result? Four Oscars including one for Milland as best actor of the year

Seedy temptation in a cheap hotel room. Oscar nominated Fredric March as Willy Loman succumbing to the sordid in the 1951 version of Arthur Miller's *Death of a Salesman* (Columbia)

A life saved. Haing S. Ngor as Cambodian translator Dith Pran saving *New York Times* reporter Sydney Schanberg (Sam Waterston) from certain death in Roland Joffe's *The Killing Fields* (Enigma/Warner Bros, 1984). Ngor received the Oscar; Waterston a nomination

(*Above*) Paul Newman's first nomination as the alcoholic Brick in Richard Brooks' 1958 version of *Cat on a Hot Tin Roof* (MGM) – and (*below*) twenty-eight years later winning the award at last for reprising his role as Eddie Felson in Scorsese's *The Color of Money* (Touchstone, 1986)

Worldly-wise housekeeper Pat Neal does her best to keep Paul Newman's arrogant and virile young Texan at bay in *Hud* (Paramount). Her efforts resulted in the best actress award of 1963

'Should I be here?' Shirley MacLaine seems to be saying in this scene from *Terms of Endearment* (Paramount). Jack Nicholson seems to be in no doubt. Certainly as far as the Oscars were concerned, getting between the sheets did the trick. Both players took top awards in 1983

Liam Neeson's sole nomination to date – for his remarkable German businessman Oskar Schindler who saved more than a thousand Jews from death in the concentration camps in World War II. The film: Steven Spielberg's *Schindler's List* (Amblin/Universal, 1993)

A hard life in the Depression. Con artists Ryan and Tatum O'Neal in *Paper Moon* (Paramount). Ryan missed out on a nomination; Tatum took the prize as 1973's best supporting actress

Seven times a nominee, never a winner! Peter O'Toole in the first of his nominated roles as T.E. Lawrence in David Lean's epic *Lawrence of Arabia* (Columbia, 1962)

The Oscar at last! Al Pacino as a blind army colonel enjoying an improvised tango in *Scent of a Woman* (Universal, 1992)

Bar-room singer Michelle Pfeiffer, best actress nominee in 1989 for *The Fabulous Baker Boys* (Gladden Films). Beauty didn't come into it on awards night; Jessica Tandy, the oldest performer ever to win an Oscar, came in first for *Driving Miss Daisy*

put paid to that, and a psychotic and a prizefighter was all he managed as far as the Oscars were concerned. A subsequent mention for his role as the torpedo boat commander in John Ford's superb World War II movie, *They Were Expendable*, would not have gone amiss.

Ron Moody

Born London, England, 8 January 1924

Oscar Nominations (1): Best Actor for Fagin in *Oliver!* (Columbia, 1968)

Alec Guinness' brilliant portrayal of Fagin in David Lean's 1948 *Oliver Twist* so incensed American audiences and distributors that it was considered anti-Semitic. When the film was ultimately released in a truncated version in 1951 it was minus twelve minutes of key scenes featuring the villainous old Jewish fence. Twenty years later, in *Oliver!*, it was a very different story, with Fagin revamped as a jolly old gent who runs his den of thieves with a light-hearted song or two. The characterisation earned Ron Moody an Oscar nomination for his performance, which although delightful in its own right was some way removed from the Dickens original. A multi-award winner, the film of *Oliver!* found favour with audiences and critics, except Renata Adler of the *New York Times* who thought it 'cast iron pastry'.

Dudley Moore

Born Dagenham, Essex, England, 19 April 1935

Oscar Nominations (1): Best Actor for Arthur Bach in *Arthur* (Warner Bros, 1981)

If little Dudley Moore could have picked a time to be nominated, it probably wouldn't have been 1981, when he was the comic relief in a year that saw such formidable contenders as Paul Newman, Burt Lancaster, Warren Beatty and the year's sentimental winner Henry Fonda all up for the award. His role of a drunken playboy who will miss out on a fortune unless he reforms and marries a socialite was a kind of throwback to the screwball

comedy roles of the thirties. It lacked the finesse of the pre-war performances of William Powell and company, but in an age when comedy was
sparse it was better than nothing. Nothing since and nothing either for his
insatiable menopausal songwriter chasing Bo Derek all over the place in *10*.

Grace Moore

Born Slabtown, Tennessee, USA, 5 December 1901; died 1947

Oscar Nominations (1): Best Actress for Mary Barrett in *One Night of
Love* (Columbia, 1934)

Opera stars didn't usually equate with big bucks for the old-time movie
moguls, but Harry Cohn's bid to make a bit of loot out of soprano Grace
Moore didn't turn out too badly, despite her tantrums and short temper
and her tendency to overeat. Nominated for her young opera singer in *One
Night of Love* (she lost to Columbia competitor Claudette Colbert in *It
Happened One Night*), she enjoyed five years at Columbia, starring with
Franchot Tone and Melvyn Douglas, and even, on one occasion, singing
'Minnie the Moocher' with Cary Grant at the piano. One Hollywood
legend has it that when she mentioned that she wanted to sing 'Butterfly' in
One Night of Love, the uncouth Harry Cohn picked up the telephone and
asked his music department how much it would cost to use 'Poor Butterfly'.
'No, no,' said Moore, '*Madame Butterfly* by Puccini.' 'You mean he stole it!'
exclaimed Cohn.

Juanita Moore

Born 1922

Oscar Nominations (1): Best Supporting Actress for Annie Johnson in
Imitation of Life (Universal-International, 1959)

Of the black actresses who have been nominated for the supporting award,
Juanita Moore tends to be remembered the least, which is a pity, for her
self-sacrificing maid who in Douglas Sirk's version of Fannie Hurst's
Imitation of Life shares her life and daughter with those of Lana Turner
belongs with the very best characterisations to be found in Hollywood

tear-jerkers. Shelley Winters won in 1959 for *The Diary of Anne Frank*. Had not three Universal stars all been in the running for the supporting Oscar – Moore's co-star Susan Kohner, who played her daughter, and little Thelma Ritter for *Pillow Talk* were both among the nominees – Moore might have made it to the rostrum instead.

Mary Tyler Moore

Born Brooklyn, New York, USA, 29 December 1936

Oscar Nominations (1): Best Actress for Beth Jarrett in *Ordinary People* (Paramount, 1980)

One of the genuine stars made by TV (the *Dick Van Dyke* and *Mary Tyler Moore* shows), Mary Tyler Moore's movie experiences have been less rewarding, even though Robert Redford's casting of her as the cold, shrewish, social-climbing mother of Timothy Hutton in *Ordinary People* made people sit up and ask: 'Is this really the Mary Tyler Moore we know and love?' She came close on Oscar night, but Sissy Spacek took the honours for her country singer Loretta Lynn in *Coal Miner's Daughter*. A multi-Emmy-winner for her TV work, and the winner also of a special Tony for *Whose Life Is It Anyway*, she has suffered with alcohol problems in her private life and the suicide of her twenty-four-year-old son.

Terry Moore

Born Los Angeles, USA, 7 January 1929

Oscar Nominations (1): Best Supporting Actress for Marie Buckholder in *Come Back Little Sheba* (Paramount, 1952)

Not too many actresses get the chance to sing 'Beautiful Dreamer' to a big ape (known to his friends as Mighty Joe Young), but Terry Moore did just that back in 1949 and remains in the memory more for that little escapade than for her Oscar-nominated role as the sexually curious student boarder of Burt Lancaster and Shirley Booth. Good at flirtatious girls with a lot more than flirting on their minds, she didn't quite manage to build on her career in the fifties, despite a contract with Fox. Her fame rests more on the fact that she was at one time Mrs Howard Hughes, which she proved in a legal battle in 1983 when the court recognised her as Hughes' widow and the mother of his stillborn child. They were married aboard Hughes' yacht in 1949.

Agnes Moorehead

Born Clinton, Massachusetts, USA, 6 December 1906; died 1974

Oscar Nominations (4): Best Supporting Actress for Fanny Amberson in *The Magnificent Ambersons* (RKO, 1942), Aspasia Conti in *Mrs Parkington* (MGM, 1944), Aggie McDonald in *Johnny Belinda* (Warner Bros, 1948) and Velma in *Hush...Hush, Sweet Charlotte* (20th Century-Fox, 1964)

Memorable in the briefest of parts as the young Kane's mother in *Citizen Kane*, Agnes Moorehead should by rights have won at least one Oscar during her thirty years in Hollywood. It was not to be. 'I guess I'll remain a bridesmaid for the rest of my life,' she sighed when she missed out for her slovenly, sarcastic housekeeper in Aldrich's piece of Grand Guignol, *Hush... Hush, Sweet Charlotte*. She knew the feeling well, having lost on three previous occasions – for her nagging spinster Fanny Amberson, the former sweetheart of pioneer Walter Pidgeon, and the stern aunt of Jane Wyman in *Johnny Belinda*. At least TV offered compensations. As Endora, the caustic witch-mother of Elizabeth Montgomery in the long-running series *Bewitched*, she became known to millions across the world.

Rita Moreno

Born Humacao, Puerto Rico, 11 December 1931

Oscars (1): Best Supporting Actress for Anita in *West Side Story* (United Artists, 1961)

'I like to be in Amereeca . . .' Who wouldn't, with the vivacious Rita Moreno cavorting about on the New York rooftops, tossing her skirts high and singing as well as acting her way to the 1961 Academy Award. Her subsequent roles were a bit of a letdown – drug addicts, strippers, etc. – although her reprise of her Broadway role in *The Ritz*, as the temperamental, gum-chewing entertainer Googie Gomez, was a knockout, and she did wonders for Jack Nicholson in the final scene of *Carnal Knowledge*.

Frank Morgan

Born New York City, USA, 1 June 1890; died 1949

Oscar Nominations (2): Best Actor for Alessandro, Duke of Florence, in *The Affairs of Cellini* (United Artists, 1934); Best Supporting Actor for 'The Pirate' in *Tortilla Flat* (MGM, 1942)

A con man! A rogue! A genial rascal who sometimes didn't seem to know what time of day it was and at others knew *exactly* what he was doing and why! That was Frank Morgan on screen, a man who spluttered more than most and whose dialogue often went along these lines: 'Aaah . . . of course . . . yes . . . Well, I never . . . er, did I say that? . . . aah now, let me see.' He missed out on an Academy nomination for his Wizard of Oz (a role originally intended for W. C. Fields), but managed a couple of mentions for his philandering sixteenth-century duke in *The Affairs of Cellini*, and the lazy, dog-loving eccentric in the film version of Steinbeck's *Tortilla Flat*. Cast as Buffalo Bill in the ill-fated *Annie Get Your Gun* (both Judy Garland and director Busby Berkeley were replaced), he died in his sleep during the early weeks of filming and was replaced by Louis Calhern.

Cathy Moriarty

Born the Bronx, New York, USA, 29 November 1960

Oscar Nominations (1): Best Supporting Actress for Vickie LaMotta in *Raging Bull* (United Artists, 1980)

Robert De Niro might have slugged it out inside the ring in Scorsese's classic *Raging Bull*, but it was Cathy Moriarty as Jake LaMotta's second wife Vickie who took most of the knocks outside the ropes, putting up with her husband's jealousy and violent rages in a performance that many deemed (and still do) worthy of more than just an Academy nomination. More at home in comedy roles in recent years (*Kindergarten Cop*, *Soapdish*), she has found *Raging Bull*-type opportunities in short supply.

Noriyuki 'Pat' Morita

Born Isleton, California, USA, 28 June 1930

Oscar Nominations (1): Best Supporting Actor for Miyagi in *The Karate Kid* (Columbia, 1984)

'Famous for one role' actors can get a bit frustrated when they try to break free from the part that has brought them success. Pat Morita, however, doesn't seem to have been bothered overmuch, having remained a popular character actor in Hollywood movies of the eighties and nineties and continuing to play his aged janitor-cum-karate-expert with no ill effects. An Oscar nominee for his original portrayal of the character in 1984, he first showed his face on screen back in the sixties as the menacing 'Oriental 2' in the 1967 musical *Thoroughly Modern Millie*. He missed out on the Academy Award, losing to Haing S. Ngor for *The Killing Fields*.

Robert Morley

Born Semley, Wiltshire, England, 26 May 1908; died 1992

Oscar Nominations (1): Best Supporting Actor for Louis XVI in *Marie Antoinette* (MGM, 1938)

A scene-stealer and a cameo player, but sometimes rather more, Robert Morley won his Oscar nomination for his very first Hollywood film, in which he played a feeble-minded Louis XVI opposite Norma Shearer. Never again nominated, despite demonstrating his range as an envious Almayer in Reed's *An Outcast of the Islands*, Katie Hepburn's missionary brother in *The African Queen*, and the tragic Oscar Wilde, he often enjoyed declaring that 'No director works with me more than once. Except a few, like Huston, men before their time!' A star of more than sixty films and a hundred plays (of which he wrote eight, including *Edward My Son*), he was most at home on a racecourse with his long-time friend and fellow actor Wilfrid Hyde-White.

☆

Chester Morris

Born New York City, USA, 16 February 1901; died 1970

Oscar Nominations (1): Best Actor for Chick Williams in *Alibi* (United Artists, 1928/29)

The determined features of Chester Morris – tough-looking face, slicked-back hair and square jaw – seemed tailor-made for the crime movies of the thirties, especially after his nomination for his first sound role, as a gangleader in *Alibi*. Things didn't quite work out that way, and instead of challenging Cagney, Bogart and the rest, he found himself languishing in a long series of mediocre roles in undistinguished movies. There was a brief revival in the forties when he played the likeable B-movie crook Boston Blackie, but B-movies were not what he had been hoping for. In 1970, after several years of ill-health, he was found dead from an overdose of barbiturates.

Paul Muni

Born Lemberg, Austria, 22 September 1895; died 1967

Oscars (1): Best Actor for the title role in *The Story of Louis Pasteur* (Warner Bros, 1936)

Oscar Nominations (4): Best Actor for James Dyke in *The Valiant* (Fox, 1928/29), James Allen in *I Am a Fugitive from a Chain Gang* (Warner Bros, 1932/33), the title role in *The Life of Emile Zola* (Warner Bros, 1937) and Dr Sam Abelman in *The Last Angry Man* (Columbia, 1959)

'Every time Paul Muni parts his beard and looks down a microscope it costs this company two million dollars!' moaned Jack Warner about Muni's inability to raise any great excitement at the box office. All of which was a little unfair, for Muni and his biographical roles brought prestige and the first major Academy Awards to the studio when Warners badly needed them. A winner for his portrait of scientist Louis Pasteur, he was also nominated on four other occasions – for his murderer awaiting execution in *The Valiant*, his criminal on the run in *I Am a Fugitive from a Chain Gang*, the French novelist Emile Zola and, when he was in his sixties, his moving portrayal of a selfless Jewish doctor working in Brooklyn in *The Last Angry Man*. An intensely private person, he liked to spend his time among books and radios and tape recorders. About acting he seemed as nonplussed as when he had started out, in the Yiddish Theatre at the age of twelve: 'I've never tried to learn the art of acting. I have been in the business for years but I still can't tell what acting is or how it is done.'

Don Murray

Born Hollywood, California, USA, 31 July 1929

Oscar Nominations (1): Best Supporting Actor for Bo Decker in *Bus Stop* (20th Century-Fox, 1956)

As the raucous young Montana cowboy who pursues and in the last reel finally lassoes disillusioned saloon singer Marilyn Monroe, Don Murray earned his one and only Oscar nomination and also a niche in cult movie history as one of Marilyn's handful of leading men. An intelligent actor of strong political and social views, he appeared in several adult movies in the late fifties (*A Hatful of Rain*, *The Hoodlum Priest*, *Advise and Consent*) but has been seen mostly in TV movies and less ambitious undertakings in recent years. In the eighties he co-starred in the TV series *Knots Landing* and appeared as the father of 'time traveller' Kathleen Turner in Coppola's *Peggy Sue Got Married*.

N

J. Carrol Naish

Born New York City, USA, 21 January 1897; died 1973

Oscar Nominations (2): Best Supporting Actor for Giuseppe in *Sahara* (Columbia, 1943) and Charley Martin in *A Medal for Benny* (Paramount, 1945)

Any nationality, any role, any dialect – J. Carrol Naish (pronounced Nash) was master of them all in the Hollywood of the thirties and forties. Chinamen, Mexicans, Arabs, Spaniards, Indians . . . they all came easily to him, as did the two roles that earned him nominations: the Italian prisoner captured by a stranded British-American unit in *Sahara*, and the aged father of an unlikely war hero in the John Steinbeck story *A Medal for Benny*. Never a major star, his small physique, pencil-thin moustache and swarthy features adorned more than two hundred films, yet despite his rich gallery of street pedlars, crooks, fishermen, pirates and the rest, it was on TV that he gained his greatest fame – first as an Italian immigrant who settles in Chicago in the comedy series *Life With Luigi*, and then, in the mid-fifties, in *The New Adventures of Charlie Chan*.

Mildred Natwick

Born Baltimore, Maryland, USA, 19 June 1908; died 1992

Oscar Nominations (1): Best Supporting Actress for Mrs Ethel Banks in *Barefoot in the Park* (Paramount, 1967)

One of the most amusing moments in Neil Simon's *Barefoot in the Park* occurs when Mildred Natwick, having staggered up five flights of stairs, totters into daughter Jane Fonda's apartment and gasps breathlessly: 'I feel as though I've gone to heaven but walked there!' When breathing more normally, she offers Jane some advice on how to keep husband Robert Redford content: 'Make him feel important. If you do, you'll have a happy marriage – like two out of every ten couples.' With lines such as those, an Oscar nomination was virtually a certainty, and the Academy duly obliged, although at the final count the voters preferred Estelle Parsons' hysterics in *Bonnie and Clyde*. Often cast as a favourite aunt or feisty mother, Mildred Natwick flitted in and out of Hollywood films for nearly fifty years. She was a regular for John Ford, and also appeared for Hitchcock as the dotty old girl who thinks she's a murderess in *The Trouble With Harry*.

Patricia Neal

Born Packard, Kentucky, USA, 20 January 1926

Oscars (1): Best Actress for Alma Brown in *Hud* (Paramount, 1963)

Oscar Nominations (1): Best Actress for Nettie Cleary in *The Subject Was Roses* (MGM, 1968)

A smart talker who knew how to make the blandest of lines crackle, Pat Neal was terrific as the cynical, worldly-wise housekeeper fending off a lecherous Paul Newman in *Hud*, and terrific yet again for her embittered mother of returning war veteran son Martin Sheen in *The Subject Was Roses*. She won, deservedly, for the former, although in many ways she merited the award more for the latter, coming as it did after she had suffered a series of strokes that damaged her nervous system and for a time confined her to a wheelchair. In 1968 she came in behind Katie Hepburn in *The Lion in Winter* and Barbra Streisand's *Funny Girl*. Her life in Britain with writer Roald Dahl was portrayed in the 1981 TV film *The Patricia Neal Story*. Glenda Jackson played Neal, Dirk Bogarde featured as Dahl.

Liam Neeson

Born Ballymena, Northern Ireland, 7 June 1952

Oscar Nominations (1): Best Actor for Oskar Schindler in *Schindler's List* (Amblin/Universal, 1993)

Steven Spielberg's casting of the 6ft 4in Irishman Liam Neeson to play the role of Oskar Schindler didn't at first seem the ideal choice; Neeson proved that it was close to being inspired, bringing pathos, power and humanity to the enigmatic German industrialist who saved more than a thousand Jews from the gas chamber in wartime Poland. An Oscar for Oskar didn't materialise, but the film paved the way for more substantial roles, including that of the famed Irish patriot Michael Collins for director Neil Jordan.

Kate Nelligan

Born London, Ontario, Canada, 16 March 1951

Oscar Nominations (1): Best Supporting Actress for Lila Wingo in *The Prince of Tides* (Columbia, 1991)

Just the one Oscar nomination for this Canadian-born actress whose sorties into movies have been brief but effective, especially as the luckless wife physically attracted to but at the same time repelled by Nazi agent Donald Sutherland in *Eye of the Needle*, and the brassy waitress who enjoys a one-night stand with Al Pacino in *Frankie and Johnny*. Her nomination was for Nick Nolte's manipulating social-climbing mother (a woman hiding a terrible secret in her past), a demanding role that required her to age from twenty to seventy. She managed it more than convincingly, although she didn't get her hands on the year's Oscar. Mercedes Ruehl clasped that in triumph for *The Fisher King*.

Paul Newman

Born Cleveland, Ohio, USA, 26 January 1925

Oscars (1): Best Actor for Eddie Felson in *The Color of Money* (Touch-stone, 1986)

Oscar Nominations (7): Best Actor for Brick Pollitt in *Cat on a Hot Tin Roof* (MGM, 1958), Eddie Felson in *The Hustler* (20th Century-Fox, 1961), Hud Bannon in *Hud* (Paramount, 1963), Luke Jackson in *Cool Hand Luke* (Warner Bros, 1967), Michael Gallagher in *Absence of Malice* (Columbia, 1981), Francis P. Galvin in *The Verdict* (20th Century-Fox, 1982) and Donald 'Sully' Sullivan in *Nobody's Fool* (Paramount/Capella Intl, 1994)

'A long time ago winning Oscars was pretty important,' said Paul Newman on one occasion. 'But it's a bit like chasing a beautiful woman. You hang in there for years, then she finally relents and you say: "I'm too tired!" ' The Academy must have thought him too tired at sixty, for they honoured him in 1985 with a special Academy Award, only to name him best actor the following year for reprising his hustling Eddie Felson in *The Color of Money*. To date he has brought his rebellious charm and engaging insolence to no fewer than eight nominated roles – his troubled Tennessee Williams hero in *Cat on a Hot Tin Roof*, pool-playing hustler, arrogant rancher's son Hud, chain-gang prisoner Cool Hand Luke, Miami businessman in *Absence of Malice*, down-at-heel lawyer in *The Verdict* and small-town loser-cum-handyman in *Nobody's Fool*. Quite a list, quite a range, quite a performer. Just one win seems inappropriate somehow!

Note: Newman received an additional nomination in 1968 as the producer of *Rachel, Rachel,* one of the five films nominated as best of the year. He has yet to receive a mention for his direction.

Haing S. Ngor

Born Cambodia, 1950; died 1996

Oscars (1): Best Supporting Actor for Dith Pran in *The Killing Fields* (Enigma/Warner Bros, 1984)

A role such as Dith Pran, the courageous translator whose skill saved the life of *New York Times* reporter Sydney Schanberg after the fall of Phnom Penh, then resulted in his own capture and escape from the Khmer Rouge, tends to come along once in a lifetime. Real-life Cambodian doctor Haing Ngor, who himself suffered torture and survived the turmoil, made the most of his opportunities, taking 1984's supporting award with consummate ease. The role remained his major film achievement, although he subsequently made the occasional film and TV appearance, most notably in Oliver Stone's *Heaven and Earth*. In February 1996 he was fatally shot outside his home on the streets of Los Angeles.

Jack Nicholson

Born Neptune, New Jersey, USA, 22 April 1937

Oscars (2): Best Actor for Randle Patrick McMurphy in *One Flew Over the Cuckoo's Nest* (United Artists, 1975); Best Supporting Actor for Garrett Breedlove in *Terms of Endearment* (Paramount, 1983)

Oscar Nominations (8): Best Supporting Actor for George Hanson in *Easy Rider* (Columbia, 1969); Best Actor for Robert Eroica Dupea in *Five Easy Pieces* (Columbia, 1970), Buddusky SMI in *The Last Detail* (Columbia, 1973) and J. J. Gittes in *Chinatown* (Paramount, 1974); Best Supporting Actor for Eugene O'Neill in *Reds* (Paramount, 1981); Best Actor for Charley Partanna in *Prizzi's Honor* (ABC/20th Century-Fox, 1985) and Francis Phelan in *Ironweed* (TriStar, 1987); Best Supporting Actor for Col. Nathan R. Jessep in *A Few Good Men* (Castle Rock/Columbia, 1992)

'I remember that someone once said that the whole thing is to keep working and pretty soon they'll think you're good.' Jack Nicholson's reasoning as to what it takes to become a top actor-star has stood him in good stead. He *has* kept working, even at the beginning of his career in the most appalling B-movies for Roger Corman, and people *do* think he's good, not least the voters of the Academy who have put more nominations his way than any other American actor, ten all told, equalling the record of Laurence Olivier and topping by one that of Spencer Tracy. Boozy lawyers, drop-outs, career sailors, private eyes, writers, Mafia hit men and tough army colonels have all fallen within his compass. So too have his remarkable portrayals of the effervescent 'mental' patient in *Cuckoo's Nest* and the former astronaut in *Terms of Endearment*. Whether there will be any more is difficult to say. The grin and mugging seem to be getting bigger; the roles smaller.

Note: Of Nicholson's ten nominations, six have been in the best actor category and four in the supporting section. Olivier's ten nominations were made up of nine best actor mentions and one support. Tracy's nine nominations were all for best actor roles.

David Niven

Born Kirriemuir, Scotland, 1 March 1909; died 1983

Oscars (1): Best Actor for Major Pollock in *Separate Tables* (United Artists, 1958)

An actor who refreshed audiences just by walking into a scene, David Niven nonetheless appeared in more mediocre and indifferent pictures than just about any other major star of the golden age. A natural as a debonair Englishman with a ready smile, he won his Oscar for a role which probed a little deeper into the kind of character he had played so often on screen – that of a jaunty but bogus colonel who is disgraced when he is charged with indecency in a public place. A star of more than eighty films, and a witty raconteur and author, he admitted in his later years that he accepted a film only after he had satisfied himself about three things: Where it was being made? Who else was in it? And how much were they paying? Only then did he read the script!

Nick Nolte

Born Omaha, Nebraska, USA, 8 February 1934

Oscar Nominations (1): Best Actor for Tom Wingo in *The Prince of Tides* (Columbia, 1991)

Anyone considering who to cast in the role of an emotional cripple suffering because of some horrendous incident in his childhood, and locked into psychiatry, would probably not have considered the rugged Nick Nolte as their first choice. It is to Barbra Streisand's credit that she insisted on him as her leading man, and to Nolte's credit that he made such a fist of it. Normally he is at his best as tough cops and reporters; in *The Prince of Tides* he was sensitive and vulnerable. The Golden Globe was his, and the Oscar looked set to follow. It went to Anthony Hopkins, usually a man of quiet charm but in 1991 up to no end of tricks as Hannibal Lecter.

O

Jack Oakie

Born Sedalia, Missouri, USA, 12 November 1903; died 1978

Oscar Nominations (1): Best Supporting Actor for Napaloni, Dictator of Bacteria, in *The Great Dictator* (United Artists, 1940)

To the question: which American actor would seem the least likely to earn himself a nomination in the early forties, the answer might well have been Jack Oakie, a round-faced, round-figured, jovial supporting performer in many Fox musical comedies of the period. Charlie Chaplin put an end to such thoughts when he cast him as a thinly disguised Mussolini in *The Great Dictator*. The laughs were there (especially in the scene where he and Chaplin try to best each other in ever-rising chairs) and so too was the nomination. On Oscar night, the question was: 'Who's it going to be, Jack Oakie or James Stephenson?' The Academy had the answer: Walter Brennan for *The Westerner*.

Merle Oberon

Born Tasmania (or according to some sources, Bombay, India),
19 February 1911; died 1979

Oscar Nominations (1): Best Actress for Kitty Vane in *The Dark Angel* (United Artists, 1935)

'Without security it is difficult for a woman to look or feel beautiful,' said the sloe-eyed, exotic Merle Oberon at her peak. Certainly she had no worries about security, being under contract in the thirties both to husband Alexander Korda in Britain and also (because Alex sublet) to Sam Goldwyn in Hollywood. She made it to the Oscar lists just the once, for her performance as the young heroine who discovers her lover has been blinded in the war in the 1935 weepie *The Dark Angel*. The subsequent years were less than kind (her marriage to Korda was dissolved in 1945), and apart from her Cathy in *Wuthering Heights* and a flamboyant outing as George Sand in *A Song to Remember*, her films rarely rated above the routine. Never a great actress, she relied on her delicate beauty to see her through, which it did, despite her being badly injured in a car crash during the filming of the abandoned *I Claudius*.

Edmond O'Brien

Born New York City, USA, 10 September 1915; died 1985

Oscars (1): Best Supporting Actor for Oscar Muldoon in *The Barefoot Contessa* (United Artists, 1954)

Oscar Nominations (1): Best Supporting Actor for Senator Raymond Clark in *Seven Days in May* (Paramount, 1964)

Sweating profusely, constantly mopping his brow and distastefully drinking milk for his ulcer, Edmond O'Brien gave easily the most convincing of all screen portraits of a Hollywood press agent in Joe Mankiewicz's *The Barefoot Contessa*. Despite competition from three *On the Waterfront* contenders – Lee J. Cobb, Karl Malden and Rod Steiger – he took the year's supporting award, confirming what many had long suspected, that he was a much more accomplished actor than his roles in routine thrillers and westerns had previously suggested. A colourful character actor in his later years – he was a crusading newspaper reporter for Ford in *The Man Who Shot Liberty Valance* and a grizzled old-timer for Peckinpah in *The Wild Bunch* – he earned his second Academy nomination for his senator loyal to President Fredric March in John Frankenheimer's political thriller *Seven Days in May*.

Arthur O'Connell

Born New York City, USA, 29 March 1908; died 1981

Oscar Nominations (2): Best Supporting Actor for Howard Bevans in *Picnic* (Columbia, 1955) and Parnell McCarthy in *Anatomy of a Murder* (Columbia, 1959)

One of Hollywood's 'average-looking-type-of-guy' character actors, Arthur O'Connell brought his somewhat doleful countenance and worried persona (and usually a drooping moustache) to more than eighty films, twice coming close to winning an Oscar but never quite making it. Nominated for his small-town bachelor finally roped into marriage by repressed schoolteacher Roz Russell, and his alcoholic assistant to James Stewart, he appeared in bit-parts and minor roles for some seventeen years before making his breakthrough in the mid-fifties. In 1941 he featured uncredited as one of the reporters seeking out the mystery behind the word 'Rosebud' in Orson Welles' classic début movie *Citizen Kane*. He died of Alzheimer's disease in 1981.

Dan O'Herlihy

Born Wexford, Ireland, 1 May 1919

Oscar Nominations (1): Best Actor for the title role in *The Adventures of Robinson Crusoe* (United Artists, 1954)

A cloak-and-sword man in his earlier, swashbuckling years, a man of mystery in the upper echelons of sinister power organisations in more recent times, Dan O'Herlihy somehow managed to squeeze a nomination out of the Academy for his Robinson Crusoe, a role that would have seemed to have been a natural for a nomination over the years but which has been recognised just the once. Unfortunately, it was O'Herlihy's misfortune to be nominated in 1954 when the *On the Waterfront* bandwagon was steamrollering all before it. Any other year . . . who knows?

Michael O'Keefe

Born Larchmont, New York, USA, 24 April 1955

Oscar Nominations (1): Best Supporting Actor for Ben Meechum in *The Great Santini* (Orion, 1980)

Nominated for one of the 'father against son' type dramas that have cropped up fairly regularly throughout Hollywood history, Michael O'Keefe made it to the lists for his sensitive portrayal of a son trying to measure up to the standards demanded of him by his bullying Marine pilot father Robert Duvall. It was Duvall who had the showy part, O'Keefe who had the more telling one. No Oscars for either, however. Robert De Niro boxed his way to the best actor award in *Raging Bull*, and O'Keefe was defeated by another young newcomer, Timothy Hutton in *Ordinary People*.

Lena Olin

Born Stockholm, Sweden, 1955

Oscar Nominations (1): Best Supporting Actress for Masha in *Enemies: A Love Story* (20th Century-Fox, 1989)

Sex is never far away whenever Lena Olin is around. Up to all kinds of tricks as the artist lover of Daniel Day-Lewis in *The Unbearable Lightness of Being*, she was in similarly hungry mood a year later, this time earning an Oscar nomination for her doomed, sexually hungry married woman hopelessly involved with concentration camp survivor Ron Silver. The sexual sparks didn't fly with Robert Redford in *Havana* but they probably will again . . . and again! Swedish-born, and the daughter of actor Stig Olin, who featured in many of Ingmar Bergman's films of the fifties, she appeared for Bergman in *Fanny and Alexander*.

Edna May Oliver

Born Malden, Massachusetts, USA, 9 November 1883; died 1942

Oscar Nominations (1): Best Supporting Actress for Mrs Sarah McKlennar in *Drums Along the Mohawk* (20th Century-Fox, 1939)

Cruelly but accurately described as 'horse-faced', the bossy Edna May Oliver was unlucky in that she played most of her best roles before Oscars were handed out for supporting performances. Hence her Betsey Trotwood in *David Copperfield*, Aunt March in *Little Women* and Red Queen in *Alice in Wonderland* all came too early for Academy consideration. It was only when John Ford cast her as the widow McKlennar, murdered by Indians during the Revolutionary War, that a belated nomination came her way. Bad luck dogged her even then. In 1939 Hollywood was more interested in the Civil War than the one that had preceded it and went for Hattie McDaniel in *Gone with the Wind*. Domineering, frequently haughty and with one of the longest and most unnerving stares in the business, Edna May never made it to the Oscar podium. She died, aged fifty-nine, in 1942.

Laurence Olivier

Born Dorking, Surrey, England, 22 May 1907; died 1989

Oscars (1): Best Actor for the title role of *Hamlet* (Rank/Two Cities, 1948)

Oscar Nominations (9): Best Actor for Heathcliff in *Wuthering Heights* (Goldwyn/United Artists, 1939), Maxim de Winter in *Rebecca* (Selznick/United Artists, 1940), the title role in *Henry V* (Rank/Two Cities, 1946), the title role in *Richard III* (Lopert Films, 1956), Archie Rice in *The Entertainer* (Woodfall, 1960), the title role in *Othello* (BHE/Warner Bros, 1965) and Andrew Wyke in *Sleuth* (20th Century-Fox, 1972); Best Supporting Actor for Szell in *Marathon Man* (Paramount, 1976); Best Actor for Ezra Lieberman in *The Boys From Brazil* (ITC/20th Century-Fox, 1978)

Overlooked by the Academy for two of his most remarkable screen roles – the wealthy restaurateur destroyed by love in *Carrie* and his ruthless Crassus in Kubrick's epic *Spartacus*, Olivier still managed to chalk up ten nominations over a forty-year award span. The Shakespearian roles one tended to take for granted; it was his other performances that took the eye – romantic as Heathcliff, autocratic as Max de Winter, broken-down as music-hall entertainer Archie Rice, malicious as the thriller-writer playing murder games in *Sleuth* and aged and defiant as the Nazi-hunter in *The Boys From Brazil*. And, of course, sadistic as that infamous Nazi dentist in *Marathon Man*. Yet even with a tally of ten acting nominations there was still the impression that he was always acting on screen, that he was always *on*. Olivier was best when toned down, not toned up!

Note: Olivier earned the Oscar as the producer of 1948's best film, *Hamlet*, and was also nominated for his direction. He was the recipient of two honorary awards, the first in 1946 for 'his outstanding achievement as actor, producer and director in bringing *Henry V* to the screen', the second in 1978 for 'the full body of his work, for the unique achievement of his entire career and his lifetime of contribution to the art of film'.

Edward James Olmos

Born Los Angeles, USA, 24 February 1947

Oscar Nominations (1): Best Actor for Jaime Escalante in *Stand and Deliver* (American Playhouse, Warner Bros, 1988)

Very much the outsider in the 1988 Oscar race (it was the year Hoffman beat off Gene Hackman's challenge in *Mississippi Burning*), Olmos offered perhaps the years' most sensitive and affecting performance as the real-life maths teacher who uses every means at his disposal to instil some knowledge into a bunch of Hispanic kids who couldn't care less whether they learned or not. A worthy and uplifting role, far removed from the one that earned him an Emmy on TV – Lt Martin Castillo in the long-running crime series *Miami Vice*.

Nancy Olson

Born Milwaukee, Wisconsin, USA, 14 July 1928

Oscar Nominations (1): Best Supporting Actress for Betty Schaefer in *Sunset Boulevard* (Paramount, 1950)

One of the few sympathetic characters in Billy Wilder's *Sunset Boulevard*, the wholesome, fresh-faced Nancy Olson earned her nomination for her young studio reader who for one brief moment looks as though she might save hack writer Bill Holden from the demands of reclusive silent star Gloria Swanson. Almost, but not quite. Holden wavers but in the end opts for greed and the role of gigolo (and death in Swanson's pool) rather than follow his natural desires. Just twenty-two when she appeared in the movie, Olson went on to make several more films with Holden (*Union Station, Force of Arms, Submarine Command*) before retiring in the mid-fifties. Married to songwriter Alan Jay Lerner (she was the third of his five wives), she returned to the screen in 1960 to make the occasional picture for Disney. In 1950 she lost on Oscar night to the dumpy, delightful and deserving Josephine Hull for *Harvey*.

Ryan O'Neal

Born Los Angeles, USA, 20 April 1941

Oscar Nominations (1): Best Actor for Oliver Barrett IV in *Love Story* (Paramount, 1970)

Only Tatum of the O'Neal family has the Oscar on her mantelpiece, although her dad came close in 1970 when he was nominated for his young Harvard law student in love with terminally ill Ali MacGraw. George C. Scott, however, strode through the nominees like he strode through his film *Patton*, and although he refused to accept the award (see p. 313), it was never a serious contest. Popular in the sixties in the long-running TV series *Peyton Place* (he featured in more than 500 episodes), O'Neal was a favourite of many directors in the early seventies, but after making a brave stab at *Barry Lyndon* for Kubrick, he faded almost as quickly as the director who had worked with him at his peak, Peter Bogdanovich.

Tatum O'Neal

Born Los Angeles, USA, 5 November 1963

Oscars (1): Best Supporting Actress for Addie Loggins in *Paper Moon* (Paramount, 1973)

A right little urchin she was, conning her way across the Midwest with Ryan, flogging Bibles to widows, smoking cigarettes and getting up to every crafty trick in the book. The smart repartee with her real-life dad helped get her the nod over Linda Blair's less than wholesome utterings in *The Exorcist*. That and a unique talent for comedy and scene-stealing. At ten years 148 days, she's still the youngest ever to win a competitive Oscar, although there have been challengers since, most recently from the eleven-year-old Anna Paquin in *The Piano*.

Barbara O'Neil

Born St Louis, Missouri, USA, 10 July 1909; died 1980

Oscar Nominations (1): Best Supporting Actress for the Duchesse de Praslin in *All This and Heaven Too* (Warner Bros, 1940)

No one really remembers Barbara O'Neil other than to recall vaguely that she played Scarlett's sensible mother in *Gone with the Wind*. That was in 1939. A year later, at Warners, she received her only Oscar nomination when she played the crazed Duchesse, a woman who was brutally murdered in mid-nineteenth-century France and whose death caused a Parisian scandal. Jane Darwell's more homely Ma Joad was more to the voters' taste, however, and O'Neil was left with a handful of none too distinguished roles, frequently of disturbed, neurotic women who were often a long way from Mrs O'Hara but pretty close to the Duchesse.

Peter O'Toole

Born Connemara, Ireland, 2 August 1932

Oscar Nominations (7): Best Actor for T. E. Lawrence in *Lawrence of Arabia* (Columbia, 1962), Henry II in *Becket* (Paramount, 1964) and *The Lion in Winter* (Avco-Embassy, 1968), Arthur Chipping in *Goodbye, Mr Chips* (MGM, 1969), Jack, 14th Earl of Gurney, in *The Ruling Class* (Avco-Embassy, 1972), Eli Cross in *The Stunt Man* (20th Century-Fox, 1980) and Alan Swann in *My Favorite Year* (MGM/UA, 1982)

'No prisoners!' cries Peter O'Toole, his face a quivering mask of hate as he leads the bloodthirsty charge against the retreating Turks in *Lawrence of Arabia*. A charge also towards an Academy Award, thought many in the know. Not so. Greg Peck was around with his finest-ever performance, as Atticus Finch, and it was he, not Pete, who collected on Oscar night, although it must have been a close-run thing. Nominated a subsequent six times, O'Toole has been in the lists for two portraits of Henry II (one as a young man, the other in crotchety middle age), the schoolmaster Arthur Chipping, an eccentric earl who believes he's Jesus Christ, a tyrannical film director (said to be based on David Lean) and an alcoholic swashbuckler. All to no avail. The chance has now probably gone for good. A tie between El Aurens and Atticus might have been the best result in 1962.

Maria Ouspenskaya

Born Tula, Russia, 29 July 1876; died 1949

Oscar Nominations (2): Best Supporting Actress for Baroness von Obersdorf in *Dodsworth* (United Artists, 1936) and Grandmother Marnet in *Love Affair* (RKO, 1939)

Already sixty when she made her American film début – a repeat of her role as the formidable baroness in the Broadway play *Dodsworth* – the Russian-born Ouspenskaya won an Oscar nomination in the year the Academy first began handing out awards for supporting roles. Sources close to the scene said it was touch and go between her and Gale Sondergaard (see p. 324), which was rather more than it was three years later when Ouspenskaya (cast this time as the grandmother of playboy Charles Boyer) came in well behind Hattie McDaniel's Mammy in *Gone with the Wind*. Tiny, very wrinkled, with luminous eyes and a thick Slavic accent, she is perhaps best remembered for her role in *The Wolf Man*, a Universal cheapie of the early forties. As the fortune-teller Maleva, she spoke the lines that have since become part of movie folklore: 'Even the man who is pure at heart and who says his prayers at night may become a wolf when the wolf bane blooms and the autumn moon is bright.' A resident of Hollywood in her later years, Ouspenskaya died tragically of burns when fire destroyed her Los Angeles apartment in 1949.

P

Al Pacino

Born New York City, USA, 25 April 1940

Oscars (1): Best Actor for Lt-Col Frank Slade in *Scent of a Woman* (Universal, 1992)

Oscar Nominations (7): Best Supporting Actor for Michael Corleone in *The Godfather* (Paramount, 1972); Best Actor for Frank Serpico in *Serpico* (Paramount, 1973), Don Michael Corleone in *The Godfather Part II* (Paramount, 1974), Sonny Wortzik in *Dog Day Afternoon* (Warner Bros, 1975) and Arthur Kirkland in *And Justice for All* (Columbia, 1979); Best Supporting Actor for Big Boy Caprice in *Dick Tracy* (Touchstone, 1990) and Ricky Roma in *Glengarry Glen Ross* (New Line, 1992)

Pacino or De Niro? The question has often been asked: 'Who's the best?' Not that either of them cares all that much, it's just the pundits who like to mull it over. As far as Oscars are concerned, De Niro has it by two to one at the moment, although with both men in their fifties, that could easily change in the years ahead. Pacino's win, when at last it came, was for his blind, embittered colonel in *Scent of a Woman*, not by any means his best role but a part reward for his missing out on his two portraits of Michael in *The Godfather* films. His other nominations? For his young cop Serpico uncovering corruption on the New York police force, bank robber trying to get funds for a sex-change operation in *Dog Day Afternoon*, volatile young lawyer in *And Justice for All* and a couple of supporting roles – his Lee J. Cobbish gang-leader in *Dick Tracy* and his desperate real-estate salesman in *Glengarry Glen Ross*. Director Sidney Lumet has said of him: 'He is literally incapable of doing anything fake.' As for the journalist who tried to interview him about his work, all he could remember when he awoke with a hangover was the single quote: 'What will you have?'

Geraldine Page

Born Kirksville, Missouri, USA, 22 November 1924; died 1987

Oscars (1): Best Actress for Mrs Watts in *The Trip to Bountiful* (Island Films, 1985)

Oscar Nominations (7): Best Supporting Actress for Angie Lowe in *Hondo* (Warner Bros, 1953); Best Actress for Alma Winemiller in *Summer and Smoke* (Paramount, 1961), and Alexandra Del Lago in *Sweet Bird of Youth* (MGM, 1962); Best Supporting Actress for Margery Chanticleer in *You're a Big Boy Now* (Seven Arts, 1966) and Gertrude in *Pete 'N' Tillie* (Universal, 1972); Best Actress for Eve in *Interiors* (United Artists, 1978); Best Supporting Actress for Mrs Ritter in *The Pope of Greenwich Village* (MGM/UA, 1984)

The win, when it came, was for a role in a chamber piece, a tale of an ageing widow who returns to her Texas hometown in search of her roots. Before that it had been neurosis and frustration all the way as she chalked up one nomination after another but never seemed to come within touching distance of the elusive Oscar. She actually won her first nomination for a rancher's wife in a John Wayne western. After that, though she really got into her stride with her repressed spinster in *Summer and Smoke*, faded movie star in *Sweet Bird of Youth* and mentally disturbed wife in *Interiors*, and in three supporting roles – the overpossessive Long Island mother in *You're a Big Boy Now*, the matchmaker in *Pete 'n' Tillie* and the mother of a dead cop in *The Pope of Greenwich Village*. No wonder someone said: 'There ain't no justice if she don't win.' She did, just a year before her premature death from a heart attack in June 1987.

Jack Palance

Born Lattimer, Pennsylvania, USA, 18 February 1919

Oscars (1): Best Supporting Actor for Curly in *City Slickers* (Warner Bros, 1991)

Oscar Nominations (2): Best Supporting Actor for Lester Blaine in *Sudden Fear* (RKO, 1952) and Jack Wilson in *Shane* (Paramount, 1953)

'Screen menace personified' was how one critic described Jack Palance, having watched him try to bump off Joan Crawford in *Sudden Fear* and then a year later try to do the same to Alan Ladd in *Shane*. Two consecutive Academy Award nominations seemed to indicate that an Oscar was there for the taking in the years that lay ahead. No one, least of all Palance, would have believed, though, that the win when it came would be thirty-eight years in the future and that instead of being a relatively youthful menace in his early thirties, Palance would be a grizzled old-timer of seventy-two. His win was for his laconic trail boss who has to put up with Billy Crystal and fellow vacationers on a holiday cattle drive. Not quite the lethal Jack Wilson in *Shane*, perhaps, but the win was well merited.

Chazz Palminteri

Oscar Nominations (1): Best Supporting Actor for Cheech in *Bullets Over Broadway* (Sweetland/Miramax, 1994)

When asked what it was like to be directed by Woody Allen in *Bullets Over Broadway*, Chazz Palminteri replied that it entailed a certain amount of discussion about basketball and baseball and the constant use of the command: 'Ready! Action! Slower!' The guidance certainly worked, helping Palminteri earn a nomination for a Runyonesque-type role, that of a hit man who is assigned to protect his boss's mistress, would-be actress Jennifer Tilly, and who turns out to have a better ear for dialogue ('You don't write like people talk') than the young playwright struggling with her play. Martin Landau came up trumps on awards night but Palminteri, a screenwriter as well as an actor (e.g. *A Bronx Tale*), remains a talent for the nineties.

Anna Paquin

Born New Zealand

Oscars (1): Best Supporting Actress for Fiona McGrath in *The Piano* (Miramax, 1993)

She won for her charming, wilful young daughter of Holly Hunter, but when she stood on the podium clutching her Oscar it seemed for a time as though she wasn't going to utter a word, which would have made a refreshing change from the speeches that were to follow. In the end she did thank the right people and in the nicest possible way and walked off the stage content in the knowledge that at the tender age of eleven she had seen off the challenges of actresses such as Winona Ryder (*The Age of Innocence*) and Emma Thompson (*In the Name of the Father*). The youngest winner since the ten-year-old Tatum O'Neal twenty years before, she won the role out of 5,000 applicants.

Eleanor Parker

Born Cedarville, Ohio, USA, 26 June 1922

Oscar Nominations (3): Best Actress for Marie Allen in *Caged* (Warner Bros, 1950), Mary McLeod in *Detective Story* (Paramount, 1951) and Marjorie Lawrence in *Interrupted Melody* (MGM, 1955)

Red-haired, cool and terrific when working from a good script; red-haired and a touch hysterical (but still terrific) when struggling with a bad one, Eleanor Parker could be both victim and shrew, although it was in the former capacity that the Academy liked her best. Nominated for her first offender hardened by prison life, her young wife who reveals a shady past to detective husband Kirk Douglas, and her Australian opera singer crippled by polio, she found the opposition too strong on each occasion – Judy Holliday, Vivien Leigh and Anna Magnani – and after a six-year golden period faded from the Oscar scene. The best of her later roles were her widow who snares Ol' Blue Eyes in Capra's *A Hole in the Head* and the baroness who gracefully acknowledges that Julie Andrews has something she hasn't – Christopher Plummer – in *The Sound of Music*.

Larry Parks

Born Olathe, Kansas, USA, 13 December 1914; died 1975

Oscar Nominations (1): Best Actor for Al Jolson in *The Jolson Story* (Columbia, 1946)

The first movie star to admit he had been a Communist when he testified before the Un-American Activities Committee in 1951, Larry Parks had essentially two movie careers – the first prior to the hearings, when he landed the prize role and an Oscar nomination for *The Jolson Story* after serving an apprenticeship at Columbia in some thirty-five B-movies; the second after the hearings, when he struggled to find anyone who would give him any kind of a role. He appeared on screen just twice after his testimony – in the 1955 British thriller *Tiger by the Tail* and in 1962 when John Huston cast him as a psychiatrist colleague of Montgomery Clift's *Freud*. Married to actress Betty Garrett, he later made infrequent appearances on stage and TV but mostly earned his living out of real estate.

Estelle Parsons

Born Lynn, Massachusetts, USA, 20 November 1927

Oscars (1): Best Supporting Actress for Blanche in *Bonnie and Clyde* (Warner Bros, 1967)

Oscar Nominations (1): Best Supporting Actress for Calla Mackie in *Rachel, Rachel* (Warner Bros, 1968)

The Oscar question 'Which performer in the *Bonnie and Clyde* cast (all five leads were nominated) won the film's sole acting award?' might not necessarily bring the answer 'Estelle Parsons'. She it was, though, who won in April 1968 for her terrified wife of Gene Hackman's Buck Barrow who is blinded by gunfire during a police raid. She almost made it two in a row when she was nominated again the following year for her spinster schoolteacher in *Rachel, Rachel*, but Ruth Gordon put paid to such aspirations by enjoying herself with satanic rituals in *Rosemary's Baby*. A teacher of acting who has often been seen in the TV show *Roseanne*, Parsons was remembered by Warren Beatty twenty years after *Bonnie and Clyde* when he cast her as Mrs Truelove in *Dick Tracy*.

Marisa Pavan

Born Cagliari, Sardinia, 19 June 1932

Oscar Nominations (1): Best Supporting Actress for Rosa Delle Rose in
The Rose Tattoo (Paramount, 1955)

Anyone sharing the screen with the dynamic Anna Magnani needed to act
their socks off to even stay in the frame; that the beautiful dark-haired
Marisa Pavan managed to hold her own and even gain a nomination as
Magnani's hot-blooded young daughter in *The Rose Tattoo* says much for her
acting, even though she failed to build on her initial success in later years.
The sister of the tragic Pier Angeli and a singer as well as an actress, she
later enjoyed a musical career on TV. Jo Van Fleet won the 1955 supporting
Oscar for her cold-blooded brothel madam in *East of Eden*.

Katina Paxinou

Born Piraeus, Greece, 1900; died 1973

Oscars (1): Best Supporting Actress for Pilar in *For Whom the Bell Tolls*
(Paramount, 1943)

The only performer to win an Oscar for portraying a Hemingway character
on screen, Katina Paxinou was the author's Spanish guerrilla leader to the
life, fiery, rebellious and defiant, dominating her once proud husband Akim
Tamiroff and gently mocking the flowering romance between freedom
fighter Gary Cooper and peasant girl Ingrid Bergman. Only a brief visitor
to Hollywood (*Hostages*, *Confidential Agent*, *Mourning Becomes Electra*), she
returned after the war to Europe where she and her husband, actor Alexis
Minotis, formed the celebrated Royal Theatre of Athens. Her subsequent
film roles were few and far between, although she enjoyed a vivid cameo in
Orson Welles' *Mr Arkadin* and was superb as the Sicilian-born widow in
Visconti's epic *Rocco and His Brothers*.

☆

David Paymer

Born Long Island, New York, USA, 30 August 1954

Oscar Nominations (1): Best Supporting Actor for Stan Yankelman in *Mr Saturday Night* (Castle Rock/Columbia, 1992)

Stealing from Billy Crystal on screen takes a bit of doing, but David Paymer managed it to some effect in *Mr Saturday Night*, the story of a veteran stand-up comedian, long past his best, who is helped and guided through life by his kindly, long-suffering agent brother. Crystal played the comic but missed out on a nomination, Paymer the brother, earning a nomination but not the award itself, which went to Gene Hackman for dishing out a nasty dose of western sadism in *Unforgiven*. Crystal has yet to make his way into the nominations lists, although he deserves something simply for being the best Oscar host since Bob Hope.

Gregory Peck

Born La Jolla, California, USA, 5 April 1916

Oscars (1): Best Actor for Atticus Finch in *To Kill a Mockingbird* (Universal, 1962)

Oscar Nominations (4): Best Actor for Father Francis Chisholm in *The Keys of the Kingdom* (20th Century-Fox, 1945), Pa Baxter in *The Yearling* (MGM, 1946), Phil Green in *Gentleman's Agreement* (20th Century-Fox, 1947) and General Frank Savage in *Twelve O'Clock High* (20th Century-Fox, 1949)

After being nominated four times in five years, and missing out on each occasion, it seemed for a time as though Greg Peck might have lost his chance of an Oscar. A priest, a Florida farmer, a crusading journalist, and a World War II bombing group commander seemed ample proof of his youthful versatility, but in the end it was fitting that he was honoured for the role that he was born to play – the widowed lawyer Atticus Finch bringing up two small children in the Depression South of the thirties. Presented with the American Film Institute Life Achievement Award in 1989, he revealed a rich sense of humour in his acceptance speech, recalling the time he was once walking through the streets of Dublin unrecognised when a woman came up to him and said respectfully: 'Beggin' your pardon, sir, but wouldn't you be James Mason in his later years?'

Sean Penn

Born Burbank, California, USA, 17 August, 1960

Oscar Nominations (1): Best Actor for Matthew Poncelet in *Dead Man Walking* (Gramercy, 1995)

The name of Sean Penn had first been linked with an Oscar back in 1994 for his lawyer in the grip of a mafioso in *Carlito's Way*. Nothing developed on that occasion, but things changed two years later, when he finally made it into the nominations for his death-row convict in *Dead Man Walking* and was the only actor to run Nicolas Cage close for the top acting prize. A director – in 1995 he filmed *The Crossing Guard* with Jack Nicholson and Anjelica Huston – as well as an actor these days, he seems destined to be there or thereabouts in both capacities before the decade has run its course. A far cry from the days when he was regarded as one of Hollywood's bad boys and married to the flamboyant pop star Madonna.

Rosie Perez

Born Brooklyn, New York, USA, 1964

Oscar Nominations (1): Best Supporting Actress for Carla Rodrigo in *Fearless* (Warner Bros, 1993)

A real contender for 1993's supporting award – she had tied with child star Anna Paquin (*The Piano*) in the vote of the Los Angeles Critics and was runner-up to Gong Li in *Farewell My Concubine* in the ballot of the New York Critics Circle – Rosie Perez must have felt that her chances on awards night were better than average for her young mother stricken with guilt over her failure to save her son from the plane crash from which she and Jeff Bridges have somehow walked unscathed. Her hopes were dashed as the winner was read out. The kid took it, the first since Tatum O'Neal twenty years earlier.

Anthony Perkins

Born New York City, USA, 4 April 1932; died 1992

Oscar Nominations (1): Best Supporting Actor for Josh Birdwell in *Friendly Persuasion* (Allied Artists, 1956)

Trick question! How many times was Anthony Perkins nominated other than for his mention for motel-keeper Norman Bates in *Psycho*? No answer, unfortunately, for the question is based on a false premise. Perkins was overlooked for poor old Norman (had it been thirty years on, round about the time of *The Silence of the Lambs*, things might have been different) and had to be content with just a supporting nomination for his young Quaker forced to come face to face with his beliefs in Wyler's Civil War epic *Friendly Persuasion*. All his grisly efforts in *Psycho* were therefore to no avail, although to be fair, his was not a one hundred per cent performance. He did not murder poor Janet Leigh in the shower. That was done by his stand-in while he was away rehearsing a play on Broadway.

Valerie Perrine

Born Galveston, Texas, USA, 3 September 1944

Oscar Nominations (1): Best Actress for Honey Bruce in *Lenny* (United Artists, 1974)

For a girl without any previous acting experience, Valerie Perrine has proved to be a natural, especially as her years as a topless Las Vegas showgirl were hardly adequate preparation for an acting career. The showy role of Lenny Bruce's stripper-junkie wife saw her into the nominations lists, and she also gave good accounts of herself as the mistress of W. C. Fields and the wonderfully named space siren Montana Wildhack in *Slaughterhouse-Five*. Unfortunately, despite her remarkable physical attributes, not a lot has happened since.

Joe Pesci

Born Newark, New Jersey, USA, 9 February 1943

Oscars (1): Best Supporting Actor for Tommy DeVito in *Goodfellas* (Warner Bros, 1990)

Oscar Nominations (1): Best Supporting Actor for Joey La Motta in *Raging Bull* (United Artists, 1980)

'I don't want to see you act, I want to see you *behave*,' Martin Scorsese told Joe Pesci when he plucked him from a Bronx restaurant and began auditioning him for his boxing classic *Raging Bull*. Pesci's 'behaviour' was obviously up to the mark, for at Oscar time he found himself among the year's five supporting nominees for his brother and manager of middle-weight champion Jake La Motta. A decade later he won the award itself in another Scorsese film, chilling the blood as the unhinged Mafia gangster Tommy DeVito. As much a comedian as a dramatic performer in recent years – he was the inept lawyer in *My Cousin Vinny* and one of the two bumbling burglars in the *Home Alone* films – Pesci worked as a barber, postal clerk, and grocer's helper before Scorsese asked him to behave.

Susan Peters

Born Spokane, Washington, USA, 3 July 1921; died 1952

Oscar Nominations (1): Best Supporting Actress for Kitty in *Random Harvest* (MGM, 1942)

One of MGM's brightest young stars of the early forties – she was nominated for her niece in love with Ronald Colman in *Random Harvest* – Susan Peters' career was cut tragically short on New Year's Day 1944, when she was injured on a hunting trip with her husband, the bullet she accidentally discharged from her gun lodging in her spine and paralysing her from the waist down. Confined to a wheelchair for the rest of her life, she attempted a comeback as a crippled woman in the small-scale picture *The Sign of the Ram*, and in 1951 actually preceded Raymond Burr's *Ironside* by playing a woman lawyer in a wheelchair in the TV series *Miss Susan*. A year later, very much a recluse, she died of a chronic kidney infection. She was thirty-one.

Michelle Pfeiffer

Born Santa Anna, California, USA, 29 April 1957

Oscar Nominations (3): Best Supporting Actress for Madame de Tourvel in *Dangerous Liaisons* (Warner Bros, 1988); Best Actress for Susie Diamond in *The Fabulous Baker Boys* (Gladden Films, 1989) and Lurene Hallett in *Love Field* (Orion, 1992)

Many Academy voters felt that in 1989, the sight of Michelle Pfeiffer sliding seductively across a piano top and singing 'Making Whoopee' was rather more fun than watching Jessica Tandy's tetchy old Southern widow in *Driving Miss Daisy*. It turned out to be Tandy's night, however, despite Pfeiffer demonstrating that she had a way with a disillusioned wisecrack as well as a song and was rather more than a pretty face. At the moment she remains one of Oscar's ladies-in-waiting, having been nominated both in 1988 as the tragic aristocrat seduced by John Malkovich in *Dangerous Liaisons* and in 1992 as the Dallas hairdresser in *Love Field*. Rather surprisingly, she failed to make the list of five nominees for her subtle rendering of Countess Olenska, the woman who enslaves Daniel Day-Lewis in Scorsese's *The Age of Innocence*.

River Phoenix

Born Madras, Oregon, USA, 24 August 1970; died 1993

Oscar Nominations (1): Best Supporting Actor for Danny Pope in *Running on Empty* (Lorimar/Warner Bros, 1988)

Unlike James Dean, who starred in three major movies before his untimely death, River Phoenix left only glimpses of what might have been, roles that didn't really stretch him a great deal – Harrison Ford's son in *The Mosquito Coast*, a young Indy Jones, and a technical whizz kid in *Sneakers*. Except, that is, his street hustler in *My Own Private Idaho*, and the part that earned him his Academy nod as the teenage son of Judd Hirsch and Christine Lahti, two sixties radicals constantly on the run from the FBI and carrying with them a son who all the time is hoping to settle down to a normal life. Under Sidney Lumet's direction, Phoenix blossomed. His death from a drug overdose at the age of twenty-three put an end to all the hopes and dreams.

Mary Pickford

Born Toronto, Canada, 18 April 1893; died 1979

Oscars (1): Best Actress for Norma Besant in *Coquette* (United Artists, 1928/29)

Trivial statistic: Mary Pickford was the first actress to weep when receiving an Oscar. More sobering one: her career lasted just four years after the award, the public refusing to accept her new image and still wanting her as the golden-curled sweet innocent she had always been – even at the age of thirty-six! 'No way,' said Pickford. 'No more of that stuff for me, I want to play the lover,' which she duly did, embarking on the role of a heartless Southern belle who busies herself ruining the lives of several men. The Oscar was hers but the career was finished. After appearing in her last film role in *Secrets* in 1933, she devoted herself to helping run United Artists, which she had formed with her husband Douglas Fairbanks, Charlie Chaplin and D. W. Griffith in 1919. She received a special Academy Award in 1975 'in recognition of her unique contribution to the film industry and the development of film as an artistic medium'.

☆

Walter Pidgeon

Born East St John, New Brunswick, Canada, 23 September 1897; died 1984

Oscar Nominations (2): Best Actor for Clem Miniver in *Mrs Miniver* (MGM, 1942) and Pierre Curie in *Madame Curie* (MGM, 1943)

Mr Dependable in every sense of the word, the stoic Walter Pidgeon earned nominations for just two of the eight films in which he co-starred with Greer Garson – *Mrs Miniver*, as the easy-going, pipe-smoking wartime hubby Clem, and *Madame Curie*, in which he put in hours of overtime helping Greer discover radium. An MGM star for nearly twenty years, he enjoyed some of his best roles on loan-outs, especially at Fox, where he played the big-game hunter stalking Hitler in Fritz Lang's *Man Hunt* and the young minister in John Ford's *How Green Was My Valley*. Ford's working methods tended to puzzle him. He said afterwards: 'When he speaks he mumbles. I listened intently to his instructions and if five words out of seventy-five were intelligible I considered it a good average. With most directors the results of such obscurity would be hopeless confusion. With Ford, no. You go out on the set and find yourself following orders you haven't heard.'

Brad Pitt

Born Shawnee, Oklahoma, USA, 1963

Oscar Nominations (1): Best Supporting Actor for Jeffrey Goines in *12 Monkeys* (Atlas Entertainment/Universal, 1995)

A break from the mould often does the trick at Oscar time; a deglamorised Brad Pitt managed it in some style in Terry Gilliam's *12 Monkeys*, as a mental asylum inmate who is always ranting on about the dangers of science and lab experiments and that the end of the world is nigh. He had a point. Bruce Willis had seen the future and travelled back thirty years to find the origins of the virus that is wiping out mankind. All Pitt's half-crazed looks and histrionics were deemed to have been worthy of a Golden Globe as best support. The Academy opted for the more naturally versatile Kevin Spacey for his gem of a role as the untrustworthy squealer in *The Usual Suspects*.

Joan Plowright

Born Scunthorpe, Brig, Lincolnshire, England, 28 October 1929

Oscar Nominations (1): Best Supporting Actress for Mrs Fisher in *Enchanted April* (Miramax, 1992)

The Brits were out in force the year Joan Plowright was up for an Oscar; Vanessa Redgrave was on the lists for twittering on about the beauty of *Howards End*, Miranda Richardson was suffering anguish over Jeremy Irons' illicit lustings in *Damage*, and Joan Plowright? She was up for her haughty widow, one of four women who find their lives transformed when they rent a medieval villa in sun-drenched Italy. Marisa Tomei did 'em all with her wisecracking girlfriend of lawyer Joe Pesci in *My Cousin Vinny*.

☆

Sidney Poitier

Born Miami, Florida, USA, 20 February 1924

Oscars (1): Best Actor for Homer Smith in *Lilies of the Field* (United Artists, 1963)

Oscar Nominations (1): Best Actor for Noah Cullen in *The Defiant Ones* (United Artists, 1958)

Incredibly, it took nearly thirty years for a black performer to be nominated for a best actor award, and then another five before the award itself was finally presented. The same actor, Sidney Poitier, was involved on both occasions, first in 1958 when he was nominated for one of the escaped convicts in *The Defiant Ones*, and then in 1963 when he won for his amiable handyman who helps some refugee nuns build a chapel in the Arizona desert. No other black actor has yet managed to emulate the achievement, although with three nominations to his credit Morgan Freeman seems the likeliest contender among contemporary actors. A dignified, quietly spoken performer, Poitier has made more than forty films, as both actor and director, since his début in 1950, among them *Guess Who's Coming to Dinner?* and *In the Heat of the Night.*

☆

Michael J. Pollard

Born Pacific, New Jersey, USA, 30 May 1939

Oscar Nominations (1): Best Supporting Actor for C. W. Moss in *Bonnie and Clyde* (Warner Bros, 1967)

For a brief moment it seemed as though Michael J. Pollard might become one of the most intriguing and cheeky of contemporary Hollywood character actors, but after winning a nomination for his dim-witted getaway driver in *Bonnie and Clyde* producers found his chubby, impish persona difficult to cast, and the initial promise quickly faded. During the seventies he became just another name below the title and has since been seen in mostly undistinguished, low-budget productions. People still remember him, though, for that one role of long ago – as the bungling car mechanic C. W. Moss whose treacherous father turns police informer and helps bring about the demise of two of the most notorious gangsters of the thirties.

Pete Postlethwaite

Born 1946

Oscar Nominations (1): Best Supporting Actor for Guiseppe Conlon in *In the Name of the Father* (Hell's Kitchen/Universal, 1993)

One of those British supporting actors who tend to make the nominations lists just the once, Pete Postlethwaite belongs with those reliable performers who bring conviction to every role in which they appear, whether it be for just a scene or two, as in *The Last of the Mohicans,* or in a role of some substance, as the father of the wrongly imprisoned Gerry Conlon in *In the Name of the Father*. Like his co-star Daniel Day-Lewis (nominated as best actor) he was among the also-rans in 1993, coming in behind Tommy Lee Jones' laconic cop in *The Fugitive*.

William Powell

Born Pittsburgh, USA, 29 July 1892; died 1984

Oscar Nominations (3): Best Actor for Nick Charles in *The Thin Man* (MGM, 1934), Godfrey Parke in *My Man Godfrey* (Universal, 1936) and Clarence Day in *Life With Father* (Warner Bros, 1947)

If Hollywood ever decides to reinstate sophisticated comedy (unlikely, but stranger things have happened) one of the actors directors should study is William Powell, whose mastery of urbane humour was second to none. Nominated three times for an Academy Award – for his suave private eye Nick Charles, his down-and-out turned butler, and his lovable, philosophising Clarence Day – he never made it to the winner's rostrum but probably uttered more witty lines than any actor in American screen history. Myrna Loy, who co-starred with him on many occasions and in all the *Thin Man* films, was never outshone and enjoyed a repartee all her own. Said she in *The Thin Man*: 'Waiter, will you serve the nuts – I mean, would you serve the guests the nuts!'

Robert Preston

Born Newton Highlands, Massachusetts, USA, 8 June 1918; died 1987

Oscar Nominations (1): Best Supporting Actor for Toddy in *Victor/ Victoria* (MGM/UA, 1982)

Few who enjoyed Robert Preston as a tough action man at Paramount in the forties, often in DeMille and Alan Ladd pics, would have wagered much on his being Oscar-nominated some forty years later for an ageing gay cabaret entertainer, but that's how things turned out, and although he didn't finish up among the winners, his gay turn in drag was a sight to see! The biggest surprise was that he failed to land a nomination for reprising his hit Broadway role as *The Music Man*. Both Yul Brynner (*The King and I*) and Rex Harrison (*My Fair Lady*) were luckier. They not only received nominations for repeating their stage roles, they won the awards as well.

Q

Randy Quaid

Born Houston, Texas, USA, 1 October 1950

Oscar Nominations (1): Best Supporting Actor for Meadows SN in *The Last Detail* (Columbia, 1973)

To steal scenes from Jack Nicholson in the early seventies required a bit of doing, but Randy Quaid managed it quite frequently in *The Last Detail* as the eighteen-year-old sailor sentenced to eight years' imprisonment for theft, who is escorted by hardened veterans Nicholson and Otis Young to a naval prison in Massachusetts. Shambling, almost child-like and naive as he is given a last 'good time' by his captors, he was a close contender at the Dorothy Chandler Pavilion in April 1974. John Houseman saw to it that he got nowhere, with his portrait of the stern law professor in *The Paper Chase*.

Anthony Quayle

Born Ainsdale, Merseyside, England, 7 September 1913; died 1989

Oscar Nominations (1): Best Supporting Actor for Cardinal Wolsey in *Anne of the Thousand Days* (Universal, 1969)

A regular in uniform on screen (sometimes, as in *The Eagle Has Landed*, even on the side of the Germans), Anthony Quayle helped rewin the war all over again in the fifties and in between received the occasional role of substance, e.g., as the husband about to leave slovenly wife Yvonne Mitchell for secretary Sylvia Syms in *Woman in a Dressing Gown*. The role for which he was Oscar-nominated – a morose-looking Cardinal Wolsey – was best described by one critic as 'demonstrating the art of making bricks without straw'.

☆

Kathleen Quinlan

Born Pasadena, California, USA, 19 November 1954

Oscar Nominations (1): Best Supporting Actress for Marilyn Lovell in *Apollo 13* (Universal, 1995)

None of the actresses playing the wives of the astronauts in *The Right Stuff* got their just rewards, despite creditable performances all round. The balance was redressed just a little in 1995 when Kathleen Quinlan made the lists for her omen-fearing wife of Jim Lovell who suffered, along with just about everyone else in the world, until the astronauts aboard *Apollo 13* made it safely back to earth. In films since 1972, and remembered for her fine performance as the teenage schizophrenic in *I Never Promised You a Rose Garden*, she came in behind the year's hot favourite, Mira Sorvino, who practised the world's oldest profession in Woody Allen's *Mighty Aphrodite*.

Anthony Quinn

Born Chihuahua, Mexico, 21 April 1915

Oscars (2): Best Supporting Actor for Eufemio Zapata in *Viva Zapata!* (20th Century-Fox, 1952) and Paul Gauguin in *Lust for Life* (MGM, 1956)

Oscar Nominations (2): Best Actor for Gino in *Wild Is the Wind* (Paramount, 1957) and Alexis Zorba in *Zorba the Greek* (20th Century-Fox, 1964)

He would have walked it had it been any other year, for if ever there was an award-winning role it was that of the grizzled, life-loving Greek peasant Zorba. Unfortunately for Anthony Quinn it wasn't any other year, it was the year of Rex Harrison in *My Fair Lady*, which meant that the rest of the nominees might as well have stayed at home. Still, Quinn couldn't really complain; he'd already earned two supporting awards for his brother of the revolutionary Emiliano Zapata and his cameo as Paul Gauguin, and also made the lists a third time for his Nevada rancher who takes on Anna Magnani in *Wild Is the Wind*. The only thing that marred his golden fifties was the fact that in those days nominations were rarely given for roles in foreign-language films, which meant that his brutish carnival strong man (for many, his finest performance) in Fellini's *La Strada* was passed over. The compensation was that the Academy voted the picture the best foreign film of the year (1956).

R

Luise Rainer

Born Vienna, Austria, 12 January 1910

Oscars (2): Best Actress for Anna Held in *The Great Ziegfeld* (MGM, 1936) and O-Lan in *The Good Earth* (MGM, 1937)

Another of Hollywood's European imports of the thirties, the diminutive Viennese Luise Rainer looked for a while as though she would transcend them all, even Garbo, when she won Oscars in successive years for her portrayal of Flo Ziegfeld's first wife, Anna Held, and the stoic Chinese peasant O-Lan in *The Good Earth*. The world should have been her oyster but her fall was as quick as her rise, and after making eight films in just three years (1935–38) she faded from the scene. She recalled later: 'For my second and third pictures I won Academy Awards. Nothing worse could have happened to me.' That said, she remained the only actress to have won two in a row until Katharine Hepburn equalled the feat thirty years later for *Guess Who's Coming to Dinner?* and *The Lion in Winter*.

Claude Rains

Born London, England, 10 November 1889; died 1967

Oscar Nominations (4): Best Supporting Actor for Senator Joseph Paine in *Mr Smith Goes to Washington* (Columbia, 1939), Captain Louis Renault in *Casablanca* (Warner Bros, 1943), Job Skeffington in *Mr Skeffington* (Warner Bros, 1944) and Alexander Sebastian in *Notorious* (RKO, 1946)

Silken, sophisticated and with a voice that could threaten with a touch of velvet and console with quiet reassurance, Claude Rains was arguably the most talented actor never to win an Oscar. For a while it seemed as though the award would come his way as he earned four nominations in a golden eight-year period – for his corrupt senator up against Jimmy Stewart's crusading Jefferson Smith, his cynical Vichy policeman Louis Renault, his blind husband of a selfish Bette Davis and his treacherous Nazi agent lusting after a vulnerable Ingrid Bergman in Hitchcock's *Notorious*. Alas, it was not to be. Dear old Charles Coburn was a popular winner in 1943 but he was really no match for Rains in *Casablanca*, who delivered to perfection the famous line, 'Round up the usual suspects' and, as he reduces a 20,000 franc bet with Bogie, the afterthought, 'Make it ten, I am only a poor corrupt official.'

Marjorie Rambeau

Born San Francisco, USA, 15 July 1889; died 1970

Oscar Nominations (2): Best Supporting Actress for Mamie Adams in *Primrose Path* (RKO, 1940) and Mrs Stewart in *Torch Song* (MGM, 1953)

A former Broadway actress who earned fame for her beauty, Marjorie Rambeau made Hollywood her home in the thirties, appearing mostly as middle-aged floozies, harlots, alcoholics and gangsters' molls. Her two supporting nominations were for roles that were a trifle more gracious – as the good-natured, sentimental mother of Ginger Rogers in *Primrose Path* and as another mom, that of neurotic musical star Joan Crawford, in *Torch Song*. An occasional performer in silent films when she was married to noted playwright-actor-director Willard Mack, she made her last screen appearance in the Lon Chaney biography, *Man of a Thousand Faces*.

Anne Ramsay

Born Nebraska, USA, 1929; died 1988

Oscar Nominations (1): Best Supporting Actress for Momma Lift in *Throw Momma from the Train* (Orion, 1987)

Anyone who can steal a movie from both Danny DeVito *and* Billy Crystal deserves some kind of recognition, and Anne Ramsay duly received hers when she was honoured with an Oscar nomination in the spring of 1988. Formidable as the tyrannical and senile mother who terrorises her son (would-be writer DeVito), she becomes the 'victim' of a swap murder plot loosely derived from Hitchcock's *Strangers on a Train*. She lost in April to Olympia Dukakis' rather more warm-hearted mother in *Moonstruck*. Just four months later she died from the throat cancer that had plagued her through filming. Married to actor Logan Ramsay (together they founded Philadelphia's Theatre of the Living Arts), she moved to Los Angeles in the early seventies. She appeared in minor roles – sometimes with her husband – before DeVito gave her her break as Momma.

Basil Rathbone

Born Johannesburg, South Africa, 13 June 1892; died 1967

Oscar Nominations (2): Best Supporting Actor for Tybalt in *Romeo and Juliet* (MGM, 1936) and Louis XI in *If I Were King* (Paramount, 1938)

Nothing for poor old Sherlock (he appeared in some fourteen Sherlock Holmes adventures) but two nominations as compensation, both for now almost forgotten Rathbone roles, as Tybalt in Cukor's 1936 version of *Romeo and Juliet*, and, unrecognisable behind heavy make-up, the wily old Louis XI in *If I Were King*. Nothing more, just a declining career that ended with a series of bizarre exploitation and horror flicks, a sad end for an actor who possessed one of the finest speaking voices in movies and who had once essayed such characters as Mr Murdstone, the Marquis St Evremonde, and, best of all, Sir Guy of Gisbourne, who in *The Adventures of Robin Hood* finishes up skewered on the point of Errol Flynn's sword!

Stephen Rea

Born Belfast, Northern Ireland, 1949

Oscar Nominations (1): Best Actor for Fergus in *The Crying Game* (Palace, 1992)

It was difficult to say who was more surprised, actor Stephen Rea or the audience, when he discovers that the girl who has taken his fancy for half the picture turns out to be a fella! Just one of the surprises in Neil Jordan's complex thriller *The Crying Game* which looked closely and with some irony at political loyalties, race and sexuality. Rea was Oscar-nominated for his

IRA gunman; Al Pacino, having waited for more than twenty years, took the top prize for his larger-than-life turn as an embittered army colonel in *Scent of a Woman*.

Robert Redford

Born Santa Monica, California, USA, 18 August 1937

Oscar Nominations (1): Best Actor for Johnny Hooker in *The Sting* (Universal, 1973)

Only one Oscar nomination for acting seems a rather meagre reward for a star who, like Gregory Peck before him, has carried the mantle of American integrity on screen for almost three decades. But one it remains – for his con man partner of Paul Newman in *The Sting*. Redford's Oscar success has been earned not for his acting but for his work behind the cameras – as best director of the much-acclaimed *Ordinary People* and, more recently, as the nominated director and co-producer of *Quiz Show*. His boyish grin, fair hair and all-American good looks have adorned more than thirty films, including *The Way We Were* opposite Barbra Streisand and the underrated *The Great Gatsby*, for which he deserved a nomination, if not more, for his finely shaded portrait of Fitzgerald's tragic hero.

Lynn Redgrave

Born London, England, 8 March 1943

Oscar Nominations (1): Best Actress for Georgy Parkin in *Georgy Girl* (Everglades/Columbia, 1966)

For a year or two in the mid-sixties, when she was nominated for her tall, plump ugly duckling adored by lecherous would-be sugar daddy James Mason, it seemed as though Lynn Redgrave would be the equal of her sister Vanessa, who by chance was also up for the 1966 actress award for her part in *Morgan*. Alas, the roles needed to enhance her career were not forthcoming, and she spent much of the seventies and eighties on American TV, displaying her jolly persona on chat shows and in the comedy series *House Calls* and *Chicken Soup*. Acclaimed by the *New York Times* for being 'as funny as Judy Holliday in *Born Yesterday*' for her *Georgy Girl*, she lost on Oscar night (as did Vanessa) to Elizabeth Taylor's no-holds-barred bitchiness in *Who's Afraid of Virginia Woolf?*

Michael Redgrave

Born Bristol, England, 20 March 1908; died 1985

Oscar Nominations (1): Best Actor for Orin Mannon in *Mourning Becomes Electra* (RKO, 1947)

'Hollywood was alright for three months,' said Michael Redgrave when he later recalled his all-too-brief stay in Tinseltown. Just a couple of films – a thriller for Fritz Lang and a ponderous version of O'Neill's *Mourning Becomes Electra* (for which he was Oscar-nominated for his doomed Orin) – were the sum of his efforts, although in some respects to earn a nomination for one out of two wasn't bad going. Nothing later, though, for his failed, burned-out schoolmaster 'Crocker' Harris in *The Browning Version* (the performance which won him the Cannes best actor award in 1951) or his boffin Dr Barnes Wallis in *The Dam Busters*. The star of some sixty films, among them many American-financed productions (*The Quiet American*, *The Heroes of Telemark*), Redgrave never returned to Hollywood.

Vanessa Redgrave

Born London, England, 30 January 1937

Oscars (1): Best Supporting Actress for the title role in *Julia* (20th Century-Fox, 1977)

Oscar Nominations (5): Best Actress for Leonie Delt in *Morgan: A Suitable Case for Treatment* (Quintra Films, 1966), Isadora Duncan in *Isadora* (Universal, 1968), the title role in *Mary, Queen of Scots* (Universal, 1971) and Olive Chancellor in *The Bostonians* (Merchant/Ivory, 1984); Best Supporting Actress for Ruth Wilcox in *Howards End* (Merchant/Ivory, 1992)

Rather more favoured than either her sister or her father, Vanessa has so far chalked up five nominations and one win in more than a quarter of a century of Academy honours. The win was for her impassioned fighter against Fascism in Nazi Germany; the nominations were for roles that demonstrated not only her talents but her remarkable versatility: her hapless wife of David Warner's round-the-bend Morgan, the famed dancer Isadora Duncan, the defiant Mary, Queen of Scots, a nineteenth-century spinster feminist, and the owner of Howards End. Quite a line-up. It would perhaps be churlish to complain about the absence from the list of her theatrical agent Peggy Ramsay in *Prick Up Your Ears*.

Joyce Redman

Born County Mayo, Ireland, 1919

Oscar Nominations (2): Best Supporting Actress for Mrs Waters/Jenny Jones in *Tom Jones* (Woodfall/United Artists, 1963) and Emilia in *Othello* (BHE/Warner Bros, 1965)

Scoff, scoff, scoff . . . It would be wrong to say that eating earned Joyce Redman her Academy Award nomination for *Tom Jones*, but chewing at her chicken bones and licking her lips over everything that came within munching distance, and all the time keeping her eye firmly fixed on Albert Finney, certainly helped. She missed out in 1963 just as she missed out a couple of years later for her sharp-tongued wife of Iago in the film version of the National Theatre production of *Othello*. Margaret Rutherford (1963) and Shelley Winters (1965) were the actresses who put paid to any Oscar aspirations she might have had.

Donna Reed

Born Denison, Iowa, USA, 27 January 1921; died 1986

Oscars (1): Best Supporting Actress for Alma/Lorene in *From Here to Eternity* (Columbia, 1953)

There may have been more appealing small-town girls than Donna Reed, although off-hand it is difficult to think of any. Ironically, she won her Oscar for playing a girl whose main ambition was to get as far away as possible from small-town life – Alma, the Hawaiian-based nightclub hostess, 'one step up from the pavement', who offers Monty Clift all the home comforts in *From Here to Eternity*. Still her best role, though, remains her Bedford Falls sweetheart who lassoes Jimmy Stewart in *It's a Wonderful Life* and, in one memorable telephone scene, makes herself irresistible to both Stewart and just about every red-blooded male in the audience. No Oscar, of course. Just a seven-year wait until Alma came along.

Lee Remick

Born Quincy, Massachusetts, USA, 14 December 1935; died 1991

Oscar Nominations (1): Best Actress for Kirsten Arnesen in *Days of Wine and Roses* (Warner Bros, 1962)

Seductive, blonde and blue-eyed, and with a look that would melt most men, Lee Remick had, in her early career, a penchant for 'come-on' characters and flirtatious Southern belles, all of whom seemed to have sex on their minds. Nominated just the once, for her wife of stressed advertising man Jack Lemmon who together with her husband plunges into the horrific depths of alcoholism, she was a star of more than fifty films and TV movies, including Preminger's *Anatomy of a Murder*. She made her screen début as a drum majorette in Kazan's *A Face in the Crowd*. Rarely has the twirling of a baton looked more attractive. She died of cancer at the much too early age of fifty-five.

Anne Revere

Born New York City, USA, 25 June 1903; died 1990

Oscars (1): Best Supporting Actress for Mrs Brown in *National Velvet* (MGM, 1945)

Oscar Nominations (2): Best Supporting Actress for Louise Soubirous in *The Song of Bernadette* (20th Century-Fox, 1943) and Mrs Green in *Gentleman's Agreement* (20th Century-Fox, 1947)

At first sight her screen mums seemed a little on the severe side, smiling only rarely and as often as not with their hair pulled back in a bun. Not a bit of it. Anne Revere was kindness itself, even presenting the young Elizabeth Taylor with the hundred sovereigns she'd won as a girl because she 'understood the importance of folly'. They gave awards for lines like that, and Miss Revere duly collected hers for *National Velvet* in the spring of 1946. Nominated also for her poverty-stricken mother of Jennifer Jones' Bernadette Soubirous, and Greg Peck's liberal-thinking mother in *Gentleman's Agreement*, she found her career cut short when she was blacklisted in 1951. She was off screen for nearly twenty years. Although never a Communist, she was a very defiant lady, maintaining: 'I'm a free-thinking Yankee rebel and nobody's going to tell *me* what to do!'

Debbie Reynolds

Born El Paso, Texas, USA, 1 April 1932

Oscar Nominations (1): Best Actress for Molly Brown in *The Unsinkable Molly Brown* (MGM, 1964)

A more accomplished performer than many give her credit for, Debbie Reynolds earned her Oscar recognition late, when all the MGM musicals had been made, except one – *The Unsinkable Molly Brown*, the story of a tough backwoods girl who in the late 1800s became one of the most celebrated and richest women of her time. Julie Andrews' magical nanny Mary Poppins was more to Hollywood's taste in 1964, but at least the nomination went some way to paying tribute to Reynolds' part in the success of many of MGM's celebrated musicals of the fifties – from the lesser-known *I Love Melvin* to the classic *Singin' in the Rain*. Well known in Hollywood for her collection of vintage film costumes and memorabilia, she is a regular nightclub entertainer, an excellent mimic and plays several musical instruments. Why didn't they ever get any of that on film?

Beah Richards

Born Vicksburg, Mississippi, USA

Oscar Nominations (1): Best Supporting Actress for Mrs Prentice in *Guess Who's Coming to Dinner?* (Columbia, 1967)

Opportunities for black actresses have remained scandalously few, even in modern times, but veteran Beah Richards has been around now for almost forty years on screen and has made the most of what has come her way. Her best year was 1967, when she earned her Oscar nomination as the worldly-wise and understanding mother of Dr Sidney Poitier (about to marry a white girl in *Guess Who's Coming to Dinner?*), played an abortionist in Norman Jewison's Oscar-winning *In the Heat of the Night* and featured for Otto Preminger in *Hurry Sundown*. Three years later she appeared as the mother of James Earl Jones in Martin Ritt's biopic of boxer Jack Johnson, *The Great White Hope*. A veteran stage actress who established herself both on and off Broadway in the fifties, she was defeated in 1967's Oscar race by Estelle Parsons in *Bonnie and Clyde*.

Miranda Richardson

Born Lancashire, England, 1958

Oscar Nominations (2): Best Supporting Actress for Ingrid Fleming in *Damage* (New Line, 1992); Best Actress for Vivienne Haigh-Wood in *Tom and Viv* (Miramax, 1994)

As versatile as any actress currently working in British cinema, Miranda Richardson should, by rights, have been among the nominees for her very first film role, as the ex-hooker turned nightclub 'hostess' Ruth Ellis, the last woman to be hanged for murder in Britain. She has since chalked up nominations for her distraught wife of Jeremy Irons' obsessed Tory MP in *Damage* and her disturbed socialite spouse of poet T. S. Eliot in *Tom and Viv*. It would be a foolish man who would bet against her winning something by the millennium.

Ralph Richardson

Born Cheltenham, Gloucestershire, England, 19 December 1902; died 1983

Oscar Nominations (2): Best Supporting Actor for Dr Austin Sloper in *The Heiress* (Paramount, 1949) and the 6th Lord of Greystoke in *Greystoke: The Legend of Tarzan, Lord of the Apes* (Warner Bros, 1984)

An actor who only occasionally brought to the screen the brilliance he so frequently displayed on stage, Ralph Richardson came closest to an Oscar when William Wyler cast him as the cruel and autocratic Dr Austin Sloper in *The Heiress*. Honoured with only a supporting nomination for what was essentially a leading role (the National Board of Review named him best actor of the year), he might have expected greater rewards three years later when David Lean cast him as an aircraft tycoon obsessed with breaking the sound barrier. The New York Critics thought him best of the year, the Academy didn't even rate him a mention. He was nominated again for his dotty old grandfather of Tarzan in his penultimate film: *Greystoke*. Needless to say, he lost.

Thelma Ritter

Born Brooklyn, New York, USA, 14 February 1905; died 1969

Oscar Nominations (6): Best Supporting Actress for Birdie in *All About Eve* (20th Century-Fox, 1950), Ellen McNulty in *The Mating Season* (Paramount, 1951), Clancy in *With a Song in My Heart* (20th Century-Fox, 1952), Moe in *Pickup on South Street* (20th Century-Fox, 1953), Alma in *Pillow Talk* (Universal-International, 1959) and Elizabeth Stroud in *Birdman of Alcatraz* (United Artists, 1962)

With her bleak expression, gravel voice and down-to-earth humour, Thelma Ritter was once acclaimed as 'a great character actress who never once got a bad notice'. She was also the best character actress never to win an Oscar – six times nominated, six times a loser. How *did* they manage it? The roll call of honour: Bette Davis' outspoken maid in *All About Eve*, a mother-in-law posing as a servant in *The Mating Season*, the nurse of crippled Susan Hayward in *With a Song in My Heart*, Doris Day's inebriated daily help in *Pillow Talk*, and the militant mother fighting for Burt Lancaster's release in *Birdman of Alcatraz*. That's five. The one missing?

Arguably the role for which she should have won, the pathetic New York waterfront tie-peddler/informer in Samuel Fuller's bleak little crime thriller *Pickup on South Street*. Nothing for her ghoulish masseuse of James Stewart in Hitchcock's *Rear Window*, although the general consensus was that there should have been.

Jason Robards

Born Chicago, USA, 22 July 1922

Oscars (2): Best Supporting Actor for Ben Bradlee in *All the President's Men* (Warner Bros, 1976) and Dashiell Hammett in *Julia* (20th Century-Fox, 1977)

Oscar Nominations (1): Best Supporting Actor for Howard Hughes in *Melvin and Howard* (Universal, 1980)

'We're about to accuse the President of the United States of being a crook. It would be nice if we were right.' So said Jason Robards as *Washington Post* editor Ben Bradlee. Such William Goldman lines, and Robards' natural grumpy cynicism, helped earn him 1976's supporting nod at Oscar time and paved the way for another win a year later, for his Dashiell Hammett in Fred Zinnemann's *Julia*. He almost made it three in five years when he was nominated for his cameo as Howard Hughes in Jonathan Demme's *Melvin and Howard*. Walter Brennan's record remained intact, however, when the young Timothy Hutton pipped Robards at the post with his performance in Redford's *Ordinary People*. A touch on the gloomy side for some audiences, Robards is renowned for his performances on Broadway in the plays of Eugene O'Neill.

Eric Roberts

Born Biloxi, Mississippi, USA, 18 April 1956

Oscar Nominations (1): Best Supporting Actor for Buck in *Runaway Train* (Cannon/Northbrook, 1985)

For a while it looked as though Eric and not his younger sister Julia would be the one to make it big in the movies, especially when Bob Fosse cast him in *Star 80* as the unstable young hustler who made *Playboy* centrefold Dorothy Stratten his Hollywood meal ticket. The film didn't catch on and Roberts' best roles since have mainly been on television. His nomination in 1985 was for one of the two convicts trapped on a runaway train hurtling through the snows of Alaska. Better than nothing, but Sis has done rather better.

Julia Roberts

Born Smyrna, Georgia, USA, 28 October 1967

Oscar Nominations (2): Best Supporting Actress for Shelby Latcherie in *Steel Magnolias* (Columbia/Tri-Star, 1989); Best Actress for Vivian Ward in *Pretty Woman* (Touchstone/Warner Bros, 1990)

Not by any means Hollywood's greatest actress of modern times, Julia Roberts nonetheless participated in one of the most enjoyable moments of nineties cinema when, to the accompaniment of Roy Orbison's title song 'Pretty Woman', she embarks on a no-holds-barred shopping spree on Rodeo Drive. As the happy Hollywood Boulevard hooker, hired for a week of sin and education by corporate raider Richard Gere ('We're similar, we both screw people for money'), she earned a surprise best actress nomination but found she was no match for the Grand Guignol antics of Kathy Bates in *Misery*. A year earlier she notched up a supporting nomination for her dying daughter of Sally Field in *Steel Magnolias*. Once again she lost out, this time to Brenda Fricker for *My Left Foot*.

Rachel Roberts

Born Llanelli, Carmarthen, Wales, 20 September 1927; died 1980

Oscar Nominations (1): Best Actress for Mrs Hammond in *This Sporting Life* (Independent Artists/British, 1963)

One would have thought that her experiences with Albert Finney in *Saturday Night and Sunday Morning* would have cured her, but no. Rachel Roberts found herself involved in an even more intense affair three years later, in *This Sporting Life*, with rugby player and former colliery worker Richard Harris. Her passionless widow drawn into a physical and often violent relationship belongs with the most remarkable female portrayals of the sixties. It didn't, unfortunately, win her the Oscar. Pat Neal took that for having much the same sort of trouble with Paul Newman in *Hud*.

Cliff Robertson

Born La Jolla, California, USA, 9 September 1925

Oscars (1): Best Actor for Charly Gordon in *Charly* (ABC-Selmur/ Cinerama, 1968)

The tears flowed in abundance, the handkerchiefs came out and the cinemas were awash as mentally retarded bakery worker Cliff Robertson became a virtual genius overnight through the wonders of brain surgery, and then, after a brief period of normality, slipped back into his original feeble-minded state. Alan Arkin really deserved the award for his deaf mute in *The Heart Is a Lonely Hunter*, but Robertson was on a roll in 1968, the sentiment was on his side and the Oscar was always going to be his. A rugged, accomplished actor who earlier in his career had portrayed the young John F. Kennedy in *PT 109*, he had originally played the role of Charly on TV in a sixty-minute special. It took him nearly a decade to bring it to the screen. He has not been nominated since.

Flora Robson

Born South Shields, Durham, England, 28 March 1902; died 1984

Oscar Nominations (1): Best Supporting Actress for Angelique Buiton in *Saratoga Trunk* (Warner Bros, 1946)

Quite how Flora Robson – English plain Jane and spinster of this parish – came to be cast as the bizarre mulatto servant of a fortune-hunting Ingrid Bergman ranks as one of the mysteries of the Hollywood casting department. Cast she was, however, and a good job she made of it too, edging into the nominations list but finding that an alcoholic Anne Baxter (another of the year's surprises) was too good for her. The role that might have earned her a nomination, Elizabeth I of England, whom she had earlier played twice (*Fire Over England*, *The Sea Hawk*), was overlooked.

May Robson

Born Melbourne, Australia, 19 April 1858; died 1942

Oscar Nominations (1): Best Actress for Apple Annie in *Lady for a Day* (Columbia, 1932/33)

Most Hollywood studios in the thirties had their stock companies of actresses who could play kindly old ladies, matrons and the like. May Robson was one of the most sought-after, especially after being nominated for her Apple Annie in Frank Capra's *Lady for a Day*, an adaptation of a Damon Runyon tale of a 'gin-sodden old hay bag' who is dolled up by some gangsters and transformed into a society matron to impress her visiting daughter. Nothing quite as good ever came her way again, although there were plenty of cooks, dowagers, grandmothers and a lovely Aunt Polly in *The Adventures of Tom Sawyer* to keep her and audiences happy.

☆

Ginger Rogers

Born Independence, Missouri, USA, 16 July 1911; died 1995

Oscars (1): Best Actress for the title role in *Kitty Foyle* (RKO, 1940)

Poor Fred Astaire never got an Oscar, except for an honorary award; Ginger, on the other hand, quickly showed what she was made of, winning just a year after the break-up of the dancing team for her office girl who falls for a socialite but eventually settles for a young doctor from her own walk of life. All good, soapy, democratic stuff, although in retrospect the award might have been more aptly bestowed for either her gangland floozie, Roxie Hart, or her impersonation of a twelve-year-old who sets her sights, Lolita-like, on an unsuspecting Ray Milland in *The Major and the Minor*. Before donning her childish disguise, she was the recipient of one of the best lines uttered in American movies of the forties. Robert Benchley was the man with the words. Eyeing her with not a little interest, he says nonchalantly: 'Why don't you step out of that wet coat and into a dry martini!'

Howard E. Rollins Jr.

Born Baltimore, Maryland, USA, 17 October 1950

Oscar Nominations (1): Best Supporting Actor for Coalhouse Walker Jr. in *Ragtime* (Paramount, 1981)

A stunning role – as a black ragtime artist who turns to crime because of racial prejudice in America in the early years of the century – earned Howard Rollins a deserved Oscar nomination but didn't for one minute convince him that he was on a roll. 'Parts for black actors are few and far between,' he commented, echoing what many black performers had been saying time and again in previous years. His subsequent work, apart from his army attorney investigating a murder on a Southern army base in *A Soldier's Story*, has been sporadic and sadly more than proved his point. He has been most successful on the smaller screen in the television series of the Oscar-winning *In the Heat of the Night*.

Mickey Rooney

Born Brooklyn, New York, USA, 23 September 1920

Oscar Nominations (4): Best Actor for Mickey Moran in *Babes in Arms* (MGM, 1939) and Homer Macauley in *The Human Comedy* (MGM, 1943); Best Supporting Actor for Dooley in *The Bold and the Brave* (RKO, 1956) and Henry Dailey in *The Black Stallion* (United Artists, 1979)

Chubby-faced and pint-sized, with a wide, toothy grin and a talent for playing just about anything on screen, Mickey Rooney was once hailed by no less an authority than James Mason as being 'the most versatile of all American screen performers'. Nominated more or less once every decade – for his young vaudevillian putting on a show in *Babes in Arms*, young telegraph messenger in *The Human Comedy*, World War II infantryman in *The Bold and the Brave* and his veteran horse-trainer in *The Black Stallion* – he was eventually presented with an honorary Oscar (to go with the special miniature he had received in 1939) when it became apparent that despite appearing in nearly 150 features, no one was going to give him a competitive Academy Award. In the end his best role was on

TV – as the mentally retarded Bill trying to cope with everyday life outside the mental institution in which he has lived for more than forty years. Glory be, he won an Emmy!

Diana Ross

Born Detroit, USA, 26 March 1945

Oscar Nominations (1): Best Actress for Billie Holiday in *Lady Sings the Blues* (Paramount, 1972)

It looked for a moment as though Diana Ross might pull it off and become the first black performer to be named best actress. The subject was right (a biopic of Billie Holiday), the music was right and the acting for a newcomer was quite remarkable, especially in the harrowing scenes of Holiday's alcoholism and drug-taking. What was wrong was that *Cabaret* was released the same year, and in showbiz parlance that meant that Liza Minnelli was a 'shoo-in' for the top award. A pity in many ways, for Ross' career had seemed destined for great things. Had she achieved her ambition of playing Josephine Baker on screen things might have been different. As it was, after playing a fashion designer in *Mahogany* and a black Dorothy in *The Wiz*, her career fizzled out and she has since concentrated on concert and recording work.

Katharine Ross

Born Los Angeles, USA, 29 January 1942

Oscar Nominations (1): Best Supporting Actress for Elaine Robinson in *The Graduate* (Embassy Pictures, 1967)

This girl *must* be a star of the seventies, said the pundits once they had glimpsed Katharine Ross in her Oscar-nominated role as Anne Bancroft's daughter in *The Graduate*, and in the western *Butch Cassidy and the Sundance Kid*. There was no must about it. When Hollywood was at a loss as to how to handle a young star on the rise and couldn't come up with the right material, they knew how to prove it. Instead of appearing in challenging roles in intelligent movies, Katharine Ross finished up in dross like *The*

Betsy, The Swarm and *The Legacy,* and on TV in *Dynasty II:The Colbys.* One American critic of the sixties had likened her to an American version of Julie Christie. Sadly, it wasn't so.

Tim Roth

Born London, England, 1962

Oscar Nominations (1): Best Supporting Actor for Cunningham in *Rob Roy* (Talisman/United Artists, 1995)

Swashbuckling villains don't usually figure among the Oscar nominees – Basil Rathbone never made it for his Sir Guy of Gisbourne, nor Douglas Fairbanks Jr. for his dashing Rupert of Hentzau – but so colourful, foppish and utterly ruthless was Tim Roth in *Rob Roy* that it would have seemed churlish to have omitted him from the 1995 lists. The Academy duly acknowledged his impudent decadence but at the final count opted for the more up-to-date criminal activities of Kevin Spacey in *The Usual Suspects.* Still, outsider that he was, Roth's versatility (he'd previously played Van Gogh for Altman in *Vincent and Theo* and appeared in the Tarantino movies *Reservoir Dogs* and *Pulp Fiction*) indicates that he may be another of today's young actors who will be among the winners in the not-too-distant future.

Gena Rowlands

Born Cambria, Wisconsin, USA, 19 June 1934

Oscar Nominations (2): Best Actress for Mabel Longhetti in *A Woman Under the Influence* (Faces International, 1974) and Gloria Swenson in *Gloria* (Columbia, 1980)

It was always a family affair with Gena Rowlands and John Cassavetes; he wrote, directed and improvised his films, she starred in them, twice proving that independent made-on-a-shoestring productions could catch Hollywood's eye at Oscar time. Her nominations: for her working-class housewife undergoing a mental breakdown, and a woman on the run and shielding an eight-year-old boy from the Mafia. The Academy preferred

Ellen Burstyn and Sissy Spacek in the respective years; Rowlands' triumph, when it came, occurred on television when she won an Emmy for her portrayal of the former First Lady in *The Betty Ford Story.*

Mercedes Ruehl

Born Queens, New York, USA, 1954

Oscars (1): Best Supporting Actress for Anne Napolitano in *The Fisher King* (TriStar, 1991)

Supporting winners in recent times have tended to enjoy their moment of Oscar glory then fade from the scene. Not Mercedes Ruehl, who followed her Oscar-winning role as the video store owner cum girlfriend of Jeff Bridges in *The Fisher King* with a stunning reprise of her Tony-winning portrayal of the backward Aunt Bella in Neil Simon's *Lost in Yonkers.* No Oscar, unfortunately, nor even a nomination, unusual for a Simon movie, many of which have collected quite a few honours over the years. Lanky and likeable, she has also been seen as a struggling single mom in *The Last Action Hero.*

Harold Russell

Born Sydney, Novia Scotia, Canada, 1914

Oscars (2): Best Supporting Actor for Homer Parrish and an Honorary Award 'for bringing hope and courage to his fellow veterans through his performance in *The Best Years of Our Lives*' (Goldwyn/RKO, 1946)

The only actor ever to receive two awards for the same role, Harold Russell was named for his handless veteran struggling to adapt to post-war civilian life in Wyler's *The Best Years of Our Lives.* A former paratroop sergeant who had lost both hands in a grenade explosion and who had appeared in an army documentary depicting the rehabilitation of an amputee, he subsequently devoted himself to working for the handicapped and returned briefly to the screen in *Inside Moves*, which looked at the difficulties of the disabled struggling with everyday life. Sadly, he became the first Oscar recipient to sell his award, in order to raise money for his wife's medical expenses.

Rosalind Russell

Born Waterbury, Connecticut, USA, 4 June 1908; died 1976

Oscar Nominations (4): Best Actress for Ruth Sherwood in *My Sister Eileen* (Columbia, 1942), Elizabeth Kenny in *Sister Kenny* (RKO, 1946), Lavinia Mannon in *Mourning Becomes Electra* (RKO, 1947) and Mame Dennis in *Auntie Mame* (Warner Bros, 1958)

Great with wisecracks ('That is a B, darling – the first letter of a seven-letter word that means your poor late father'), Rosalind Russell would have been better served had the Academy named her more frequently for the sophisticated comedy roles that made her name. She was excellent, of course, as the eccentric Mame and as one of the two sisters enjoying Greenwich Village in *My Sister Eileen*. But Sister Kenny? And Lavinia in *Mourning Becomes Electra*? Surely her woman reporter exchanging barbs with Cary Grant in *His Girl Friday* and her prize bitch in *The Women* would have been better bets. Not that she would have agreed with the assessment: 'In all those types of films I wore a tan suit, a grey suit, a beige suit and then a négligé for the seventh reel near the end when I would admit to my best friend on the telephone that what I really wanted was to become a little housewife.' She was awarded a special Oscar for her charity work in 1972.

Margaret Rutherford

Born London, England, 11 May 1892; died 1972

Oscars (1): Best Supporting Actress for the Duchess of Brighton in *The VIPs* (MGM, 1963)

By rights, Margaret Rutherford should have won her Oscar for her bicycle-riding spiritualist Madame Arcati in David Lean's *Blithe Spirit* (1944), but Hollywood tended to reward its own in the forties and it was another twenty years before she was finally honoured for her eccentric duchess, one of the many star passengers stranded at the fog-bound London Airport in *The VIPs*. Stoutly built, with eyes set in deep pouches and resting on many chins beneath a fierce jaw, she was a veteran of more than a hundred plays and forty films. She was once asked whether she was as eccentric as she appeared on screen. She replied: 'I hope I'm an individual. I suppose an eccentric is a super-individual. Perhaps an eccentric is just off-centre – ex-centric. But that contradicts a belief of mine that we've got to be centrifugal.'

Robert Ryan

Born Chicago, USA, 11 November 1909; died 1973

Oscar Nominations (1): Best Supporting Actor for Montgomery in *Crossfire* (RKO, 1947)

When filmgoers listed Robert Ryan as one of the screen's all-time best heavies, Ryan shrugged and commented: 'I guess they never saw me in most of my pictures. Still, I've never stopped working so I can't complain.' He made more than ninety all told, although he reckoned only four or five were any good – *The Set-Up* (his favourite), about an ageing boxer who refuses to throw a fight, *Bad Day at Black Rock*, *Lonelyhearts*, *The Wild Bunch*, and *Crossfire*, for which he was nominated for his sadistic anti-Semitic marine who murders a man he meets in a nightclub simply because the man is Jewish. A politically active actor from the late forties until his death, he could never explain why he didn't become a target of Joe McCarthy: 'I was involved in the things he was throwing rocks at but I never was a target. Looking back, I suspect my Irish name, my being a Catholic and an ex-Marine sort of softened the blow.'

Winona Ryder

Born Winona, Minnesota, USA, 29 October 1971

Oscar Nominations (2): Best Supporting Actress for May Welland in *The Age of Innocence* (Columbia, 1993); Best Actress for Jo March in *Little Women* (Columbia, 1994)

With her sweet smile, lovely complexion and classical youthful beauty, Winona Ryder looks as though butter wouldn't melt in her mouth. Since starting her screen career at eighteen, however, she has been the thirteen-year-old child bride of Dennis Quaid's Jerry Lee Lewis, befriended ghosts in *Beetlejuice*, embarked on high-school homicide, and fallen victim to the fangs of Dracula. Not much to melt the butter there, nor in her two Oscar-nominated roles, as the well-bred young society woman who snares Daniel Day-Lewis and the rebellious tomboy Jo in *Little Women*. Very definitely more than just a pretty face.

S

Eva Marie Saint

Born Newark, New Jersey, USA, 4 July 1924

Oscars (1) Best Supporting Actress for Edie Doyle in *On the Waterfront* (Columbia, 1954)

Hitchcock tried to turn her into one of his ice-cool blondes in *North by Northwest*, Preminger took her on a tour of Israel with Paul Newman in *Exodus*, and Edward Dmytryk plonked her down in *Raintree County*, yet true stardom eluded her and for Eva Marie Saint it was always a case of being the 'nearly girl', almost but not quite. Her finest screen role remained her first, for which she won her Oscar as Marlon Brando's girlfriend and shared some of the most emotional screen moments of the early fifties. Sensitive and fragile, she has appeared in fewer than twenty films in her forty-year career. Elia Kazan, who directed her in *On the Waterfront*, never used her again. If he had, perhaps things might have been different.

George Sanders

Born St Petersburg, Russia, 3 July 1906; died 1972

Oscars (1): Best Supporting Actor for Addison DeWitt in *All About Eve* (20th Century-Fox, 1950)

World-weary one minute, lazily offensive the next, the voice of George Sanders was like that of no other actor on screen. For more than thirty years he presented a gallery of cads, crooks, romantic heroes and, best of all, cynical men about town. In *The Picture of Dorian Gray* (as Lord Henry Wotton) he uttered Oscar Wilde's epigrams with delicious aplomb, and in *All About Eve* (as the drama critic Addison DeWitt) he allowed himself to purr in admiration at the hysterics of Bette Davis and be wryly amused by the social climbing of Anne Baxter. Never much enamoured with his career as an actor, he died in April 1972 after taking five tubes of Nembutal. His body was found in a small Spanish resort hotel. His suicide note read: 'Dear World, I am leaving because I am bored. I feel I have lived long enough. I am leaving you with your worries in this sweet cesspool. Good luck.' He was sixty-five.

Chris Sarandon

Born Beckley, West Virginia, USA, 24 July 1942

Oscar Nominations (1): Best Supporting Actor for Leon Shermer in *Dog Day Afternoon* (Warner Bros, 1975)

Just the one nomination, for his role as Al Pacino's gay lover in *Dog Day Afternoon*, and nothing since. An all-too-familiar story among so many Oscar nominees, but at least Sarandon had his moment, got to dress up as Pacino's transvestite 'second wife', and took part in one of the most bizarre movies of the seventies – the true story of a three-man raid on New York's First Brooklyn Savings Bank to help finance a sex-change operation! Poor Charles Durning was the cop trying to make sense of it all; Sarandon and Pacino were the ones who stole the film and earned the Academy mentions.

Susan Sarandon

Born New York City, USA, 4 October 1946

Oscars (1): Best Actress for Sister Helen Prejean in *Dead Man Walking* (Gramercy Pictures/Polygram, 1995)

Oscar Nominations (4): Best Actress for Sally in *Atlantic City* (Paramount, 1981), Louise Sawyer in *Thelma and Louise* (MGM, 1991), Michaela Odone in *Lorenzo's Oil* (Universal, 1992) and Reggie Love in *The Client* (Warner Bros, 1994)

She would have been great in a Howard Hawks western – a strong, independent woman who does her own thing, knows her own mind and takes no bullshit from men. Imagine her opposite John Wayne! Hawks, though, is long gone and so too, more or less, is the western. Instead, the modern-day reality – five nominations in fifteen years and an Oscar at last for her portrayal of the real-life Catholic nun who becomes the spiritual adviser to convicted killer Sean Penn in *Dead Man Walking*. Her best performance? Possibly, although her earlier nominated roles were by no means negligible – her would-be croupier for Louis Malle in *Atlantic City*, get-up-and-go waitress in *Thelma and Louise*, crusading mother caring for a brain diseased child, and her anti-establishment lawyer in *The Client*. More to come? Quite possibly!

Telly Savalas

Born Garden City, New York, USA, 21 January 1924; died 1994

Oscar Nominations (1): Best Supporting Actor for Feto Gomez in *Birdman of Alcatraz* (United Artists, 1962)

'Who loves ya baby?' was Telly Savalas' stock phrase in his halcyon days as TV's New York cop Kojak. Before the advent of his lollipop-sucking policeman, however, very few people loved Telly on the big screen, when his stock-in-trade was playing malevolent heavies and degenerates of every description. The Academy nominated him just the once, for his fellow convict and bird-keeper holed up in Alcatraz with Burt Lancaster. Three years later, director George Stevens requested he shave his head for Pontius Pilate in *The Greatest Story Ever Told*. He left it that way, and the rest was history. Two Emmy awards for his Kojak work went some way to making up for his lack of Oscar success.

Diana Scarwid

Born Savannah, Georgia, USA, 27 August 1955

Oscar Nominations (1): Best Supporting Actress for Louise in *Inside Moves* (Goodmark/AFD, 1980)

Desperately moving as the young bar waitress who falls frustratingly in love with failed suicide and cripple John Savage, Diana Scarwid had the good fortune to make the nominations of 1980 but the misfortune to be hampered by her independent film's lack of publicity and distribution. Had today's practice of mailing video cassettes to voters been more prevalent in the early eighties, the result might have been different. As it was, Miss Scarwid trailed in behind Mary Steenburgen (for *Melvin and Howard*) and has never again been close to an Oscar. In 1981 she appeared as the adult Christina Crawford in Frank Perry's Joan Crawford biography, *Mommie Dearest*.

Roy Scheider

Born Orange, New Jersey, USA, 10 November 1932

Oscar Nominations (2): Best Supporting Actor for Buddy Russo in *The French Connection* (20th Century-Fox, 1971); Best Actor for Joe Gideon in *All That Jazz* (Columbia/20th Century-Fox, 1979)

By rights he should have become one of *the* stars of the eighties, but despite Oscar nominations for two accomplished roles in the previous decade – for his detective partner of Gene Hackman's Popeye Doyle and his Bob Fosse-style Broadway director/choreographer in *All That Jazz* – Roy Scheider has never quite broken through to the big time and in recent years has been seen mostly as a likeable co-star in mainly routine productions. It was the seventies that saw him at his best when he suffered more than most, sweating blood as he drove a truck of nitroglycerine through the South American jungles in *Sorcerer*, failed to avoid Olivier's deadly sleeve knife in *Marathon Man*, and uttered the memorable line: 'I think we need a bigger boat' when first catching sight of his quarry in *Jaws*.

Maximilian Schell

Born Vienna, Austria, 8 December 1930

Oscars (1): Best Actor for Hans Rolfe in *Judgment at Nuremberg* (United Artists, 1961)

Oscar Nominations (2): Best Actor for Arthur Goldman in *The Man in the Glass Booth* (Landau/AFT, 1975); Best Supporting Actor for Johann in *Julia* (20th Century-Fox, 1977)

The trouble with Maximilian Schell's early Oscar success was that it tended to typecast him as a villain. Not surprising, really, in that his fiercely nationalistic lawyer spent most of Stanley Kramer's film defending the undefendable, the Nazi officials on trial at Nuremberg. Still, there were some bright moments in the sixties, especially in the caper movie *Topkapi*, and he added to his Oscar laurels with nominations for two very different performances in the subsequent decade – as a wealthy Jewish businessman accused of being a war criminal, and as Vanessa Redgrave's emissary who shares but one affecting scene with Jane Fonda in Fred Zinnemann's film of *Julia*. Jason Robards, who enjoyed rather more scenes in the picture, took the supporting award for his portrait of Dashiell Hammett.

Note: Schell's remarkable documentary of Marlene Dietrich, *Marlene*, was nominated for an Academy Award as the best documentary feature of 1984.

Joseph Schildkraut

Born Vienna, Austria, 22 March 1895; died 1964

Oscars (1): Best Supporting Actor for Captain Alfred Dreyfus in *The Life of Emile Zola* (Warner Bros, 1937)

Anyone trying to name the movies of Joseph Schildkraut (even the most avid of movie buffs) would be in a spot of bother, for although he made more than fifty, only a handful were of any quality. His Oscar was won for his wrongly imprisoned Jewish army officer, condemned to Devil's Island because of anti-Semitism in the hierarchy of the French military. The only surprise was that he didn't add to his tally for his superb role as the young Anne's kindly, dignified father in Fox's 1959 film version of *The Diary of Anne Frank*. He had first played the part on the Broadway stage; George Stevens directed him in the movie version. Not even a nomination. One for the black book.

Paul Scofield

Born Hurstpierpoint, Sussex, England, 21 January 1922

Oscars (1): Best Actor for Sir Thomas More in *A Man for All Seasons* (Columbia, 1966)

Oscar Nominations (1): Best Supporting Actor for Mark Van Doren in *Quiz Show* (Hollywood Pictures/Buena Vista, 1994)

A stage actor who is a sometime film performer, Paul Scofield triumphed in 1966 for repeating his stage role of Sir Thomas More in *A Man for All Seasons*. Whether or not it was a superior portrayal to the defeated history professor of Richard Burton in *Who's Afraid of Virginia Woolf?* is a moot point, but 1966 was certainly Burton's best chance of the award, and in a colossal battle of the giants the evening finished up: *Man for All Seasons*, six awards, *Virginia Woolf*, five, the latter film taking the two actress awards (Taylor and Dennis). A gentle, quietly spoken, dignified man who has enhanced dozens of plays but only a handful of films, Scofield was nominated last for his university lecturer father of game-show contestant Ralph Fiennes in Robert Redford's *Quiz Show*.

George C. Scott

Born Wise, Virginia, USA, 18 October 1926

Oscars (1): Best Actor for General George S. Patton in *Patton* (20th Century-Fox, 1970)

Oscar Nominations (3): Best Supporting Actor for Claude Dancer in *Anatomy of a Murder* (Columbia, 1959) and Bert Gordon in *The Hustler* (20th Century-Fox, 1961); Best Actor for Dr Herbert Bock in *The Hospital* (United Artists, 1971)

'The ceremonies are a two-hour meat parade, a public display with contrived suspense for economic reasons,' said George C. Scott when he found himself up for the top Oscar for his brilliant rendering of World War II general Patton. He wouldn't turn up and he wouldn't accept it if he won. Would he win? It was Goldie Hawn who found out as she opened the envelope and squealed: 'Oh, my God . . . the winner is George C. Scott!' The film's producer Frank McCarthy graciously accepted, but Scott was as good as his word and never claimed the statuette. A regular among the nominees in the sixties and seventies – for his city-smart lawyer up against Jimmy Stewart, his ruthless, soured-by-life manager of Paul Newman's hustler, and his at-the-end-of-his-tether doctor in *The Hospital* – he has failed to live up to his initial brilliance and in recent times has preferred to concentrate on reviving for the TV screen such classic Dickensian roles as Scrooge and Fagin.

Martha Scott

Born Jamesport, Missouri, USA, 22 September 1914

Oscar Nominations (1): Best Actress for Emily Webb in *Our Town* (United Artists, 1940)

The lovely Martha Scott won her nomination when they used to award Pulitzer Prizes for writing plays about small-town America. Thornton Wilder won his for essaying the ordinary day-to-day happenings in the lives of the inhabitants of the New England town of Grover's Corners in the early years of the century. Scott repeated her Broadway role as the vibrant, hard-working daughter of the town's newspaper editor; a twenty-two-year-old Bill Holden played her boyfriend. His first Oscar nomination was still ten years away. Hers was then and there. The chance, though, went begging. Ginger Rogers had just hung up her dancing shoes and had a point or two to prove as a dramatic actress. She proved it and won for her working girl Kitty Foyle. The most embarrassed man of the evening? Sam Wood. He had directed both Ginger and Martha to their Oscar nominations and had to stay friends with them both.

George Segal

Born New York City, USA, 13 February 1934

Oscar Nominations (1): Best Supporting Actor for Nick in *Who's Afraid of Virginia Woolf?* (Warner Bros, 1966)

Very much a star of the sixties and early seventies, George Segal's easy-going, natural manner was perfectly suited to the lightweight comedies and spy thrillers of the time. Nominated just the once, for enduring with his faculty wife Sandy Dennis an evening of 'fun and games' with Taylor and Burton, he was described by one critic as looking permanently 'cynical and worried'. None of which was too surprising considering he was involved with neo-Nazis in *The Quiller Memorandum*, a mass murderer in *No Way to Treat a Lady*, sudden unemployment in *Fun with Dick and Jane*, and, best of all, a highly sexed Glenda Jackson who in *A Touch of Class* proved to him that he wasn't quite as fit as he thought he was. One surprise in retrospect: no nomination for his best role as the cynical, opportunistic PoW, *King Rat*.

Peter Sellers

Born Southsea, Hampshire, England, 8 September 1925; died 1980

Oscar Nominations (2): Best Actor for Group Captain Lionel Mandrake/President Merkin Muffley/Dr Strangelove in *Dr Strangelove; Or How I Learned to Stop Worrying and Love the Bomb* (Columbia, 1964) and Chance in *Being There* (Lorimar, 1979)

More of a mimic than an actor, Peter Sellers earned Academy acclaim for his three roles in *Dr Strangelove* – the RAF pilot, the American President and the ex-Nazi scientist of the title – and for his somewhat quieter, simple-minded gardener in *Being There*. The role for which he should perhaps have been nominated, and the one that helped rescue his sagging career in the sixties and seventies, was that of the accident-prone Inspector Clouseau in the *Pink Panther* films. 'I suspect everyone, I suspect no one,' he would say, slowly eyeing all the wrong people and then leaning nonchalantly on a door that wasn't there! Audiences laughed, and Herbert Lom's Chief Inspector Dreyfus simply added another twitch to his already haggard features.

Omar Sharif

Born Alexandria, Egypt, 10 April 1932

Oscar Nominations (1): Best Supporting Actor for Sherif Ali in *Lawrence of Arabia* (Columbia, 1962)

Riding through the mirage did it, of course. That and being cast as *Doctor Zhivago* and opposite Barbra Streisand in *Funny Girl*. Yet by the end of the decade when the large-scale movies in which he had made his name had all but run their course, Omar Sharif was already past his peak and facing many years of mostly undistinguished productions. Nominated for his Sherif Ali in *Lawrence*, his dark eyes and flashing smile counted for nothing on Oscar night, when the voters opted for the distinctly less romantic features of Ed Begley. Before riding into stardom for David Lean, Sharif was one of the most popular Egyptian actors of the fifties, appearing as a romantic hero in more than twenty movies. He is one of the world's most famous bridge players and leads a professional team that has won many international tournaments.

Robert Shaw

Born Westhoughton, Manchester, England, 9 August 1927; died 1978

Oscar Nominations (1): Best Supporting Actor for Henry VIII in *A Man for All Seasons* (Columbia, 1966)

Jovial and charming one minute, cunning and dangerous the next, Robert Shaw's volatile Henry VIII was the only role that brought him close to an Oscar, just as it did Richard Burton three years later in *Anne of the Thousand Days*. Only Laughton, however, triumphed as the lusty monarch, and Shaw found more fame in the subsequent decade when he was taken to the cleaners by con men Paul Newman and Robert Redford in *The Sting* and swallowed whole by the shark in *Jaws*. A playwright and novelist as well as an actor, he died prematurely from a heart attack at the age of fifty-one.

Norma Shearer

Born Montreal, Canada, 10 August 1900; died 1983

Oscars (1): Best Actress for Jerry in *The Divorcee* (MGM, 1929/30)

Oscar Nominations (5): Best Actress for Lally in *Their Own Desire* (MGM, 1929/30), Jan Ashe in *A Free Soul* (MGM, 1930/31), Elizabeth Barrett in *The Barretts of Wimpole Street* (MGM, 1934), Juliet in *Romeo and Juliet* (MGM, 1936) and the title role in *Marie Antoinette* (MGM, 1938)

Norma Shearer's Oscar tally was impressive, one win and five nominations within the space of nine years. But was she that good an actress (Garbo managed only four), and would she have made it to the nominations quite so often had she not been married to MGM's boy wonder production executive Irving Thalberg? Many think not, but the list is there for the perusing – an Oscar for her vengeful wife of a philandering husband, and nominations for being in love with Robert Montgomery, the mistress of gang leader Clark Gable, an ailing Elizabeth Barrett, an over-age (thirty-six!) Juliet and a glittering Marie Antoinette. She retired from the screen some five years after her husband's premature death, after declining the lead in *Mrs Miniver*, a more rewarding role than any for which she had been nominated in the thirties.

Note: As in the case of George Arliss (see p. 11) Norma Shearer received nominations for two films in 1929/30 – *The Divorcee* and *Their Own Desire* – but on Oscar night was named only for her performance in the former movie. No official reason was given by the Academy. After 1929/30 performers were nominated for roles in one film only.

Sam Shepard

Born Fort Sheridan, Illinois, USA, 5 November 1943

Oscar Nominations (1): Best Supporting Actor for Chuck Yeager in *The Right Stuff* (The Ladd Company/Warner Bros, 1983)

It was a gift of a part – Chuck Yeager, the first man to break the sound barrier – but actor/playwright Sam Shepard made the most of it, emerging as the only acting nominee in Philip Kaufman's underrated *The Right Stuff*. Like the other actors up for 1983's supporting nod, he realised, however, that a nomination was the most he was likely to get. The reason? The competition included Jack Nicholson's boozy, womanising former astronaut who beds down with Shirley MacLaine in *Terms of Endearment*. Shepard could have broken the sound barrier a million times and still not come close!

Talia Shire

Born Lake Success, New York, USA, 25 April 1946

Oscar Nominations (2): Best Supporting Actress for Connie Corleone in *The Godfather Part II* (Paramount, 1974); Best Actress for Adrian in *Rocky* (United Artists, 1976)

All *The Godfather*s and all the *Rocky*s! Talia Shire appeared in every one, first as Al Pacino's sluttish sister, then as the shy young girlfriend and later wife of Rocky, wincing away as the punches rained in during numbers I, II, III, IV and V. The result: a supporting nomination for all the Mafia fun and games in the second of the three *Godfather* films and a best actress nod for her long-suffering partner of Mr Stallone. No Oscars, though. They went in 1974 to Ingrid Bergman in *Murder on the Orient Express* and in 1976 to Faye Dunaway in *Network*. The younger sister of director Francis Ford Coppola, she has somehow found time to make the occasional film between all the mayhem and fisticuffs, but has recently concerned herself with film production.

Anne Shirley

Born New York City, USA, 17 April 1918; died 1993

Oscar Nominations (1): Best Supporting Actress for Laurel Dallas in *Stella Dallas* (United Artists, 1937)

Some performers know when to retire, most don't. Luckily for Anne Shirley, she belonged in the former category, calling it a day at the age of twenty-seven after more than sixty films and an Oscar nomination for her young daughter of Barbara Stanwyck's self-sacrificing working-class mom, Stella Dallas. On screen from the age of five, initially as Dawn O'Day, she enjoyed her most accomplished roles at RKO in the early forties, most notably as one of Raymond Chandler's rare nice girls tending the wounds of Dick Powell in *Farewell My Lovely*. She was married three times – to actor John Payne, producer Adrian Scott (one of the Hollywood Ten) and writer Charles Lederer.

Elisabeth Shue

Born 1963

Oscar Nominations (1): Best Actress for Sera in *Leaving Las Vegas* (Lumiere Pictures/MGM-UA, 1995)

It may have been because she came cheap (*Leaving Las Vegas* cost just $3.5 million and was shot in under five weeks) that director Mike Figgis cast her as the young hooker who befriends Nicolas Cage's terminal alcoholic. Certainly few of Elisabeth Shue's previous films had indicated that she was capable of such a touching performance. Lightweight roles had generally been the order of the day, not doom-laden dramas with unhappy endings that focus on the decline of a couple of losers. A deserved nominee in a year when, for a change, the best actress category was of some quality, she began the year brightly by winning several of the top critical awards but was unfortunate to lose momentum in the six-week run-up to the Oscar ceremony.

Sylvia Sidney

Born the Bronx, New York, USA, 8 August 1910

Oscar Nominations (1): Best Supporting Actress for Rita's Mother in *Summer Wishes, Winter Dreams* (Columbia, 1973)

The large, soulful eyes and waif-like vulnerability were perfect for the Depression years, but not, it seems, quite enough to find Sylvia Sidney a place among the decade's Oscar nominees, even though the best directors frequently sought her services – Mamoulian, Vidor, Lang, Wyler – and she enjoyed a little piece of movie history by becoming one of the first actresses to be photographed in 'outdoor Technicolor', in *The Trail of the Lonesome*

Pine. The Academy remained unimpressed, until 1973, when they at last nominated her, for her role as the mother of Joanne Woodward in *Summer Wishes, Winter Dreams*. Even then the fates were against her. Tatum O'Neal and Linda Blair were battling it out for the supporting award for their performances in *Paper Moon* and *The Exorcist*. What chance for a sixty-three-year-old? Sadly, none.

Simone Signoret

Born Wiesbaden, Germany, 25 March 1921; died 1985

Oscars (1): Best Actress for Alice Aisgill in *Room at the Top* (Romulus, 1959)

Oscar Nominations (1): Best Actress for La Condesa in *Ship of Fools* (Columbia, 1965)

Age usually diminishes the charms of actresses who in their youth practised the art of screen seduction and flaunted their sensual appeal. Not in the case of Simone Signoret, who in 1952 was close to perfection as the destructive Apache moll in Jacques Becker's *Casque d'Or* and seven years later reached her peak as Laurence Harvey's tragic ageing mistress in *Room at the Top*. The Oscar was hers, plus an award at Cannes and the satisfaction of becoming the first (and to date only) French actress to be named best of the year, albeit in a British film. Nominated subsequently for her political activist, one of the luckless passengers on board Katherine Anne Porter's *Ship of Fools*, she later brought her earthy sexuality to a whole range of world-weary madams, hookers and alcoholics, and featured in 1975's best foreign-language film, *Madame Rosa*, as a former prostitute and concentration camp victim living in the Arab quarter of Paris.

Jean Simmons

Born London, England, 31 January 1929

Oscar Nominations (2): Best Supporting Actress for Ophelia in *Hamlet* (Two Cities/Rank, 1948); Best Actress for Mary Wilson in *The Happy Ending* (United Artists, 1969)

Only too aware that demure, virginal heroines in Hollywood epics (with which she had been saddled for much of her Hollywood career) didn't figure in the Oscar lists, Jean Simmons opted for a spot of disillusionment in 1969 and did herself proud as the suburban wife fed up with sixteen years of marriage and seeking fulfilment elsewhere. The film, *The Happy Ending*, brought her her second nomination, although there was no happy ending on Oscar night, Maggie Smith taking on all-comers as Miss Brodie and coming out triumphant as always. Nominated earlier when she was just nineteen for her Ophelia in Olivier's *Hamlet*, Simmons first made her mark on screen with the song 'Let Him Go, Let Him Tarry'. She was memorable as the young Estella in David Lean's *Great Expectations*.

Frank Sinatra

Born Hoboken, New Jersey, USA, 12 December 1915

Oscars (1): Best Supporting Actor for Angelo Maggio in *From Here to Eternity* (Columbia, 1953)

Oscar Nominations (1): Best Actor for Frankie Machine in *The Man with the Golden Arm* (United Artists, 1955)

As comebacks go, Sinatra's still ranks top of the list – three years in the wilderness after a mediocre career at MGM, a loss of confidence and popularity as a vocalist, and then . . . the role of the rebellious little private Maggio in *From Here to Eternity*. He played the part for just $8,000, swept back to the top with an Oscar and hasn't looked back since. As if to prove it had been no fluke, he earned another nomination two years later, as the drug-addicted Frankie Machine in Otto Preminger's *The Man with the Golden Arm*. Awarded the 1970 Jean Hersholt Humanitarian Award for his charity work, he has performed three Oscar-winning songs: 'Three Coins in the Fountain'; 'All the Way' (*The Joker Is Wild*); and 'High Hopes' (*A Hole in the Head*). Only Crosby, with four, has done better.

Gary Sinise

Born near Chicago, USA, 1955

Oscar Nominations (1): Best Supporting Actor for Lt Dan Taylor in *Forrest Gump* (Paramount, 1994)

He was in there somewhere, was Gary Sinise – as the crippled Vietnam veteran whose story is intertwined with that of the hero – although he did tend to get a bit lost amongst all the *Forrest Gump* razzmatazz on Oscar night. A subsequent co-star of Tom Hanks in *Apollo 13* (as the crew member who was dropped just prior to launch date), he has drifted more into mainstream cinema in recent times, after spending his early years as one of the co-founders of Chicago's Steppenwolf Theatre Company. In 1992 he directed and starred in (as George) a respectable remake of *Of Mice and Men*. Why was he not among the Gump winners? Answer: Martin Landau devoured all as Bela Lugosi!

Lila Skala

Born Vienna, Austria, 28 November 1896; died 1994

Oscar Nominations (1): Best Supporting Actress for Mother Maria in *Lilies of the Field* (United Artists, 1963)

In 1963 it was the Brits against the rest in the supporting actress category, the Brits being made up of Edith Evans, Diane Cilento, Joyce Redman (*Tom Jones*) and Margaret Rutherford (*The VIPs*), the rest consisting of Lila Skala for her Mother Superior who persuades handyman Sidney Poitier to build her German nuns a new chapel in the desert. He agreed and won an Oscar. She finished up an also-ran, being no match for Rutherford at her most eccentric. Still, the nomination kick-started her film career, which later embraced TV shows and films and daily soaps. She lived until she was well into her nineties.

Maggie Smith

Born Ilford, Essex, England, 28 December 1934

Oscars (2): Best Actress for the title role in *The Prime of Miss Jean Brodie* (20th Century-Fox, 1969); Best Supporting Actress for Diana Barrie in *California Suite* (Columbia, 1978)

Oscar Nominations (3): Best Supporting Actress for Desdemona in *Othello* (BHE/Warner Bros, 1965); Best Actress for Aunt Augusta in *Travels with My Aunt* (MGM, 1972); Best Supporting Actress for Charlotte Bartlett in *A Room with a View* (Merchant Ivory/Cinecom, 1986)

'You've got to have a sentimental reason for them to vote for you. Any decent actress can give a good performance, but a dying husband – that would have insured everything,' said Maggie Smith, eyeing hubby Michael Caine in the vain hope that he might go down with something. He didn't oblige, but a year later the Academy did, naming her best supporting actress for her fictional Oscar nominee in Neil Simon's *California Suite*. Already a best actress winner for her Scottish schoolteacher in *The Prime of Miss Jean Brodie*, Smith's nominations have spanned more than two decades, taking in a tragic Desdemona, an eccentric aunt and a spinster chaperone. Nigh on perfect in all of them, it would not have been amiss had she won for all five. Not that she didn't pick well. Her five nominated roles were by Shakespeare, Muriel Spark, Graham Greene, Neil Simon and E. M. Forster.

Carrie Snodgress

Born Chicago, USA, 27 October 1946

Oscar Nominations (1): Best Actress for Tina Balser in *Diary of a Mad Housewife* (Universal, 1970)

A role of a housewife who's just about had it up to her neck with kids and married life, takes a writer lover and ends up in psychological group therapy sessions was just what the doctor ordered for any actress wanting to make her name in the early seventies. Carrie Snodgress seized the opportunity with both hands and came out as the best thing in Frank Perry's social satire that, although uneven, had its moments, most of them when Snodgress was on screen. Her subsequent career has produced little of note, although she was hauntingly effective as the widowed mother attracted by Clint Eastwood's *Pale Rider*. A portrayal of an emancipated woman from an earlier age – Glenda Jackson's Gudrun Brangwen in *Women in Love* – took the honours in 1970.

Gale Sondergaard

Born Litchfield, Minnesota, USA, 15 February 1899; died 1985

Oscars (1): Best Supporting Actress for Faith Paleologue in *Anthony Adverse* (Warner Bros, 1936)

Oscar Nominations (1): Best Supporting Actress for Lady Thiang in *Anna and the King of Siam* (20th Century-Fox, 1946)

The first recipient of the best supporting actress Oscar – for her scheming housekeeper in *Anthony Adverse* – the tall, imposing Gale Sondergaard complemented her Oscar win with a nomination ten years later for her Number One wife of Rex Harrison in *Anna and the King of Siam*. A favourite Hollywood *femme fatale*, both in dramatic parts and in comedy (she appeared in four films with Bob Hope), she fell victim to the Hollywood Un-American Activities Committee in the post-war years, and along with her husband, director Herbert J. Biberman, was blacklisted for her alleged Communist sympathies. She did not, as is popularly believed, receive an Oscar nomination for her most famous role – that of the Eurasian wife who finally puts an end to Bette Davis with the twist of a knife in *The Letter*!

Mira Sorvino

Oscars (1): Best Supporting Actress for Linda Ash in *Mighty Aphrodite* (Miramax, 1995)

A sweet-natured bimbo who is a hooker who has a heart of gold who is the mother of Woody Allen's adopted child and who needs a partner in life! What self-respecting actress could refuse such a role, especially in an Allen movie and one that allows your screen character to go by the professional working name of 'Judy Cum'! Mira Sorvino, daughter of actor Paul

Sorvino, duly made the most of her opportunities, and on 25 March 1996 became the third actress to win an Oscar for a performance in a Woody Allen film, following Diane Keaton for *Annie Hall* and the double winner Dianne Wiest (*Hannah and Her Sisters, Bullets Over Broadway*). The film critic of the *Boston Globe* described her thus: 'She is funny and hugely appealing. She's got looks and brains and heart and timing. More than that the gods don't give you.' It was a fair assessment. The Academy voters obviously agreed.

Ann Sothern

Born Valley City, North Dakota, USA, 22 January 1909

Oscar Nominations (1): Best Supporting Actress for Tisha Doughty in *The Whales of August* (Alive Films, 1987)

A spirited, lighthearted actress who gained popularity in the forties as MGM's scatterbrained blonde adventuress 'Maisie', Ann Sothern looked for a while as though she would be stuck forever as 'Queen of the Bs'. A piece of inspired casting by writer/director Joseph Mankiewicz, who selected her as one of the suspicious spouses in *A Letter to Three Wives*, at last brought her critical acclaim, but by then she was turning her attention to television, where she enjoyed success in *Private Secretary* and *The Ann Sothern Show*. She made only sporadic screen appearances in her later years, most notably as a National Committee woman in Gore Vidal's political satire *The Best Man*. She won her belated Oscar nomination at the age of seventy-eight (after more than seventy films) for her long-time friend of the aged, widowed sisters Bette Davis and Lillian Gish in *The Whales of August*.

Sissy Spacek

Born Quitman, Texas, USA, 25 December 1949

Oscars (1): Best Actress for Loretta Lynn in *Coal Miner's Daughter* (Universal, 1980)

Oscar Nominations (4): Best Actress for Carrie White in *Carrie* (United Artists, 1976), Beth Horman in *Missing* (Universal, 1982), Mae Garvey in *The River* (Universal, 1984) and Babe Magrath Botrelle in *Crimes of the Heart* (DeLaurentiis Entertainment, 1986)

Bette Davis gave her the nod as being the best of all the young contemporary American actresses: 'She seems as though she can do just about anything and she doesn't care how she looks when she's doing it,' she said. The Academy shared her admiration, honouring Spacek five times in a ten-year period when it seemed as though she could do no wrong, winning for her country singer Loretta Lynn and earning nominations for her telekinetic tricks as Carrie, searching in South America with Jack Lemmon for her missing husband, struggling as a farmer's wife, and evoking eccentricity as a Southern belle accused of murdering her husband in *Crimes of the Heart*. She enjoyed some of her best lines in the last-named film. Responding to Jessica Lange's question as to why she had put her head in the oven, she says: 'Oh, I don't know, Meg. I'm having a bad day – it's been a real bad day.'

Kevin Spacey

Born South Orange, New Jersey, USA, 26 July 1959

Oscars (1): Best Supporting Actor for 'Verbal' Kint in *The Usual Suspects* (Gramercy, 1995)

Dip in and pull out a player seemed to be the order of the day when it came to selecting an actor from the cast of *The Usual Suspects*. Kevin Spacey was the Academy's choice, just as he had been that of the National Board of Review and the New York Critics Circle, who named him for not one but four 1995 performances – in *The Usual Suspects*, *Outbreak*, *Seven* and *Swimming with Sharks*. One was enough for the Academy – his crippled New York squealer who survives a ship explosion in San Pedro harbour and lives to tell cop Chazz Palminteri the tale. The voters said best support; Brad Pitt and the others went away to nurse their wounds.

Robert Stack

Born Los Angeles, USA, 13 January 1919

Oscar Nominations (1): Best Supporting Actor for Kyle Hadley in *Written on the Wind* (Universal-International, 1956)

A Texas oil man with no strength of character and coming apart at the seams because of too much money and an excess of booze! How could Robert Stack lose with credentials such as those? Lose he did, however, and although a nomination came his way, he could do nothing but sit and watch, in March 1957, when Anthony Quinn strolled with ease to his second Oscar for playing just a scene or two as Van Gogh in *Lust for Life*. As things turned out, it didn't matter a great deal, for *The Untouchables* was on Stack's TV horizon and with it a 1960 Emmy award for his Eliot Ness. Kevin Costner, later to become the cinema's Eliot Ness, was four years old at the time.

Sylvester Stallone

Born New York City, USA, 6 July 1946

Oscar Nominations (1): Best Actor for Rocky Balboa in *Rocky* (United Artists, 1976)

A stumble and mumble actor for most of the time, Sylvester Stallone nonetheless made the nominations lists for his portrayal of the heroic boxer Rocky who slugs his way to success in the first of the interminable *Rocky* sagas. Always impressed by screen actors displaying the noble art of fisticuffs, e.g., Wallace Beery (*The Champ*), John Garfield (*Body and Soul*), Kirk Douglas (*Champion*), the Academy would have been more daring if they had awarded Stallone a nomination for his trade union leader in Norman Jewison's *FIST*, a biography closely modelled on the career of Teamster boss Jimmy Hoffa. Peter Finch won the top acting prize in 1976, the year Stallone was nominated – both as a performer and a screenwriter – for *Rocky*.

Terence Stamp

Born London, England, 22 July 1939

Oscar Nominations (1): Best Supporting Actor for the title role in *Billy Budd* (Allied Artists, 1962)

One of the most handsome young stars to emerge from Britain's new-wave cinema of the sixties, Terence Stamp looked for a while as though he would be among those who would stay the course and not fall by the wayside. Alas, after an Oscar nomination for his ill-fated young foretopman Billy Budd, and acclaim (but no Oscar nomination) for his psychotic kidnapper in Wyler's *The Collector*, the wayside seemed to be his destination. Unable to find a niche for himself in Hollywood, he faded in the seventies and these days turns up mostly in character roles and movie cameos.

Kim Stanley

Born Tularosa, New Mexico, USA, 11 February 1925

Oscar Nominations (2): Best Actress for Myra Savage in *Seance on a Wet Afternoon* (Attenboro-Forbes/Artixo, 1964); Best Supporting Actress for Lillian Farmer in *Frances* (Brooksfilm/EMI, 1982)

'Hers is by far the best acting performance of the year' said Hedda Hopper of Kim Stanley's medium on the verge of a total breakdown in *Seance on a Wet Afternoon*. The New York Critics agreed. So did the National Board of Review. Best actress, they voted. The theme, though, was perhaps a bit too intense for Academy voters – a woman who cannot accept the birth of her stillborn child and slowly loses her grip on reality – who rewarded her with just a nomination. The Oscar they handed to Julie Andrews for her rather less complicated magical nanny Mary Poppins. Ho-hum! Stanley was nominated again eighteen years later for her unstable mother of unstable thirties movie actress, Frances Farmer.

☆

Barbara Stanwyck

Born Brooklyn, New York, USA, 16 July 1907; died 1990

Oscar Nominations (4): Best Actress for the title role in *Stella Dallas* (Goldwyn, United Artists, 1937), Sugarpuss O'Shea in *Ball of Fire* (Goldwyn, RKO, 1941), Phyllis Dietrichson in *Double Indemnity* (Paramount, 1944) and Leona Stevenson in *Sorry, Wrong Number* (Paramount, 1948)

At her best when playing self-assured, often aggressive women, Barbara Stanwyck used to say: 'I'm a tough old broad from Brooklyn. I intend to go on acting until I'm ninety and they won't need to paste my face with make-up.' She made it to eighty-two, some eight years short of her target, but even so it was quite a life, quite a career and some Oscar record – four nominations in just over a decade and all for roles that belong in the annals of Hollywood history – the self-sacrificing mother Stella Dallas, the burlesque dancer Sugarpuss O'Shea, the most deadly of *femme fatales* in *Double Indemnity*, and, as a kind of revenge for what she got up to in that film, a bedridden heiress who hears her murder being plotted over the telephone. No wonder they gave her a special Oscar in 1981, and no wonder Walter Matthau summed her up thus: 'When she was good she was very very good but when she was bad she was terrific.'

Maureen Stapleton

Born Troy, New York, USA, 21 June 1925

Oscars (1): Best Supporting Actress for Emma Goldman in *Reds* (Paramount, 1981)

Oscar Nominations (3): Best Supporting Actress for Fay Doyle in *Lonelyhearts* (United Artists, 1958), Inez Guerrero in *Airport* (Universal, 1970) and Pearl in *Interiors* (United Artists, 1978)

Only a few performers can genuinely be said to have never given a bad screen performance; Maureen Stapleton is indisputably one of them. Nominated for her very first screen role, as the cripple's wife in *Lonelyhearts*, she had to wait another twenty-three years before the Academy smiled on her. During that time she was nominated thrice – for her frightened wife of madman Van Heflin in *Airport*, 'the other woman' E. G. Marshall brings home to meet the family in Woody Allen's *Interiors* and finally for the role that eventually landed her her Oscar, the revolutionary Emma Goldman in Warren Beatty's *Reds*. An actress who has appeared in some twenty-five films and many TV movies, she has been a leading exponent of the work of Tennessee Williams on the Broadway stage.

Mary Steenburgen

Born Newport, Arkansas, USA, 8 February 1953

Oscars (1): Best Supporting Actress for Lynda Dummar in *Melvin and Howard* (Universal, 1980)

One American critic likened her to Judy Holliday, another called her the new Jean Arthur. She was, of course, neither, just Mary Steenburgen, a vivacious actress-comedienne who came up trumps in the 1980 supporting department with her portrait of a two-time wife and divorcee who finds that a grizzled old-timer calling himself Howard Hughes has left her husband $150 million in a Mormon will. Steenburgen took the award in March of 1981, proving that the Academy voters liked the film even though its studio, Universal, may have been right in delaying its release by seventeen months. No one went to see it.

Rod Steiger

Born Westhampton, New York, USA, 14 April 1925

Oscars (1): Best Actor for Bill Gillespie in *In the Heat of the Night* (United Artists, 1967)

Oscar Nominations (2): Best Supporting Actor for Charley Malloy in *On the Waterfront* (Columbia, 1954); Best Actor for Sol Nazerman in *The Pawnbroker* (Ely Landau/American International, 1965)

Extraordinarily powerful when in full flow but at his most effective when in quieter, more restrained mood, Steiger found his way to the podium for his bigoted Southern sheriff forced to accept the aid of black cop Sidney Poitier in a murder investigation. Many, indeed most, thought he should have been up there a couple of years earlier for his pawnbroker with horrendous memories of the Holocaust, surely one of the great performances of the post-war American cinema. Two Oscars would have been the best result. He was nominated in the fifties for one of his early roles as the crooked lawyer brother of Marlon Brando in *On the Waterfront*.

James Stephenson

Born Yorkshire, England, 14 April 1888; died 1941

Oscar Nominations (1): Best Supporting Actor for Howard Joyce in *The Letter* (Warner Bros, 1940)

He was so close to the Oscar, was James Stephenson, for his lawyer who defends the murderous Bette Davis in *The Letter* that for many the result seemed a foregone conclusion. Had he won (Walter Brennan nipped in to take his third award in five years for *The Westerner*) it would have been just reward for a Warner stock player who had appeared in a remarkable thirty-seven films in five years and was looked upon by the studio as an up-and-coming character actor – even at the age of fifty-three. Sadly, he got no further than *The Letter*. Just five months after the Oscar ceremony he died of a heart attack, and one of Hollywood's most promising careers was cut off in its prime.

Jan Sterling

Born New York City, USA, 3 April 1923

Oscar Nominations (1): Best Supporting Actress for Sally McKee in *The High and the Mighty* (Warner Bros, 1954)

Hollywood liked Jan Sterling best as a disillusioned cynic, a blonde floozie who has had a bad experience of life. Her Oscar nomination in *The High and the Mighty* was for just such a role, as a fading and slightly shop-soiled beauty en route by plane to marry a man she has never met. It was goodish Sterling but not great Sterling. That was reserved for her heartless, money-grabbing wife in Wilder's *Ace in the Hole*. Eyeing Kirk Douglas' ruthless reporter with not a little contempt, she sneers: 'I met a lot of hard-boiled eggs in my life – but you, you're twenty minutes!' Great dialogue, no Oscar. Worse, no nomination.

James Stewart

Born Indiana, Pennsylvania, USA, 20 May 1908

Oscars (1): Best Actor for Mike Connor in *The Philadelphia Story* (MGM, 1940)

Oscar Nominations (4): Best Actor for Jefferson Smith in *Mr Smith Goes to Washington* (Columbia, 1939), George Bailey in *It's a Wonderful Life* (RKO, 1946), Elwood P. Dowd in *Harvey* (Universal-International, 1950) and Paul Biegler in *Anatomy of a Murder* (Columbia, 1959)

The slow drawl and hesitant manner, the fumbling and anxious searching for the right word . . . for many, Jimmy Stewart was always the same. The more discerning, though, rated him as one of Hollywood's greatest actors and deserving of rather more than his solitary Oscar win. The Oscar when it came was presented for his magazine reporter enamoured with Katie Hepburn in *The Philadelphia Story*, although many, himself included, felt the award was compensation for his having missed out a year earlier for his crusading senator in Frank Capra's *Mr Smith Goes to Washington*. His subsequent nominations were all for post-war performances – for his small-town 'at-the-end-of-his-tether' family man in Capra's *It's a Wonderful Life*, his proud, inebriated companion of the invisible six-foot rabbit Harvey, and his defence lawyer in *Anatomy of a Murder*. Fredric March, Jose Ferrer and Charlton Heston triumphed in the respective years. The only black mark against the Academy? Why no mention for his obsessed detective in *Vertigo*, arguably his greatest role? He was honoured with a special Oscar in 1984 for 'his fifty years of memorable performances and for his high ideals both on and off the screen'.

Dean Stockwell

Born North Hollywood, California, USA, 5 March 1936

Oscar Nominations (1): Best Supporting Actor for Tony 'the Tiger' Russo in *Married to the Mob* (Orion, 1988)

Dean Stockwell had been around for so long when he eventually received his belated Oscar nomination that many actors who had starred with him when he was a child must have checked their birth certificates to make sure they weren't older than they really were! Named for his suave, well-dressed Mafia don ('all slime under the silk') in Jonathan Demme's gangster farce *Married to the Mob*, he finished among the runners-up to Kevin Kline's ex-CIA assassin in *A Fish Called Wanda*. Still remembered for his young war orphan in Joe Losey's *The Boy with Green Hair*, and just nine when he co-starred with Gene Kelly and Frank Sinatra in *Anchors Aweigh*, he has become popular in recent years for his role in the TV series *Quantum Leap*.

Lewis Stone

Born Worcester, Massachusetts, USA, 15 November 1879; died 1953

Oscar Nominations (1): Best Actor for Count Pahlen in *The Patriot* (Paramount, 1928/29)

He's best remembered for his stern but kindly judge-father of Mickey Rooney in the Andy Hardy pictures, but it was in the silent days that Lewis Stone shone brightest, both as a swashbuckling hero (*The Prisoner of Zenda*) and villain (*Scaramouche*), and in Lubitsch's *The Patriot*, in which he won his only Oscar nomination, for his prime minister who agrees to the assassination of Russia's mad Czar, Paul I. An MGM star for twenty-nine years, he worked at the studio for just twelve weeks a year when he was in his seventies, although Louis B. Mayer insisted on paying him for forty! The only surprise as far as the Oscars were concerned? No nominations for any of his character roles of the thirties and forties.

Sharon Stone

Born Meadville, Pennsylvania, USA, 10 March 1958

Oscars (1): Best Actress for Ginger McKenna in *Casino* (Universal, 1995)

Just about the only thing likely to enable audiences to forget (for a moment!) that Sharon Stone was *sans* knickers when she uncrossed her legs during the interrogation scene in *Basic Instinct* was an Oscar proving that she had acting ability as well as looks and an attractive pair of thighs. Director Martin Scorsese got her close to the winning post when he cast her as the tortured, two-timing and ultimately pathetic wife of big-time gambler Robert De Niro. 'I'm thirty-seven now, I'm getting on a bit,' she wailed in interviews prior to the awards. She shouldn't worry. *Casino* didn't win her the ultimate accolade but it did demonstrate that she is a formidable actress deserving of rather more than the sex flicks with which she was associated in her earlier years. An Academy Award in the not too distant future is by no means out of the question.

Beatrice Straight

Born Old Westbury, New York, USA, 2 August 1918

Oscars (1): Best Supporting Actress for Louise Schumacher in *Network* (United Artists, 1976)

One of the rare performers to give an interesting acceptance speech on Oscar night – she praised Paddy Chayefsky for 'writing what we all feel but cannot express' – Beatrice Straight achieved the seemingly impossible by winning her Oscar for just one scene. The film was *Network* and the scene, not surprisingly, was a real humdinger, as she reacts emotionally and in the end forlornly to husband William Holden's admission that he is having an affair with another woman. Her competition in 1976 included Lee Grant, Piper Laurie and the young Jodie Foster, all of whom had many more lines to conquer, but in 1976 one scene was enough. The scene took three days to rehearse and three days to shoot.

Lee Strasberg

Born Budzanow, Austria, 17 November 1901; died 1982

Oscar Nominations (1): Best Supporting Actor for Hyman Roth in *The Godfather, Part II* (Paramount, 1974)

Al Pacino made the suggestion: how about Lee Strasberg for the role of the Jewish gangster Hyman Roth in the long-awaited *Godfather, Part II?* Director Ford Coppola thought it a good idea, persuaded the Actor's Studio boss to practise what he preached, and the result was an Oscar nomination first time out. Not bad for a seventy-three-year-old. Perhaps he should have started earlier. Former Strasberg pupil Robert De Niro, nominated for his performance in the same film, bested his mentor by taking the supporting award for his portrait of the young Don Corleone.

Robert Strauss

Born New York City, USA, 8 November 1913; died 1975

Oscar Nominations (1): Best Supporting Actor for 'Animal' Stosh in
Stalag 17 (Paramount, 1953)

All in all, the burly Robert Strauss didn't earn too many good roles in his
career, but he made the most of the one classic he did get (the clownish
PoW 'Animal', forever fantasising about Betty Grable in Billy Wilder's
Stalag 17) by printing his acceptance speech in the trade papers shortly after
receiving his nomination from the Academy. His cheek amused Hollywood
but it didn't win him the award (it was Sinatra's year), and at the end of the
day he had to make do with just his nomination certificate. Billy Wilder
used him again, as the wide-eyed janitor in *The Seven-Year Itch* but *Stalag 17*
(in which he had also appeared on Broadway) remained the high spot of a
mostly disappointing screen career.

☆

Meryl Streep

Born Summit, New Jersey, USA, 22 June 1949

Oscars (2): Best Supporting Actress for Joanna Kramer in *Kramer vs.
Kramer* (Columbia, 1979); Best Actress for Sophie Zawistowska in *Sophie's
Choice* (ITC/Universal, 1982)

Oscar Nominations (8): Best Supporting Actress for Linda in *The Deer
Hunter* (EMI/Universal, 1978); Best Actress for Sarah Woodruff/Anna in
The French Lieutenant's Woman (United Artists, 1981), Karen Silkwood in
Silkwood (20th Century-Fox, 1983), Karen Blixen-Finecke in *Out of Africa*
(Universal, 1985), Helen Archer in *Ironweed* (TriStar, 1987), Lindy
Chamberlain in *A Cry in the Dark* (Warner Bros, 1988), Suzanne Vale in
Postcards from the Edge (Columbia, 1990) and Francesca Johnson in *The
Bridges of Madison County* (Warner Bros, 1995)

For some she is rather like an acting machine, lacking emotion and bringing
her mannerisms and range of accents to the surface of roles rather than to
the substance that lies beneath; for others she's the most accomplished

actress of her time, and was voted so by the magazine *American Film*, which named her the best actress of the eighties. Certainly no performer since Bette Davis and Greer Garson has so dominated things in the awards stakes. A double winner in the space of three years, she was honoured for her deserting young mother in *Kramer*, and for her tragic Sophie, who is forced by the Germans to choose which of her two children will survive the gas chamber. Her other nominations: her girlfriend of deer-hunter Robert De Niro, a French lieutenant's woman, a nuclear plant worker, the celebrated Danish author Karen Blixen, a former singer suffering the horrors of the Depression, the Australian mother in the dingo baby case, and a drug-addicted movie actress struggling to make a comeback. Most recently she made the lists for the tenth time (equalling the tally of Bette Davis) for her Midwestern housewife romanced by photographer Clint Eastwood in *The Bridges of Madison County*.

Barbra Streisand

Born Brooklyn, New York, USA, 24 April 1942

Oscars (1): Best Actress for Fanny Brice in *Funny Girl* (Columbia, 1968)

Oscar Nominations (1): Best Actress for Katie Morosky in *The Way We Were* (Columbia, 1973)

A great singer and a formidable screen actress, Barbra Streisand's Oscar record is impressive but perhaps could and should have been better. A winner first time out for repeating her Broadway role as Fanny Brice (she shared the award with Katharine Hepburn in the only best actress tie in Oscar history), she added to her laurels five years later with a nomination for her political activist in Sydney Pollack's *The Way We Were*, in which she enjoyed one of the film's best lines when she asks, rather contemptuously, of Robert Redford, 'Do you smile *all* the time?' Overlooked for her work as a director (*Yentl, The Prince of Tides*), and somewhat surprisingly for her young rock star on the rise in *A Star Is Born*, she nonetheless earned Oscar recognition for her work on the film by winning a best song award for 'Evergreen', which she wrote with lyricist Paul Williams.

Note: Streisand was nominated in 1992 for co-producing with Andrew Karsch her Columbia movie *The Prince of Tides*.

Margaret Sullavan

Born Norfolk, Virginia, USA, 16 May 1911; died 1960

Oscar Nominations (1): Best Actress for Pat Hollmann in *Three Comrades* (MGM, 1938)

No one was quite so radiant on screen or so difficult to work with as the husky-voiced Margaret Sullavan, whose reign in Hollywood lasted for less than a decade (1933–41) but whose ill-temper, violent outbursts and rows with directors became legendary. 'Perhaps I'll get used to this bizarre place called Hollywood but I doubt it,' she snapped on one occasion between movies. She never did, and returned to the New York stage whenever possible. Nominated just the once, for her lovely performance as the tubercular wife of Robert Taylor in MGM's version of Remarque's *Three Comrades* (the New York Critics voted her the year's best), she suffered from deafness in her later years. She put an end to her traumatic life by taking an overdose of barbiturates. She was forty-nine.

Janet Suzman

Born Johannesburg, South Africa, 9 February 1939

Oscar Nominations (1): Best Actress for the Empress Alexandra in *Nicholas and Alexandra* (Columbia/Horizon, 1971)

Producer Sam Spiegel decided that British actors would be best for most of the Russians in *Nicholas and Alexandra*, just as William Wyler had decided they would be best for the Romans in his 1959 epic *Ben-Hur*. As it turned out, the Brits came nowhere at nomination time, and only South African-born Janet Suzman made the lists, for her portrayal of the Empress, a woman terrified that her child will die of haemophilia and who falls under the spell of the peasant monk Rasputin. Quite what Alexandra got up to with Rasputin has only been hinted at in the history books; there were no such mysteries about call girl Jane Fonda's activities in *Klute*, a terrifying thriller which earned Fonda 1971's best actress nod over the formidable Miss Suzman.

Gloria Swanson

Born Chicago, USA, 27 March 1897; died 1983

Oscar Nominations (3): Best Actress for the title role in *Sadie Thompson* (United Artists, 1927/28), Marion Donnell in *The Trespasser* (United Artists, 1929/30) and Norma Desmond in *Sunset Boulevard* (Paramount, 1950)

The Academy never disclose the number of votes polled by each nominee, which is a pity, for it might reveal some interesting contests. The one year the rule should perhaps have been broken was 1950. How many votes, for instance, did Gloria Swanson's faded silent movie queen get, as against those garnered by Bette Davis' Margo Channing in *All About Eve*, or Judy Holliday's Billie Dawn in *Born Yesterday*? They all had great dialogue, of course, Swanson more than most, as she claimed that 'she was big, it was the pictures that got small' and that she was 'ready for [her] close-up now, Mr DeMille'. She lost on Oscar night (no performer in *Sunset Boulevard* won), just as she had done in the late silent days when she was nominated for Somerset Maugham's South Seas prostitute Sadie Thompson and her young stenographer in the tear-jerking melodrama *The Trespasser*. An unlucky Oscar performer, then, but just how many votes did her Norma Desmond lose by? A thousand . . . a hundred . . . ten . . . one?

$\mathcal{T}$

Russ Tamblyn

Born Los Angeles, USA, 30 December 1934

Oscar Nominations (1): Best Supporting Actor for Norman Page in *Peyton Place* (20th Century-Fox, 1957)

Considering that George Chakiris won his Oscar for his Puerto Rican gangleader in *West Side Story*, it would seem reasonable to assume that Russ Tamblyn earned his nomination for his leader of the rival gang, the Jets. Wrong. Tamblyn's nomination came not for *West Side Story* but for his clean-cut young teenager amorously involved with Lana Turner's daughter in *Peyton Place*. The musicals had more or less finished by then; so too, unfortunately, had his acrobatic dancing, which had so enhanced MGM's song-and-dance movies in the fifties.

Akim Tamiroff

Born Baku, Russia, 29 October 1899; died 1972

Oscar Nominations (2): Best Supporting Actor for General Yang in *The General Dies at Dawn* (Paramount, 1936) and Pablo in *For Whom the Bell Tolls* (Paramount, 1943)

Described by one critic as 'both alarming and subtle', the swarthy Akim Tamiroff essayed villains of the mysterious foreigner variety, playing anything from emirs to Russian pirates, saloon-keepers to French legionnaires. The Academy preferred him as a ruthless Chinese bandit and a drunken Spanish guerrilla leader but never felt compelled to go beyond the nomination stage. A long-time friend of Orson Welles, he appeared in several of Welles' films (*Mr Arkadin, Touch of Evil, The Trial*) and was his Sancho Panza in the unfinished and unseen *Don Quixote*. He once revealed that he had offered to take lessons to rid himself of his heavy Russian accent, only to be told by Paramount that if he did he would be dismissed forthwith!

Jessica Tandy

Born London, England, 7 June 1907; died 1994

Oscars (1): Best Actress for Miss Daisy Werthan in *Driving Miss Daisy* (Warner Bros, 1989)

Oscar Nominations (1): Best Supporting Actress for Ninny Threadgoode in *Fried Green Tomatoes at the Whistle Stop Café* (Universal, 1991)

She was the first actress to play Blanche DuBois on stage, but lost the screen role to Vivien Leigh, and she failed to make it above character roles because Hollywood thought her lacking in sex appeal. She also, perhaps in frustration as well as horror, screamed the place down in Hitchcock's *The Birds* when she came across a neighbouring farmer and found him dead in his kitchen with his eyes pecked out! Age brought its compensations and rewards. At eighty, she played another Southern belle, a crusty, dictatorial old matron who befriends her black chauffeur of many years in *Driving Miss Daisy*, and became the oldest performer to win an Academy Award. Nominated again for her elderly eccentric recalling her past in *Fried Green Tomatoes*, she made her last film appearance in *Nobody's Fool*, directed by Robert Benton and dedicated to her memory.

Elizabeth Taylor

Born London, England, 27 February 1932

Oscars (2): Best Actress for Gloria Wandrous in *Butterfield 8* (MGM, 1960) and Martha in *Who's Afraid of Virginia Woolf?* (Warner Bros, 1966)

Oscar Nominations (3): Best Actress for Susanna Drake in *Raintree County* (MGM, 1957), Maggie Pollitt in *Cat on a Hot Tin Roof* (MGM, 1958) and Catherine Holly in *Suddenly, Last Summer* (Columbia, 1959)

She blazed away in *Butterfield 8*, did Liz Taylor. 'Mama, face it; I was the slut of all time,' she yells at a bewildered Mildred Dunnock, and to her current *amour*, Laurence Harvey: 'I started at Amherst and I worked my way through the alphabet to Yale. I'm stuck there.' So much for promiscuity.

Anthony Quinn's Zorba finds comfort with ageing madam Lila Kedrova in 1964's *Zorba the Greek* (20th Century-Fox). Kedrova found comfort with the Oscar as best support of the year; Quinn was nominated in the best actor category

The finale of Hitchcock's *Notorious* (RKO, 1946): Cary Grant and Ingrid Bergman make their escape; the figures framed in the doorway wait to inform Claude Rains (*right*) of his fate. A four-time Oscar nominee, Rains was nominated as one of the year's best supporting actors

A beguiling serenity and a quiet cunning. Winona Ryder, nominated as best supporting actress in 1993 for her lovely fiancée of Daniel Day-Lewis in *The Age of Innocence* (Columbia). She was defeated by Anna Paquin in *The Piano*

A winner at the fifth attempt. Susan Sarandon, best actress of 1995 for her socially conscious nun, Sister Helen Prejean, in *Dead Man Walking* (Gramercy/Polygram)

Thomas More, Lord Chancellor of England (*left*), played in Academy Award-winning style by Paul Scofield in Fred Zinnemann's film version of Robert Bolt's stage play *A Man for All Seasons* (Columbia, 1966). Sharing things in this scene: Nigel Davenport as the Duke of Norfolk

Spot the Oscar winner! Answer: the guy on the far right (Kevin Spacey) who may or may not be who he says he is. Spacey won 1995's best supporting actor award for his role in *The Usual Suspects* (Gramercy)

The way they were: Robert Redford and Barbra Streisand in Columbia's popular tearjerker of 1973. Streisand won a best actress nomination; Redford was named for his work in another of the year's top films, *The Sting*

Troubled thoughts of unrequited love. A pensive Kate Winslet and Emma Thompson consider the future in *Sense and Sensibility* (Columbia, 1995). Both were nominated for acting awards; Thompson won for her screenplay

Richard Todd, best actor nominee in 1949 for his dying Scottish soldier in *The Hasty Heart* (Warner Bros). Sharing things with him in this scene: nurse Patricia Neal

Two of the most inept hit men in the business: John Travolta (best actor nominee) and Samuel L. Jackson (supporting nominee) in Quentin Tarantino's *Pulp Fiction* (Miramax, 1994). The bodies fell but the Oscars went elsewhere

(*Above*) Katharine Hepburn and Spencer Tracy in their first film together, *Woman of the Year* (MGM, 1942), in which she was nominated and he missed out; and (*below*) off-set on their last picture *Guess Who's Coming to Dinner?* (Columbia, 1967) which won Kate her second best actress Oscar. Their total Oscar tally: 6 wins and 15 nominations, all in the major acting categories

New York and the lower depths. Would-be stud Jon Voight and crippled hustler Dustin Hoffman struggle through poverty and loneliness in the Big Apple in *Midnight Cowboy* (United Artists, 1969). Oscar nominations for both but not the award. John Wayne took that for *True Grit*

All it needed was the eye patch! John Wayne, a winner at last for his one-eyed Rooster Cogburn in *True Grit* (Paramount, 1969)

Sigourney Weaver and co-star in *Gorillas in the Mist* (Warner Bros/Universal, 1988). Weaver was nominated as best actress for her portrait of Dian Fossey

Three sisters but only one Oscar winner – Dianne Wiest (*right*) in Woody Allen's 1986 hit *Hannah and Her Sisters* (Orion). Her relations: Mia Farrow (*left*) and Barbara Hershey

Still, all the histrionics worked and the Oscar came her way, to be followed six years later by a second, for her blowsy Martha in *Virginia Woolf*. The role for which she should have been named (she received only a nomination) was her Maggie the Cat in Tennessee Williams' *Cat on a Hot Tin Roof*, in which she was perfectly cast and had never looked better. Nominated also for another Tennessee Williams role, as the girl close to madness in *Suddenly, Last Summer*, she was first mentioned in the listings for her Southern belle in *Raintree County*, proving that she would have made an admirable Scarlett had Metro ever decided to remake the Margaret Mitchell classic.

Emma Thompson

Born London, England, 15 April 1959

Oscars (1): Best Actress for Margaret Schlegel in *Howards End* (Merchant Ivory/Sony Pictures Classics, 1992)

Oscar Nominations (3): Best Actress for Miss Kenton in *The Remains of the Day* (Merchant Ivory/Columbia, 1993); Best Supporting Actress for Gareth Peirce in *In the Name of the Father* (Hell's Kitchen/Universal, 1993); Best Actress for Elinor Dashwood in *Sense and Sensibility* (Mirage/Columbia, 1995)

Something of a regular at recent Oscar shows, but with still only the one acting award to show for her efforts (for her young inheritor of the house Howards End), Emma Thompson has also enjoyed the rather more dubious distinction of being the only actress, apart from Sigourney Weaver, to have been nominated as best actress and supporting actress in the same year and not won in either category. Weaver is crying the loudest, for she hasn't an Oscar to fall back on. Thompson has, and has recently added to her achievements with a writing award for *Sense and Sensibility*. Unable to do much wrong in most people's eyes, she has shown misjudgement on occasion, especially when agreeing to co-star in the pregnant man Schwarzenegger comedy *Junior*. Her two-in-one-year nominations were for her English solicitor of Gerry Conlon in *In the Name of the Father* and her loyal housekeeper in *The Remains of the Day*.

Uma Thurman

Born Boston, USA, 29 April 1970

Oscar Nominations (1): Best Supporting Actress for Mia Wallace in *Pulp Fiction* (Miramax, 1994)

A newcomer to the Oscar lists, the sexy, slinky young Uma Thurman found herself in line for the award for her gangster's wife out for a night on the town with dim hit man John Travolta in *Pulp Fiction* – a night that begins in something of a frenzy in a gimmicky restaurant and ends in near-tragedy with an accidental overdose of heroin. Oscar night didn't finish all that well either; Dianne Wiest, the choice of just about all the critics in the run-up to the awards, took the Oscar for *Bullets Over Broadway*. Thurman, though, is definitely one for the future.

Lawrence Tibbett

Born Bakersfield, California, USA, 16 November 1896; died 1960

Oscar Nominations (1): Best Actor for Yegor in *The Rogue Song* (MGM, 1929/30)

One of the first surprise Oscar nominees, Metropolitan Opera star Lawrence Tibbett somehow found himself among the Oscar candidates of 1930 for his portrayal of the Russian mountain bandit who sings in *The Rogue Song*. Hollywood's penchant for musicals may have had something to do with his inclusion, but none of the pundits gave him the remotest chance of winning and he didn't disappoint them. Still, he did earn a distinction of sorts, becoming the first screen star to be nominated for his début film, a record that lasted for ten years until Orson Welles came along with *Citizen Kane*!

Gene Tierney

Born Brooklyn, New York, USA, 20 November 1920; died 1991

Oscar Nominations (1): Best Actress for Ellen Berent in *Leave Her to Heaven* (20th Century-Fox, 1945)

A woman of exotic and quite unusual beauty – high cheekbones, brown-red hair and green eyes – Gene Tierney came closest to winning an Oscar not for *Laura*, as is sometimes supposed, but for her paranoid wife driven to murder because of obsessive jealousy in *Leave Her to Heaven*. One of those actresses lucky enough to photograph well in early Technicolor, she was at her most effective in bitchy, aristocratic roles, notably as another jealous lady, the lethal Isabel Bradley in Somerset Maugham's *The Razor's Edge*. The subject of gossip because of her links with the young John Kennedy and Prince Aly Khan, she made the headlines when she suffered a nervous breakdown and became a voluntary patient in a mental home. Otto Preminger brought her out of retirement to play a Washington hostess in *Advise and Consent*, but she preferred a publicity-free retirement in Texas, where she contented herself working for charities.

Jennifer Tilly

Born 1961

Oscar Nominations (1): Best Supporting Actress for Olive Neal in *Bullets Over Broadway* (Miramax, 1994)

If ever an actress deserved to be bumped off in a movie it was the Oscar-nominated Jennifer Tilly in Woody Allen's *Bullets Over Broadway*. It was gangster playwright Chazz Palminteri who did the rubbing out, unable to stand what her squeaky Judy Holliday/Jean Hagen-type voice and dumb persona were doing to his precious lines of dialogue and blowing her away one dark night on the waterfront of New York. Jennifer Tilly's co-star, Dianne Wiest, won the year's supporting award for her performance as the theatrical *grande dame* in the same film.

Meg Tilly

Born Long Beach, California, USA, 14 February 1960

Oscar Nominations (1): Best Supporting Actress for Sister Agnes in *Agnes of God* (Columbia, 1985)

Donning a nun's habit has certainly helped in the nomination department over the years, Ingrid Bergman, Deborah Kerr, Loretta Young, Celeste Holm and Audrey Hepburn being among those who have taken to life behind convent walls. Meg Tilly joined the group in 1985 for her troubled young nun (and mother) who has no recollection of her baby's conception or delivery and may be a saint or a murderer. An intriguing and frequently moving role that offered rather more food for thought than Anjelica Huston's wisecracking Mafia girl in *Prizzi's Honor*. But guess who won? Meg hasn't been in the running since, although sister Jennifer chalked up a nomination in 1994 for her floozie actress in *Bullets Over Broadway*.

Richard Todd

Born Dublin, Ireland, 11 June 1919

Oscar Nominations (1): Best Actor for 'The Scot' in *The Hasty Heart* (Warner Bros, 1949)

One of several new stars to emerge in the British cinema in the post-war years, the thirty-year-old Richard Todd looked set for a rewarding Hollywood career when he earned an Oscar nomination for his truculent Scottish soldier having to come to terms with his imminent death in *The Hasty Heart*. The career did take off to some extent (there were a few films at Fox, including *The Virgin Queen* opposite Bette Davis, and three romps for Disney in England), but he was at his best as one of the stiff-upper-lip brigade in British war films of the fifties when it was invariably a case of 'Try John Mills or if he can't do it check on Jack Hawkins. Or if he's unavailable try Richard Todd' . . . or the other way round!

☆

Marisa Tomei

Born Brooklyn, New York, USA, 4 December 1964

Oscars (1): Best Supporting Actress for Mona Lisa Vito in *My Cousin Vinny* (20th Century-Fox, 1992)

The wisecracking girlfriend/mistress has been a key ingredient of Hollywood comedy from the moment movies found their voice. Marisa Tomei proved the role had lost none of its old appeal when she played the leggy girlfriend of novice lawyer Joe Pesci in *My Cousin Vinny*. Pesci won his case in court; Tomei took the Oscar and saw off a formidable challenge from a British threesome: Miranda Richardson (*Damage*), Vanessa Redgrave (*Howards End*), and Joan Plowright (*Enchanted April*). Not a lot has happened to her since, although Richard Attenborough used her to some effect as silent star Mabel Normand in his *Chaplin*.

Lily Tomlin

Born Detroit, USA, 1 September 1939

Oscar Nominations (1): Best Supporting Actress for Linnea Reese in *Nashville* (Paramount, 1975)

Just about everyone in Robert Altman's *Nashville* seemed as though they were in with a chance of some kind of an acting award, although in the end only two of the film's performers made it into the Oscar lists – Ronee Blakley (see p. 36) and Lily Tomlin, who earned her nod for her portrayal of a distressed gospel singer. The New York Critics liked her and gave her their vote; the Academy liked her but gave her only a nomination, preferring Lee Grant in *Shampoo*. The only cast member to win for *Nashville* was Keith Carradine, who missed being nominated in the acting categories but won for composing and singing the year's best song, 'I'm Easy'.

Franchot Tone

Born Niagara Falls, New York, USA, 27 February 1905; died 1968

Oscar Nominations (1): Best Actor for Roger Byam in *Mutiny on the Bounty* (MGM, 1935)

A crack on the jaw from actor Tom Neal in a restaurant, surgery to put his looks back together again and a marriage to actress Barbara Payton (about whom they were brawling) for just fifty-three days! Franchot Tone's ability to hit the headlines for the wrong reasons put his solitary Oscar achievement in the shade, although he did achieve an Academy record of sorts, being one of three performers – Laughton and Gable were the others – to be nominated as best actor for the same film. His midshipman loyal to Captain Bligh came nowhere on Oscar night, Victor McLaglen's *The Informer* taking the main award. Excellent on screen as dashing society sophisticates, Tone was married four times. His first wife, when he was an MGM star in the thirties, was Joan Crawford.

☆

Topol

Born Tel Aviv, Israel, 9 September 1935

Oscar Nominations (1): Best Actor for Tevye in *Fiddler on the Roof* (United Artists, 1971)

Anyone cast as the Jewish milkman Tevye in the 1971 film of the musical *Fiddler on the Roof* was already halfway to an Oscar nomination, and so it transpired when the Israeli actor Topol, who had played Tevye for a year on the London stage, found himself up against one of the toughest detectives the screen has ever known – Gene Hackman's Popeye Doyle – and lost. There were those who felt that had director Norman Jewison opted for Zero Mostel, who had first created the role on Broadway, the result might have been different, especially after Mostel's success some three years earlier in Mel Brooks' *The Producers*. Topol, though, was the younger man (thirty-five to fifty-five), and it's doubtful if even Mostel could have improved on his portrayal, especially his 'If I Were a Rich Man', which remains a musical *tour de force*.

Rip Torn

Born Temple, Texas, USA, 6 February 1931

Oscar Nominations (1): Best Supporting Actor for Marsh Turner in *Cross Creek* (Universal, 1983)

Mean, moody and nasty for the most part on screen, Rip Torn enjoyed a nice change of pace when Martin Ritt thought him suitable for the tragic, poverty-stricken Florida backwoods farmer in *Cross Creek*. The Academy thought him suitable too, naming him as one of the year's five supporting nominees. Alas, it was the wrong year to make the lists. Jack Nicholson had the award in his pocket before the nominations were even announced, for his boozy astronaut in *Terms of Endearment*.

Lee Tracy

Born Atlanta, Georgia, USA, 14 April 1898; died 1968

Oscar Nominations (1): Best Supporting Actor for Art Hockstader in *The Best Man* (United Artists, 1964)

The screen's perfect fast-talking newspaperman, Lee Tracy brought his machine-gun delivery to dozens of 'hold-the-front-page'-type movies during a screen career that lasted for more than thirty-five years. He came closest to winning his Oscar for his very last film, when he was nominated for his ailing US President in Gore Vidal's scathing political satire *The Best Man*. Of his type casting as a newshawk, he agreed that it had hindered the development of his movie career. 'I should have quit playing newspapermen after three or four parts in the movies, but the money kept coming in and I liked it,' he said with a smile. Ironically, he missed out on his most famous newshound, Hildy Johnson, whom he had played on Broadway in *The Front Page*. On screen the part went to Pat O'Brien.

Spencer Tracy

Born Milwaukee, Wisconsin, USA, 5 April 1900; died 1967

Oscars (2): Best Actor for Manuel in *Captains Courageous* (MGM, 1937) and Father E. Flanagan in *Boys' Town* (MGM, 1938)

Oscar Nominations (7): Best Actor for Father Mullin in *San Francisco* (MGM, 1936), Stanley T. Banks in *Father of the Bride* (MGM, 1950), John J. Macreedy in *Bad Day at Black Rock* (MGM, 1955), the Old Man in *The Old Man and the Sea* (Warner Bros, 1958), Henry Drummond in *Inherit the Wind* (United Artists, 1960), Judge Dan Haywood in *Judgment at Nuremberg* (United Artists, 1961) and Matt Drayton in *Guess Who's Coming to Dinner?* (Columbia, 1967)

For many he was quite simply the best of all time; for others he should have embraced more ambitious films that stretched his talents to the limit. Whatever one's view, he remains one of the half-dozen best that Hollywood has produced, enjoying a marvellous on-screen teaming with his long-time love Katharine Hepburn and becoming the only actor (until Tom Hanks repeated the feat in the nineties) to win Oscars in consecutive years – for his Portuguese fisherman in *Captains Courageous* and his Father Flanagan in *Boys' Town*. His other nominations: for a priest caught up with Clark Gable in the San Francisco earthquake, a harassed father of bride Elizabeth Taylor, a one-armed army veteran clad in black, Hemingway's Cuban fisherman in *The Old Man and the Sea*, the Darrow-type lawyer defending the right to teach Darwin's theory in Tennessee, a Nuremberg judge, and, in his last film, an ageing father coming face to face with his principles. Seven nominations and two wins. A remarkable achievement. Clark Gable's view of his acting: 'All he had to do was show up and be photographed.' Tracy's reply to the question as to what he looked for most in a script: 'Days off!'

Henry Travers

Born Berwick-upon-Tweed, Northumberland, England, 5 March 1874; died 1965

Oscar Nominations (1): Best Supporting Actor for Mr Ballard in *Mrs Miniver* (MGM, 1942)

A gentle, British-born little actor who brought to life on screen such dignified figures as mayors, professors and doctors, Henry Travers won his

Oscar nomination for his kindly stationmaster who enters his 'Miniver rose' in the local flower show. A bit never-never-land, perhaps, but Henry Travers was at home in such worlds, and quite how he came to be overlooked for his guardian angel Clarence Oddbody (Angel Second Class) who saves James Stewart from suicide in *It's a Wonderful Life* only the voters of the time will ever know. A late starter (he was fifty-nine when he first appeared on screen in *Reunion in Vienna* in 1933), he made more than fifty films in his sixteen-year career. His very last role was as a judge in the long-forgotten Ronald Reagan movie *The Girl from Jones Beach*.

John Travolta

Born Englewood, New Jersey, USA, 18 February 1954

Oscar Nominations (2): Best Actor for Tony Manero in *Saturday Night Fever* (Paramount, 1977) and Vincent Vega in *Pulp Fiction* (Miramax, 1994)

'Staying Alive' – the title of one of John Travolta's numbers in *Saturday Night Fever* – seemed to say it all as far as his movie career was concerned. He managed it, just, keeping his name in front of the public with the jaw-dropping dross of the *Look Who's Talking* films and then earning his second Oscar nomination for his long-haired hit man in Quentin Tarantino's *Pulp Fiction*. Tom Hanks (*Forrest Gump*) kept him in his seat on Oscar night, just as Richard Dreyfuss had done some seventeen years earlier with his performance in *The Goodbye Girl*.

Claire Trevor

Born New York City, USA, 8 March 1909

Oscars (1): Best Supporting Actress for Gaye Dawn in *Key Largo* (Warner Bros, 1948)

Oscar Nominations (2): Best Supporting Actress for Francey in *Dead End* (United Artists, 1937) and May Hoist in *The High and the Mighty* (Warner Bros, 1954)

Much admired by male audiences for her warm-hearted floozies and women who long ago had lost their reputations, Claire Trevor won her Oscar for playing true to type – as the alcoholic former nightclub singer 'owned' by mobster Edward G. Robinson in *Key Largo*. Nominated also for her streetwalker in *Dead End* and her ageing beauty with money and memories in *The High and the Mighty*, she later broadened her range to include *femmes fatales* and hard, calculating, shrewish women such as the wife of the luckless Eddie Mayehoff in *How to Murder Your Wife* and the spouse of film director Edward G who, in *Two Weeks in Another Town*, refers to her as 'my lawful wedded nightmare'. A long, long way from the warmth of dance-hall gal Dallas in *Stagecoach* for which (shame on the Academy!) she was overlooked at nomination time.

Massimo Troisi

Born 1953; died 1994

Oscar Nominations (1): Best Actor for Mario Ruoppolo in *The Postman* (Miramax, 1995)

The trouble with being a European nominee in a foreign-language movie is that a nomination is all you're likely to get, for no 'foreign' actor has yet managed to pull off the major prize. The late Massimo Troisi, the first posthumous best actor nominee since Peter Finch some twenty years earlier, was no exception, despite his affecting and moving portrayal of a gentle village postman whose life is changed because of his friendship with an exiled Chilean poet. The surprise among 1995's nominees, Troisi was also among those nominated for the screenplay of the film. He died just twelve hours after shooting had been completed. His nomination for the Oscar was announced some twenty months after his death.

Note: The only European actress to win for a performance in a foreign-language film is Sophia Loren, who was named in 1961 for her role in DeSica's *Two Women*.

Tom Tully

Born Durango, Colorado, USA, 1908; died 1982

Oscar Nominations (1): Best Supporting Actor for Captain Devriess in *The Caine Mutiny* (Columbia, 1954)

Considering he was an ex-navy man, it was perhaps fitting that Tom Tully earned his Oscar nomination for *The Caine Mutiny*, even though seamen were not usually his forte on screen. Cops, saloon-keepers, bar-tenders, even the occasional politician, were more his scene, amiable enough guys on the face of it but sometimes a little more cunning and untrustworthy under the surface. His role in *The Caine Mutiny* was as the easy-going skipper in charge of *The Caine* before Bogie's Queeg took over and gave 'em hell! Edmond O'Brien won the supporting nod in 1954 for his sweating press agent in *The Barefoot Contessa*.

Kathleen Turner

Born Springfield, Missouri, USA, 19 June 1954

Oscar Nominations (1): Best Actress for the title role in *Peggy Sue Got Married* (TriStar, 1986)

The nomination should have been for her sultry *femme fatale* in *Body Heat* ('You're not too bright, are you?' she says to William Hurt. 'I like that in a man'). Failing that, she should have earned a mention for her double-crossing hit girl in *Prizzi's Honor*, in which she was involved with another slow thinker, Jack Nicholson. On both occasions the Academy looked the other way and instead nominated Kathleen Turner for her lighter touch, as the girl who goes time-travelling back to her high-school days. An OK performance, but one in the class of Matty Walker in *Body Heat* or Irene Walker (a lethal cousin perhaps!) in *Prizzi's Honor*? Not really.

Lana Turner

Born Wallace, Idaho, USA, 8 February 1920; died 1995

Oscar Nominations (1): Best Actress for Constance MacKenzie in
Peyton Place (20th Century-Fox, 1957)

During her 'sweater girl' years at MGM, Lana Turner only once came close
to an Oscar nomination, when she was memorably teamed with John
Garfield and cast as the murdering *femme fatale* in *The Postman Always Rings
Twice*. Possibly because Barbara Stanwyck had essayed a similar role in
Double Indemnity just two years earlier, she was overlooked. Her luck
changed in early middle age when she embarked on a series of lush soap
operas and melodramas, most notably the film version of the bestselling
Peyton Place, in which she played a small-town New Hampshire widow
caught up in the problems of her teenage daughter. Her nomination was
well deserved, although it was a bright new star, Joanne Woodward (then
twenty-seven), who took the award, for *The Three Faces of Eve*. Nine years
later Turner's drunken mum on the skids in the remake of *Madame X* was
also considered a possible Oscar performance. Alas, she was required to
deliver such dialogue as: 'He fished me out of the sewers of Mexico and got
me dirt cheap', and any talk of an Oscar went out of the window!

☆

Susan Tyrrell

Born San Francisco, USA, 1946

Oscar Nominations (1): Best Supporting Actress for Oma in *Fat City*
(Rastar/Columbia 1972)

Floozies and losers . . . they've been a staple diet for actresses young and
old over the years, never more so than in John Huston's boxing story *Fat
City*, a film in which just about everyone was a loser, from Stacy Keach's
washed-up fighter to his drunken girlfriend Susan Tyrrell. Her scenes with
Keach as they argue, rage and almost drive each other crazy seemed
improvised. Knowing Huston, they probably were. Whatever, they were
enough to get her into the Oscar lists for the first and only time. Eileen
Heckart, much more in control of things as the domineering mother in
Butterflies Are Free, was the year's supporting winner.

Cicely Tyson

Born New York City, USA, 19 December 1933

Oscar Nominations (1): Best Actress for Rebecca Morgan in *Sounder* (20th Century-Fox, 1972)

The closest Cicely Tyson has come to an Oscar was in March of 1978 when she and King Vidor arrived on stage to present the director's award to Woody Allen for *Annie Hall*, discovered that no one was on hand to accept on his behalf and just walked off with it into the wings. Six years earlier she had been in competition with Diana Ross (*Lady Sings the Blues*) for her sharecropper's wife struggling through the Depression in Martin Ritt's *Sounder*, a year when, for the first time in Academy history, three of the leading acting nominees – Paul Winfield also received a mention for *Sounder* – were black. It made no difference. Liza Minnelli was the year's best actress for *Cabaret*; *Godfather* Brando the lead actor. Tyson's best work has mostly been on TV, notably in *Roots* and *The Autobiography of Miss Jane Pittman*, in which she gave a remarkable performance as a 110-year-old former slave.

U

Liv Ullmann

Born Tokyo, Japan, 16 December 1939

Oscar Nominations (2): Best Actress for Kristina in *The Emigrants* (Svensk Filmindustri, Sweden, 1972) and Dr Jenny Isaksson in *Face to Face* (Cinematograph, AB, 1976)

Always ill at ease in Hollywood movies (*Forty Carats, Lost Horizon*), the radiant blonde beauty Liv Ullmann functioned best in Sweden, where she brought her remarkable emotional range to a long line of Ingmar Bergman films. Surprisingly nominated just the twice for the major prize, she reached the final five in 1972 when she played a Swedish farmer's wife migrating to America in Jan Troell's *The Emigrants* and in 1976 for her psychiatrist who suffers a slow, painful nervous breakdown in Bergman's *Face to Face*. Liza Minnelli (*Cabaret*) and Faye Dunaway (*Network*) were deemed to have given superior performances in the respective years. Ullmann's performances in the Bergman films *Persona, Cries and Whispers* and *Scenes from a Marriage* all went unnoticed.

Miyoshi Umeki

Born Otaru, Hokkaido, Japan, 1929

Oscars (1): Best Supporting Actress for Katsumi in *Sayonara* (Warner Bros, 1957)

The betting was on either Elsa Lanchester (*Witness for the Prosecution*) or Diane Varsi (*Peyton Place*). Failing that, Carolyn Jones for her brief scene in *The Bachelor Party*. No one really considered Japanese actress Miyoshi Umeki for her tragic war bride in *Sayonara*. She surprised them all, joining Red Buttons, who played her American army husband in the film, as one of the decade's double winners in the supporting category. Despite her Oscar, her subsequent film roles were few and far between, although she enjoyed success in both the stage and screen versions of the Rodgers and Hammerstein musical *Flower Drum Song*.

Mary Ure

Born Glasgow, Scotland, 18 February 1933; died 1975

Oscar Nominations (1): Best Supporting Actress for Clara Dawes in *Sons and Lovers* (20th Century-Fox, 1960)

Heartwarming as Clara, the emancipated Nottingham woman who initiates Dean Stockwell into the pleasures of sex, the blonde-haired Mary Ure offered rather more than what poor Mr Stockwell had been trying to obtain from Heather Sears during the first forty minutes of screen time. An Oscar nomination duly followed, although in a year of 'bad girls', Shirley Jones took the award for providing for Burt Lancaster exactly what Ure had provided for Stockwell, the only difference being that hers was a business, Ure's was for love. Also memorable as the long-suffering victim of Jimmy Porter's abuse in *Look Back in Anger*, Mary Ure was just forty-two when she died of an accidental overdose of barbiturates.

Peter Ustinov

Born London, England, 16 April 1921

Oscars (2): Best Supporting Actor for Lentulus Batiatus in *Spartacus* (Universal, 1960) and Arthur Simpson in *Topkapi* (United Artists, 1964)

Oscar Nominations (1): Best Supporting Actor for Nero in *Quo Vadis?* (MGM, 1951)

Something about Peter Ustinov's portly persona seemed to trigger off the word 'epic' in the minds of Hollywood producers. It's difficult to see quite why, but all the costume stuff certainly seemed to pay dividends, especially as far as Oscars were concerned – a nomination for his unstable and distinctly unmusical Nero in *Quo Vadis?*, nothing for *The Egyptian* but the award itself for his cunning master of a gladiator school in *Spartacus*. He added to his laurels four years later by coming up to date a bit and winning for his slow-thinking strong man Arthur Simpson in Dassin's caper movie *Topkapi*. Rumour has it that he keeps his awards in a glass case in his bathroom, as that is the only place he can admire them in due modesty.

Note: Ustinov was also nominated, along with Ira Wallach, for his 1968 story and screenplay for MGM's *Hot Millions*.

$\mathcal{V}$

Brenda Vaccaro

Born Brooklyn, New York, USA, 18 November, 1939

Oscar Nominations (1): Best Supporting Actress for Linda Riggs in *Jacqueline Susann's Once Is Not Enough* (Paramount, 1975)

Every so often a movie as glossy and ludicrous as *Once Is Not Enough* makes it into the Academy's lists – usually for costume design or art direction, but occasionally for acting as well. Brenda Vaccaro was the 'lucky lady' who found herself among 1975's supporting nominees for her kooky magazine editor who eventually gets fired after sleeping with her boss. Utter tosh, of course; Vaccaro was more effective a few years earlier as the 'classy' lady in *Midnight Cowboy* who embarks on a turn with stud Jon Voight and then complains about the quality of his performance.

Jo Van Fleet

Born Oakland, California, USA, 30 December 1919

Oscars (1): Best Supporting Actress for Kate in *East of Eden* (Warner Bros, 1955)

An Oscar for her début role as James Dean's brothel-madam mother in Kazan's *East of Eden* should have ensured a long career for Jo Van Fleet, but her subsequent screen roles have been few and far between and usually in the mother mould. Her real-life westerner Big Nose Kate in John Sturges' *Gunfight at the OK Corral* was something of a change of pace; so too was her second film with Kazan, *Wild River*, in which at the age of forty she played an eighty-year-old widow who refuses to move from her home when the Tennessee Valley Authority threaten to flood her land. A second Oscar or nomination would not have come amiss.

Diane Varsi

Born San Mateo, California, USA, 1937; died 1992

Oscar Nominations (1): Best Supporting Actress for Allison MacKenzie in *Peyton Place* (20th Century-Fox, 1957)

A 'Fox Showcase Star', i.e., one of the young performers the Fox studio was hoping to groom for stardom in the late fifties, Diane Varsi said thanks but no thanks after just four films, one Oscar nomination (for her writer who reveals the steamy secrets of Peyton Place) and a stormy relationship with her studio. Stating at the time that she was 'running away from destruction', she later tried for a comeback, but Hollywood studios proved they had long memories and her roles were few and far between. Of the Fox Showcase Group, only Joanne Woodward went on to greater things. In 1957, the year of *Peyton Place*, she won for best actress for *The Three Faces of Eve*. Diane Varsi lost to Miyoshi Umeki in *Sayonara*.

Robert Vaughn

Born New York City, USA, 30 November 1932

Oscar Nominations (1): Best Supporting Actor for Chet Gwynn in *The Young Philadelphians* (Warner Bros, 1959)

A household name on television in the sixties for his Napoleon Solo in *The Man from UNCLE* series, the urbane, smooth-talking Robert Vaughn managed to make inroads into the Academy lists just the once before his TV fame – for his wealthy young Korean war veteran who is accused of murder and defended in court by Paul Newman. No surprise that he got off! Not a great deal of note since, at least on the big screen, although his gunfighter who has lost his nerve in *The Magnificent Seven*, and his assistant district attorney forever on the back of honest cop Steve McQueen in *Bullitt* remain firmly etched in the memory.

☆

Jon Voight

Born Yonkers, New York, USA, 29 December 1938

Oscars (1): Best Actor for Luke Martin in *Coming Home* (United Artists, 1978)

Oscar Nominations (2): Best Actor for Joe Buck in *Midnight Cowboy* (United Artists, 1969) and Manny in *Runaway Train* (Cannon/Northbrook, 1985)

United Artists offered Jane Fonda a million dollars not to sign Jon Voight as the crippled Vietnam veteran in *Coming Home*. Not enough box-office clout, was their view. Find a star! Fonda refused, arguing that it was her project and she would cast who she wanted. It was a wise decision. Voight had been a class act since his Oscar-nominated New York stud in *Midnight Cowboy* and delivered in style, earning the year's best actor award and joining Fonda (best actress) on the Academy's roll of honour. He has since been nominated a third time for his tough-as-nails escaped convict on the run with fellow inmate Eric Roberts in *Runaway Train*.

Erich Von Stroheim

Born Vienna, Austria, 22 September 1885; died 1957

Oscar Nominations (1): Best Supporting Actor for Max Von Mayerling in *Sunset Boulevard* (Paramount, 1950)

When Billy Wilder lured former silent director Von Stroheim back to mainstream Hollywood by casting him as Rommel in *Five Graves to Cairo*, he welcomed him with the words: 'It's an honour to be directing you Mr Von Stroheim. You were always ten years ahead of your time.' To which Von Stroheim replied: 'Twenty, Mr Wilder, twenty!' Popularly known as 'the man you love to hate' and famous for his closely cropped bullet head, Von Stroheim appeared again for Wilder seven years later, this time as Max, the devoted butler and former husband of faded silent movie queen Gloria Swanson. It marked the only occasion the Academy honoured Von Stroheim, who, as always when he worked in Hollywood, emerged a loser, George Sanders taking the supporting award for *All About Eve*. Allowed to show his directorial genius only in his series of memorable silent epics – *Foolish Wives, Greed, The Wedding March* – Von Stroheim spent most of his later years in France, where he was presented with an award somewhat more significant than the Oscar, the French Legion of Honor, for his services to the film art.

Max Von Sydow

Born Lund, Sweden, 10 April 1929

Oscar Nominations (1): Best Actor for Pappa Lasse in *Pelle the Conqueror* (A Per Holst/Kaerne Films Prod-Denmark, 1988)

It seemed for a while as though the gaunt Max Von Sydow spent most of his time playing chess with Death, agonising in deep contemplation on remote islands and debating as to whether or not he was approaching madness. That was in his Ingmar Bergman days, before Hollywood got hold of him and cast him as Christ in *The Greatest Story Ever Told*, a hired assassin in *Three Days of the Condor* and Ming the Merciless in *Flash Gordon* – to name but three of many. His best results, though, have still been in Scandinavia, where he played his Oscar-nominated role of the immigrant widower who, with his young son, tries to make a new life for himself in early twentieth-century Denmark. A leading actor in a dozen films by Bergman, he appeared in two that earned the director the best foreign-language film award – *The Virgin Spring* and *Through a Glass Darkly*.

W

Christopher Walken

Born Astoria, Queens, New York, USA, 31 March 1943

Oscars (1): Best Supporting Actor for Nikanor Chevotarevich ('Nick') in
The Deer Hunter (EMI/Universal, 1978)

His young Pennsylvania steelworker destroyed by war in Cimino's Vietnam
epic *The Deer Hunter* was arguably the finest character performance in
American cinema in the seventies. All the more disappointing, then, that
Christopher Walken has failed to live up to his initial promise and really
only made his mark as a couple of super-villains in mainstream cinema, one
up against James Bond in *A View to a Kill*, the other at odds with Batman in
Batman Returns. His quietly sadistic oddball drill sergeant in Neil Simon's
satirical *Biloxi Blues* revealed a talent for comedy, but the quality roles have
been few and far between.

Julie Walters

Born Birmingham, England, 22 February 1950

Oscar Nominations (1): Best Actress for Rita in *Educating Rita* (Acorn,
1983)

One of those actresses who lights up a scene no matter how indifferent the
material, Julie Walters made a dream screen début as the working-class
hairdresser who enrols in an English course run by university professor
Michael Caine and succeeds in changing not only her life but his as well. A
Tony-winner for the role on stage, she couldn't quite match it with an
Oscar, earning her nomination in the year the Academy finally decided to
award the prize to Shirley MacLaine, who had been waiting patiently since
her first nomination twenty-five years before. Walters' brothel madam in
Personal Services and her American dancer in *Stepping Out* have been the
pick of her subsequent screen performances.

Jack Warden

Born Newark, New Jersey, USA, 18 September 1920

Oscar Nominations (2): Best Supporting Actor for Lester in *Shampoo* (Columbia, 1975) and Max Corkle in *Heaven Can Wait* (Paramount, 1978)

One of those character actors who has 'saved' films just by being in them, Jack Warden has twice been bemused by the screen antics of Warren Beatty and twice been Oscar-nominated for his bemusement – first as the philandering husband of Lee Grant who can't quite make out whether hairdresser Beatty is straight or gay, then as a football manager who is equally undecided as to whether Beatty has returned from the dead or is just plain out of his mind! Overlooked on both occasions by the Academy, he has been described by one director as 'being so versatile he could play a baby if you put a bib on him'. A well-known face since the fifties, he first came to public attention in *12 Angry Men* as the salesman jury member anxious to find the defendant guilty of murder so that he can get to a ball game in time.

☆

H. B. Warner

Born London, England, 26 October 1876; died 1958

Oscar Nominations (1): Best Supporting Actor for Chang in *Lost Horizon* (Columbia, 1937)

Hollywood legend has it that when he was cast as Christ in DeMille's silent *King of Kings*, an inebriated H. B. Warner was discovered naked in his dressing room, entwined around an equally naked female extra. The stone-cold-sober extra demanded money to keep quiet about the fact that she had slept with Christ, DeMille paid up and Warner went on to receive acclaim for his screen performance which may or may not have been better than the one he'd achieved off camera. His sole Oscar nomination was for his number two lama, Chang, in Frank Capra's *Lost Horizon*, although post-war audiences remember him best for the same director's *It's a Wonderful Life* as the grief-stricken pharmacist who, because of the news of the death of his son, prescribes the wrong medicine for a patient. In Hollywood from 1914, and described by Capra as 'a fine actor of courtly grace', he was used by Billy Wilder as one of the 'waxworks' who play their weekly game of bridge with Gloria Swanson in *Sunset Boulevard*.

Lesley Ann Warren

Born New York, USA, 16 August 1947

Oscar Nominations (1): Best Supporting Actress for Norma in *Victor/Victoria* (MGM, 1982)

Sizzlingly effective as the sexpot girlfriend of gangster James Garner in *Victor/Victoria*, and a knockout with the number 'Chicago, Illinois', Lesley Ann Warren seemed set for big things when she made it to the Oscar lists in 1982. Unfortunately, what should have been a great launching point for a lively career proved to be something of a damp squib. The Oscar went to Jessica Lange for *Tootsie*, the quality follow-up roles did not materialise and the films that did, among them *Cop* and *Life Stinks*, were of little consequence. A star of Disney family films in the seventies, Warren was a regular in the popular TV series *Mission Impossible*. She has been seen mainly in TV films in recent years.

Denzel Washington

Born Mount Vernon, New York, USA, 28 December 1954

Oscars (1): Best Supporting Actor for Trip in *Glory* (TriStar/Columbia, 1989)

Oscar Nominations (2): Best Supporting Actor for Steve Biko in *Cry Freedom* (Universal, 1987); Best Actor for the title role in *Malcolm X* (Warner Bros, 1992)

Along with Morgan Freeman and Whoopi Goldberg, one of the three black actors to have really made his mark in Hollywood in the last decade, Denzel Washington has managed to steer clear of black stereotypes and essay a rich variety of characters, earning an Oscar for one of them – the embittered former slave in *Glory* – and nominations for two more – the South African activist Steve Biko, and the black revolutionary leader Malcolm X. More recently he enjoyed a welcome change of pace as Don Pedro, Prince of Aragon, in *Much Ado About Nothing*. No black actor has yet won two Academy Awards. Denzel Washington might conceivably be the first to do so.

Ethel Waters

Born Chester, Pennsylvania, USA, 31 October 1896; died 1977

Oscar Nominations (1): Best Supporting Actress for Granny Dysey Johnson in *Pinky* (20th Century-Fox, 1949)

'I hate to sing. I do it for a living. I'd rather act,' said Ethel Waters when looking back on her career as a musical star and dramatic actress. Certainly it is as an actress that she'll best be remembered, as far as the cinema is concerned, earning acclaim for her grandmother of Jeanne Crain, the girl who passes for white in *Pinky*, and for repeating her Broadway role of the eloquent cook of the Southern household in *The Member of the Wedding*. She was Oscar-nominated for the former role, deservedly so; she was overlooked for the latter, which goes down in the debit column as one of the Academy's most unfortunate oversights.

Sam Waterston

Born Cambridge, Massachusetts, USA, 15 November 1940

Oscar Nominations (1): Best Actor for Sydney Schanberg in *The Killing Fields* (Enigma/Warner Bros, 1984)

Thoughtful, intelligent, discerning . . . the virtues of the slim, gaunt-looking Sam Waterston have tended to have been seen to their best advantage on TV rather than in the cinema, notably as the atomic physicist Robert Oppenheimer, and as William L. Shirer, author of *The Rise and Fall of the Third Reich.* He was, though, a near-perfect Nick Carraway for Jack Clayton in *The Great Gatsby*, and has been a regular in minor roles for Woody Allen over the years. No Oscar mentions for his work with Allen. Just a nomination for his *New York Times* reporter saved from death by the bravery of interpreter Dith Pran.

Lucile Watson

Born Quebec, Canada, 27 May 1879; died 1962

Oscar Nominations (1): Best Supporting Actress for Fanny Farrelly in *Watch on the Rhine* (Warner Bros, 1943)

A bit domineering at times, haughty at others, and quite impeccable as 'Lady this' or 'Lady that', Lucile Watson belonged to Hollywood's grand old ladies club of the 1940s, reaching the nominations lists just the once as Bette Davis' Washington mother in *Watch on the Rhine*. Too bad it was 1943, the year of the peasant (Katina Paxinou in *For Whom the Bell Tolls*) and not the sophisticate. Not that she let it worry her. She carried on undaunted in similar vein for another seventeen films before calling it a day at seventy-two.

John Wayne

Born Winterset, Iowa, USA, 26 May 1907; died 1979

Oscars (1): Best Actor for Rooster Cogburn in *True Grit* (Paramount, 1969)

Oscar Nominations (1): Best Actor for Sgt John M. Stryker in *Sands of Iwo Jima* (Republic, 1949)

'Come up and see a fat old man sometime!' yelled John Wayne at the close of *True Grit*. As director Henry Hathaway froze the frame of man and horse in mid-leap it suddenly seemed like a celebration of a lifetime's work. The Academy certainly thought so. On Oscar night Barbra Streisand read out the words many in Hollywood thought they would never hear: 'And the winner is John Wayne!' to which the western star exclaimed, 'Wow. If I'd have known, I'd have put that eyepatch on thirty-five years earlier.' Nominated just once before, for his battle-hardened World War II Marine sergeant (but never for any of his western roles with John Ford), Wayne's down-to-earth approach to film-making was summed up by his comment: 'There's too much pretentious nonsense talked about the artistic problems of making pictures. I've never had a goddamn artistic problem in my life and I've worked with the best of them.'

Note: Wayne did not make the nominations for his direction of his epic *The Alamo* but did earn recognition as a producer when the film was nominated as one of the five best pictures of the year.

Sigourney Weaver

Born New York, USA, 8 October 1949

Oscar Nominations (3): Best Actress for Ripley in *Aliens* (20th Century-Fox, 1986) and Dian Fossey in *Gorillas in the Mist* (Warner Bros/Universal, 1988); Best Supporting Actress for Katherine Parker in *Working Girl* (20th Century-Fox, 1988)

The general rule of thumb regarding double Oscar nominations in the same year has been that if a performer is named in both the major and supporting categories (and for different films), he or she will almost certainly pick up one of the awards. Fay Bainter, Teresa Wright, Jessica Lange, Al Pacino and Holly Hunter have all benefited in this way. The exceptions have been Emma Thompson and the unlucky Sigourney Weaver, who in 1988 was up for her Dian Fossey in *Gorillas in the Mist* and her double-crossing Wall Street executive in *Working Girl*. She lost, first to Jodie Foster (*The Accused*) and then to Geena Davis (*The Accidental Tourist*). Reprising her role of astronaut Ripley didn't do her much good either. Destroying monsters on other planets has never been regarded as a serious occupation, and she was in the lists basically to make up the numbers. At her most effective in serious, thoughtful films, she nonetheless managed to take the breath away as the possessed 'Gate Keeper' who mutates into a hell hound in *Ghostbusters*.

Clifton Webb

Born Indianapolis, Indiana, USA, 19 November 1891; died 1966

Oscar Nominations (3): Best Supporting Actor for Waldo Lydecker in *Laura* (20th Century-Fox, 1944) and Elliott Templeton in *The Razor's Edge* (20th Century-Fox, 1946); Best Actor for Lynn Belvedere in *Sitting Pretty* (20th Century-Fox, 1948)

'Laura considered me the wisest, the wittiest, the most interesting man she'd ever met. I was in complete accord with her on that point.' Only the waspish delivery of the suave Clifton Webb could do justice to such lines, and the writers at the Fox studio delighted in supplying them for nearly twenty years. Three times an Oscar nominee, Webb was honoured for his acid New York columnist Waldo Lydecker, Somerset Maugham's pompous socialite Elliott Templeton and perhaps most famously his babysitter Lynn Belvedere, who in *Sitting Pretty* gained a place in movie history (and the eternal thanks of frustrated parents across the world) by turning a bowl of oatmeal over the head of the baby who has been peppering him with cereal throughout breakfast! Born Webb Parmallee Hollenbeck, and a famous singer and dancer on Broadway before entering films, Webb was well known for his elegant taste in clothes. He was credited with having introduced into the man's wardrobe such items as the white dresscoat dinner jacket and the double-breasted waistcoat.

Tuesday Weld

Born New York City, USA, 27 August 1943

Oscar Nominations (1): Best Supporting Actress for Katherine Dunn in *Looking for Mr Goodbar* (Paramount, 1977)

Just the one nomination – for her impulsive older sister of Diane Keaton in *Looking for Mr Goodbar* – is the sum of Tuesday Weld's Oscar achievements. Not much, considering she's been around for more than forty years, enlivened many inferior films with her predatory teenagers and sex kittens and made entertaining ones seem even better with her range of performance. Keaton had the major role in *Goodbar* – that of a repressed teacher who seeks excitement in singles bars and dangerous one-night stands; Weld was the controversial film's only acting nominee.

Orson Welles

Born Kenosha, Wisconsin, USA, 6 May 1915; died 1985

Oscar Nominations (1): Best Actor for Charles Foster Kane in *Citizen Kane* (RKO, 1941)

'I started at the top and worked my way down,' Orson Welles would say, usually with a chuckle, occasionally with sadness, when talking to the press. As far as the Oscars were concerned, it was an all-too-accurate assessment, for after *Citizen Kane* (apart from an honorary award in 1970) the Academy never looked in his direction again, even though, in that memorable year of 1941, he was nominated four times – as producer, director, writer and actor. He succeeded only in the writing category (an award he shared with Herman Mankiewicz), losing out as best actor to Gary Cooper's *Sergeant York*. Frequently at odds with the Hollywood establishment, he was subsequently passed over for his suave black marketeer Harry Lime in *The Third Man* and his corrupt sheriff Hank Quinlan in *Touch of Evil*. Prone to obesity (he weighed twenty-two stone when he died), he consoled himself in later years by making huge sums for his voice-over commercials for lager and sherry. He said of the Hollywood of the eighties: 'We live in a snake pit here . . . I hate it but I just don't allow myself to face the fact that I hold it in contempt because it keeps turning out to be the only place to go.'

Oskar Werner

Born Vienna, Austria, 13 November 1922; died 1984

Oscar Nominations (1): Best Actor for Dr Schumann in *Ship of Fools* (Columbia, 1965)

To earn your only Oscar nomination in a year which saw Richard Burton, Rod Steiger and a boozy Lee Marvin all up for the award, and all in top form, is, to say the least, unlucky. Oskar Werner would have been better served had he made it into the supporting lists for his brilliant little East German agent in *The Spy Who Came in from the Cold*. As it was, his dying ship's doctor embroiled in a romance with Simone Signoret in *Ship of Fools* was very much the outsider of the 1965 bunch. He was overlooked in 1962 for his Jules who had the good fortune to share Jeanne Moreau with Henry Serre in Truffaut's masterpiece *Jules and Jim*.

Stuart Whitman

Born San Francisco, USA, 1 February 1926

Oscar Nominations (1): Best Actor for Jim Fuller in *The Mark* (Stross-Buchman-Continental, British, 1961)

A rugged, goodish actor who made some rugged, goodish movies for Fox during his contract years at the studio, Stuart Whitman took a chance by accepting a role that would be controversial even in today's cinema – that of an alleged sex criminal who has served a three-year sentence for molesting a ten-year-old girl and is struggling to rehabilitate himself. His acting won him a nomination but went unrewarded in April 1962, when the Academy opted for Maximilian Schell in *Judgment at Nuremberg*. Whitman has apparently been more astute in his financial investments than in his general choice of movies (of which he has made more than a hundred), and at the last count had amassed a personal fortune of some $100 million.

James Whitmore

Born White Plains, New York, USA, 1 October 1921

Oscar Nominations (2): Best Supporting Actor for Sergeant Kinnie in *Battleground* (MGM, 1949); Best Actor for President Truman in *Give 'Em Hell Harry!* (Theatrovision/Avco Embassy, 1975)

Some called him a Spencer Tracy lookalike, which didn't really make much sense because if you've got one Tracy why do you need another? Others saw him as one of the best character actors in Hollywood, who never quite got the breaks he deserved. His two Oscar nominations came twenty-five years apart, the first for his tough platoon sergeant, battling it out in the Bastogne in the final days of World War Iī, the second for his magnificent one-man show as Harry Truman. He lost on both occasions, although when one recalls his soft-shoe shuffle with Keenan Wynn to

'Brush Up Your Shakespeare' in *Kiss Me Kate*, it doesn't seem to matter all that much. Three minutes of musical magic made up for all the lack of Oscar success!

Dame May Whitty

Born Liverpool, England, 19 June 1865; died 1948

Oscar Nominations (2): Best Supporting Actress for Mrs Bramson in *Night Must Fall* (MGM, 1937) and Lady Beldon in *Mrs Miniver* (MGM, 1942)

Dame May Whitty said of her role in *Night Must Fall*: 'It's just a thriller and won't run. The part is an old beast in a wheelchair but I'd better do it.' She made the right decision. Emlyn Williams' play did run and allowed her to play the old beast (an elderly woman terrified by a young psychopath who has charmed his way into her house) in London, on Broadway and eventually in Hollywood, where, at the age of seventy-two, she earned herself an Oscar nomination first time out. Seen mostly as aunts, mothers and grandmothers, she was a regular at many American studios during the forties (appearing in twenty-seven films in just eleven years) but primarily at MGM, where she earned her second Oscar nomination as the lady of the manor in Wyler's *Mrs Miniver*. Much loved for her mischievous Miss Froy, who disappears without trace in Hitchcock's classic *The Lady Vanishes*, she revealed her villainous side in the B-movie *My Name Is Julia Ross*, in which she played a scheming dowager with a psychologically unstable son who plans a nasty fate for her new secretary. Humorous and in no way pompous in real life, Dame May once summed up her acting career as 'a bit of variety and sandwiches'.

Richard Widmark

Born Sunrise, Minnesota, USA, 26 December 1914

Oscar Nominations (1): Best Supporting Actor for Tommy Udo in *Kiss of Death* (20th Century-Fox, 1947)

It was as a 'mean bastard' that the public liked him best, and it was for the ultimate in mean bastards, the giggling psychopath Tommy Udo (his début role) that Richard Widmark received his sole Oscar nomination. After that he never took the Academy's eye again, although his vicious racist hoodlum in *No Way Out* and, in later, mellower years, his ageing rodeo cowboy in *When the Legends Die* were both worthy of consideration. In the western *Alvarez Kelly* he showed that he had lost none of his old sadism when, as a Confederate guerrilla, he tries to persuade Bill Holden to rustle 2,500 head of cattle. When Holden refuses he shoots off one of his fingers and says, 'You have ten days to decide. One finger per day!'

Dianne Wiest

Born Kansas City, Missouri, USA, 28 March 1948

Oscars (2): Best Supporting Actress for Holly in *Hannah and Her Sisters* (Orion, 1986) and Helen Sinclair in *Bullets Over Broadway* (Miramax, 1994)

Oscar Nominations (1): Best Supporting Actress for Helen in *Parenthood* (Universal, 1989)

As neurotic as they come in her first Oscar-winning role, as Mia Farrow's desperate showbiz sister trying to start up a catering business, and as far removed from reality as it was possible to get in her second, as the *grande dame* actress in *Bullets Over Broadway*, Dianne Wiest must have wondered why she was passed over for arguably her best Woody Allen portrayal, as the young Woody's Aunt Beah, always searching for her ideal man in *Radio Days*. She did get a third nomination but not for a Woody Allen film – for her divorcee mother with a mountain of problems in *Parenthood*.

Jack Wild

Born 1952

Oscar Nominations (1): Best Supporting Actor for the Artful Dodger in *Oliver!* (Columbia, 1968)

''Ere 'e is, Fagin, my friend Oliver Twist!' Any number of child actors playing the Artful Dodger have uttered Dickens' words on screen over the years. Only the fifteen-year-old Jack Wild has been able to accompany them with a chorus or two by Lionel Bart. Not that it did him much good on awards night; an actor old enough to be Wild's grandad, the sixty-one-year-old Jack Albertson, took the supporting Oscar for *The Subject Was Roses*. An occasional child actor in the early seventies, Wild was seen recently in *Robin Hood, Prince of Thieves*.

Cornel Wilde

Born New York City, USA, 13 October 1915; died 1989

Oscar Nominations (1): Best Actor for Frederic Chopin in *A Song to Remember* (Columbia, 1945)

American critic James Agee alleged that Cornel Wilde had just two facial expressions and used them both too often. The verdict was perhaps a little harsh, but there's no doubting that Wilde was fortunate to break through to stardom for his Chopin in Columbia's bizarre biopic of 1945. Coughing blood on to the white keyboard and having to endure such insults as 'Discontinue that so-called *polonaise* jumble you've been playing for days' from Merle Oberon's George Sand, he suffered enough to earn an Oscar nomination but lost to Ray Milland, who went through another kind of private hell in *The Lost Weekend*. Best known for his swashbucklers and period dramas, he later emerged as a highly competent independent producer-director of pictures that dealt with environmental concerns, e.g., *The Naked Prey* and *No Blade of Grass*. An expert swordsman who qualified for the US fencing team in the 1936 Olympics, he was of Hungarian ancestry and spoke several languages. In his heyday he was popularly supposed to sleep with a sword under his pillow and to breakfast in doublet and hose!

Gene Wilder

Born Milwaukee, Wisconsin, USA, 11 June 1935

Oscar Nominations (1): Best Supporting Actor for Leo Bloom in *The Producers* (Avco-Embassy, 1968)

The kind of comedian who gets his laughs by conveying a delayed hysteria that sometimes comes close to apoplexy, Gene Wilder has only once entered the acting lists – for his meek accountant who in *The Producers* conspires with impoverished producer Zero Mostel to make a fortune out of a flop Broadway musical (the appalling *Springtime for Hitler*), only to see their hopes dashed when the show is a smash. Nothing, unfortunately, for Mostel, even though he had some of Mel Brooks' best lines: 'How could this happen?' he wails. 'I was so careful. I picked the wrong play, the wrong director, the wrong cast. Where did I go *right*?'

Note: Wilder shared a 1974 writing nomination with Mel Brooks for their screenplay of *Young Frankenstein*.

Cara Williams

Born Brooklyn, New York, USA, 29 June 1925

Oscar Nominations (1): Best Supporting Actress for 'The Woman' in *The Defiant Ones* (United Artists, 1958)

No one really remembers her in *The Defiant Ones*. They remember convicts Tony Curtis and Sidney Poitier shackled by the wrist and on the run. And Theodore Bikel as the sheriff pursuing them. Even the baying dogs. But the woman? Where and who was she? She came in somewhere around the halfway mark, a lonely mother starved of affection who gives solace to Tony Curtis and almost sends Sidney Poitier to his death in quicksands. Only a few scenes, but the nomination was hers. Not the award, though; the rather more reserved Wendy Hiller took that for *Separate Tables*.

Robin Williams

Born Chicago, USA, 21 July 1952

Oscar Nominations (3): Best Actor for Adrian Cronauer in *Good Morning, Vietnam* (Touchstone, 1987), John Keating in *Dead Poets Society* (Touchstone, 1989) and Parry in *The Fisher King* (TriStar, 1991)

A 'love him or loathe him' kind of actor, Robin Williams either drives audiences crazy with his ghastly mugging and constant overdrive or has them in fits and rolling in the aisles. Most feel he was at his best as the frenzied armed forces disc jockey in *Good Morning, Vietnam* and the schoolteacher forever telling his students to 'seize the day' in *Dead Poets Society*, although his mystical vagrant Parry in Terry Gilliam's *The Fisher King* remains for many his most substantial screen achievement. Dressing up as *Mrs Doubtfire* didn't do a lot for him, but an Oscar would seem to be his for the taking once he tones down a bit and the right role comes along.

Chill Wills

Born Seagoville, Texas, USA, 18 July 1903; died 1978

Oscar Nominations (1): Best Supporting Actor for 'Beekeeper' in *The Alamo* (United Artists, 1960)

Sometimes cruelly referred to as being best known as the voice of Francis the Talking Mule (the animal 'star' of a series of Universal programmers of the fifties), the gravel-voiced Chill Wills lent his amiable personality to more than a hundred films, most of them westerns. The only actor to emerge with a nomination from John Wayne's epic *The Alamo* (he was cast as comic relief as a character called 'Beekeeper') he hired his own press agent to help support his cause. The move created embarrassment when one of the ads publicising his performance included a picture of the cast of the film, superimposed with the words: 'We of *The Alamo* cast are praying harder – than the real Texans prayed for their lives in the Alamo – for Chill Wills to win the supporting Oscar'. God wasn't listening. Peter Ustinov won for providing the comic relief in *Spartacus*.

Paul Winfield

Born Los Angeles, USA, 22 May 1940

Oscar Nominations (1): Best Actor for Nathan Lee Morgan in *Sounder* (20th Century-Fox, 1972)

Another of the actors to have benefited from the direction of Martin Ritt, Paul Winfield would, in any normal year, have been a strong contender for his black sharecropper jailed because of stealing food to feed his family in 1930s Louisiana. Nineteen seventy-two was, unfortunately, not a normal year. Brando (*The Godfather*), Olivier and Caine (*Sleuth*) and O'Toole (*The Ruling Class*) were all in contention, and for Winfield it was really a case of turning up and enjoying the evening. Which he did! No nominations since, more's the pity.

Oprah Winfrey

Born Kosciusko, Mississippi, USA, 29 January 1954

Oscar Nominations (1): Best Supporting Actress for Sofia in *The Color Purple* (Warner Bros, 1985)

Nowadays America's most popular TV talk show host, but back in 1985 an actress still finding her feet as the strong-willed and rebellious Sofia in Spielberg's *The Color Purple*. Quincy Jones was the man responsible for getting her into the picture, having seen her host *AM Chicago* just prior to filming; at Oscar time she and Margaret Avery (see p. 14) both figured among the year's supporting actress nominees. The studio vote was split. Neither won.

Debra Winger

Born Cleveland, Ohio, USA, 17 May 1955

Oscar Nominations (3): Best Actress for Paula Pokrifki in *An Officer and a Gentleman* (Paramount, 1982), Emma Horton in *Terms of Endearment* (Paramount, 1983) and Joy Gresham in *Shadowlands* (Savoy Pictures, 1993)

As talented as any contemporary American actress when working from the right script and with the right director (not always the easiest of combinations to find), Debra Winger's gutsy, down-to-earth characters seem at times so real that they might have been photographed walking down a small-town street or relaxing in a local bar. No one has yet managed to make the most of her fiery persona, although the Academy has nominated her three times – for her millworker set on Richard Gere, her dying daughter of Shirley MacLaine, and the American lover of children's writer C. S. Lewis (arguably the best of the three) in *Shadowlands*. No Oscars as yet, although it would have been interesting to see what she would have made of the Holly Hunter part in *Broadcast News* had pregnancy not forced her to withdraw from the role. Jack Nicholson's assessment of her talents: 'Real smart . . . dedicated . . . resourceful . . . the girl's got boom!'

Mare Winningham

Born Phoenix, Arizona, USA, 6 May 1959

Oscar Nominations (1): Best Supporting Actress for the title role of *Georgia* (Miramax, 1995)

It was the name of Jennifer Jason Leigh that was on everyone's lips when the film *Georgia* was mentioned as a possible Oscar contender. In the end, though, it was the little-known Mare Winningham who made the lists, for her famed country singer who carries her success with ease and always puts it second to her husband and family. Rather different from her tormented sister Leigh, a rock 'n' roll urchin dependent on drugs and booze, who lacks her sister's talent and envies her maturity and success. Sibling rivalry at its most intense! The fairest solution would have been to have nominated both Leigh and Winningham in the best actress category. As it was, Winningham finished up with a supporting nod and Leigh with nothing at all, a situation with which she was all too familiar, having been overlooked by the Academy just a year before for her superb portrayal of Dorothy Parker.

Kate Winslet

Born 1975

Oscar Nominations (1): Best Supporting Actress for Marianne Dashwood in *Sense and Sensibility* (Mirage/Columbia, 1995)

The women rated highly among the nominations for *Sense and Sensibility*: Emma Thompson (actress and screenplay) nabbed two, producer Lindsay Doran one and Kate Winslet a supporting nod for her tempestuous young Marianne who is swept off her feet by a bounder, finds that good looks and youthful charm aren't all they're cracked up to be and in the end settles for sombre bachelor Alan Rickman, a wiser and happier woman. A name for the future (she was one of the notorious New Zealand girls whose obsessions drive them to murder in *Heavenly Creatures*), she lost on awards night to the hot favourite, Mira Sorvino.

Shelley Winters

Born St Louis, Missouri, USA, 18 August 1922

Oscars (2): Best Supporting Actress for Mrs Van Daan in *The Diary of Anne Frank* (20th Century-Fox, 1959) and Rose-Ann D'Arcey in *A Patch of Blue* (MGM, 1965)

Oscar Nominations (2): Best Actress for Alice Tripp in *A Place in the Sun* (Paramount, 1951); Best Supporting Actress for Belle Rosen in *The Poseidon Adventure* (20th Century-Fox, 1972)

'You gotta play mothers,' said Shelley Winters when she was getting on a bit. 'If you don't you won't get a long career in Hollywood.' She took her own advice, winning awards for two very different moms – Mrs Van Daan, one of those trapped with the Anne Frank family in George Stevens' film of 1959, and the amoral mother who tries to ruin her daughter's relationship with a black man in *A Patch of Blue*. She might well have made it three had she won in 1972 for her Jewish momma who, in *The Poseidon Adventure*, saves Gene Hackman from drowning at the cost of her own life. A best actress nominee for her factory girl who finds herself in the way of

Montgomery Clift's progress in *A Place in the Sun*, she was and has remained a talented comedienne. She has said of wedded bliss: 'In Hollywood all marriages are happy. It's trying to live together afterwards that causes the problems.'

Natalie Wood

Born San Francisco, USA, 20 July 1938; died 1981

Oscar Nominations (3): Best Supporting Actress for Judy in *Rebel Without a Cause* (Warner Bros, 1955); Best Actress for Wilma Dean Loomis in *Splendor in the Grass* (Warner Bros, 1961) and Angie Rossini in *Love with the Proper Stranger* (Paramount, 1963)

The nervous smile, gently hysterical laugh and innocent, appealing eyes worked their magic on audiences in the sixties, just as they had a decade earlier when Natalie Wood appeared as a child star. They worked their magic too on the Academy voters, who nominated her three times – for her troubled teenage friend of Jimmy Dean in *Rebel Without a Cause*, her sexually frustrated high-school girl in Kazan's *Splendor in the Grass* and her pregnant girlfriend (her most affecting role) of bemused musician Steve McQueen, whose method of proposing marriage was 'better wed than dead'! Unfortunately, she was also considered by some to be too limited in style and was unlucky enough to be adopted by the *Harvard Lampoon* who initiated the annual Natalie Wood award for the worst performance by an actress. She died tragically, drowning in a yachting accident in 1981.

Peggy Wood

Born Brooklyn, New York, USA, 9 February 1892; died 1978

Oscar Nominations (1): Best Supporting Actress for the Mother Abbess in *The Sound of Music* (20th Century-Fox, 1965)

Nuns two, Austrian aristocrats and Nazis nil! That was the final score when the acting nominations were announced for *The Sound of Music*, Julie Andrews earning her second nomination in consecutive years for her novice Maria, and being joined on the lists by Peggy Wood, whose main contribution to the proceedings was to sing 'Climb Every Mountain'. For many viewers who had suffered silently and endured the film's 174 minutes, that's exactly what they felt they had been doing. Others were in seventh heaven. Only an occasional performer in movies, Peggy Wood earned fame on Broadway in operatic roles in *Maytime* and *Bitter Sweet*. She also featured in the TV series *Mama* (1949–57).

Alfre Woodard

Born Tulsa, Oklahoma, USA, 8 November 1953

Oscar Nominations (1): Best Supporting Actress for Geechee in *Cross Creek* (Universal, 1983)

She's known these days for her work on TV in *Hill Street Blues* and *St Elsewhere*, but in the early eighties she was more or less unknown until she was cast as the young black housekeeper of Marjorie Kinnan Rawlings in *Cross Creek*. The result was an Oscar nomination, which wasn't too surprising considering the film's director was Martin Ritt, who more than any other film-maker brought quality roles to black actors in the seventies and eighties, e.g., James Earl Jones in *The Great White Hope* and Paul Winfield and Cicely Tyson in *Sounder*. Woodard came in behind Linda Hunt (*The Year of Living Dangerously*) on Oscar night, but subsequent Emmys for *Hill Street Blues* and *LA Law* have softened the blow somewhat.

James Woods

Born Vernal, Utah, USA, 18 April 1947

Oscar Nominations (1): Best Actor for Richard Boyle in *Salvador* (Hemdale, 1986)

Just the once has James Woods made it to the Oscar lists, but once has been enough to reveal that his talents lie somewhat beyond the hoods, crooks and menacing figures he has usually been required to play on screen. His nomination was for his sleazy newshound who takes off with his out-of-work disc jockey buddy James Belushi to make some quick money in El Salvador, only to find himself face to face with Fascism and the oppression of a people embroiled in an horrific civil war. A strong argument could be made that Woods deserved the 1986 nod; the Academy voters, though, were in sentimental mood. Paul Newman it was, for *The Color of Money*.

Joanne Woodward

Born Thomasville, Georgia, USA, 27 February 1930

Oscars (1): Best Actress for Eve in *The Three Faces of Eve* (20th Century-Fox, 1957)

Oscar Nominations (3): Best Actress for Rachel Cameron in *Rachel, Rachel* (Warner Bros, 1968), Rita Walden in *Summer Wishes, Winter Dreams* (Columbia, 1973) and India Bridge in *Mr and Mrs Bridge* (Miramax, 1990)

An Oscar-winner at twenty-seven for what amounted to three performances in one – as the split personality housewife in *The Three Faces of Eve* – Joanne Woodward has tended to crop up in the nominations about once every decade: in the sixties for her spinster schoolteacher finding love for the first time, the seventies for her chic wife suffering a mid-life crisis, and then the nineties for her submissive, strait-laced Kansas wife in *Mr and Mrs Bridge*. Only in the eighties was she missing, something of an oversight by the Academy, who ignored her Southern belle mother Amanda in Paul Newman's 1987 remake of *The Glass Menagerie*. Directed by hubby on three occasions (*Rachel, Rachel, The Effect of Gamma Rays on Man-in-the-Moon Marigolds* and *Menagerie*), she has appeared with him on several occasions on screen but had to wait for close on thirty years before he at last placed an Oscar (for *The Color of Money*) alongside hers on the mantelpiece.

Monty Woolley

Born New York City, USA, 17 August 1888; died 1963

Oscar Nominations (2): Best Actor for Howard in *The Pied Piper* (20th Century-Fox, 1942); Best Supporting Actor for Colonel Smollett in *Since You Went Away* (Selznick/United Artists, 1944)

Rudeness was his trademark, so too was his acerbic wit. He employed them both in more than thirty films, earning nominations for two now all-but-forgotten roles – his prickly Englishman who helps some British children escape the Nazis in the spring of 1940, and his crusty old boarder of Claudette Colbert – but missing out for his most famous role, that of the insufferable theatre critic Sheridan Whiteside who insults everyone he comes in contact with in *The Man Who Came to Dinner*. Nurse Mary Wickes was the unluckiest cast member. Roared a ferocious Woolley: 'You have the touch of a sex-starved cobra . . . My Great-Aunt Jennifer ate a box of chocolates every day of her life. She lived to be 102 and when she had been dead three days she looked healthier than you do now!'

Teresa Wright

Born New York City, USA, 27 October 1918

Oscars (1): Best Supporting Actress for Carol Beldon in *Mrs Miniver* (MGM, 1942)

Oscar Nominations (2): Best Supporting Actress for Alexandra Giddens in *The Little Foxes* (RKO, 1941); Best Actress for Eleanor Gehrig in *The Pride of the Yankees* (RKO, 1942)

A remarkable golden period when she was just twenty-four seemed to indicate there was a big future ahead for the charming Teresa Wright, whose sweet nature enhanced several small-town movies of the forties but whose luck seemed to run out, at least as far as the Oscars were concerned, once the war was over. A winner for her daughter-in-law of Greer Garson's *Mrs Miniver*, and nominated the same year as best actress for her wife of baseball hero Lou Gehrig, she also made the lists for her début role as the luckless daughter of Bette Davis and Herbert Marshall in William Wyler's *The Little Foxes*. Quite how she was overlooked for her adoring niece of suave murderer Joe Cotten in Hitchcock's *Shadow of a Doubt* remains a mystery. She appeared for a third time for Wyler as the girlfriend of returning war veteran Dana Andrews in *The Best Years of Our Lives*.

Margaret Wycherly

Born London, England, 1881; died 1956

Oscar Nominations (1): Best Supporting Actress for Mother York in *Sergeant York* (Warner Bros, 1941)

An actress who thrived on playing devoted mothers on screen, Margaret Wycherly came closest to winning an Oscar when Howard Hawks cast her as the Tennessee ma of World War I pacifist hero Sergeant York. Her real *tour de force*, however, occurred eight years later, when Raoul Walsh suggested that she change her sharp little features from sympathetic to darkly murderous in his gangster movie *White Heat*. At the film's climax, the mother-fixated James Cagney blasts away on top of a giant gas tank and blows himself to smithereens with the cry 'Top of the world, Ma!' Everyone remembers the scene. Everyone remembers Cagney. No one remembers who played Ma. Answer: Margaret Wycherly.

Jane Wyman

Born St Joseph, Missouri, USA, 4 January 1914

Oscars (1): Best Actress for Belinda McDonald in *Johnny Belinda* (Warner Bros, 1948)

Oscar Nominations (3): Best Actress for Ma Baxter in *The Yearling* (MGM, 1946), Louise in *The Blue Veil* (RKO, 1951) and Helen Phillips in *Magnificent Obsession* (Universal-International, 1954)

Take plenty of hankies, was usually the advice given by critics when praising a Jane Wyman film of the post-war years. It was good advice, especially when watching her stunning performance as the deaf-mute rape victim Johnny Belinda. The tears flowed too in her nominated roles as Greg Peck's Florida farming wife in *The Yearling*, the self-sacrificing nanny in *The Blue Veil,* and the wealthy blind widow loved by Rock Hudson in *Magnificent Obsession.* As if to prove she did have a lighter side, she also contributed to Bing Crosby's Oscar-winning song of 1951, 'In the Cool, Cool, Cool of the Evening'. And as if to prove she had a darker side, she played a ruthless matriarch in the popular TV series of the eighties, *Falcon Crest.*

Ed Wynn

Born Philadelphia, USA, 9 November 1886; died 1966

Oscar Nominations (1): Best Supporting Actor for Albert Dussell in *The Diary of Anne Frank* (20th Century-Fox, 1959)

Best remembered for his little old man who can't stop laughing and keeps floating to the ceiling in *Mary Poppins,* Ed Wynn earned his Oscar nomination for a much more sombre role – as the garrulous old dentist who hides from the Nazis with the Anne Frank family in Amsterdam. A regular in movies only in his seventies – he incorporated just about every facet of showbusiness (vaudeville, Broadway, radio, TV) in his career – he enjoyed himself mostly at the Disney studio, where he occasionally co-starred with his son, Keenan (*The Absent-Minded Professor, Son of Flubber*), who had done much to help his father through the leaner times, of which there had been many. Keenan, who featured in more than 150 movies and TV films (mostly at MGM), never once rated an Oscar nomination.

Diana Wynyard

Born London, England, 16 January 1906; died 1964

Oscar Nominations (1): Best Actress for Jane Marryot in *Cavalcade* (Fox, 1932/33)

An occasional film actress who brought a charm and grace to her screen performances, Diana Wynyard was nominated just the once, for *Cavalcade,* as the mother of the family through whose experiences thirty years of British history unfolds, from the Boer War to the outbreak of

World War I and its aftermath. Best remembered for being driven close to madness by her lethal husband Anton Walbrook in *Gaslight* (Charles Boyer did the same to Ingrid Bergman in the Hollywood remake), she also appeared in Korda's sumptuous version of Oscar Wilde's *An Ideal Husband*, and in H.G. Wells' *Kipps*, which was directed by her husband of four years, Carol Reed.

Y

Susannah York

Born London, England, 9 January 1941

Oscar Nominations (1): Best Supporting Actress for Alice in *They Shoot Horses, Don't They?* (Palomar, 1969)

One of the loveliest examples of the English rose-type actress (especially as the sexually awakening adolescent in *The Greengage Summer*), Susannah York had graduated to Oscar nominee status by her late twenties, being named for her pathetic Harlow-type actress subjected to humiliation in one of Hollywood's Depression dance marathons. A horrendous screaming fit and breakdown in the shower probably brought her to the notice of the voters, although she didn't rate herself too highly in the part: 'I don't think I have much of a chance and I didn't think much of myself in it,' she said bluntly before the ceremony. No more nominations since, but plenty of challenging, provocative and often boldly sexual roles, for such directors as Aldrich, Skolimowski and Altman.

Burt Young

Born Queens, New York, USA, 30 April 1940

Oscar Nominations (1): Best Supporting Actor for Paulie in *Rocky* (United Artists, 1976)

It's pleasant to be able to latch on to a meal ticket if you've spent most of your screen time in routine and at times rather mundane productions. The stocky, chubby-faced Burt Young found his in the five *Rocky* films, in which he played Stallone's understanding, somewhat put-upon brother-in-law, who was always around in a crisis. Nominated for his first portrayal in 1976, he used his *Rocky* earnings to develop his talents as a screenwriter and director and to appear in stage productions. He would have made an admirable Scorsese player had not the director been more occupied with De Niro, Keitel, Pesci and company. No nominations since.

Gig Young

Born St Cloud, Minnesota, USA, 4 November 1913; died 1978

Oscars (1): Best Supporting Actor for Rocky in *They Shoot Horses, Don't They?* (Palomar, 1969)

Oscar Nominations (2): Best Supporting Actor for Boyd Copeland in *Come Fill the Cup* (Warner Bros, 1951) and Dr Hugo Pine in *Teacher's Pet* (Paramount, 1958)

The change of image did it for Gig Young. Once his likeable, clean-cut features were allowed to remain unshaven and take on an unkempt, sleazy look, he was halfway home for his ruthless dance marathon MC. 'Yowsir, yowsir, yowsir!' he yells as the dance goes round and round. 'There can be only one winner but isn't that the American way?' Nominated twice before, for his alcoholic rich boy in *Come Fill the Cup* and Doris Day's psychologist boyfriend in *Teacher's Pet*, he found that real life offered less than glittering prizes. Married five times, his life ended in tragedy when police discovered his body, along with that of his bride of three weeks, a thirty-one-year-old German actress, in a Manhattan apartment. He was holding a gun. The police concluded that he had shot his wife and then turned the gun on himself.

Loretta Young

Born Salt Lake City, Utah, USA, 6 January 1913

Oscars (1): Best Actress for Katrin Holstrom in *The Farmer's Daughter* (RKO, 1947)

Oscar Nominations (1): Best Actress for Sister Margaret in *Come to the Stable* (20th Century-Fox, 1949)

Unfairly described by one critic as 'the most beautiful clothes horse ever to become a movie star', Loretta Young proved her pedigree by coming from nowhere to defeat hot favourite Rosalind Russell and win 1947's best actress award for her Swedish Minnesota farming girl who runs for

Congress. Nominated again two years later, for her nun trying to raise funds for a children's hospital, she switched to television in the fifties, where she did even better, winning three Emmys to put alongside her Oscar. The critics were right about her beauty – large blue eyes, high cheekbones – and were eventually proved correct about the clothes as well, when she dressed to the hilt every week on primetime television in *The Loretta Young Show*.

Roland Young

Born London, England, 11 November 1887; died 1953

Oscar Nominations (1): Best Supporting Actor for Cosmo Topper in *Topper* (Roach/MGM, 1937)

Often seen as slightly dim, slow-witted little Englishmen who for much of the time didn't seem to know quite what they were doing or where they were, Roland Young won an Oscar nomination for being haunted by the spirits of freewheeling sophisticates Cary Grant and Constance Bennett. His bewildered banker, however, was up against formidable opposition – Joseph Schildkraut's portrait of the condemned French army captain Dreyfus in *The Life of Emile Zola* – and although he subsequently played his ghost-beset Cosmo in two popular sequels, his sole reward remained his nomination for the first film in the series.

Oscars Chronology

A companion year-order list of all acting, directing and best film nominees and **winners** from 1927 to the present.

1927/28

Production: *The Last Command* (Paramount); *The Racket* (Paramount); *Seventh Heaven* (Fox); *The Way of All Flesh* (Paramount); **Wings (Paramount)**

Actor: Richard Barthelmess in *The Noose*; Richard Barthelmess in *The Patent Leather Kid*; Charles Chaplin in *The Circus*; **Emil Jannings in *The Last Command*; Emil Jannings in *The Way of All Flesh***

Actress: Louise Dresser in *A Ship Comes In*; **Janet Gaynor in *Seventh Heaven*; Janet Gaynor in *Street Angel*; Janet Gaynor in *Sunrise*;** Gloria Swanson in *Sadie Thompson*

Direction: **Frank Borzage for *Seventh Heaven*;** Herbert Brenon for *Sorrell and Son*; King Vidor for *The Crowd*. Comedy Direction (not given after this year): Charles Chaplin for *The Circus*; **Lewis Milestone for *Two Arabian Knights*;** Ted Wilde for *Speedy*

1928/29

Production: *Alibi* (United Artists); ***The Broadway Melody* (MGM);** *Hollywood Revue* (MGM); *In Old Arizona* (Fox); *The Patriot* (Paramount)

Actor: **Warner Baxter in *In Old Arizona*;** Chester Morris in *Alibi*; Paul Muni in *The Valiant*; George Bancroft in *Thunderbolt*; Lewis Stone in *The Patriot*

Actress: Ruth Chatterton in *Madame X*; Betty Compson in *The Barker*; Jeanne Eagels in *The Letter*; Bessie Love in *The Broadway Melody*; **Mary Pickford in *Coquette***

Direction: Lionel Barrymore for *Madame X*; Harry Beaumont for *The Broadway Melody*; Irving Cummings for *In Old Arizona*; **Frank Lloyd for *The Divine Lady*;** Frank Lloyd for *Weary River*; Frank Lloyd for *Drag*; Ernst Lubitsch for *The Patriot*

1929/30

Production: ***All Quiet on the Western Front* (Universal);** *The Big House* (MGM); *Disraeli* (Warner Bros); *The Divorcee* (MGM); *The Love Parade* (Paramount)

Actor: **George Arliss in *Disraeli*;** George Arliss in *The Green Goddess*; Wallace Beery in *The Big House*; Maurice Chevalier in *The Love Parade*;

Maurice Chevalier in *The Big Pond*; Ronald Colman in *Bulldog Drummond*; Ronald Colman in *Condemned*; Lawrence Tibbett in *The Rogue Song*

Actress: Nancy Carroll in *The Devil's Holiday*; Ruth Chatterton in *Sarah and Son*; Greta Garbo in *Anna Christie*; Greta Garbo in *Romance*; **Norma Shearer in *The Divorcee***; Norma Shearer in *Their Own Desire*; Gloria Swanson in *The Trespasser*

Direction: Clarence Brown for *Anna Christie*; Clarence Brown for *Romance*; Robert Z. Leonard for *The Divorcee*; Ernst Lubitsch for *The Love Parade*; **Lewis Milestone for *All Quiet on the Western Front***; King Vidor for *Hallelujah*

1930/31

Production: ***Cimarron* (RKO Radio)**; *East Lynne* (Fox); *The Front Page* (United Artists); *Skippy* (Paramount); *Trader Horn* (MGM)

Actor: **Lionel Barrymore in *A Free Soul***; Jackie Cooper in *Skippy*; Richard Dix in *Cimarron*; Fredric March in *The Royal Family of Broadway*; Adolphe Menjou in *The Front Page*

Actress: Marlene Dietrich in *Morocco*; **Marie Dressler in *Min and Bill***; Irene Dunne in *Cimarron*; Ann Harding in *Holiday*; Norma Shearer in *A Free Soul*

Direction: Clarence Brown for *A Free Soul*; Lewis Milestone for *The Front Page*; Wesley Ruggles for *Cimarron*; Josef von Sternberg for *Morocco*; **Norman Taurog for *Skippy***

1931/32

Production: *Arrowsmith* (United Artists); *Bad Girl* (Fox); *The Champ* (MGM); *Five Star Final* (First National); ***Grand Hotel* (MGM)**; *One Hour With You* (Paramount); *Shanghai Express* (Paramount); *The Smiling Lieutenant* (Paramount)

Actor: **Wallace Beery in *The Champ***; Alfred Lunt in *The Guardsman*; **Fredric March in *Dr Jekyll and Mr Hyde***

Actress: Marie Dressler in *Emma*; Lynn Fontanne in *The Guardsman*; **Helen Hayes in *The Sin of Madelon Claudet***

Direction: **Frank Borzage for *Bad Girl***; King Vidor for *The Champ*; Josef von Sternberg for *Shanghai Express*

1932/33

Production: ***Cavalcade* (Fox)**; *A Farewell to Arms* (Paramount); *Forty-Second Street* (Warner Bros); *I Am a Fugitive from a Chain Gang* (Warner Bros); *Lady for a Day* (Columbia); *Little Women* (RKO Radio); *The Private Life of Henry VIII* (London Films); *She Done Him Wrong* (Paramount); *Smilin' Thru* (MGM); *State Fair* (Fox)

Actor: Leslie Howard in *Berkeley Square*; **Charles Laughton in *The Private Life of Henry VIII***; Paul Muni in *I Am a Fugitive from a Chain Gang*

Actress: **Katharine Hepburn in *Morning Glory***; May Robson in *Lady for a Day*; Diana Wynyard in *Cavalcade*

Direction: Frank Capra for *Lady for a Day*; George Cukor for *Little Women*; **Frank Lloyd for *Cavalcade***

1934

Production: *The Barretts of Wimpole Street* (MGM); *Cleopatra* (Paramount); *Flirtation Walk* (First National); *The Gay Divorcee* (RKO Radio); *Here Comes the Navy* (Warner Bros); *The House of Rothschild* (Twentieth Century); *Imitation of Life* (Universal); **It Happened One Night (Columbia)**; *One Night of Love* (Columbia); *The Thin Man* (MGM); *Viva Villa* (MGM); *The White Parade* (Fox)

Actor: **Clark Gable in *It Happened One Night***; Frank Morgan in *Affairs of Cellini*; William Powell in *The Thin Man*

Actress: **Claudette Colbert in *It Happened One Night***; Grace Moore in *One Night of Love*; Norma Shearer in *The Barretts of Wimpole Street*

Direction: **Frank Capra for *It Happened One Night***; Victor Schertzinger for *One Night of Love*; W. S. Van Dyke for *The Thin Man*

1935

Production: *Alice Adams* (RKO Radio); *The Broadway Melody of 1936* (MGM); *Captain Blood* (Warner Bros); *David Copperfield* (MGM); *The Informer* (RKO Radio); *Les Miserables* (Twentieth Century); *Lives of a Bengal Lancer* (Paramount); *A Midsummer Night's Dream* (Warner Bros); **Mutiny on the Bounty (MGM)**; *Naughty Marietta* (MGM); *Ruggles of Red Gap* (Paramount); *Top Hat* (RKO Radio)

Actor: Clark Gable in *Mutiny on the Bounty*; Charles Laughton in *Mutiny on the Bounty*; **Victor McLaglen in *The Informer***; Franchot Tone in *Mutiny on the Bounty*

Actress: Elisabeth Bergner in *Escape Me Never*; Claudette Colbert in *Private Worlds*; **Bette Davis in *Dangerous***; Katharine Hepburn in *Alice Adams*; Miriam Hopkins in *Becky Sharp*; Merle Oberon in *The Dark Angel*

Direction: **John Ford for *The Informer***; Henry Hathaway for *Lives of a Bengal Lancer*; Frank Lloyd for *Mutiny on the Bounty*

1936

Production: *Anthony Adverse* (Warner Bros); *Dodsworth* (Goldwyn UA); **The Great Ziegfeld (MGM)**; *Libeled Lady* (MGM); *Mr Deeds Goes to Town* (Columbia); *Romeo and Juliet* (MGM); *San Francisco* (MGM); *The Story of Louis Pasteur* (Warner Bros); *A Tale of Two Cities* (MGM); *Three Smart Girls* (Universal)

Actor: Gary Cooper in *Mr Deeds Goes to Town*; Walter Huston in *Dodsworth*; **Paul Muni in *The Story of Louis Pasteur***; William Powell in *My Man Godfrey*; Spencer Tracy in *San Francisco*

Actress: Irene Dunne in *Theodora Goes Wild*; Gladys George in *Valiant Is the Word for Carrie*; Carole Lombard in *My Man Godfrey*; **Luise Rainer in The Great Ziegfeld**; Norma Shearer in *Romeo and Juliet*

Supporting Actor: Mischa Auer in *My Man Godfrey*; **Walter Brennan in Come and Get It**; Stuart Erwin in *Pigskin Parade*; Basil Rathbone in *Romeo and Juliet*; Akim Tamiroff in *The General Died at Dawn*

Supporting Actress: Beulah Bondi in *The Gorgeous Hussy*; Alice Brady in

My Man Godfrey; Bonita Granville in *These Three*; Maria Ouspenskaya in *Dodsworth*; **Gale Sondergaard in *Anthony Adverse***
Direction: **Frank Capra for *Mr Deeds Goes to Town***; Gregory LaCava for *My Man Godfrey*; Robert Z. Leonard for *The Great Ziegfeld*; W. S. Van Dyke for *San Francisco*; William Wyler for *Dodsworth*

1937

Production: *The Awful Truth* (Columbia); *Captains Courageous* (MGM); *Dead End* (Goldwyn, UA); *The Good Earth* (MGM); *In Old Chicago* (20th Century-Fox); ***The Life of Emile Zola* (Warner Bros)**; *Lost Horizon* (Columbia); *One Hundred Men and a Girl* (Universal); *Stage Door* (RKO Radio); *A Star Is Born* (Selznick International, UA)
Actor: Charles Boyer in *Conquest*; Fredric March in *A Star Is Born*; Robert Montgomery in *Night Must Fall*; Paul Muni in *The Life of Emile Zola*; **Spencer Tracy in *Captains Courageous***
Actress: Irene Dunne in *The Awful Truth*; Greta Garbo in *Camille*; Janet Gaynor in *A Star Is Born*; **Luise Rainer in *The Good Earth***; Barbara Stanwyck in *Stella Dallas*
Supporting Actor: Ralph Bellamy in *The Awful Truth*; Thomas Mitchell in *The Hurricane*; **Joseph Schildkraut in *The Life of Emile Zola***; H. B. Warner in *Lost Horizon*; Roland Young in *Topper*
Supporting Actress: **Alice Brady in *In Old Chicago***; Andrea Leeds in *Stage Door*; Anne Shirley in *Stella Dallas*; Claire Trevor in *Dead End*; Dame May Whitty in *Night Must Fall*
Direction: William Dieterle for *The Life of Emile Zola*; Sidney Franklin for *The Good Earth*; Gregory LaCava for *Stage Door*; **Leo McCarey for *The Awful Truth***; William Wellman for *A Star Is Born*

1938

Production: *The Adventures of Robin Hood* (Warner Bros); *Alexander's Ragtime Band* (20th Century-Fox); *Boys' Town* (MGM); *The Citadel* (MGM); *Four Daughters* (Warner Bros); *La Grande Illusion* (France); *Jezebel* (Warner Bros); *Pygmalion* (MGM); *Test Pilot* (MGM); ***You Can't Take It With You* (Columbia)**
Actor: Charles Boyer in *Algiers*; James Cagney in *Angels with Dirty Faces*; Robert Donat in *The Citadel*; Leslie Howard in *Pygmalion*; **Spencer Tracy in *Boys' Town***
Actress: Fay Bainter in *White Banners*; **Bette Davis in *Jezebel***; Wendy Hiller in *Pygmalion*; Norma Shearer in *Marie Antoinette*; Margaret Sullavan in *Three Comrades*
Supporting Actor: **Walter Brennan in *Kentucky***; John Garfield in *Four Daughters*; Gene Lockhart in *Algiers*; Robert Morley in *Marie Antoinette*; Basil Rathbone in *If I Were King*
Supporting Actress: **Fay Bainter in *Jezebel***; Beulah Bondi in *Of Human Hearts*; Spring Byington in *You Can't Take It With You*; Billie Burke in *Merrily We Live*; Miliza Korjus in *The Great Waltz*
Direction: **Frank Capra for *You Can't Take It With You***; Michael Curtiz for *Angels with Dirty Faces*; Michael Curtiz for *Four Daughters*; Norman Taurog for *Boys' Town*; King Vidor for *The Citadel*

1939
Production: *Dark Victory* (Warner Bros); **Gone with the Wind (Selznick/ MGM)**; *Goodbye, Mr Chips* (MGM); *Love Affair* (RKO Radio); *Mr Smith Goes to Washington* (Columbia); *Ninotchka* (MGM); *Of Mice and Men* (United Artists); *Stagecoach* (United Artists); *The Wizard of Oz* (MGM); *Wuthering Heights* (Goldwyn, UA)
Actor: **Robert Donat in Goodbye, Mr Chips**; Clarke Gable in *Gone with the Wind*; Laurence Olivier in *Wuthering Heights*; Mickey Rooney in *Babes in Arms*; James Stewart in *Mr Smith Goes to Washington*
Actress: Bette Davis in *Dark Victory*; Irene Dunne in *Love Affair*; Greta Garbo in *Ninotchka*; Greer Garson in *Goodbye, Mr Chips*; **Vivien Leigh in Gone with the Wind**
Supporting Actor: Brian Aherne in *Juarez*; Harry Carey in *Mr Smith Goes to Washington*; Brian Donlevy in *Beau Geste*; **Thomas Mitchell in Stagecoach**; Claude Rains in *Mr Smith Goes to Washington*
Supporting Actress: Olivia de Havilland in *Gone with the Wind*; Geraldine Fitzgerald in *Wuthering Heights*; **Hattie McDaniel in Gone with the Wind**; Edna May Oliver in *Drums Along the Mohawk*; Maria Ouspenskaya in *Love Affair*
Direction: Frank Capra for *Mr Smith Goes to Washington*; **Victor Fleming for Gone with the Wind**; John Ford for *Stagecoach*; Sam Wood for *Goodbye, Mr Chips*; William Wyler for *Wuthering Heights*

1940
Production: *All This, and Heaven Too* (Warner Bros); *Foreign Correspondent* (United Artists); *The Grapes of Wrath* (20th Century-Fox); *The Great Dictator* (United Artists); *Kitty Foyle* (RKO Radio); *The Letter* (Warner Bros); *The Long Voyage Home* (United Artists); *Our Town* (United Artists); *The Philadelphia Story* (MGM); **Rebecca (Selznick, United Artists)**
Actor: Charles Chaplin in *The Great Dictator*; Henry Fonda in *The Grapes of Wrath*; Raymond Massey in *Abe Lincoln in Illinois*; Laurence Olivier in *Rebecca*; **James Stewart in The Philadelphia Story**
Actress: Bette Davis in *The Letter*; Joan Fontaine in *Rebecca*; Katharine Hepburn in *The Philadelphia Story*; **Ginger Rogers in Kitty Foyle**; Martha Scott in *Our Town*
Supporting Actor: Albert Basserman in *Foreign Correspondent*; **Walter Brennan in The Westerner**; William Gargan in *They Knew What They Wanted*; Jack Oakie in *The Great Dictator*; James Stephenson in *The Letter*
Supporting Actress: Judith Anderson in *Rebecca*; **Jane Darwell in The Grapes of Wrath**; Ruth Hussey in *The Philadelphia Story*; Barbara O'Neil in *All This and Heaven Too*; Marjorie Rambeau in *Primrose Path*
Direction: George Cukor for *The Philadelphia Story*; **John Ford for The Grapes of Wrath**; Alfred Hitchcock for *Rebecca*; Sam Wood for *Kitty Foyle*; William Wyler for *The Letter*

1941
Production: *Blossoms in the Dust* (MGM); *Citizen Kane* (RKO Radio); *Here Comes Mr Jordan* (Columbia); *Hold Back the Dawn* (Paramount); **How Green Was My Valley (20th Century-Fox)**; *The Little Foxes* (Goldwyn,

RKO Radio); *The Maltese Falcon* (Warner Bros); *One Foot in Heaven* (Warner Bros) *Sergeant York* (Warner Bros); *Suspicion* (RKO Radio)

Actor: **Gary Cooper in *Sergeant York***; Cary Grant in *Penny Serenade*; Walter Huston in *All That Money Can Buy*; Robert Montgomery in *Here Comes Mr Jordan*; Orson Welles in *Citizen Kane*

Actress: Bette Davis in *The Little Foxes*; **Joan Fontaine in *Suspicion***; Greer Garson in *Blossoms in the Dust*; Olivia de Havilland in *Hold Back the Dawn*; Barbara Stanwyck in *Ball of Fire*

Supporting Actor: Walter Brennan in *Sergeant York*; Charles Coburn in *The Devil and Miss Jones*; **Donald Crisp in *How Green Was My Valley***; James Gleason in *Here Comes Mr Jordan*; Sydney Greenstreet in *The Maltese Falcon*

Supporting Actress: Sara Allgood in *How Green Was My Valley*; **Mary Astor in *The Great Lie***; Patricia Collinge in *The Little Foxes*; Teresa Wright in *The Little Foxes*; Margaret Wycherly in *Sergeant York*

Direction: **John Ford for *How Green Was My Valley***; Alexander Hall for *Here Comes Mr Jordan*; Howard Hawks for *Sergeant York*; Orson Welles for *Citizen Kane*; William Wyler for *The Little Foxes*

1942

Production: *The Invaders* (British – GB *The 49th Parallel*); *Kings Row* (Warner Bros); *The Magnificent Ambersons* (RKO Radio); **Mrs Miniver (MGM)**; *The Pied Piper* (20th Century-Fox); *The Pride of the Yankees* (Goldwyn, RKO); *Random Harvest* (MGM); *The Talk of the Town* (Columbia); *Wake Island* (Paramount); *Yankee Doodle Dandy* (Warner Bros)

Actor: **James Cagney in *Yankee Doodle Dandy***; Ronald Colman in *Random Harvest*; Gary Cooper in *The Pride of the Yankees*; Walter Pidgeon in *Mrs Miniver*; Monty Woolley in *The Pied Piper*

Actress: Bette Davis in *Now, Voyager*; **Greer Garson in *Mrs Miniver***; Katharine Hepburn in *Woman of the Year*; Rosalind Russell in *My Sister Eileen*; Teresa Wright in *The Pride of the Yankees*

Supporting Actor: William Bendix in *Wake Island*; **Van Heflin in *Johnny Eager***; Walter Huston in *Yankee Doodle Dandy*; Frank Morgan in *Tortilla Flat*; Henry Travers in *Mrs Miniver*

Supporting Actress: Gladys Cooper in *Now, Voyager*; Agnes Moorehead in *The Magnificent Ambersons*; Susan Peters in *Random Harvest*; Dame May Whitty in *Mrs Miniver*; **Teresa Wright in *Mrs Miniver***

Direction: Michael Curtiz for *Yankee Doodle Dandy*; John Farrow for *Wake Island*; Mervyn LeRoy for *Random Harvest*; Sam Wood for *Kings Row*; **William Wyler for *Mrs Miniver***

1943

Production: ***Casablanca* (Warner Bros)**; *For Whom the Bell Tolls* (Paramount); *Heaven Can Wait* (20th Century-Fox); *The Human Comedy* (MGM); *In Which We Serve* (British); *Madame Curie* (MGM); *The More the Merrier* (Columbia); *The Ox-Bow Incident* (20th Century-Fox); *The Song of Bernadette* (20th Century-Fox); *Watch on the Rhine* (Warner Bros)

Actor: Humphrey Bogart in *Casablanca*; Gary Cooper in *For Whom the Bell Tolls*; **Paul Lukas in *Watch on the Rhine***; Walter Pidgeon in *Madame*

Curie; Mickey Rooney in *The Human Comedy*
Actress: Jean Arthur in *The More the Merrier*; Ingrid Bergman in *For Whom the Bell Tolls*; Joan Fontaine in *The Constant Nymph*; Greer Garson in *Madame Curie*; **Jennifer Jones in *The Song of Bernadette***
Supporting Actor: Charles Bickford in *The Song of Bernadette*; **Charles Coburn in *The More the Merrier***; J. Carrol Naish in *Sahara*; Claude Rains in *Casablanca*; Akim Tamiroff in *For Whom the Bell Tolls*
Supporting Actress: Gladys Cooper in *The Song of Bernadette*; Paulette Goddard in *So Proudly We Hail*; **Katina Paxinou in *For Whom the Bell Tolls***; Anne Revere in *The Song of Bernadette*; Lucile Watson in *Watch on the Rhine*
Direction: Clarence Brown for *The Human Comedy*; **Michael Curtiz for *Casablanca***; Henry King for *The Song of Bernadette*; Ernst Lubitsch for *Heaven Can Wait*; George Stevens for *The More the Merrier*

1944

Production: *Double Indemnity* (Paramount); *Gaslight* (MGM); ***Going My Way* (Paramount)**; *Since You Went Away* (Selznick International, UA); *Wilson* (20th Century-Fox)
Actor: Charles Boyer in *Gaslight*; **Bing Crosby in *Going My Way***; Barry Fitzgerald in *Going My Way*; Cary Grant in *None But the Lonely Heart*; Alexander Knox in *Wilson*
Actress: **Ingrid Bergman in *Gaslight***; Claudette Colbert in *Since You Went Away*; Bette Davis in *Mr Skeffington*; Greer Garson in *Mrs Parkington*; Barbara Stanwyck in *Double Indemnity*
Supporting Actor: Hume Cronyn in *The Seventh Cross*; **Barry Fitzgerald in *Going My Way***; Claude Rains in *Mr Skeffington*; Clifton Webb in *Laura*; Monty Woolley in *Since You Went Away*
Supporting Actress: **Ethel Barrymore in *None But the Lonely Heart***; Jennifer Jones in *Since You Went Away*; Angela Lansbury in *Gaslight*; Aline MacMahon in *Dragon Seed*; Agnes Moorehead in *Mrs Parkington*
Direction: Alfred Hitchcock for *Lifeboat*; Henry King for *Wilson*; **Leo McCarey for *Going My Way***; Otto Preminger for *Laura*; Billy Wilder for *Double Indemnity*

1945

Production: *Anchors Aweigh* (MGM); *The Bells of St Mary's* (RKO Radio); ***The Lost Weekend* (Paramount)**; *Mildred Pierce* (Warner Bros); *Spellbound* (Selznick International, UA)
Actor: Bing Crosby in *The Bells of St Mary's*; Gene Kelly in *Anchors Aweigh*; **Ray Milland in *The Lost Weekend***; Gregory Peck in *The Keys of the Kingdom*; Cornel Wilde in *A Song to Remember*
Actress: Ingrid Bergman in *The Bells of St Mary's*; **Joan Crawford in *Mildred Pierce***; Greer Garson in *The Valley of Decision*; Jennifer Jones in *Love Letters*; Gene Tierney in *Leave Her to Heaven*
Supporting Actor: Michael Chekhov in *Spellbound*; John Dall in *The Corn Is Green*; **James Dunn in *A Tree Grows in Brooklyn***; Robert Mitchum in *The Story of GI Joe*; J. Carrol Naish in *A Medal for Benny*
Supporting Actress: Eve Arden in *Mildred Pierce*; Ann Blyth in *Mildred*

Pierce; Angela Lansbury in *The Picture of Dorian Gray*; Joan Lorring in *The Corn Is Green*; **Anne Revere in *National Velvet***
Direction: Clarence Brown for *National Velvet*; Alfred Hitchcock for *Spellbound*; Leo McCarey for *The Bells of St Mary's*; Jean Renoir for *The Southerner*; **Billy Wilder for *The Lost Weekend***

1946
Production: ***The Best Years of Our Lives* (Goldwyn, RKO)**; *Henry V* (Rank/Two Cities/British); *It's a Wonderful Life* (RKO Radio); *The Razor's Edge* (20th Century-Fox); *The Yearling* (MGM)
Actor: **Fredric March in *The Best Years of Our Lives***; Laurence Olivier in *Henry V*; Larry Parks in *The Jolson Story*; Gregory Peck in *The Yearling*; James Stewart in *It's a Wonderful Life*
Actress: **Olivia de Havilland in *To Each His Own***; Celia Johnson in *Brief Encounter*; Jennifer Jones in *Duel in the Sun*; Rosalind Russell in *Sister Kenny*; Jane Wyman in *The Yearling*
Supporting Actor: Charles Coburn in *The Green Years*; William Demarest in *The Jolson Story*; Claude Rains in *Notorious*; **Harold Russell in *The Best Years of Our Lives***; Clifton Webb in *The Razor's Edge*
Supporting Actress: Ethel Barrymore in *The Spiral Staircase*; **Anne Baxter in *The Razor's Edge***; Lillian Gish in *Duel in the Sun*; Flora Robson in *Saratoga Trunk*; Gale Sondergaard in *Anna and the King of Siam*
Direction: Clarence Brown for *The Yearling*; Frank Capra for *It's a Wonderful Life*; David Lean for *Brief Encounter*; Robert Siodmak for *The Killers*; **William Wyler for *The Best Years of Our Lives***

1947
Production: *The Bishop's Wife* (Goldwyn, RKO); *Crossfire* (RKO Radio); ***Gentleman's Agreement* (20th Century-Fox)**; *Great Expectations* (Rank-Cineguild/British); *Miracle on 34th Street* (20th Century-Fox)
Actor: **Ronald Colman in *A Double Life***; John Garfield in *Body and Soul*; Gregory Peck in *Gentleman's Agreement*; William Powell in *Life With Father*; Michael Redgrave in *Mourning Becomes Electra*
Actress: Joan Crawford in *Possessed*; Susan Hayward in *Smash-Up – The Story of a Woman*; Dorothy McGuire in *Gentleman's Agreement*; Rosalind Russell in *Mourning Becomes Electra*; **Loretta Young in *The Farmer's Daughter***
Supporting Actor: Charles Bickford in *The Farmer's Daughter*; Thomas Gomez in *Ride the Pink Horse*; **Edmund Gwenn in *Miracle on 34th Street***; Robert Ryan in *Crossfire*; Richard Widmark in *Kiss of Death*
Supporting Actress: Ethel Barrymore in *The Paradine Case*; Gloria Grahame in *Crossfire*; **Celeste Holm in *Gentleman's Agreement***; Marjorie Main in *The Egg and I*; Anne Revere in *Gentleman's Agreement*
Direction: George Cukor for *A Double Life*; Edward Dmytryk for *Crossfire*; **Elia Kazan for *Gentleman's Agreement***; Henry Koster for *The Bishop's Wife*; David Lean for *Great Expectations*

1948
Production: ***Hamlet* (Rank-Two Cities/British)**; *Johnny Belinda* (Warner Bros); *The Red Shoes* (Rank-Archers/British); *The Snake Pit*

(20th Century-Fox; *The Treasure of the Sierra Madre* (Warner Bros)

Actor: Lew Ayres in *Johnny Belinda*; Montgomery Clift in *The Search*; Dan Dailey in *When My Baby Smiles at Me*; **Laurence Olivier in *Hamlet***; Clifton Webb in *Sitting Pretty*

Actress: Ingrid Bergman in *Joan of Arc*; Olivia de Havilland in *The Snake Pit*; Irene Dunne in *I Remember Mama*; Barbara Stanwyck in *Sorry, Wrong Number*; **Jane Wyman in *Johnny Belinda***

Supporting Actor: Charles Bickford in *Johnny Belinda*; Jose Ferrer in *Joan of Arc*; Oscar Homolka in *I Remember Mama*; **Walter Huston in *The Treasure of the Sierra Madre***; Cecil Kellaway in *The Luck of the Irish*

Supporting Actress: Barbara Bel Geddes in *I Remember Mama*; Ellen Corby in *I Remember Mama*; Agnes Moorehead in *Johnny Belinda*; Jean Simmons in *Hamlet*; **Claire Trevor in *Key Largo***

Direction: **John Huston for *The Treasure of the Sierra Madre***; Anatole Litvak for *The Snake Pit*; Jean Negulesco for *Johnny Belinda*; Laurence Olivier for *Hamlet*; Fred Zinnemann for *The Search*

1949

Production: ***All the King's Men* (Columbia)**; *Battleground* (MGM); *The Heiress* (Paramount); *A Letter to Three Wives* (20th Century-Fox); *Twelve O'Clock High* (20th Century-Fox)

Actor: **Broderick Crawford in *All the King's Men***; Kirk Douglas in *Champion*; Gregory Peck in *Twelve O'Clock High*; Richard Todd in *The Hasty Heart*; John Wayne in *Sands of Iwo Jima*

Actress: Jeanne Crain in *Pinky*; **Olivia de Havilland in *The Heiress***; Susan Hayward in *My Foolish Heart*; Deborah Kerr in *Edward, My Son*; Loretta Young in *Come to the Stable*

Supporting Actor: John Ireland in *All the King's Men*; **Dean Jagger in *Twelve O'Clock High***; Arthur Kennedy in *Champion*; Ralph Richardson in *The Heiress*; James Whitmore in *Battleground*

Supporting Actress: Ethel Barrymore in *Pinky*; Celeste Holm in *Come to the Stable*; Elsa Lanchester in *Come to the Stable*; **Mercedes McCambridge in *All the King's Men***; Ethel Waters in *Pinky*

Direction: **Joseph L. Mankiewicz for *A Letter to Three Wives***; Carol Reed for *The Fallen Idol*; Robert Rossen for *All the King's Men*; William A. Wellman for *Battleground*; William Wyler for *The Heiress*

1950

Production: ***All About Eve* (20th Century-Fox)**; *Born Yesterday* (Columbia); *Father of the Bride* (MGM); *King Solomon's Mines* (MGM); *Sunset Boulevard* (Paramount)

Actor: Louis Calhern in *The Magnificent Yankee*; **Jose Ferrer in *Cyrano de Bergerac***; William Holden in *Sunset Boulevard*; James Stewart in *Harvey*; Spencer Tracy in *Father of the Bride*

Actress: Anne Baxter in *All About Eve*; Bette Davis in *All About Eve*; **Judy Holliday in *Born Yesterday***; Eleanor Parker in *Caged*; Gloria Swanson in *Sunset Boulevard*

Supporting Actor: Jeff Chandler in *Broken Arrow*; Edmund Gwenn in *Mister 880*; Sam Jaffe in *The Asphalt Jungle*; **George Sanders in *All***

About Eve; Erich Von Stroheim in *Sunset Boulevard*
Supporting Actress: Hope Emerson in *Caged*; Celeste Holm in *All About Eve*; **Josephine Hull in *Harvey***; Nancy Olson in *Sunset Boulevard*; Thelma Ritter in *All About Eve*
Direction: George Cukor for *Born Yesterday*; John Huston for *The Asphalt Jungle*; **Joseph L. Mankiewicz for *All About Eve***; Carol Reed for *The Third Man*; Billy Wilder for *Sunset Boulevard*

1951

Production: ***An American in Paris* (MGM)**; *Decision Before Dawn* (20th Century-Fox); *A Place in the Sun* (Paramount); *Quo Vadis?* (MGM); *A Streetcar Named Desire* (Warner Bros)
Actor: **Humphrey Bogart in *The African Queen***; Marlon Brando in *A Streetcar Named Desire*; Montgomery Clift in *A Place in the Sun*; Arthur Kennedy in *Bright Victory*; Fredric March in *Death of a Salesman*
Actress: Katharine Hepburn in *The African Queen*; **Vivien Leigh in *A Streetcar Named Desire***; Eleanor Parker in *Detective Story*; Shelley Winters in *A Place in the Sun*; Jane Wyman in *The Blue Veil*
Supporting Actor: Leo Genn in *Quo Vadis?*; **Karl Malden in *A Streetcar Named Desire***; Kevin McCarthy in *Death of a Salesman*; Peter Ustinov in *Quo Vadis?*; Gig Young in *Come Fill the Cup*
Supporting Actress: Joan Blondell in *The Blue Veil*; Mildred Dunnock in *Death of a Salesman*; Lee Grant in *Detective Story*; **Kim Hunter in *A Streetcar Named Desire***; Thelma Ritter in *The Mating Season*
Direction: John Huston for *The African Queen*; Vincente Minnelli for *An American in Paris*; William Wyler for *Detective Story*; **George Stevens for *A Place in the Sun***; Elia Kazan for *A Streetcar Named Desire*

1952

Production: ***The Greatest Show on Earth* (Paramount)**; *High Noon* (United Artists); *Ivanhoe* (MGM); *Moulin Rouge* (United Artists); *The Quiet Man* (Republic)
Actor: Marlon Brando in *Viva Zapata!*; **Gary Cooper in *High Noon***; Kirk Douglas in *The Bad and the Beautiful*; Jose Ferrer in *Moulin Rouge*; Alec Guinness in *The Lavender Hill Mob*
Actress: **Shirley Booth in *Come Back Little Sheba***; Joan Crawford in *Sudden Fear*; Bette Davis in *The Star*; Julie Harris in *The Member of the Wedding*; Susan Hayward in *With a Song in My Heart*
Supporting Actor: Richard Burton in *My Cousin Rachel*; Arthur Hunnicutt in *The Big Sky*; Victor McLaglen in *The Quiet Man*; Jack Palance in *Sudden Fear*; **Anthony Quinn in *Viva Zapata!***
Supporting Actress: **Gloria Grahame in *The Bad and the Beautiful***; Jean Hagen in *Singin' in the Rain*; Colette Marchand in *Moulin Rouge*; Terry Moore in *Come Back Little Sheba*; Thelma Ritter in *With a Song in My Heart*
Direction: Cecil B. DeMille for *The Greatest Show on Earth*; **John Ford for *The Quiet Man***; John Huston for *Moulin Rouge*; Joseph L. Mankiewicz for *Five Fingers*; Fred Zinnemann for *High Noon*

1953

Production: ***From Here to Eternity* (Columbia)**; *Julius Caeser* (MGM); *The Robe* (20th Century-Fox); *Roman Holiday* (Paramount); *Shane* (Paramount)

Actor: Marlon Brando in *Julius Caesar*; Richard Burton in *The Robe*; Montgomery Clift in *From Here to Eternity*; **William Holden in *Stalag 17***; Burt Lancaster in *From Here to Eternity*

Actress: Leslie Caron in *Lili*; Ava Gardner in *Mogambo*; **Audrey Hepburn in *Roman Holiday***; Deborah Kerr in *From Here to Eternity*; Maggie McNamara in *The Moon Is Blue*

Supporting Actor: Eddie Albert in *Roman Holiday*; Brandon De Wilde in *Shane*; Jack Palance in *Shane*; **Frank Sinatra in *From Here to Eternity***; Robert Strauss in *Stalag 17*

Supporting Actress: Grace Kelly in *Mogambo*; Geraldine Page in *Hondo*; Marjorie Rambeau in *Torch Song*; **Donna Reed in *From Here to Eternity***; Thelma Ritter in *Pickup on South Street*

Direction: George Stevens for *Shane*; Charles Walters for *Lili*; Billy Wilder for *Stalag 17*; William Wyler for *Roman Holiday*; **Fred Zinnemann for *From Here to Eternity***

1954

Production: *The Caine Mutiny* (Columbia); *The Country Girl* (Paramount); ***On the Waterfront* (Columbia)**; *Seven Brides for Seven Brothers* (MGM); *Three Coins in the Fountain* (20th Century-Fox)

Actor: Humphrey Bogart in *The Caine Mutiny*; **Marlon Brando in *On the Waterfront***; Bing Crosby in *The Country Girl*; James Mason in *A Star Is Born*; Dan O'Herlihy in *The Adventures of Robinson Crusoe*

Actress: Dorothy Dandridge in *Carmen Jones*; Judy Garland in *A Star Is Born*; Audrey Hepburn in *Sabrina*; **Grace Kelly in *The Country Girl***; Jane Wyman in *Magnificent Obsession*

Supporting Actor: Lee J. Cobb in *On the Waterfront*; Karl Malden in *On the Waterfront*; **Edmond O'Brien in *The Barefoot Contessa***; Rod Steiger in *On the Waterfront*; Tom Tully in *The Caine Mutiny*

Supporting Actress: Nina Foch in *Executive Suite*; Katy Jurado in *Broken Lance*; **Eva Marie Saint in *On the Waterfront***; Jan Sterling in *The High and the Mighty*; Claire Trevor in *The High and the Mighty*

Direction: Alfred Hitchcock for *Rear Window*; **Elia Kazan for *On the Waterfront***; George Seaton for *The Country Girl*; William A. Wellman for *The High and the Mighty*; Billy Wilder for *Sabrina*

1955

Production: *Love Is a Many-Splendored Thing* (20th Century-Fox); ***Marty* (United Artists)**; *Mister Roberts* (Warner Bros); *Picnic* (Columbia); *The Rose Tattoo* (Paramount)

Actor: **Ernest Borgnine in *Marty***; James Cagney in *Love Me or Leave Me*; James Dean in *East of Eden*; Frank Sinatra in *The Man with the Golden Arm*; Spencer Tracy in *Bad Day at Black Rock*

Actress: Susan Hayward in *I'll Cry Tomorrow*; Katharine Hepburn in *Summertime*; Jennifer Jones in *Love Is a Many-Splendored Thing*; **Anna**

Magnani in *The Rose Tattoo*; Eleanor Parker in *Interrupted Melody*

Supporting Actor: Arthur Kennedy in *Trial*; **Jack Lemmon in *Mister Roberts***; Joe Mantell in *Marty*; Sal Mineo in *Rebel Without a Cause*; Arthur O'Connell in *Picnic*

Supporting Actress: Betsy Blair in *Marty*; Peggy Lee in *Pete Kelly's Blues*; Marisa Pavan in *The Rose Tattoo*; **Jo Van Fleet in *East of Eden***; Natalie Wood in *Rebel Without a Cause*

Direction: Elia Kazan for *East of Eden*; David Lean for *Summertime*; Joshua Logan for *Picnic*; **Delbert Mann for *Marty***; John Sturges for *Bad Day at Black Rock*

1956

Production: ***Around the World in 80 Days* (United Artists)**; *Friendly Persuasion* (Allied Artists); *Giant* (Warner Bros); *The King and I* (20th Century-Fox); *The Ten Commandments* (Paramount)

Actor: **Yul Brynner in *The King and I***; James Dean in *Giant*; Kirk Douglas in *Lust for Life*; Rock Hudson in *Giant*; Laurence Olivier in *Richard III*

Actress: Carroll Baker in *Baby Doll*; **Ingrid Bergman in *Anastasia***; Katharine Hepburn in *The Rainmaker*; Nancy Kelly in *The Bad Seed*; Deborah Kerr in *The King and I*

Supporting Actor: Don Murray in *Bus Stop*; Anthony Perkins in *Friendly Persuasion*; **Anthony Quinn in *Lust for Life***; Mickey Rooney in *The Bold and the Brave*; Robert Stack in *Written on the Wind*

Supporting Actress: Mildred Dunnock in *Baby Doll*; Eileen Heckart in *The Bad Seed*; Mercedes McCambridge in *Giant*; Patty McCormack in *The Bad Seed*; **Dorothy Malone in *Written on the Wind***

Direction: Michael Anderson for *Around the World in 80 Days*; William Wyler for *Friendly Persuasion*; **George Stevens for *Giant***; Walter Lang for *The King and I*; King Vidor for *War and Peace*

1957

Production: ***The Bridge on the River Kwai* (Columbia)**; *Peyton Place* (20th Century-Fox); *Sayonara* (Warner Bros); *12 Angry Men* (United Artists); *Witness for the Prosecution* (United Artists)

Actor: Marlon Brando in *Sayonara*; Anthony Franciosa in *A Hatful of Rain*; **Alec Guinness in *The Bridge on the River Kwai***; Charles Laughton in *Witness for the Prosecution*; Anthony Quinn in *Wild Is the Wind*

Actress: Deborah Kerr in *Heaven Knows, Mr Allison*; Anna Magnani in *Wild Is the Wind*; Elizabeth Taylor in *Raintree County*; Lana Turner in *Peyton Place*; **Joanne Woodward in *The Three Faces of Eve***

Supporting Actor: **Red Buttons in *Sayonara***; Vittoria De Sica in *A Farewell to Arms*; Sessue Hayakawa in *The Bridge on the River Kwai*; Arthur Kennedy in *Peyton Place*; Russ Tamblyn in *Peyton Place*

Supporting Actress: Carolyn Jones in *The Bachelor Party*; Elsa Lanchester in *Witness for the Prosecution*; Hope Lange in *Peyton Place*; **Miyoshi Umeki in *Sayonara***; Diane Varsi in *Peyton Place*

Direction: **David Lean for *The Bridge on the River Kwai***; Mark Robson for *Peyton Place*; Joshua Logan for *Sayonara*; Sidney Lumet for *12 Angry Men*; Billy Wilder for *Witness for the Prosecution*

1958

Production: *Auntie Mame* (Warner Bros); *Cat on a Hot Tin Roof* (MGM); *The Defiant Ones* (United Artists); **Gigi (MGM)**; *Separate Tables* (United Artists)

Actor: Tony Curtis in *The Defiant Ones*; Paul Newman in *Cat on a Hot Tin Roof*; **David Niven in *Separate Tables***; Sidney Poitier in *The Defiant Ones*; Spencer Tracy in *The Old Man and the Sea*

Actress: **Susan Hayward in *I Want to Live***; Deborah Kerr in *Separate Tables*; Shirley MacLaine in *Some Came Running*; Rosalind Russell in *Auntie Mame*; Elizabeth Taylor in *Cat on a Hot Tin Roof*

Supporting Actor: Theodore Bikel in *The Defiant Ones*; Lee J. Cobb in *The Brothers Karamazov*; **Burl Ives in *The Big Country***; Arthur Kennedy in *Some Came Running*; Gig Young in *Teacher's Pet*

Supporting Actress: Peggy Cass in *Auntie Mame*; **Wendy Hiller in *Separate Tables***; Martha Hyer in *Some Came Running*; Maureen Stapleton in *Lonelyhearts*; Cara Williams in *The Defiant Ones*

Direction: Richard Brooks for *Cat on a Hot Tin Roof*; Stanley Kramer for *The Defiant Ones*; **Vincente Minnelli for *Gigi***; Robert Wise for *I Want to Live*; Mark Robson for *The Inn of the Sixth Happiness*

1959

Production: *Anatomy of a Murder* (Columbia); **Ben-Hur (MGM)**; *The Diary of Anne Frank* (20th Century-Fox); *The Nun's Story* (Warner Bros); *Room at the Top* (Romulus Films/British)

Actor: Laurence Harvey in *Room at the Top*; **Charlton Heston in *Ben-Hur***; Jack Lemmon in *Some Like It Hot*; Paul Muni in *The Last Angry Man*; James Stewart in *Anatomy of a Murder*

Actress: Doris Day in *Pillow Talk*; Audrey Hepburn in *The Nun's Story*; Katharine Hepburn in *Suddenly, Last Summer*; **Simone Signoret in *Room at the Top***; Elizabeth Taylor in *Suddenly, Last Summer*

Supporting Actor: **Hugh Griffith in *Ben-Hur***; Arthur O'Connell in *Anatomy of a Murder*; George C. Scott in *Anatomy of a Murder*; Robert Vaughn in *The Young Philadelphians*; Ed Wynn in *The Diary of Anne Frank*

Supporting Actress: Hermione Baddeley in *Room at the Top*; Susan Kohner in *Imitation of Life*; Juanita Moore in *Imitation of Life*; Thelma Ritter in *Pillow Talk*; **Shelley Winters in *The Diary of Anne Frank***

Direction: **William Wyler for *Ben-Hur***; George Stevens for *The Diary of Anne Frank*; Fred Zinnemann for *The Nun's Story*; Jack Clayton for *Room at the Top*; Billy Wilder for *Some Like It Hot*

1960

Production: *The Alamo* (United Artists); **The Apartment (United Artists)**; *Elmer Gantry* (United Artists); *Sons and Lovers* (20th Century-Fox); *The Sundowners* (Warner Bros)

Actor: Trevor Howard in *Sons and Lovers*; **Burt Lancaster in *Elmer Gantry***; Jack Lemmon in *The Apartment*; Laurence Olivier in *The Entertainer*; Spencer Tracy in *Inherit the Wind*

Actress: Greer Garson in *Sunrise at Campobello*; Deborah Kerr in *The Sundowners*; Shirley MacLaine in *The Apartment*; Melina Mercouri in

Never on Sunday; **Elizabeth Taylor in *Butterfield 8***
Supporting Actor: Peter Falk in *Murder Inc.*; Jack Kruschen in *The Apartment*; Sal Mineo in *Exodus*; **Peter Ustinov in *Spartacus***; Chill Wills in *The Alamo*
Supporting Actress: Glynis Johns in *The Sundowners*; **Shirley Jones in *Elmer Gantry***; Shirley Knight in *The Dark at the Top of the Stairs*; Janet Leigh in *Psycho*; Mary Ure in *Sons and Lovers*
Direction: Jack Cardiff for *Sons and Lovers*; Jules Dassin for *Never on Sunday*; Alfred Hitchcock for *Psycho*; **Billy Wilder for *The Apartment***; Fred Zinnemann for *The Sundowners*

1961
Production: *Fanny* (Warner Bros); *The Guns of Navarone* (Columbia); *The Hustler* (20th Century-Fox); *Judgment at Nuremberg* (United Artists); ***West Side Story* (United Artists)**
Actor: Charles Boyer in *Fanny*; Paul Newman in *The Hustler*; **Maximilian Schell in *Judgment at Nuremberg***; Spencer Tracy in *Judgment at Nuremberg*; Stuart Whitman in *The Mark*
Actress: Audrey Hepburn in *Breakfast at Tiffany's*; Piper Laurie in *The Hustler*; **Sophia Loren in *Two Women***; Geraldine Page in *Summer and Smoke*; Natalie Wood in *Splendor in the Grass*
Supporting Actor: **George Chakiris in *West Side Story***; Montgomery Clift in *Judgment at Nuremberg*; Peter Falk in *Pocketful of Miracles*; Jackie Gleason in *The Hustler*; George C. Scott in *The Hustler*
Supporting Actress: Fay Bainter in *The Children's Hour*; Judy Garland in *Judgment at Nuremberg*; Lotte Lenya in *The Roman Spring of Mrs Stone*; Una Merkel in *Summer and Smoke*; **Rita Moreno in *West Side Story***
Direction: J. Lee Thompson for *The Guns of Navarone*; Robert Rossen for *The Hustler*; Stanley Kramer for *Judgment at Nuremberg*; Federico Fellini for *La Dolce Vita*; **Robert Wise and Jerome Robbins for *West Side Story***

1962
Production: ***Lawrence of Arabia* (Columbia)**; *The Longest Day* (20th Century-Fox); *The Music Man* (Warner Bros); *Mutiny on the Bounty* (MGM); *To Kill a Mockingbird* (Universal-International)
Actor: Burt Lancaster in *Birdman of Alcatraz*; Jack Lemmon in *Days of Wine and Roses*; Marcello Mastroianni in *Divorce, Italian Style*; Peter O'Toole in *Lawrence of Arabia*; **Gregory Peck in *To Kill a Mockingbird***
Actress: **Anne Bancroft in *The Miracle Worker***; Bette Davis in *What Ever Happened to Baby Jane?*; Katharine Hepburn in *Long Day's Journey into Night*; Geraldine Page in *Sweet Bird of Youth*; Lee Remick in *Days of Wine and Roses*
Supporting Actor: **Ed Begley in *Sweet Bird of Youth***; Victor Buono in *What Ever Happened to Baby Jane?*; Telly Savalas in *Birdman of Alcatraz*; Omar Sharif in *Lawrence of Arabia*; Terence Stamp in *Billy Budd*
Supporting Actress: Mary Badham in *To Kill a Mockingbird*; **Patty Duke in *The Miracle Worker***; Shirley Knight in *Sweet Bird of Youth*; Angela Lansbury in *The Manchurian Candidate*; Thelma Ritter in *Birdman of Alcatraz*

Direction: Frank Perry for *David and Lisa*; Pietro Germi for *Divorce, Italian Style*; **David Lean for *Lawrence of Arabia***; Arthur Penn for *The Miracle Worker*; Robert Mulligan for *To Kill a Mockingbird*

1963

Production: ***Tom Jones* (United Artists)**; *America, America* (Warner Bros); *Cleopatra* (20th Century-Fox); *How the West Was Won* (MGM); *Lilies of the Field* (United Artists)

Actor: Albert Finney in *Tom Jones*; Richard Harris in *This Sporting Life*; Rex Harrison in *Cleopatra*; Paul Newman in *Hud*; **Sidney Poitier in *Lilies of the Field***

Actress: Leslie Caron in *The L-Shaped Room*; Shirley MacLaine in *Irma La Douce*; **Patricia Neal in *Hud***; Rachel Roberts in *This Sporting Life*; Natalie Wood in *Love with the Proper Stranger*

Supporting Actor: Nick Adams in *Twilight of Honour*; Bobby Darin in *Captain Newman MD*; **Melvyn Douglas in *Hud***; Hugh Griffith in *Tom Jones*; John Huston in *The Cardinal*

Supporting Actress: Diane Cilento in *Tom Jones*; Edith Evans in *Tom Jones*; Joyce Redman in *Tom Jones*; **Margaret Rutherford in *The VIPs***; Lilia Skala in *Lilies of the Field*

Direction: **Tony Richardson for *Tom Jones***; Elia Kazan for *America, America*; Otto Preminger for *The Cardinal*; Federico Fellini for *8½*; Martin Ritt for *Hud*

1964

Production: *Becket* (Paramount); *Dr Strangelove* (Columbia); *Mary Poppins* (Walt Disney); ***My Fair Lady* (Warner Bros)**; *Zorba the Greek* (20th Century-Fox)

Actor: **Rex Harrison in *My Fair Lady***; Peter O'Toole in *Becket*; Anthony Quinn in *Zorba the Greek*; Peter Sellers in *Dr Strangelove*; Richard Burton in *Becket*

Actress: **Julie Andrews in *Mary Poppins***; Anne Bancroft in *The Pumpkin Eater*; Sophia Loren in *Marriage, Italian Style*; Debbie Reynolds in *The Unsinkable Molly Brown*; Kim Stanley in *Seance on a Wet Afternoon*

Supporting Actor: John Gielgud in *Becket*; Stanley Holloway in *My Fair Lady*; Edmond O'Brien in *Seven Days in May*; Lee Tracy in *The Best Man*; **Peter Ustinov in *Topkapi***

Supporting Actress: Gladys Cooper in *My Fair Lady*; Edith Evans in *The Chalk Garden*; Grayson Hall in *Night of the Iguana*; **Lila Kedrova in *Zorba the Greek***; Agnes Moorehead in *Hush... Hush, Sweet Charlotte*

Direction: Peter Glenville for *Becket*; Stanley Kubrick for *Dr Strangelove*; Robert Stevenson for *Mary Poppins*; **George Cukor for *My Fair Lady***; Michael Cacoyannis for *Zorba the Greek*

1965

Production: *Darling* (Embassy/British); *Dr Zhivago* (MGM); *Ship of Fools* (Columbia); ***The Sound of Music* (20th Century-Fox)**; *A Thousand Clowns* (United Artists)

Actor: Richard Burton in *The Spy Who Came in from the Cold*; **Lee Marvin** in *Cat Ballou*; Laurence Olivier in *Othello*; Rod Steiger in *The Pawnbroker*; Oskar Werner in *Ship of Fools*

Actress: Julie Andrews in *The Sound of Music*; **Julie Christie in *Darling***; Samantha Eggar in *The Collector*; Elizabeth Hartman in *A Patch of Blue*; Simone Signoret in *Ship of Fools*

Supporting Actor: **Martin Balsam in *A Thousand Clowns***; Ian Bannen in *Flight of the Phoenix*; Tom Courtenay in *Dr Zhivago*; Michael Dunn in *Ship of Fools*; Frank Finlay in *Othello*

Supporting Actress: Ruth Gordon in *Inside Daisy Clover*; Joyce Redman in *Othello*; Maggie Smith in *Othello*; **Shelley Winters in *A Patch of Blue***; Peggy Wood in *The Sound of Music*

Direction: William Wyler for *The Collector*; John Schlesinger for *Darling*; David Lean for *Dr Zhivago*; **Robert Wise for *The Sound of Music***; Hiroshi Teshigahara for *Woman of the Dunes*

1966

Production: *Alfie* (Paramount/British); ***A Man for All Seasons* (Columbia)**; *The Russians Are Coming, The Russians Are Coming* (United Artists); *The Sand Pebbles* (20th Century-Fox); *Who's Afraid of Virginia Woolf?* (Warner Bros)

Actor: Alan Arkin in *The Russians Are Coming, The Russians Are Coming*; Richard Burton in *Who's Afraid of Virginia Woolf?*; Michael Caine in *Alfie*; Steve McQueen in *The Sand Pebbles*; **Paul Scofield in *A Man for All Seasons***

Actress: Anouk Aimee in *A Man and a Woman*; Ida Kaminska in *The Shop on Main Street*; Lynn Redgrave in *Georgy Girl*; Vanessa Redgrave in *Morgan: A Suitable Case for Treatment*; **Elizabeth Taylor in *Who's Afraid of Virginia Woolf?***

Supporting Actor: Mako in *The Sand Pebbles*; James Mason in *Georgy Girl*; **Walter Matthau in *The Fortune Cookie***; George Segal in *Who's Afraid of Virginia Woolf?*; Robert Shaw in *A Man for All Seasons*

Supporting Actress: **Sandy Dennis in *Who's Afraid of Virginia Woolf?***; Wendy Hiller in *A Man for All Seasons*; Jocelyn LaGarde in *Hawaii*; Vivien Merchant in *Alfie*; Geraldine Page in *You're a Big Boy Now*

Direction: Michelangelo Antonioni for *Blow Up*; Claude Lelouch for *A Man and a Woman*; **Fred Zinnemann for *A Man for All Seasons***; Richard Brooks for *The Professionals*; Mike Nichols for *Who's Afraid of Virginia Woolf?*

1967

Production: *Bonnie and Clyde* (Warner Bros); *Doctor Dolittle* (20th Century-Fox); *The Graduate* (United Artists); *Guess Who's Coming to Dinner?* (Columbia); ***In the Heat of the Night* (United Artists)**

Actor: Warren Beatty in *Bonnie and Clyde*; Dustin Hoffman in *The Graduate*; Paul Newman in *Cool Hand Luke*; **Rod Steiger in *In the Heat of the Night***; Spencer Tracy in *Guess Who's Coming to Dinner?*

Actress: Anne Bancroft in *The Graduate*; Faye Dunaway in *Bonnie and Clyde*; Edith Evans in *The Whisperers*; Audrey Hepburn in *Wait Until Dark*; **Katharine Hepburn in *Guess Who's Coming to Dinner?***

Supporting Actor: John Cassavetes in *The Dirty Dozen*; Gene Hackman in *Bonnie and Clyde*; Cecil Kellaway in *Guess Who's Coming to Dinner?*; **George Kennedy in *Cool Hand Luke***; Michael J. Pollard in *Bonnie and Clyde*

Supporting Actress: Carol Channing in *Thoroughly Modern Millie*; Mildred Natwick in *Barefoot in the Park*; **Estelle Parsons in *Bonnie and Clyde***; Beah Richards in*Guess Who's Coming to Dinner?*; Katharine Ross in *The Graduate*

Direction: Arthur Penn for *Bonnie and Clyde*; **Mike Nichols for *The Graduate***; Stanley Kramer for *Guess Who's Coming to Dinner?*; Richard Brooks for *In Cold Blood*; Norman Jewison for *In the Heat of the Night*

1968

Production: *Funny Girl* (Columbia); *The Lion in Winter* (Avco Embassy); ***Oliver!* (Columbia)**; *Rachel, Rachel* (Warner Bros); *Romeo and Juliet* (Paramount)

Actor: Alan Arkin in *The Heart Is a Lonely Hunter*; Alan Bates in *The Fixer*; Ron Moody in *Oliver!*; Peter O'Toole in *The Lion in Winter*; **Cliff Robertson in *Charly***

Actress: **Katharine Hepburn in *The Lion in Winter***; Patricia Neal in *The Subject Was Roses*; Vanessa Redgrave in *Isadora*; **Barbra Streisand in *Funny Girl***; Joanne Woodward in *Rachel, Rachel*

Supporting Actor: **Jack Albertson in *The Subject Was Roses***; Seymour Cassel in *Faces*; Daniel Massey in *Star!*; Jack Wild in *Oliver!*; Gene Wilder in *The Producers*

Supporting Actress: Lynn Carlin in *Faces*; **Ruth Gordon in *Rosemary's Baby***; Sondra Locke in *The Heart Is a Lonely Hunter*; Kay Medford in *Funny Girl*; Estelle Parsons in *Rachel, Rachel*

Direction: Gillo Pontecorvo for *The Battle of Algiers*; Franco Zeffirelli for *Romeo and Juliet*; Anthony Harvey for *The Lion in Winter*; **Carol Reed for *Oliver!***; Stanley Kubrick for *2001: A Space Odyssey*

1969

Production: *Anne of the Thousand Days* (Universal); *Butch Cassidy and the Sundance Kid* (20th Century-Fox); *Hello, Dolly!* (20th Century-Fox); ***Midnight Cowboy* (United Artists)**; *Z* (Algeria/France)

Actor: Richard Burton in *Anne of the Thousand Days*; Dustin Hoffman in *Midnight Cowboy*; Peter O'Toole in *Goodbye, Mr Chips*; Jon Voight in *Midnight Cowboy*; **John Wayne in *True Grit***

Actress: Genevieve Bujold in *Anne of the Thousand Days*; Jane Fonda in *They Shoot Horses, Don't They?*; Liza Minnelli in *The Sterile Cuckoo*; Jean Simmons in *The Happy Ending*; **Maggie Smith in *The Prime of Miss Jean Brodie***

Supporting Actor: Rupert Crosse in *The Reivers*; Elliott Gould in *Bob and Carol and Ted and Alice*; Jack Nicholson in *Easy Rider*; Anthony Quayle in *Anne of the Thousand Days*; **Gig Young in *They Shoot Horses, Don't They?***

Supporting Actress: Cathy Burns in *Last Summer*; Dyan Cannon in *Bob and Carol and Ted and Alice*; **Goldie Hawn in *Cactus Flower***; Sylvia Miles in

Midnight Cowboy; Susannah York in *They Shoot Horses, Don't They?*
Direction: Arthur Penn for *Alice's Restaurant*; George Roy Hill for *Butch Cassidy and the Sundance Kid*; **John Schlesinger for *Midnight Cowboy***; Sydney Pollack for *They Shoot Horses, Don't They?*; Costa-Gavras for *Z*

1970
Production: *Airport* (Universal); *Five Easy Pieces* (Columbia); *Love Story* (Paramount); *M·A·S·H* (20th Century-Fox); ***Patton* (20th Century-Fox)**
Actor: Melvyn Douglas in *I Never Sang for My Father*; James Earl Jones in *The Great White Hope*; Jack Nicholson in *Five Easy Pieces*; Ryan O'Neal in *Love Story*; **George C. Scott in *Patton***
Actress: Jane Alexander in *The Great White Hope*; **Glenda Jackson in *Women in Love***; Ali MacGraw in *Love Story*; Sarah Miles in *Ryan's Daughter*; Carrie Snodgress in *Diary of a Mad Housewife*
Supporting Actor: Richard Castellano in *Lovers and Other Strangers*; Chief Dan George in *Little Big Man*; Gene Hackman in *I Never Sang for My Father*; **John Mills in *Ryan's Daughter***; John Marley in *Love Story*
Supporting Actress: Karen Black in *Five Easy Pieces*; Lee Grant in *The Landlord*; **Helen Hayes in *Airport***; Sally Kellerman in *M·A·S·H*; Maureen Stapleton in *Airport*
Direction: Federico Fellini for *Satyricon*; Arthur Hiller for *Love Story*; Robert Altman for *M·A·S·H*; **Franklin J. Schaffner for *Patton***; Ken Russell for *Women in Love*

1971
Production: *A Clockwork Orange* (Warner Bros); *Fiddler on the Roof* (United Artists); ***The French Connection* (20th Century-Fox)**; *The Last Picture Show* (Columbia); *Nicholas and Alexandra* (Columbia)
Actor: Peter Finch in *Sunday Bloody Sunday*; **Gene Hackman in *The French Connection***; Walter Matthau in *Kotch*; George C. Scott in *The Hospital*; Topol in *Fiddler on the Roof*
Actress: **Jane Fonda in *Klute***; Julie Christie in *McCabe and Mrs Miller*; Glenda Jackson in *Sunday Bloody Sunday*; Vanessa Redgrave in *Mary, Queen of Scots*; Janet Suzman in *Nicholas and Alexandra*
Supporting Actor: Jeff Bridges in *The Last Picture Show*; Leonard Frey in *Fiddler on the Roof*; Richard Jaeckel in *Sometimes a Great Notion*; **Ben Johnson in *The Last Picture Show***; Roy Scheider in *The French Connection*
Supporting Actress: Ellen Burstyn in *The Last Picture Show*; Barbara Harris in *Who Is Harry Kellerman?*; **Cloris Leachman in *The Last Picture Show***; Margaret Leighton in *The Go-Between*; Ann-Margret in *Carnal Knowledge*
Direction: Stanley Kubrick for *A Clockwork Orange*; Norman Jewison for *Fiddler on the Roof*; **William Friedkin for *The French Connection***; Peter Bogdanovich for *The Last Picture Show*; John Schlesinger for *Sunday Bloody Sunday*

1972

Production: *Cabaret* (Allied Artists); *Deliverance* (Warner Bros); *The Emigrants* (Sweden); **The Godfather (Paramount)**; *Sounder* (20th Century-Fox)

Actor: **Marlon Brando in The Godfather**; Michael Caine in *Sleuth*; Laurence Olivier in *Sleuth*; Peter O'Toole in *The Ruling Class*; Paul Winfield in *Sounder*

Actress: **Liza Minnelli in Cabaret**; Diana Ross in *Lady Sings the Blues*; Maggie Smith in *Travels with My Aunt*; Cicely Tyson in *Sounder*; Liv Ullmann in *The Emigrants*

Supporting Actor: Eddie Albert in *The Heartbreak Kid*; James Caan in *The Godfather*; Robert Duvall in *The Godfather*; Al Pacino in *The Godfather*; **Joel Grey in Cabaret**

Supporting Actress: **Eileen Heckart in Butterflies Are Free**; Geraldine Page in *Pete 'n' Tillie*; Susan Tyrrell in *Fat City*; Shelley Winters in *The Poseidon Adventure*; Jeannie Berlin in *The Heartbreak Kid*

Direction: **Bob Fosse for Cabaret**; John Boorman for *Deliverance*; Jan Troell for *The Emigrants*; Francis Ford Coppola for *The Godfather*; Joseph L. Mankiewicz for *Sleuth*

1973

Production: *American Graffiti* (Universal); *Cries and Whispers* (Sweden); *The Exorcist* (Warner Bros); **The Sting (Universal)**; *A Touch of Class* (Avco Embassy)

Actor: Marlon Brando in *Last Tango in Paris*; **Jack Lemmon in Save the Tiger**; Jack Nicholson in *The Last Detail*; Al Pacino in *Serpico*; Robert Redford in *The Sting*

Actress: Ellen Burstyn in *The Exorcist*; **Glenda Jackson in A Touch of Class**; Marsha Mason in *Cinderella Liberty*; Barbra Streisand in *The Way We Were*; Joanne Woodward in *Summer Wishes, Winter Dreams*

Supporting Actor: Vincent Gardenia in *Bang the Drum Slowly*; Jack Gilford in *Save the Tiger*; **John Houseman in The Paper Chase**; Jason Miller in *The Exorcist*; Randy Quaid in *The Last Detail*

Supporting Actress: Linda Blair in *The Exorcist*; Candy Clark in *American Graffiti*; Madeline Kahn in *Paper Moon*; **Tatum O'Neal in Paper Moon**; Sylvia Sidney in *Summer Wishes, Winter Dreams*

Direction: George Lucas for *American Graffiti*; Ingmar Bergman for *Cries and Whispers*; William Friedkin for *The Exorcist*; **George Roy Hill for The Sting**; Bernardo Bertolucci for *Last Tango in Paris*

1974

Production: *Chinatown* (Paramount); *The Conversation* (Paramount); **The Godfather, Part II (Paramount)**; *Lenny* (United Artists); *The Towering Inferno* (20th Century-Fox/Warner Bros)

Actor: **Art Carney in Harry and Tonto**; Albert Finney in *Murder on the Orient Express*; Dustin Hoffman in *Lenny*; Jack Nicholson in *Chinatown*; Al Pacino in *The Godfather, Part II*

Actress: **Ellen Burstyn in Alice Doesn't Live Here Anymore**; Diahann Carroll in *Claudine*; Faye Dunaway in *Chinatown*; Valerie Perrine in

Lenny; Gena Rowlands in *A Woman Under the Influence*

Supporting Actor: Fred Astaire in *The Towering Inferno*; Jeff Bridges in *Thunderbolt and Lightfoot*; **Robert De Niro in *The Godfather, Part II***; Michael V. Gazzo in *The Godfather, Part II*; Lee Strasberg in *The Godfather, Part II*

Supporting Actress: **Ingrid Bergman in *Murder on the Orient Express***; Valentina Cortese in *Day for Night*; Madeline Kahn in *Blazing Saddles*; Diane Ladd in *Alice Doesn't Live Here Anymore*; Talia Shire in *The Godfather, Part II*

Direction: Roman Polanski for *Chinatown*; François Truffaut for *Day for Night*; **Francis Ford Coppola for *The Godfather, Part II***; Bob Fosse for *Lenny*; John Cassavetes for *A Woman Under the Influence*

1975

Production: *Barry Lyndon* (Warner Bros); *Dog Day Afternoon* (Warner Bros); *Jaws* (Universal); *Nashville* (Paramount); **One Flew Over the Cuckoo's Nest (United Artists)**

Actor: Walter Matthau in *The Sunshine Boys*; **Jack Nicholson in *One Flew Over the Cuckoo's Nest***; Al Pacino in *Dog Day Afternoon*; Maximilian Schell in *The Man in the Glass Booth*; James Whitmore in *Give 'Em Hell Harry!*

Actress: Isabelle Adjani in *The Story of Adèle H*; Ann-Margret in *Tommy*; **Louise Fletcher in *One Flew Over the Cuckoo's Nest***; Glenda Jackson in *Hedda*; Carol Kane in *Hester Street*

Supporting Actor: **George Burns in *The Sunshine Boys***; Brad Dourif in *One Flew Over the Cuckoo's Nest*; Burgess Meredith in *The Day of the Locust*; Chris Sarandon in *Dog Day Afternoon*; Jack Warden in *Shampoo*

Supporting Actress: Ronee Blakley in *Nashville*; **Lee Grant in *Shampoo***; Sylvia Miles in *Farewell My Lovely*; Lily Tomlin in *Nashville*; Brenda Vaccaro in *Once Is Not Enough*

Direction: Federico Fellini for *Amarcord*; Stanley Kubrick for *Barry Lyndon*; Sidney Lumet for *Dog Day Afternoon*; Robert Altman for *Nashville*; **Milos Forman for *One Flew Over the Cuckoo's Nest***

1976

Production: *All the President's Men* (Warner Bros); *Bound for Glory* (United Artists); *Network* (United Artists); **Rocky (United Artists)**; *Taxi Driver* (Columbia)

Actor: Robert De Niro in *Taxi Driver*; **Peter Finch in *Network***; Giancarlo Giannini in *Seven Beauties*; William Holden in *Network*; Sylvester Stallone in *Rocky*

Actress: Marie-Christine Barrault in *Cousin, Cousine*; **Faye Dunaway in *Network***; Talia Shire in *Rocky*; Sissy Spacek in *Carrie*; Liv Ullmann in *Face to Face*

Supporting Actor: Ned Beatty in *Network*; Burgess Meredith in *Rocky*; Laurence Olivier in *Marathon Man*; **Jason Robards in *All the President's Men***; Burt Young in *Rocky*

Supporting Actress: Jane Alexander in *All the President's Men*; Jodie Foster

in *Taxi Driver*; Lee Grant in *Voyage of the Damned*; Piper Laurie in *Carrie*; **Beatrice Straight in *Network***
Direction: Alan J. Pakula for *All the President's Men*; Ingmar Bergman for *Face to Face*; Sidney Lumet for *Network*; **John G. Avildsen for *Rocky***; Lina Wertmuller for *Seven Beauties*

1977
Production: ***Annie Hall* (United Artists)**; *The Goodbye Girl* (MGM-Warner Bros); *Julia* (20th Century-Fox); *Star Wars* (20th Century-Fox); *The Turning Point* (20th Century-Fox)
Actor: Woody Allen in *Annie Hall*; Richard Burton in *Equus*; **Richard Dreyfuss in *The Goodbye Girl***; Marcello Mastroianni in *A Special Day*; John Travolta in *Saturday Night Fever*
Actress: Anne Bancroft in *The Turning Point*; Jane Fonda in *Julia*; **Diane Keaton in *Annie Hall***; Shirley MacLaine in *The Turning Point*; Marsha Mason in *The Goodbye Girl*
Supporting Actor: Mikhail Baryshnikov in *The Turning Point*; Peter Firth in *Equus*; Alec Guinness in *Star Wars*; **Jason Robards in *Julia***; Maximilian Schell in *Julia*
Supporting Actress: Leslie Browne in *The Turning Point*; Quinn Cummings in *The Goodbye Girl*; Melinda Dillon in *Close Encounters of the Third Kind*; **Vanessa Redgrave in *Julia***; Tuesday Weld in *Looking for Mr Goodbar*
Direction: **Woody Allen for *Annie Hall***; Steven Spielberg for *Close Encounters of the Third Kind*; Fred Zinnemann for *Julia*; George Lucas for *Star Wars*; Herbert Ross for *The Turning Point*

1978
Production: *Coming Home* (United Artists); ***The Deer Hunter* (EMI/Universal)**; *Heaven Can Wait* (Paramount); *Midnight Express* (Columbia); *An Unmarried Woman* (20th Century-Fox)
Actor: Warren Beatty in *Heaven Can Wait*; Gary Busey in *The Buddy Holly Story*; Robert De Niro in *The Deer Hunter*; Laurence Olivier in *The Boys From Brazil*; **Jon Voight in *Coming Home***
Actress: Ingrid Bergman in *Autumn Sonata*; Ellen Burstyn in *Same Time, Next Year*; Jill Clayburgh in *An Unmarried Woman*; **Jane Fonda in *Coming Home***; Geraldine Page in *Interiors*
Supporting Actor: Bruce Dern in *Coming Home*; Richard Farnsworth in *Comes a Horseman*; John Hurt in *Midnight Express*; **Christopher Walken in *The Deer Hunter***; Jack Warden in *Heaven Can Wait*
Supporting Actress: Dyan Cannon in *Heaven Can Wait*; Penelope Milford in *Coming Home*; **Maggie Smith in *California Suite***; Maureen Stapleton in *Interiors*; Meryl Streep in *The Deer Hunter*
Best Direction: Hal Ashby for *Coming Home*; **Michael Cimino for *The Deer Hunter***; Warren Beatty and Buck Henry for *Heaven Can Wait*; Woody Allen for *Interiors*; Alan Parker for *Midnight Express*

1979
Production: *All That Jazz* (Columbia/20th Century-Fox); *Apocalypse Now* (United Artists); *Breaking Away* (20th Century-Fox); ***Kramer vs. Kramer***

(Columbia); *Norma Rae* (20th Century-Fox)

Actor: **Dustin Hoffman in *Kramer vs. Kramer***; Jack Lemmon in *The China Syndrome*; Al Pacino in *And Justice for All*; Roy Scheider in *All That Jazz*; Peter Sellers in *Being There*

Actress: Jill Clayburgh in *Starting Over*; **Sally Field in *Norma Rae***; Jane Fonda in *The China Syndrome*; Marsha Mason in *Chapter Two*; Bette Midler in *The Rose*

Supporting Actor: **Melvyn Douglas in *Being There***; Robert Duvall in *Apocalypse Now*; Frederic Forrest in *The Rose*; Justin Henry in *Kramer vs. Kramer*; Mickey Rooney in *The Black Stallion*

Supporting Actress: Jane Alexander in *Kramer vs. Kramer*; Barbara Barrie in *Breaking Away*; Candice Bergen in *Starting Over*; Mariel Hemingway in *Manhattan*; **Meryl Streep in *Kramer vs. Kramer***

Direction: Bob Fosse in *All That Jazz*; Francis Ford Coppola for *Apocalypse Now*; Peter Yates for *Breaking Away*; **Robert Benton for *Kramer vs. Kramer***; Edouard Molinaro for *La Cage aux Folles*

1980

Production: *Coal Miner's Daughter* (Universal); *The Elephant Man* (Paramount); ***Ordinary People* (Paramount)**; *Raging Bull* (United Artists); *Tess* (Columbia)

Actor: **Robert De Niro in *Raging Bull***; Robert Duvall in *The Great Santini*; John Hurt in *The Elephant Man*; Jack Lemmon in *Tribute*; Peter O'Toole in *The Stunt Man*

Actress: Ellen Burstyn in *Resurrection*; Goldie Hawn in *Private Benjamin*; Mary Tyler Moore in *Ordinary People*; Gena Rowlands in *Gloria*; **Sissy Spacek in *Coal Miner's Daughter***

Supporting Actor: Judd Hirsch in *Ordinary People*; **Timothy Hutton in *Ordinary People***; Michael O'Keefe in *The Great Santini*; Joe Pesci in *Raging Bull*; Jason Robards in *Melvin and Howard*

Supporting Actress: Eileen Brennan in *Private Benjamin*; Eva Le Gallienne in *Resurrection*; Cathy Moriarty in *Raging Bull*; Diana Scarwid in *Inside Moves*; **Mary Steenburgen in *Melvin and Howard***

Direction: David Lynch for *The Elephant Man*; **Robert Redford for *Ordinary People***; Martin Scorsese for *Raging Bull*; Richard Rush for *The Stunt Man*; Roman Polanski for *Tess*

1981

Production: *Atlantic City* (Paramount); ***Chariots of Fire* (The Ladd Company/Warner Bros)**; *On Golden Pond* (ITC/Universal); *Raiders of the Lost Ark* (Paramount); *Reds* (Paramount)

Actor: Warren Beatty in *Reds*; **Henry Fonda in *On Golden Pond***; Burt Lancaster in *Atlantic City*; Dudley Moore in *Arthur*; Paul Newman in *Absence of Malice*

Actress: **Katharine Hepburn in *On Golden Pond***; Diane Keaton in *Reds*; Marsha Mason in *Only When I Laugh*; Susan Sarandon in *Atlantic City*; Meryl Streep in *The French Lieutenant's Woman*

Supporting Actor: James Coco in *Only When I Laugh*; **John Gielgud in**

Arthur; Ian Holm in *Chariots of Fire*; Jack Nicholson in *Reds*; Howard E.
Rollins Jr. in *Ragtime*

Supporting Actress: Melinda Dillon in *Absence of Malice*; Jane Fonda in *On
Golden Pond*; Joan Hackett in *Only When I Laugh*; Elizabeth McGovern in
Ragtime; **Maureen Stapleton in *Reds***

Direction: Louis Malle for *Atlantic City*; Hugh Hudson for *Chariots of Fire*;
Mark Rydell for *On Golden Pond*; Steven Spielberg for *Raiders of the Lost
Ark*; **Warren Beatty for *Reds***

1982

Production: *E. T. The Extra-Terrestrial* (Universal); ***Gandhi* (Columbia)**;
Missing (Universal); *Tootsie* (Columbia); *The Verdict* (20th Century-Fox)

Actor: Dustin Hoffman in *Tootsie*; **Ben Kingsley in *Gandhi***; Jack
Lemmon in *Missing*; Paul Newman in *The Verdict*; Peter O'Toole in *My
Favorite Year*

Actress: Julie Andrews in *Victor/Victoria*; Jessica Lange in *Frances*; Sissy
Spacek in *Missing*; **Meryl Streep in *Sophie's Choice***; Debra Winger in
An Officer and a Gentleman

Supporting Actor: Charles Durning in *The Best Little Whorehouse in Texas*;
Louis Gossett, Jr. in *An Officer and a Gentleman*; John Lithgow in
The World According to Garp; James Mason in *The Verdict*; Robert Preston
in *Victor/Victoria*

Supporting Actress: Glenn Close in *The World According to Garp*; Teri Garr
in *Tootsie*; **Jessica Lange in *Tootsie***; Kim Stanley in *Frances*; Lesley Ann
Warren in *Victor/Victoria*

Direction: Wolfgang Peterson for *Das Boot*; Steven Spielberg for *E. T. The
Extra-Terrestrial*; **Richard Attenborough for *Gandhi***; Sydney Pollack
for *Tootsie*; Sidney Lumet for *The Verdict*

1983

Production: *The Big Chill* (Columbia); *The Dresser* (Goldcrest/Columbia);
The Right Stuff (The Ladd Co/Warner Bros); *Tender Mercies* (EMI/
Universal); ***Terms of Endearment* (Paramount)**

Actor: Michael Caine in *Educating Rita*; Tom Conti in *Reuben, Reuben*; Tom
Courtenay in *The Dresser*; **Robert Duvall in *Tender Mercies***; Albert
Finney in *The Dresser*

Actress: Jane Alexander in *Testament*; **Shirley MacLaine in *Terms of
Endearment***; Meryl Streep in *Silkwood*; Julie Walters in *Educating Rita*;
Debra Winger in *Terms of Endearment*

Supporting Actor: Charles Durning in *To Be or Not to Be*; John Lithgow in
Terms of Endearment; **Jack Nicholson in *Terms of Endearment***; Sam
Shepard in *The Right Stuff*; Rip Torn in *Cross Creek*

Supporting Actress: Cher in *Silkwood*; Glenn Close in *The Big Chill*; **Linda
Hunt in *The Year of Living Dangerously***; Amy Irving in *Yentl*; Alfre
Woodard in *Cross Creek*

Direction: Peter Yates for *The Dresser*; Ingmar Bergman for *Fanny and
Alexander*; Mike Nichols for *Silkwood*; Bruce Beresford for *Tender Mercies*;
James L. Brooks for *Terms of Endearment*

1984

Production: *Amadeus* **(Zaentz/Orion)**; *The Killing Fields* (Enigma/ Warner Bros); *A Passage to India* (G.W. Films/Columbia); *Places in the Heart* (Tri-Star); *A Soldier's Story* (Columbia)

Actor: **F. Murray Abraham in *Amadeus*;** Jeff Bridges in *Starman*; Albert Finney in *Under the Volcano*; Tom Hulce in *Amadeus*; Sam Waterston in *The Killing Fields*

Actress: Judy Davis in *A Passage to India*; **Sally Field in *Places in the Heart*;** Jessica Lange in *Country*; Vanessa Redgrave in *The Bostonians*; Sissy Spacek in *The River*

Supporting Actor: Adolph Caesar in *A Soldier's Story*; John Malkovich in *Places in the Heart*; Noriyuki 'Pat' Morita in *The Karate Kid*; **Haing S. Ngor in *The Killing Fields*;** Ralph Richardson in *Greystoke: The Legend of Tarzan, Lord of the Apes*

Supporting Actress: **Peggy Ashcroft in *A Passage to India*;** Glenn Close in *The Natural*; Lindsay Crouse in *Places in the Heart*; Christine Lahti in *Swing Shift*; Geraldine Page in *The Pope of Greenwich Village*

Direction: **Milos Forman for *Amadeus*;** Woody Allen for *Broadway Danny Rose*; Roland Joffe for *The Killing Fields*; David Lean for *A Passage to India*; Robert Benton for *Places in the Heart*

1985

Production: *The Color Purple* (Warner Bros); *Kiss of the Spider Woman* (Island Alive); *Out of Africa* **(Universal)**; *Prizzi's Honor* (ABC/20th Century-Fox); *Witness* (Paramount)

Actor: Harrison Ford in *Witness*; James Garner in *Murphy's Romance*; **William Hurt in *Kiss of the Spider Woman*;** Jack Nicholson in *Prizzi's Honor*; Jon Voight in *Runaway Train*

Actress: Anne Bancroft in *Agnes of God*; Whoopi Goldberg in *The Color Purple*; Jessica Lange in *Sweet Dreams*; **Geraldine Page in *The Trip to Bountiful*;** Meryl Streep in *Out of Africa*

Supporting Actor: **Don Ameche in *Cocoon*;** Klaus Maria Brandauer in *Out of Africa*; William Hickey in *Prizzi's Honor*; Robert Loggia in *Jagged Edge*; Eric Roberts in *Runaway Train*

Supporting Actress: Margaret Avery in *The Color Purple*; **Anjelica Huston in *Prizzi's Honor*;** Amy Madigan in *Twice in a Lifetime*; Meg Tilly in *Agnes of God*; Oprah Winfrey in *The Color Purple*

Direction: Hector Babenco for *Kiss of the Spider Woman*; **Sydney Pollack for *Out of Africa*;** John Huston for *Prizzi's Honor*; Akira Kurosawa for *Ran*; Peter Weir for *Witness*

1986

Production: *Children of a Lesser God* (Paramount); *Hannah and Her Sisters* (Orion); *The Mission* (Warner Bros); *Platoon* **(Hemdale/Orion)**; *A Room with a View* (Merchant Ivory/Cinecom)

Actor: Dexter Gordon in *'Round Midnight*; Bob Hoskins in *Mona Lisa*; William Hurt in *Children of a Lesser God*; **Paul Newman in *The Color of Money*;** James Woods in *Salvador*

Actress: Jane Fonda in *The Morning After*; **Marlee Matlin in *Children of a***

Lesser God; Sissy Spacek in *Crimes of the Heart*; Kathleen Turner in *Peggy Sue Got Married*; Sigourney Weaver in *Aliens*

Supporting Actor: Tom Berenger in *Platoon*; **Michael Caine in *Hannah and Her Sisters***; Willem Dafoe in *Platoon*; Denholm Elliott in *A Room with a View*; Dennis Hopper in *Hoosiers*

Supporting Actress: Tess Harper in *Crimes of the Heart*; Piper Laurie in *Children of a Lesser God*; Mary Elizabeth Mastrantonio in *The Color of Money*; Maggie Smith in *A Room with a View*; **Dianne Wiest in *Hannah and Her Sisters***

Direction: David Lynch for *Blue Velvet*; Woody Allen for *Hannah and Her Sisters*; Roland Joffe for *The Mission*; **Oliver Stone for *Platoon***; James Ivory for *A Room with a View*

1987

Production: *Broadcast News* (20th Century-Fox); *Fatal Attraction* (Paramount); *Hope and Glory* (Davros/Columbia); **The Last Emperor (Hemdale/Columbia)**; *Moonstruck* (MGM)

Actor: William Hurt in *Broadcast News*; **Michael Douglas in *Wall Street***; Robin Williams in *Good Morning, Vietnam*; Marcello Mastroianni in *Dark Eyes*; Jack Nicholson in *Ironweed*

Actress: **Cher in *Moonstruck***; Meryl Streep in *Ironweed*; Sally Kirkland in *Anna*; Glenn Close in *Fatal Attraction*; Holly Hunter in *Broadcast News*

Supporting Actor: Albert Brooks in *Broadcast News*; Morgan Freeman in *Street Smart*; **Sean Connery in *The Untouchables***; Denzel Washington in *Cry Freedom*; Vincent Gardenia in *Moonstruck*

Supporting Actress: Norma Aleandro in *Gaby – A True Story*; Ann Sothern in *The Whales of August*; **Olympia Dukakis in *Moonstruck***; Anne Archer in *Fatal Attraction*; Anne Ramsey in *Throw Momma from the Train*

Direction: **Bernardo Bertolucci for *The Last Emperor***; John Boorman for *Hope and Glory*; Lasse Hallstrom for *My Life as a Dog*; Norman Jewison for *Moonstruck*; Adrian Lyne for *Fatal Attraction*

1988

Production: *The Accidental Tourist* (Warner Bros); *Dangerous Liaisons* (Lorimar/Warner Bros); *Mississippi Burning* (Orion); **Rain Man (United Artists)**; *Working Girl* (20th Century-Fox)

Actor: Gene Hackman in *Mississippi Burning*; Tom Hanks in *Big*; **Dustin Hoffman in *Rain Man***; Edward James Olmos in *Stand and Deliver*; Max Von Sydow in *Pelle the Conqueror*

Actress: Glenn Close in *Dangerous Liaisons*; **Jodie Foster in *The Accused***; Melanie Griffith in *Working Girl*; Meryl Streep in *A Cry in the Dark*; Sigourney Weaver in *Gorillas in the Mist*

Supporting Actor: Alec Guinness in *Little Dorrit*; **Kevin Kline in *A Fish Called Wanda***; Martin Landau in *Tucker: The Man and His Dream*; River Phoenix in *Running on Empty*; Dean Stockwell in *Married to the Mob*

Supporting Actress: Joan Cusack in *Working Girl*; **Geena Davis in *The Accidental Tourist***; Frances McDormand in *Mississippi Burning*; Michelle Pfeiffer in *Dangerous Liaisons*; Sigourney Weaver in *Working Girl*

Direction: Charles Crichton for *A Fish Called Wanda*; **Barry Levinson for**

Rain Man; Mike Nichols for *Working Girl*; Alan Parker for *Mississippi Burning*; Martin Scorsese for *The Last Temptation of Christ*

1989
Production: *Born on the Fourth of July* (Universal); *Dead Poets Society* (Buena Vista/Touchstone); **Driving Miss Daisy (Warner Bros)**; *Field of Dreams* (Universal); *My Left Foot* (Miramax/Ferndale Films)
Actor: Kenneth Branagh in *Henry V*; Tom Cruise in *Born on the Fourth of July*; Morgan Freeman in *Driving Miss Daisy*; **Daniel Day-Lewis in *My Left Foot***; Robin Williams in *Dead Poets Society*
Actress: Isabelle Adjani in *Camille Claudel*; Pauline Collins in *Shirley Valentine*; Jessica Lange in *Music Box*; Michelle Pfeiffer in *The Fabulous Baker Boys*; **Jessica Tandy in *Driving Miss Daisy***
Supporting Actor: Danny Aiello in *Do the Right Thing*; Dan Aykroyd in *Driving Miss Daisy*; Marlon Brando in *A Dry White Season*; Martin Landau in *Crimes and Misdemeanors*; **Denzel Washington in *Glory***
Supporting Actress: **Brenda Fricker in *My Left Foot***; Anjelica Huston in *Enemies:A Love Story*; Lena Olin in *Enemies:A Love Story*; Julia Roberts in *Steel Magnolias*; Dianne Wiest in *Parenthood*
Direction: **Oliver Stone for *Born on the Fourth of July***; Woody Allen for *Crimes and Misdemeanors*; Peter Weir for *Dead Poets Society*; Kenneth Branagh for *Henry V*; Jim Sheridan for *My Left Foot*

1990
Production: *Awakenings* (Columbia); **Dances With Wolves (Orion/Tig)**; *Ghost* (Paramount); *The Godfather Part III* (Paramount), *Goodfellas* (Warner Bros)
Actor: Kevin Costner in *Dances With Wolves*; Robert De Niro in *Awakenings*; Gerard Depardieu in *Cyrano de Bergerac*; Richard Harris in *The Field*; **Jeremy Irons in *Reversal of Fortune***
Actress: **Kathy Bates in *Misery***; Anjelica Huston in *The Grifters*; Julia Roberts in *Pretty Woman*; Meryl Streep in *Postcards from the Edge*; Joanne Woodward in *Mr and Mrs Bridge*
Supporting Actor: Bruce Davison in *Longtime Companion*; Andy Garcia in *The Godfather Part III*; Graham Greene in *Dances With Wolves*; Al Pacino in *Dick Tracy*; **Joe Pesci in *Goodfellas***
Supporting Actress: Annette Bening in *The Grifters*; Lorraine Bracco in *Goodfellas*; **Whoopi Goldberg in *Ghost***; Diane Ladd in *Wild at Heart*; Mary McDonnell in *Dances With Wolves*
Direction: **Kevin Costner for *Dances With Wolves***; Francis Ford Coppola for *The Godfather Part III*; Martin Scorsese for *Goodfellas*; Stephen Frears for *The Grifters*; Barbet Schroeder for *Reversal of Fortune*

1991
Production: *Beauty and the Beast* (Buena Vista, Walter Disney Pictures); *Bugsy* (Tristar); *JFK* (Warner Bros); *The Prince of Tides* (Columbia); **The Silence of the Lambs (Orion)**
Actor: Warren Beatty in *Bugsy*; Robert De Niro in *Cape Fear*; **Anthony Hopkins in *The Silence of the Lambs***; Nick Nolte in *The Prince of*

Tides; Robin Williams in *The Fisher King*
Actress: Geena Davis in *Thelma and Louise*; Laura Dern in *Rambling Rose*; **Jodie Foster in *The Silence of the Lambs***; Bette Midler in *For the Boys*; Susan Sarandon in *Thelma and Louise*
Supporting Actor: Tommy Lee Jones in *JFK*; Harvey Keitel in *Bugsy*; Ben Kingsley in *Bugsy*; Michael Lerner in *Barton Fink*; **Jack Palance in *City Slickers***
Supporting Actress: Diane Ladd in *Rambling Rose*; Juliette Lewis in *Cape Fear*; Kate Nelligan in *The Prince of Tides*; **Mercedes Ruehl in *The Fisher King***; Jessica Tandy in *Fried Green Tomatoes at the Whistle Stop Café*
Direction: John Singleton for *Boyz N the Hood*; Barry Levinson for *Bugsy*; Oliver Stone for *JFK*; **Jonathan Demme for *The Silence of the Lambs***; Ridley Scott for *Thelma and Louise*

1992

Production: *The Crying Game* (Palace Pictures); *A Few Good Men* (Columbia); *Howards End* (Merchant Ivory/Sony Pictures Classics); *Scent of a Woman* (Universal); ***Unforgiven* (Warner Bros)**
Actor: Robert Downey, Jr. in *Chaplin*; Clint Eastwood in *Unforgiven*; **Al Pacino in *Scent of a Woman***; Stephen Rea in *The Crying Game*; Denzel Washington in *Malcolm X*
Actress: Catherine Deneuve in *Indochine*; Mary McDonnell in *Passion Fish*; Michelle Pfeiffer in *Love Field*; Susan Sarandon in *Lorenzo's Oil*; **Emma Thompson in *Howards End***
Supporting Actor: Jaye Davidson in *The Crying Game*; **Gene Hackman in *Unforgiven***; Jack Nicholson in *A Few Good Men*; Al Pacino in *Glengarry Glen Ross*; David Paymer in *Mr Saturday Night*
Supporting Actress: Judy Davis in *Husbands and Wives*; Joan Plowright in *Enchanted April*; Vanessa Redgrave in *Howards End*; Miranda Richardson in *Damage*; **Marisa Tomei in *My Cousin Vinny***
Direction: Neil Jordan for *The Crying Game*; James Ivory for *Howards End*; Robert Altman for *The Player*; Martin Brest for *Scent of a Woman*; **Clint Eastwood for *Unforgiven***

1993

Production: *The Fugitive* (Warner Bros); *In the Name of the Father* (Hell's Kitchen/Universal); *The Piano* (Miramax); *The Remains of the Day* (Merchant Ivory Productions); ***Schindler's List* (Universal/Amblin)**
Actor: Daniel Day-Lewis in *In the Name of the Father*; Laurence Fishburne in *What's Love Got to Do With It?*; **Tom Hanks in *Philadelphia***; Anthony Hopkins in *The Remains of the Day*; Liam Neeson in *Schindler's List*
Actress: Angela Bassett in *What's Love Got to Do With It?*; Stockard Channing in *Six Degrees of Separation*; **Holly Hunter in *The Piano***; Emma Thompson in *The Remains of the Day*; Debra Winger in *Shadowlands*
Supporting Actor: Leonardo DiCaprio in *What's Eating Gilbert Grape?*; Ralph Fiennes in *Schindler's List*; **Tommy Lee Jones in *The Fugitive***;

John Malkovich in *In the Line of Fire*; Pete Postlethwaite in *In the Name of the Father*

Supporting Actress: Holly Hunter in *The Firm*; **Anna Paquin in The Piano**; Rosie Perez in *Fearless*; Winona Ryder in *The Age of Innocence*; Emma Thompson in *In the Name of the Father*

Direction: Robert Altman for *Short Cuts*; Jane Campion for *The Piano*; James Ivory for *The Remains of the Day*; Jim Sheridan for *In the Name of the Father*; **Steven Spielberg for Schindler's List**

1994

Production: **Forrest Gump (Paramount)**; *Four Weddings and a Funeral* (Working Title/Gramercy Pictures); *Pulp Fiction* (Miramax); *Quiz Show* (Buena Vista/Hollywood Pictures); *The Shawshank Redemption* (Castle Rock/Columbia)

Actor: Morgan Freeman in *The Shawshank Redemption*; **Tom Hanks in Forrest Gump**; Nigel Hawthorne in *The Madness of King George*; Paul Newman in *Nobody's Fool*; John Travolta in *Pulp Fiction*

Actress: Jodie Foster in *Nell*; **Jessica Lange in Blue Sky**; Miranda Richardson in *Tom and Viv*; Winona Ryder in *Little Women*; Susan Sarandon in *The Client*

Supporting Actor: Samuel L. Jackson in *Pulp Fiction*; **Martin Landau in Ed Wood**; Chazz Palminteri in *Bullets Over Broadway*; Paul Scofield in *Quiz Show*; Gary Sinise in *Forrest Gump*

Supporting Actress: Rosemary Harris in *Tom and Viv*; Helen Mirren in *The Madness of King George*; Uma Thurman in *Pulp Fiction*; Jennifer Tilly in *Bullets Over Broadway*; **Dianne Wiest in Bullets Over Broadway**

Direction: Woody Allen for *Bullets Over Broadway*; **Robert Zemeckis for Forrest Gump**; Quentin Tarantino for *Pulp Fiction*; Robert Redford for *Quiz Show*; Krzysztof Kieslowski for *Red*

1995

Production: *Apollo 13* (Universal); *Babe* (Universal); **Braveheart (Paramount/20th Century-Fox)**; *The Postman* (Miramax-Italy); *Sense and Sensibility* (Columbia)

Actor: **Nicolas Cage in Leaving Las Vegas**; Richard Dreyfuss in *Mr Holland's Opus*; Anthony Hopkins in *Nixon*; Sean Penn in *Dead Man Walking*; Massimo Troisi in *The Postman*

Actress: **Susan Sarandon in Dead Man Walking**; Elisabeth Shue in *Leaving Las Vegas*; Sharon Stone in *Casino*; Meryl Streep in *The Bridges of Madison County*; Emma Thompson in *Sense and Sensibility*

Supporting Actor: James Cromwell in *Babe*; Ed Harris in *Apollo 13*; Brad Pitt in *12 Monkeys*; Tom Roth in *Rob Roy*; **Kevin Spacey in The Usual Suspects**

Supporting Actress: Joan Allen in *Nixon*; Kathleen Quinlan in *Apollo 13*; **Mira Sorvino in Mighty Aphrodite**; Mare Winningham in *Georgia*; Kate Winslet in *Sense and Sensibility*

Direction: Chris Noonan for *Babe*; **Mel Gibson for Braveheart**; Tim Robbins for *Dead Man Walking*; Mike Figgis for *Leaving Las Vegas*; Michael Radford for *The Postman*

Index of Movies